S0-DJW-515

EMPLOYMENT FOR POVERTY REDUCTION AND FOOD SECURITY

EMPLOYMENT FOR POVERTY REDUCTION AND FOOD SECURITY

Edited by Joachim von Braun

International Food Policy Research Institute
Washington, D.C.

Published in 1995 by the

International Food Policy Research Institute
1200 Seventeenth Street, N.W.
Washington, D.C. 20036-3006
U.S.A.

Library of Congress Cataloging-in-Publication Data

Employment for poverty reduction and food security / edited by
    Joachim von Braun.
    p.   cm.— (Occasional paper)
    Includes bibliographical references.
    ISBN 0-89629-332-7
    1. Poor—Employment—Government policy—Developing coun-
tries. 2. Full employment policies—Developing countries. 3. Nutrition policy—Developing countries. 4. Poor—Developing countries—Nutrition. 5. Economic assistance, Domestic—Developing
countries. 6. Food relief—Developing countries. I. von Braun,
Joachim, 1950–   . II. Series: Occasional papers (International Food
Policy Research Institute)
HD5852.E568   1995   95-40061
362.5'89'091724—dc20   CIP

Cover art by Leonie von Braun

Contents

Tables, Illustrations, and Boxes

Tables

Illustrations

Boxes

Foreword

Rapid expansion of employment in low-income countries is one of the biggest challenges of development. The growth in labor supply in developing countries will remain large for a long time to come. Incomes of the poor in rural areas will depend more and more on productive off-farm work, and in the rapidly expanding urban areas, food security will depend largely on jobs and wage rates. As Joachim von Braun says in the introductory chapter of this volume, "Today, understanding the labor market is as relevant for food policy design as understanding the food market."

While economic growth generally leads to reduction of poverty, the process often takes an unacceptably long time. In this volume, employment policies and programs are analyzed in terms of their potential for addressing the problems of poverty and economic growth simultaneously. The conclusions are encouraging.

As these chapters reveal, direct action for employment in low-income countries has considerable potential for reducing poverty. Linking infrastructure improvement with jobs for the poor has considerable appeal. The strong participation of women is an important feature of the programs. Clearly, however, these studies show that participation of the people in the design of the programs and strong managerial capacities for efficient implementation are preconditions for sustainable employment programs that effectively reduce poverty and food insecurity.

The volume builds on and is related to a number of IFPRI research findings: earlier IFPRI research indicated that agriculture can be stimulated by improved infrastructure, with favorable effects for rural income and employment generation both on and off the farm. IFPRI research has also shown that the commercialization of agriculture, fostered by improved market systems and other institutional innovations, greatly expands rural employment opportunities. Moreover, in famine-prone areas, job creation programs have had some positive effects on food security, as IFPRI studies in Ethiopia and Sudan have shown. In the context of all these and other policies and programs, IFPRI research has pointed out in considerable detail that the effects of the interventions vary for diverse population groups and often by gender. All these findings have a bearing on the research and policy conclusions presented in this volume.

Lawrence Haddad
Director
Food Consumption and Nutrition Division

Acknowledgments

Policy-oriented study of the relationships between food security and employment requires a conceptual and analytical understanding of both issues individually, as well as of their interactions. While the International Food Policy Research Institute (IFPRI) has long-standing experience in the study of food security, cooperation with scholars from other institutions with a background in employment studies, for example the International Labour Office (ILO), was particularly important for this work.

The volume contains chapters by eminent scholars in the field, as well as from practitioners from implementing agencies such as the ILO and the World Food Programme (WFP), who could draw on the extensive program experience of their respective organizations. It has been particularly valuable that they have joined in this effort by IFPRI to derive policy conclusions from new research in the area of employment for food security.

Most of the chapters in this volume result from long-term (1988–94) multicountry research by IFPRI on employment policies for poverty reduction and food security. The findings and policy conclusions of the research were discussed at an international policy workshop (held at Airlie House, Virginia, in October 1993), in which program managers and policymakers shared their experience with employment programs for poverty reduction and reviewed related research results. The criticism and insights voiced by the workshop participants, as well as by others who have reviewed the papers, were an essential contribution.

In particular, thanks go to the contributors to this volume and the following experts (affiliation at the time in parentheses): Aseffa Abreha (Public Works Task Force, Prime Minister's Office, Ethiopia), Ide Adamou (Early Warning System, Government of Niger), Ehtisham Ahmed (IMF), M. Asaduzzaman (Bangladesh Institute for Development Studies, Bangladesh), Gideon Asfaw (Ministry of Natural Resources, Ethiopia), Liang Dachao (State Planning Commission, China), Christopher Delgado (IFPRI), Bathusi Dintwa (Undersecretary, Ministry of Local Government, Lands and Housing, Botswana), Bernd Dreesmann (EURONAID, a group of European NGOs involved in food aid), Guenter Dresrusse (Food and Agriculture Organization of the United Nations), Zhang Guize (Employment Program, Sichuan, China), M. A. Hakim (Secretary, Ministry of Relief, Bangladesh), M. Mokammel Haque (Planning Commission, Bangladesh), Hans von Haugwitz (Deutsche Gesellschaft für Technische

Zusammenarbeit [GTZ]), Francis Idachaba (University of Agriculture, Nigeria), Emmanuel Jimenez (World Bank), Julius Kanyasi (Labor-Intensive Public Works Program, Prime Minister's Office, Tanzania), Wolfgang Kunze (GTZ), N. J. Kurian (Nepal), Fang Lei (Department of Planning, China), Qian Lijia (An Hui, China), A. H. Maan (Director, Ministry of Food and Agriculture, Pakistan), N. J. Manamela (Ministry of Finance, Botswana), July Moyo (Permanent Secretary, Ministry of Transport and Energy, Zimbabwe), Harris M. Mule (Kenya), Roger Nignon (Director, NIGETIP, Niger), Gerard Oonk (Netherlands), Klaus Pilgram (GTZ), Per Pinstrup-Andersen (IFPRI), James Smith (U.S. Agency for International Development), Paul Streeten, Tshikala Tshibaka (IFPRI) and Wang Xinhuai (Director, Poverty Alleviation, State Planning Commission, China).

The support of GTZ, which funded the workshop, is gratefully acknowledged.

Many of the chapters in this volume are based on detailed field research involving primary data collection, which could be carried out only by committed field-research teams supported and guided by national institutions. Their fruitful cooperation facilitated the generation of useful local and national know-how regarding program implementation. It yielded the basis for international comparative studies and was therefore central to the project's success.

Thanks go to Rajul Pandya-Lorch, Lynette Aspillera, and Laurie Goldberg (all at IFPRI) for their fine assistance in assuring a successful workshop and to Jay Willis (IFPRI) for his unparalleled word-processing skills.

Finally, the outstanding contribution of Paul Streeten to the conceptualization and focusing of the policy issues raised in this volume must be recognized in particular. In a commentary at the workshop, Paul Streeten reminded us that "People talk about 'political will,' which is a phrase that I would ban from the vocabulary of development studies. If we do not have action, which is the manifestation of will, the will is not there either. It is not political will that we ought to be studying, but how to create the political base."

It remains the objective of the contributors that the research process that led to this volume, the findings reported here, and the appropriate follow-up by relevant national and international institutions do actually result in strengthening of the political base for employment policies that foster poverty reduction and food security.

Joachim von Braun

1
EMPLOYMENT FOR POVERTY REDUCTION AND FOOD SECURITY: CONCEPT, RESEARCH ISSUES, AND OVERVIEW

Joachim von Braun

Closer Links between Employment, Poverty, and Food Security

Today, understanding the labor market is as important for addressing the food security problems of the rural and urban poor in developing countries as understanding the food market. It is now widely accepted that food security is at least as much a matter of poverty—limited access to food— as it is a matter of supply—limited availability of food (Drèze and Sen 1989). Food security is defined here as access by all people at all times to the food required for a healthy life (von Braun et al. 1992).

The studies presented in this volume point out the rapidly increasing dependence of the absolutely destitute—those lacking food security—on the labor market, and argue in favor of placing strong emphasis on employment in any poverty-reduction strategy. Of course, such strategies must also address the huge challenges of producing, transporting, and marketing an adequate food supply for the rapidly growing populations in low-income countries (Pinstrup-Andersen 1994).

Too little attention has been paid to the idea of investing in productive and remunerative employment for the poor as an alternative to subsidizing food (or capital). During the 1980s, however, many countries shifted their policies in this direction, that is, away from food subsidies and toward more developmental policies for poverty reduction or are now striving to implement such policies. The potential and limitations of food subsidies are now well understood (Pinstrup-Andersen 1988, 1993). The feeling now is that it is necessary to address the problems of poverty and hunger in conjunction with the issue of economic growth in order to bring about a sustainable reduction of poverty (Radwan, Chapter 2, this volume; World Bank 1990; Lipton and van der Gaag 1993). Due to its potential effectiveness and sustainability, a strategy of "food security through employment" may also facilitate resource mobilization and domestic as well as international development assistance.

The distribution of food insecurity is becoming more concentrated among the landless and the urban poor, and, in a regional sense, in Africa and South Asia. With increasingly limited land resources per capita in rural areas, the poor in many low-income countries lack resources. Most of the poor have only a single resource: their own labor. Utilizing that resource effectively and increasing its productivity are the objectives of employment policies and related human-resource improvement for eradicating poverty. The challenge of creating jobs in low-income countries where the workforce is expanding rapidly is already tremendous; the labor force is growing while other resources (such as land and capital) are becoming increasingly scarce.

There seems to be no generalized, comprehensive strategy for dealing with open unemployment in high-income countries, where the total working-age population is stagnating or declining. Seemingly even more intractable are the problems of underemployment and low labor productivity in low-income countries, where the labor force continues to grow rapidly and where lack of remunerative employment for the poor often means lack of food security. The world's total working-age population (adults aged 15–64) is expected to grow from 3.3 billion in 1990 to 4.6 billion in 2010 (ILO 1986). This represents a 39 percent increase in only two decades, and this growth will take place almost entirely in the developing countries among the poorest segments of the world's population. Greater focus on employment as an approach to reducing poverty in the coming years seems to be justified by a number of global trends:

- The labor force of low-income countries is growing more rapidly now than in any period in history.
- The relationship between growth rate of output and growth rate of employment appears weak, with the latter lagging behind the former.
- Rapid population growth is paralleled by increasing scarcity of one resource—land—which further limits the earnings of the rural poor from farming.
- In the context of structural adjustment, the cost of unskilled labor has fallen precipitously relative to the cost of capital in many low-income countries, particularly in Africa.
- Due to past and present civil unrest, many areas of the world require extensive reconstruction, which can be carried out in a labor-intensive manner.

In general, an enhanced resource base (terracing, watershed protection, and so forth) and improved infrastructure are prerequisites for achieving sustained economic growth. Such infrastructure improvements may be created and maintained through labor-intensive programs, and are further stimulated by the reduced labor-to-capital cost ratio referred to above. Especially in Sub-Saharan Africa, infrastructural constraints are severely hampering economic development, partly because of their dampening role for incentives to facilitate supply response (Platteau 1993).

Employment-Poverty Links
in Theory and Strategies

Achieving a high level of employment—preferably "full employment"—is virtually a universal goal among policymakers. Employment expansion figured centrally among the concerns of early development theories (Lewis 1955; Fei and Ranis 1964). Due to their highly aggregate conceptualization and slight regard for the institutional complexities of rural and urban labor markets in low-income countries, however, some early theories had only limited usefulness as instruments for guiding policy. Too broad an aggregation of labor, and an equally undifferentiated treatment of capital (that is, the assumption of its homogeneity) in economic growth models have plagued theory and prevented human resources from being appropriately incorporated in development theory (Schultz 1981).

Also, economic development theory offered but little guidance in regard to employment strategies and the institutional aspects of implementation. In the 1980s, strategies for reducing poverty by providing for basic needs were pursued—at best—parallel to growth-oriented concepts, or were even seen as competing with them (Streeten 1981). Employment considerations did play a role in the development strategy debate, however, within the context of the analysis of the food and agriculture sector's key role in the development process (Mellor 1986). More recently, expanded analysis of the economic aspects of institutions—including those related to labor—offers new insights for developing and implementing poverty reduction strategies by taking a more comprehensive approach toward treatment of the potential and limitations of the role of markets and government (Bardhan 1989; Hoff, Braverman, and Stiglitz 1993).

Since the mid-1980s, it has been recognized more and more widely that (1) expanding employment is central to reducing poverty and that (2) working toward that goal via policy action means taking into consideration macroeconomic relationships, microeconomic allocation of resources, technology, and a range of institutional conditions (Todaro 1989). A comprehensive, multicountry study conducted by Horton, Kanbur, and

Mazumdar (1994) on labor markets undergoing economic stabilization and adjustment asks two important sets of questions: first, how well have labor markets functioned and have they facilitated or impeded macro adjustment efforts? And, second, what effects have these adjustments had on the labor market? On the first set of questions, by and large, the authors, reporting on studies in individual countries, "argue that the labor markets performed well" (Horton, Kanbur, and Mazumdar 1994, 54). Rather diverse findings are reported on the second question, however. Direct policy and program action for employment of the poorest—such as that considered here—is not dealt with by the Horton, Kanbur, and Mazumdar study so that the two studies complement one another. It is interesting to note that many countries undergoing structural adjustment increased their employment programs for poverty reduction without much initial involvement of the international institutions guiding the adjustment policies (that is, the International Monetary Fund and the World Bank). This changed only to a limited extent in the early 1990s, when the long-term potential for reducing poverty through employment became more widely recognized.

Broadening strategic thinking on employment-growth-poverty links, Streeten (1994) places employment into the context of an antipoverty strategy with a mix of four components: structural reform, employment creation, social services, and participation. Streeten (1994, 62) argues that "... market-friendly policies should be accompanied by people-friendly markets," and people-friendly markets should be built on participatory institutions, human investment (in nutrition, education, and so forth), and efficient, labor-intensive, environmentally benign technologies.

Past Experiences and Reviews

The attempt to target poverty through employment is not really new; historically, the Poor Employment Act of 1817 in Great Britain represented a major milestone in the development of economic policy regarding public action to reduce poverty through development (Flinn 1961). India, too, has a long history of employment programs for reducing poverty (Dev, Chapter 5, this volume). Ishikawa (1967) has emphasized the critical role of communal labor mobilization in the context of economic development in Asia.

A comparative study by Burki et al. (1976) concluded that public works can make a significant contribution to reducing poverty, provided there is sustained political commitment and close attention to detail in the design and administration of the program. Such commitment was lacking, however, until the underlying economic conditions changed in the 1980s and, even then, the institutional response to new conditions has come slowly, particularly among the organizations set on a development track focusing on capital investment. In an illuminating Philippine case study of communal works in irrigation rehabilitation, Kikuchi, Dozina, and Hayami (1978) identify critical economic and organizational conditions for mobilization of labor at the community level. First, incentives must be high in order to stimulate participation and, second, they must be appropriately organized by accepted leaders of the community. Very high benefit-cost ratios are found in this study. These benefits were found to be widely distributed among small farmers and landless people. The landless gained more than proportionally (according to income comparisons before and after the project), but landlords (mostly absentee) did not contribute resources to the project, despite major windfall gains in income from it. Kikuchi, Dozina, and Hayami (1978) call for an institution to be promoted that would be designed to expropriate such windfalls by taxation and other means to return the resources to the local community for further investment in the rural infrastructure, a conceptual issue that will be discussed further.

A more recent review of labor-intensive schemes for rural development by Gaude et al. (1987), based on the findings of special public works programs, comes to rather favorable conclusions concerning their impact. Also, Clay (1986) notes the relative success of major South Asian schemes using food as wage goods, but—a highly provisional assessment—sees only limited scope for organizing labor-intensive works on any significant scale in Africa. Now, in the mid-1990s, it can be seen with the clarity of hindsight that the scope and scale of these programs in Africa has already changed drastically (see Chapters 6, 7, and 8 in this volume).

Conceptual Framework and Research Questions

While it is now widely accepted that productive and remunerative employment is fundamental to overcoming food entitlement failure among the poor (Drèze and Sen 1989), there is still only limited understanding and agreement as to how to go about providing such employment. An understanding of household and family decisions is certainly one prerequisite, as comprehensively demonstrated in more general contexts of development and food policy by Strauss and Thomas (1994) and by Haddad (1994). Another prerequisite, as pointed out earlier, is an understanding of the dynamics of labor markets under different macroeconomic conditions. Furthermore, employment policies and programs for poverty reduction involve an extensive set of institutional and operational issues, which are a focus of this volume.

Short- and Long-Term Linkages

Development-oriented strategies for poverty reduction are of growing interest to governments, nongovernmental organizations, and development-assistance and other agencies. Such strategies function both by creating assets that benefit the poor and by raising the productivity of the poor through education, public health, and other human-resource-related measures. Figure 1.1 places employment programs in that context. While asset creation and productivity enhancement are not necessarily mutually exclusive, they operate on different time scales. Education programs, for instance, are geared toward improving human resources over the long run, whereas employment programs can potentially create income for the poor very quickly.

Employment programs are not a panacea, but they may be one important element in an economically sustainable, development-oriented, poverty-eradication strategy. They should not be viewed as alternatives to social security policies for the vulnerable, but as complements to policies in support of nonemployable population segments, such as children, the elderly, and the disabled (Ahmad et al. 1990).

While there seems to be plenty of scope for a renewed focus on employment policies and programs for reducing poverty and food insecurity, short-term job provision is not the main goal. The proper aim of employment policies is sustainable, remunerative employment based on higher labor productivity. While it is not a major focus of this book, it should be stressed at the outset that higher labor productivity can be achieved only when employment programs are combined with asset generation, the utilization of technology, and the enhancement of human resources. Thus, employment policies are to be viewed within a larger context of complementary development policies.

Employment programs offer certain features that make them an attractive complement to a bundle of development instruments for poverty reduction. An appropriate assessment of the degree to which employment programs can improve food security must place them within the context of a defined development strategy, as discussed, and of alternative (and possibly complementary) policy instruments (for instance, macroeconomic policy, trade and price stabilization policies, food and agricultural production policies, and so forth).

Labor-intensive employment programs have both transfer benefits and stabilization benefits, decreasing the risk of consumption shortfalls among the poor (Ravallion 1990). Of course, both resources and effective management are required to generate these food security benefits (Kinsey 1987).

Figure 1.1—Employment programs for poverty reduction and food security: The main short-term and long-term links

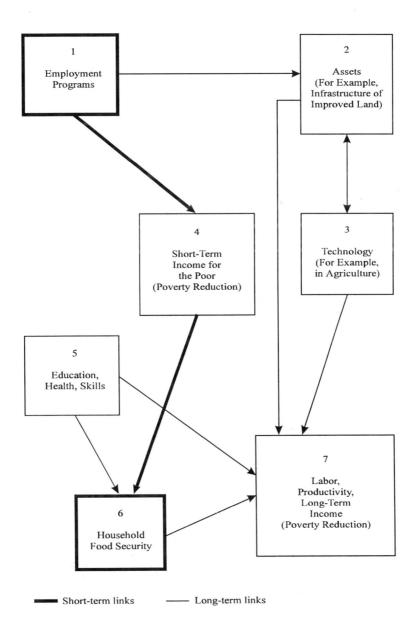

8

Figure 1.2—Employment for poverty reduction and food security: Linkages and policy and program concerns

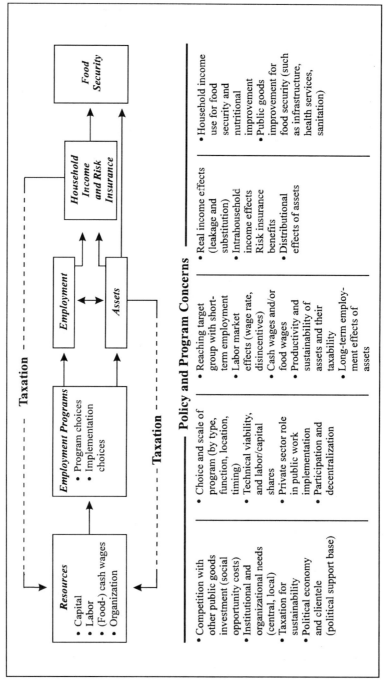

Source: Adapted from von Braun, Teklu, and Webb 1991.

Figure 1.2 outlines policy and program concerns relating to five key areas of the employment program-food security interface:

- resources for labor-intensive programs;
- public works programs and implementation choices;
- creation of short-term employment and long-term assets;
- household income and risk insurance; and
- household food-security outcome.

Policy and program concerns arising in each of these spheres are listed in the lower part of Figure 1.2. These concerns and the related research questions that are briefly discussed below also establish the issues addressed by many of the chapters in this volume.

Resources for Labor-Intensive Employment Programs

Four types of resources are required for effective labor-intensive employment programs, as shown on the left-hand side of Figure 1.2: investment capital (for asset creation), labor, wage payments, and organizational capabilities. The investment of resources for employment means, of course, that the resources are no longer available for use in other investments, whether public or private, and that the resources must therefore be valued at their economic returns to society (social opportunity costs). In the long run, employment programs and their institutions ought to achieve economic sustainability when incremental incomes and assets, created through them, become taxable.

Employment programs, like any other poverty-reduction tool, cannot escape the necessity of having a political support base. Narrowly targeted programs, while theoretically desirable on the grounds of their economic efficiency, often lack such a support base. Nevertheless, a sustainable political support base may emerge from narrow targeting of short-term benefits for those participating directly in the scheme, coupled with a wider distribution of benefits from created assets. This, however, needs to be explored in specific program circumstances.

Program and Implementation Choices

Labor-intensive programs with food security goals attempt to maximize poverty reduction and thereby achieve food security, while also encouraging growth and providing development-oriented public goods (that is, infrastructure). This approach appears to be ideal, but in reality the pressure to implement fast-acting job-creation programs increases when, for instance, an economy has emergencies to deal with, which may result in the acceptance of trade-offs between jobs tomorrow and sustainable assets next year. Optimality criteria are not easily established. Theoretically, the shadow price of labor versus that of capital in the macroeconomic environment ought to determine the choice of technology in the long run. The issue of trade-offs between employment and asset creation is most acute when employment programs are used as crisis-mitigating instruments of limited duration that compete with other instruments such as free food distribution or relief camps. Under such circumstances, a case may be made for programs designed to be more employment-focused than asset-focused in the short run. Excessive emphasis on short-term employment effects for the target group may, however, result in programs lacking technical and economic viability. On the other hand, disregarding the short-term targeting feature of public works programs may overlook their key potential for improving short-term food security through their transfer and stabilization benefits.

Employment programs are not necessarily public-sector works, but may also be implemented through the private sector. In fact, at the worker level, employment in public programs should not be considered permanent; otherwise, the flexibility in employment arrangements and the targeting feature of such programs may be lost.

Depending on the type and function of a program's specific activities, community participation and decentralization to local government levels in planning and implementation are vital for achieving distributional benefits and long-term viability. Local participation seems to be of paramount importance for the labor-based development of community-level infrastructure that enhances food security both directly and indirectly. The selection of appropriate methods for bringing about such participation and decentralization is an issue of local conditions. Local leadership can clearly affect the opportunities for participatory organization of community works programs (Kikuchi, Dozina, and Hayami 1978).

Wage rate determination in employment programs is one of the most critical policy decisions in such programs. It is generally tempting to set wage rates in public employment programs at inappropriately high levels (for instance, at the minimum wage in the public sector), which then results in employment rationing under prevailing fiscal constraints. This may in turn lead to a greater proportion of the poorest segments of interested employees being excluded (Ravallion, Datt, and Chaudhuri 1990). Two considerations come into play here: first, labor market characteristics and labor-capital price ratios, both of which determine the choice of technology in public works programs within a specific setting and season of implementation; and, second, wage rates for the food-insecure (including reservation wage rates of self-employed or subsistence farmers) who participate in the labor market. These two considerations suggest, on the one hand, that wage rates ought not to be too low to reach into the desired skill and productivity levels and, on the other hand, that wage rates ought not to be too high to maintain the self-targeting feature of public works programs under fiscal constraints. Such broad conclusions, however, are not particularly helpful for program operators. An effort must be made to arrive at more specific conclusions regarding wage rate determination in specific types of program settings (see Chapters 11 and 12).

Whether wages in labor-intensive programs should be paid in the form of cash or kind (food) depends on local circumstances relating to the risk of market failure. A priori it seems that the scale of programs and the thinness of food markets should be core considerations. The incremental employment and increased cash income of the poor translate readily into increased food demand. But market supply must be adequate in order to avoid local inflationary effects on food prices, which would adversely impinge on poor, nonparticipating households. Such market supply can, however, be constrained by infrastructure, prices, government policies, or a combination of the three. What results have food versus cash payments in different program settings actually yielded, and what do program participants say about the alternatives under various circumstances? These questions will be explored in particular in the chapters on Bangladesh (Chapter 3), China (Chapter 4), and Ethiopia (Chapter 8).

In the absence of such programs, households are compelled to search for alternative employment and income sources. Three behavioral parameters at the household level are critical for the actual food-security outcome of employment programs: (1) substitution in employment, (2) substitution in income sources, which determines the net effect of income (gross income from public works minus foregone income), and (3) household consumption behavior vis-à-vis income from employment programs versus other earned income. To arrive at an appropriate valuation of the costs and benefits of employment programs, it would be necessary to assess the social opportunity costs of time for the poor. What actually are the alternatives of participants in employment programs, if any, and what are the key behavioral parameters? These questions shall be addressed in specific program and country settings.

It is the asset-creating effect of employment programs that makes them sustainable developmental instruments, rather than merely a form of social transfer. To the extent that assets created by public works programs result in privately held assets—some irrigation infrastructure, for example—it is, of course, legitimate to tax them. There is little dispute that productive assets created by public works programs are frequently regressively distributed—a further argument for linking taxation to them.

The sustainability of the provision of public goods through employment programs must largely be achieved through the public sector budget. The more prominent a role public works programs play in a state or country, the more attention must be paid to ensuring that assets and income generated by public works programs contribute to replenishing resources via taxation (see Figure 1.2). A simulation analysis with a general equilibrium model for India appears to confirm the superiority of rural public works programs over alternatives for poverty reduction, particularly when such public works programs are financed through taxation, rather than by reducing other investments (Parikh and Srinivasan 1993). This highlights the necessity of keeping the mode of financing and the opportunity cost of resources used in public works programs in perspective when assessing their net benefits. Attempts to address this issue satisfactorily give rise to complex, unresolved modeling issues (that is, for wage formation in the labor market, government's public expenditure behavior, and so forth).

Household Income and Risk Insurance

Direct welfare effects for poor households resulting from employment programs consist of (1) income enhancement within a short period of time through wage employment, (2) risk insurance, where programs are designed with the desirable feature of employment guarantees, and (3) employment and income effects, both direct and indirect, over the long run from the assets created.

Combined, these three effects simultaneously address both transitory and structural food-security problems confronting the poor. The relative importance of each of the three welfare effects differs according to household type and the applicable food-security risk profile. With respect to the distribution of the benefits and burdens of incremental employment, it is not only the effects at the aggregate household level that matter, but also the issue of which person(s) from the household actually participate in the employment program—men, women, or children—which may affect intrahousehold resource control and allocation (Haddad 1994; Alderman et al. 1995). Within the context of employment programs, much about these issues has remained unclear in the past and is being studied in specific socioeconomic and cultural contexts in this volume.

Household Food Security Outcome

The actual effect of employment programs on food security, then, is determined by the level of household real income effects, over both the short and the long run, and household consumption and expenditure behavior. While increased income generally has favorable effects on food consumption, the already-mentioned issue of intrahousehold resource control may have a further impact on household spending for food and nutritional improvement (that is, male versus female spending preferences in some settings). Important related research issues addressed in some of the studies in this volume are women's time allocation to employment programs, quality of child care, and direct and indirect effects on child labor.

The 1980s and 1990s have seen a tremendous proliferation of poverty-reducing employment programs, especially in Asia and Africa (von Braun, Teklu, and Webb 1991). The question is why this has occurred recently, but not earlier? In other words, what prompted so many countries to initiate these types of programs when they did, or, in the case of countries that already had such programs existing, to expand them substantially?

The central questions examined here are what results have such programs yielded thus far? Or, in other words, what impact have the programs had on poor people over the short term and on development (through asset creation) over the long term? And, most importantly, how can the effectiveness, efficiency, and sustainability of such policies and programs be enhanced?

One question of relevance in devising a poverty-reduction strategy is what role, if any, the government and public action should play in creating employment? While failures in labor markets and exploitive institutional arrangements may require the attention of public policy in support of the poor, there is also the risk of public institutional and organizational failure. Especially in cases where governance problems and weaknesses in the legal system loom large, they undermine the country's potential for economic development and also probably reduce the scope for employment programs.

The specific objectives of the research assembled in this volume are, in brief,

- to analyze the changing linkages between poverty and employment at an international and national level, taking into account changing economic and political circumstances;
- to review and synthesize recent experience with employment policies that address the rural and urban poor under different national conditions in order to facilitate sharing these experiences internationally;
- to identify the conditions—including political-economic ones—under which various types of employment policies and programs for poverty reduction and food security seem to work well (this analysis must also consider the complementarities of employment programs with other development actions in pursuit of coherent policies); and

- to assess the institutional and organizational requirements for efficient, effective, and sustainable labor-intensive employment programs at different levels (community and regional), including implementation issues such as where to locate programs, what type of organizations to form at specific levels of program operation, how to formulate wage rates, and so forth.

Overview

The purpose of this overview is to give readers a general idea of the rationale behind the structure and contents of this volume.

It starts with an exploration of the relationships between employment and poverty in a growth strategy. Samir Radwan (Chapter 2) takes a forward-looking approach in addressing relevant policy prescriptions for poverty reduction, given major trends in the international and regional economies, particularly globalization, the need to regenerate growth, and the shift from state-sponsored to market-oriented development strategies. Radwan calls for a poverty-reduction strategy, undertaken as an integral part of the growth process, with major emphasis on employment. The broad elements of the suggested strategy are, first, a macroeconomic framework consistent with the objective of poverty reduction; second, a major attack on poverty through increasing investment for employment creation; and, third, public action for poverty reduction, including investment in the next generation's education and health, as well as social protection for those who cannot be reached through conventional policy instruments.

The next sections of the book are structured according to regions and countries, and each section addresses different findings from employment policies and programs for the improvement of food security. The focus of these chapters ranges from policy and program design and effectiveness issues to political-economy considerations, participation, and sustainability issues, and intrahousehold effects. Operational aspects figure prominently in the analysis of program findings.

The selection of countries and programs dealt with here was not at random. When the research project on which many of the chapters are based was first being designed, a conceptual framework for the study of employment programs was developed, and a comprehensive review of the current regional distribution, design, and documented results of employment policies for poverty reduction and food security was undertaken (von Braun, Teklu, and Webb 1991). That review included 13 African countries; the Asian countries of China, India, and Bangladesh; and findings from a case study in Latin America (Guatemala). That global review was supplemented by the experience of bilateral and multilateral organizations, such as the International Labour Office (ILO), the World Food Programme (WFP), the World Bank, Gesellschaft für Technische Zusammenarbeit (GTZ), the United States Agency for International Development (USAID), as well as nongovernmental organizations involved in employment programs.

Based on these reviews, national and program studies were selected from countries with significant absolute poverty and food security problems, including the largest countries with particularly large programs (China, India); those with particularly long-standing and interesting histories (Maharashtra, Bangladesh); some with recent and innovative programs (Niger, Botswana); and some with a specific focus on food-crisis mitigation (Ethiopia). While it became obvious at the outset that regions in Asia and Africa had generated much in the way of results from which everyone could learn, little experience and few research-based findings were available from Latin America.

The experience with Bangladesh's food-for-work program as well as alternatives to it are studied by Akhter Ahmed et al. in Chapter 3. China's varied experience with labor-intensive public works in poor areas is then analyzed by Zhu Ling and Jiang Zhongyi in Chapter 4. The programs of China are of particular interest to countries that are in the process of transforming from primarily state-dominated economic systems to market-oriented ones and have to cope with complex poverty and mounting infrastructure problems at the same time.

Among the most interesting employment policies and programs targeted toward the poor are those of India, especially the Employment Guarantee Scheme of Maharashtra. The results of this program are reviewed by Mahendra Dev (Chapter 5).

Africa's experience with employment programs is growing rapidly. Labor-intensive public works located in the drought-prone areas of Botswana and Tanzania are studied by Tesfaye Teklu (Chapter 6). The diverse performances and experiences of these programs in Botswana and Tanzania underscore the key role that institutional arrangements play in programs' sustainability.

In a comparison between rural and urban experiences with employment programs in Niger and Zimbabwe, Patrick Webb highlights program-design issues, that is, private-sector versus public-sector implementation, and presents findings on household-level participation, particularly women's participation (Chapter 7).

Africa's largest employment programs—those in Ethiopia—are reviewed by Patrick Webb and Shubh Kumar in Chapter 8, which looks at the experience gained with different types of employment programs and contrasts modes of payment (cash or food) in an environment where famine looms large as a risk.

In Latin America, employment policies and programs have been partly integrated in social investment fund initiatives; the results are reviewed by José Wurgaft in Chapter 9.

Each of the studies sheds light on several aspects of labor-intensive employment programs. Table 1.1 provides a guide to the experience gleaned from the national programs studied. The table is structured according to the nature of poverty and food security conditions, on the one hand, and the characteristics of the employment policies and programs studied and their economic and political environment, on the other.

The various countries' poverty and food-security conditions are grouped into two categories: (1) disasters, crises, and famines, and (2) chronic poverty and food insecurity (rural and urban). Further distinctions are made between the various countries' institutional conditions for labor-intensive employment programs (for instance, political support base, organizational base), their financial support base, and the implementation and specific investment focus of their programs (for instance, building infrastructure or improving natural resources).

Each country or program viewed in this structured manner may appear multiple times in Table 1.1, as some of the studies cover different aspects of policies and programs and deal with several different poverty and food-security contexts. Treating the national studies this way maximizes the insights gained into the key policy research issues pointed out in the previous section.

The last section of the volume deals with generalized issues and policy conclusions. In this section, issues relating to the development and relief potential of food aid for employment are discussed by John Shaw (Chapter 10). This is followed by a comprehensive review of implementation issues relating to employment programs (Chapter 11), in which Jean Majeres draws on the long-standing experience of the International Labour Office (ILO). The book concludes with a synthesis of the findings and the lessons they offer for the formulation of future policy (Chapter 12).

Table 1.1—A guide to the reviewed experience of countries with poverty-reducing and food-security–enhancing employment programs

Aspects of Employment Policies and Programs	Poverty and Food Security Conditions in Countries Studied	
	Disasters, Crises, and Famines	Chronic Poverty and Food Insecurity
Countries' institutional conditions for employment programs		
Strong political support base for programs	Bangladesh, India, Botswana, Ethiopia	Bangladesh, India, Botswana, Niger
Strong organization base for programs (or long experience)	India, Botswana, Ethiopia	China, India, Botswana, Niger
Financial support base for programs		
Mainly domestic	China, India, Botswana	China, India, Botswana
Much international or NGO support	Bangladesh, Niger, Ethiopia	Bangladesh, Niger, Tanzania, Latin American cases
Implementation		
Mainly public	China, India, Botswana	China, India, Botswana, Tanzania, Zimbabwe
Private and public	Bangladesh, Ethiopia	Bangladesh, Ethiopia, Latin American cases
Focus of programs		
Building infrastructure	Bangladesh, Botswana, Niger, Ethiopia	Bangladesh, China, Botswana, Tanzania, Zimbabwe
Natural resource conservation and improvement	India, Niger, Ethiopia	China, India, Niger, Zimbabwe, Ethiopia

REFERENCES

Ahmad, E., J. Drèze, J. Hills, and A. Sen, eds. 1991. *Social security in developing countries*. Oxford: Clarendon Press.

Alderman, H., P. A. Chiappori, L. Haddad, J. Hoddinott, and R. Kanbur. 1995. Unitary versus collective models of the household: Is it time to shift the burden of proof? *World Bank Research Observer* 10 (1): 1–19.

Bardhan, P., ed. 1989. *The economic theory of agrarian institutions*. Oxford: Clarendon Press.

Braun, J. von, T. Teklu, and P. Webb. 1991. *Labor-intensive public works for food security: Experience in Africa*. Working Papers on Food Subsidies 6. Washington, D.C.: International Food Policy Research Institute.

Braun, J. von, H. Bouis, S. Kumar, and R. Pandya-Lorch. 1992. *Improving food security of the poor: Concept, policy, and programs*. Washington, D.C.: International Food Policy Research Institute.

Burki, S. J., D. G. Davies, R. H. Hook, and J. W. Thomas. 1976. Public works programs in developing countries: A comparative analysis. World Bank Staff Paper 224. Washington, D.C.: World Bank.

Clay, E. J. 1986. Rural public works and food-for-work: A survey. *World Development* 14 (10/11): 1237–1252.

Drèze, J., and A. Sen. 1989. *Hunger and public action*. Oxford: Clarendon Press.

Fei, J. C. H., and G. Ranis. 1964. *Development of the labor surplus economy: Theory and policy*. New Haven, Conn., U.S.A.: Yale University Press.

Flinn, M. W. 1961. The Poor Employment Act of 1817. *Economic History Review* 14: 82–92.

Gaude, J., A. Guichaona, B. Martens, and S. Miller. 1987. Rural development and labor-intensive schemes: Impact studies of some pilot programs. *International Labor Review* 126 (4): 423–446.

Haddad, L. 1994. Strengthening food policy through intrahousehold analysis. *Food Policy* 19 (4): 347–356.

Hoff, K., A. Braverman, and J. E. Stiglitz, eds. 1993. *The economics of rural organization: Theory, practice, and policy*. Oxford: Oxford University Press.

Horton, S., R. Kanbur, and D. Mazumdar, eds. 1994. *Labor markets in an era of adjustment*, Vols. 1, 2. EDI Development Studies. Washington, D.C.: World Bank.

ILO (International Labour Office). 1986. *Economically active population estimates: 1950-1980; Projections 1985–2025*. Six volumes. Geneva.

Ishikawa, S. 1967. *Economic development in Asian perspective*. Tokyo: Kino Kuniya.

Kikuchi, M., G. Dozina, and Y. Hayami. 1978. Economics of community work programs: A communal irrigation project in the Philippines. *Economic Development and Cultural Change* 26 (2): 211–226.

Kinsey, B. H. 1987. *Creating rural employment*. London: Croom Helm.

Lewis, W. A. 1955. *The theory of economic growth*. Homewood, Ill., U.S.A.: Richard D. Irwin.

Lipton, M., and J. van der Gaag, eds. 1993. *Including the poor*. Washington, D.C.: World Bank.

Mellor, J. W. 1986. Agriculture on the road to industrialization. In *Development strategies reconsidered*, ed. J. P. Lewis and V. Kallab. U.S.-Third World Perspectives 5. New Brunswick, N.J., U.S.A.: Transaction Books.

Parikh, K., and T. N. Srinivasan. 1993. Poverty alleviation policies in India. In *Including the poor*, ed. M. Lipton and J. van der Gaag, 392–410. Washington, D.C.: World Bank.

Pinstrup-Andersen, P., ed. 1988. *Food subsidies in developing countries: Costs, benefits, and policy options*. Baltimore, Md., U.S.A.: Johns Hopkins University Press for the International Food Policy Research Institute.

_____. ed. 1993. *The political economy of food and nutrition policies*. Baltimore, Md., U.S.A.: Johns Hopkins University Press.

_____. 1994. *World food trends and future food security*. Food Policy Report. Washington, D.C.: International Food Policy Research Institute.

Platteau, J. P. 1993. *Sub-Saharan Africa as a special case: The crucial role of (infra)structural constraints.* Serie Recherche No. 128, 1993/6. Namur: Facultes Universitaires Notre Dame de La Paix.

Ravallion, M. 1990. *Reaching the poor through rural public employment. A survey of theory and evidence.* World Bank Discussion Paper 94. Washington, D.C.: World Bank.

Ravallion, M., G. Datt, and S. Chaudhuri. 1990. Higher wages for relief work can make many of the poor worse off: Recent evidence from Maharashtra's Employment Guarantee Scheme. World Bank, Washington, D.C. Mimeo.

Schultz, T. W. 1981. *Investing in people: The economics of population quality.* Berkeley, Calif., U.S.A.: University of California Press.

Strauss, J., and D. Thomas. 1994. Human resources: Empirical modeling of household and family decisions. For *Handbook of development economies*, Vol. 3, ed. T. N. Srinivasan and J. R. Behrman. Working Paper Series 97-07. Santa Monica, Calif., U.S.A.: Rand, Labor and Population Program.

Streeten, P. 1981. *First things first: Meeting basic human needs in developing countries.* Oxford: Oxford University Press.

_____. 1994. *Strategies for human development, global poverty, and unemployment.* Copenhagen: Handelstioejskolens Forlag.

Todaro, M. P. 1989. *Economic development in the Third World.* New York: Longman.

World Bank. 1990. *Poverty, world development report.* Oxford: Oxford University Press.

2
CHALLENGES AND SCOPE FOR AN EMPLOYMENT-INTENSIVE GROWTH STRATEGY

Samir Radwan

The main objective of this chapter is to explore new approaches to policy for poverty reduction, given the major trends in the international and regional economies, particularly globalization, the need to generate new growth, and the shift from state-sponsored to market-oriented development strategies.

The literature abounds with poverty studies that contain concepts, measurements, determinants, and policies to reduce poverty. This chapter takes stock of what has been learned and attempts to provide the broad outlines of a growth-oriented strategy for poverty alleviation. The chapter begins with a brief study of the magnitude of the problem, continues with a schematic presentation of different approaches to poverty reduction, and ends by outlining an employment-focused strategy for poverty alleviation.

Trends in Poverty Incidence

Poverty reduction has emerged as a central theme in development.[1] Generally speaking, poverty has been increasing at the same rate as population growth (2 percent) in developing countries (Chen, Datt, and Ravallion 1993).

According to World Bank estimates (Table 2.1), around 30 percent of the population in developing countries lived in poverty in 1990, on the basis of an absolute poverty line of $31 per person per month. Close to one-half of the population was in poverty in South Asia and Sub-Saharan Africa, compared with one-third in the Middle East and North Africa, a quarter in Latin America and the Caribbean, and a little over one-tenth in East Asia. The global incidence of poverty remained almost unchanged between the two years quoted in the table—1985 and 1990—although the absolute number of poor people increased because of population growth.

---

[1]This section, which draws on work of the International Labour Office (ILO 1993, 1–4) was the result of a collective effort undertaken under the auspices of the International Institute of Labour Studies in Geneva.

Table 2.1—Poverty in the developing world, 1985–90

Region	Percentage of Population Below the Poverty Line		Number of Poor Persons	
	1985	1990	1985	1990
	(percent)		(millions)	
All developing countries	30.5	29.7	1,050	1,133
South Asia	51.8	49.0	532	562
East Asia	13.2	11.3	182	169
Sub-Saharan Africa	47.6	47.8	184	216
Middle East and North Africa	30.6	33.1	60	73
Latin America and the Caribbean	22.4	25.5	87	108

Source: World Bank 1992.

Asia, with its rapid income growth, was the most successful in alleviating poverty. But poverty increased in Africa, Latin America, and the Middle East. These figures are, of course, only indicative; there is a great deal of subjectivity in estimates of the extent of poverty. These numbers illustrate the enormity and persistence of the problem, however.

Poverty is by no means confined to the developing countries of the regions included in Table 2.1, although the nature of poverty in industrialized countries is different. The recent growth in poverty in Central and Eastern Europe following the collapse of socialist systems of public provisioning surely poses a threat to economic reconstruction.

In developing countries, the poor tend to be concentrated in rural areas, where average real incomes are much lower than in urban areas. But there is also much extreme poverty in the cities, where the poor typically live in slums or squatter settlements, and often have to contend with overcrowding, bad sanitation, and contaminated water. In recent years, civil wars and the breakdown of law and order have also resulted in much extreme deprivation, sometimes associated with large-scale movements of refugees and the misery of refugee camps.

In the longer term, there have been significant changes in the nature and causes of poverty and of the processes that lead to poverty in developing countries. Major structural transformations have occurred since the 1960s, involving the relocation of vast numbers of rural people to the urban areas. In most Latin American countries, over two-thirds of the population now live in the cities, compared with only one-third 30 years ago. In Sub-Saharan Africa, urbanization has proceeded at annual rates of 6–8 percent and one-third of the population is now urban compared with only 10 percent or so at the start of the 1960s. The rural population is already a minority in most of the Asian newly industrialized countries (NICs). But whereas urbanization in the NICs has increased in line with employment opportunities, in most other developing countries rural-urban migration has occurred at much higher rates than warranted by the absorptive capacity of the formal sector. Consequently, unemployment and underemployment have grown, with the informal sector having to bear the brunt of urban labor absorption.

Other factors that have led to changes in the incidence of poverty include a series of structural changes in the world economy. One such change is the growing polarization in the labor market. As enterprises attempt to reduce costs in the face of increasingly fierce global competition, the number of jobs with higher incomes and employment security declines. Advantages are restricted to a core group of workers who possess human capital acquired from formal education and on-the-job training. Around them is a larger group of "secondary" workers who are often employed under fixed-term or temporary contracts. Finally, there is an army of sub-contracted informal workers and a host of small enterprises in which employment conditions are much less generous. This process of labor differentiation can be observed in both developed and developing countries alike.

In the rural areas, too, significant changes have occurred. Because of land shortage or changes in landholding patterns, landlessness has increased and the new entrants to the rural labor force are increasingly forced into wage labor. The number of net buyers of food has begun to rival the surplus producers and the self-sufficient, even in Africa.

The long-term trends toward urbanization and landlessness have been exacerbated by the now two-decade-long crisis in Latin America and Africa and the structural adjustment programs that were implemented to contend with the crisis. Asia has been somewhat protected from these two trends, although some of the impacts are discernible even there. While the crisis originated in the tradables sector—effectively the agriculture sector—because commodity prices declined, its most visible effect was to spur the declines in real wages in urban areas: a fall of 30–50 percent in wages was common in the Sub-Saharan countries and similar declines occurred in many countries in Latin America. The structural adjustment programs, which emphasized restraints on wages and the removal of subsidies on staple foods, contributed to the fall in real wages. Plummeting wages, combined with a decrease in the numbers of people in formal wage employment, has sometimes led to the evaporation of wage incomes in urban areas, especially in Africa. African countries have become "informalized," not only in the sense that the urban wage class has been reduced to a minority, but also in the sense that most wages are earned in the informal sector. Similar trends exist in Latin America. In East Asia, however, rapid economic expansion has, in fact, resulted in the contraction of informal activities.

In the rural areas, the effects of the crisis and concomitant adjustment programs have varied. Wage workers have been hardest hit—their wages have fallen along with those of their urban counterparts and for similar reasons—the repeal or decline of minimum wages and the freeing of food prices. Export crop producers have been less affected by the crisis, as declines in world prices were often offset by devaluation.

The breakdown of the extended—and even the nuclear—family is another factor explaining the changing composition of the poor. As a result of education and migration, the bonds of the extended family are loosening. One result is that more households are headed by women, who often command lower wages than men.

The aging of the population is also likely to shape the composition of the poor in the future. In developed countries, old people are protected by private pensions, social insurance, and other forms of social assistance. But in developing countries, such provisions hardly exist; without countervailing policies, poverty is therefore likely to worsen among old people.

In general, the poor usually lack assets as well as income, including the "human capital" embodied in skills and knowledge. Vulnerability to ill health is common as a consequence and cause of poverty, and is often associated with malnutrition. Poor women are particularly disadvantaged, since they are discriminated against in the labor market and are vulnerable to ill health as a consequence of child bearing. Ill health reduces the poor's capacity for work—and so diminishes their main or only asset.

The poor are a heterogeneous group, since poverty has many causes and it affects many different groups. It is possible to identify cultural, social, and ethnic background; family situation; or the area and housing that people live in as characteristics that help to identify the poor. But even if all these characteristics were the same for all families with the same income or the same pattern of deprivation, it is quite possible that they would adopt different strategies to overcome their situation. For example, declining incomes in both rural and urban areas have resulted in excessive diversification of economic roles, with most families increasing their activities in several sectors to make ends meet. Changes have been most noticeable in the urban areas where, for example, families have resorted to a variety of income-earning activities, including even urban farming. This mixing of economic roles makes it more difficult to identify groups in poverty. The usual "indicators" of poverty, such as wages and farm prices, can no longer be taken as guides to family income, since the composition of family income varies between groups and over time. By and large, the vulnerable groups include smallholders, the farm workers, urban wage earners, and informal-sector workers. But because of the diversity of survival strategies, this characterization may well be too imprecise for the design of effective policy. Because the economic and social situations of the poor are diverse, too simple a notion of poverty is likely to lead to inappropriate policy.

Approaches to Poverty Reduction

Currently, the interest in poverty reduction results from the experience of developing countries in the postwar period. While these countries achieved a reasonable rate of growth of GDP, poverty did not shrink, and, in many cases, it grew.

Two general approaches to poverty reduction may be distinguished: (1) the "trickle-down approach," where growth is regarded as a condition for poverty reduction; and (2) the targeting approach, where nonmarket interventions by the state are prescribed in the fight against poverty (for example, the basic needs approach, food for work, public works, and so forth).

It may be useful to summarize the specific strategies for poverty reduction by referring to the experience of the International Labour Office (ILO) (ILO 1993, 27-51). The following sections will attempt to provide a critical summary of these approaches, which are largely rooted in the second approach to poverty reduction stated above, to illustrate both the potential and the limitations of these various interventions for poverty reduction.

Changing the Distribution of Assets

Land and Physical Capital. A significant amount of the ILO's work on poverty has stressed the importance of asset redistribution. The main rationale for this approach has been that the distribution of asset ownership is a major determinant of income distribution in developing countries. The vast majority of the economically active population in these countries works in the rural and informal sectors where self-employment predominates. The returns of self-employment are largely determined by the productive assets available to the self-employed, whether they are engaged in peasant farming, nonfarm rural activity, or the urban informal sector. As a consequence, there is a strong correlation between asset deprivation and poverty.

While many of the urban poor are struggling to subsist in the informal sector from what they can produce with improvised equipment, the rural poor are mostly landless or have farms too small to yield an adequate income. Agrarian reform has therefore been frequently advocated in the ILO's work as an efficient policy instrument to deal with rural poverty, especially in Asia and Latin America. It was argued that unequal distribution of land ownership and archaic land tenure arrangements were direct causes of poverty. The poor's access to other inputs, especially credit, is also curtailed by their lack of access to land. Moreover, land reform can lead to an increase in productivity since there is an inverse correlation between farm size and output per unit of land, so the advocacy of land reform was also based on efficiency grounds.

A second part of the rationale for the focus on asset distribution also relates to efficiency. This part was based on the observation that the secondary effects of an unequal distribution of assets reinforce the poverty directly caused by the inadequacy of productive assets. In the rural economy, unequal land distribution results in a concentration of economic and political power that negatively affects the poor.

In the late 1970s, significant attention was paid to the issue of asset distribution. For example, the study on poverty and landlessness in rural Asia (ILO 1977) argued that because of unequal agrarian structure, rural poverty increased in spite of economic growth. A redistribution of assets (land and tenancy reform) was therefore necessary. This challenged the orthodox "trickle down" view, which predicted that the promotion of agricultural growth through land-augmenting policies (such as new seeds, irrigation investments, and small farmer programs) would automatically lead to a decline in the incidence of rural poverty.

Subsequent work on agrarian systems incorporated the premise that asset redistribution was a key element in development strategies by evaluating the effectiveness of different types of land ownership and rural development. This work contrasted agrarian systems based on a highly concentrated pattern of land ownership with postreform systems such as egalitarian peasant farming and various forms of communal agriculture. Its broad conclusion was that agrarian reform was potentially a powerful means for ensuring equitable growth and poverty reduction, and that these postreform models were viable in both socialist and market economies.

This broad conclusion should, however, be tempered by other considerations. For instance, in many countries, land reform was a necessary, but not sufficient, instrument for poverty reduction. In densely populated economies, land was often too scarce to make a meaningful distribution possible. In such situations, a first round of land redistribution may have produced some positive results, but productivity gains were soon eroded, particularly through population growth. The provision of inputs and the adoption of correct pricing policies were perhaps as important as land reform in determining returns to land and labor.

Finally, surveys of countries that undertook land reform (Radwan 1977; Collier and Radwan 1986) have shown that while the distribution of assets explains about half the variation in poverty incidence, the other half is determined by the skill endowment of the household or its access to remittances from migrant members. Such results point to the need for complementary policies to deal with such things as the lack of access to credit and education and weak bargaining power in the labor markets. In the light of this and the strength of the interests opposed to asset redistribution, such policies have made limited contributions to poverty reduction in most countries, despite their theoretical importance.

Human Capital. Investments in education and training are a potentially powerful instrument for reducing income disparities and for raising the productivity and earnings of the poor. Increased literacy and basic education enhance the capabilities of the poor in several ways. In the rural economy, improved educational levels have been shown to raise productivity in peasant agriculture because educated farmers appear eager to absorb information on new techniques of production and to innovate. More generally, education also enhances farmers' ability to respond to market opportunities in both farm and nonfarm rural activities, and it offers a route to training and, through this, to better jobs. In the urban economy, improved access to further education and training for the poor is a key escape route from poverty to more higher skilled and better paying jobs. Training is also an important component of support services provided to raise productivity and incomes in the informal sector. The ILO's mandate in human resource development is largely confined to vocational training outside the regular school system.[2]

Since the late 1970s, the organization has developed new operational activities in the area of targeted training programs for poor or disadvantaged groups. These have included the skills development for self-reliance and training for rural gainful activities programs, which have offered training and complementary support in order to promote rural income-generating activities (ILO 1982). A program for promoting income-generating activities for women was also developed. From 1986 onward, the issue of training for the informal sector also began to be addressed in ILO research. This highlighted the problem that preemployment training in formal institutions benefited only the relatively small proportion of the labor force that was being prepared for skilled employment in the formal sector. Public expenditures on training provided few benefits to the large numbers already in or destined for informal-sector employment, raising the issue of equity. This

---

[2]Within the UN system, responsibility for primary and higher levels of education, as well as for technical and vocational education within schools, rests with the United Nations Educational, Scientific, and Cultural Organization (UNESCO). As a result, the ILO's work has rarely touched on the broader questions of how the level and allocation of educational expenditures might reduce poverty.

later ILO work addressed the possibility of greater outreach by training institutions to the informal sector, the need to emphasize training for self-employment, and the means through which traditional apprenticeship systems in the informal sector could be upgraded and rendered more effective.

These new areas of work represent a welcome shift toward greater sensitivity to poverty and equity issues.[3] But these new areas of ILO work may not be cost-effective and they may be difficult to replicate. Training interventions must also be linked to other support measures, since it is rarely the case that training on its own can succeed in raising the incomes of the poor.

Restructuring Production at the Sectoral Level

Promoting Production and Employment in the Informal and Small-Scale Sectors. Since its initial conceptualization, popularized by the ILO's Employment Strategy Mission to Kenya in 1972, the "informal sector" has been looked upon as a large source of employment potential. One of the mission's main findings was that the major employment problem was not unemployment, but the existence of large numbers of the "working poor," involved in the production of goods and services, whose activities were not recognized, recorded, protected, or regulated. Many such workers are self-employed, and research on the causes of poverty among them shows that it can often be traced to inadequate access to productive assets, an issue discussed above.

Clearly, informal-sector workers are a group that should be targeted for poverty reduction. But systematic policy design has been inhibited by several factors: the haziness of the concept of the informal sector and the heterogeneity of the activities that it encompasses; the lack of organization of informal sector workers and producers and their lack of direct representation in the ILO; the difficulty of applying universal labor standards, both because of the difficulty of enforcement and because of the inability of many informal producers to comply; and the very real difficulties faced by formal organizations such as the ILO and its constituents in dealing with nonformalized

---

[3]Recently, the ILO has paid more attention to the promotion and application of its standards on human resources development and training (Convention No. 142 on human resources development of 1975 and the corresponding Recommendations No. 150). These standards emphasize equality of access and other equity issues and provide a clear mandate for policy action at the macro and other levels that are more closely linked to issues of poverty reduction.

situations. While the ultimate objective of ILO action is to integrate progressively the informal sector into the formal economy, and to apply the protective measures articulated in international labor standards to this group, it is clear that the informal sector's employment-creating potential must be maintained.[4] Analysis of the constraints imposed upon the informal sector by existing institutional, legal, and regulatory structures suggests that, while it is important to provide basic social protection to informal sector producers and workers, it would be unrealistic to try to bring them into compliance with all existing labor legislation. Most informal sector producers are unable to comply with such regulatory structures, and such a move would only cause them to retreat further into the hidden economy.

However, if action in the informal sector is to help reduce poverty, access to skills, capital, and markets is clearly crucial. In ILO work, promotion of informal sector productivity has been undertaken through targeted programs of support to small producers. These programs are designed to help producers provide more employment and income opportunities. Specifically, the ILO has sought to improve access to credit and technology and provide technical training and information relevant to product marketing. The support programs are based on the concept of participatory development, which contains three guiding principles: autonomy through reliance on the target groups' own resources (financial, technical, and human); organizational structures that ensure the effective participation of the beneficiaries; and empowerment, by building the institutional capacity to overcome economic and social constraints.

Employment Creation in the Rural Economy. The potential for increasing employment in agriculture through technological change and agrarian reform is considerable, as East Asian experiences in particular have shown. But even under the most optimistic scenarios, it seems unlikely that developing countries' agriculture will be able to absorb the growing numbers of entrants to the labor market. The result may be an increasing stream of rural-urban migration that swells the ranks of the urban informal sector or the urban unemployed, or an intensification of rural underemployment and deprivation. To deal with this situation, the ILO proposed a "rural-focused, employment-oriented strategy of development" in 1988. The main thrust of such a strategy would be to increase labor absorption in the rural areas by linking a dynamic nonfarm rural economy to an agriculture

---

[4]This has been explicitly referred to in the Employment Policy (Supplementary Provisions) Recommendations No. 169, 1984.

sector experiencing rapid productivity growth due to the adoption of innovative and appropriate technology.

Evidence from recent research on the experience of some developing countries suggests that such a strategy is feasible. The basic objective of the strategy is to create conditions for maximum labor absorption in the rural economy through three basic measures. First, agricultural growth must be accelerated through land-augmenting technological progress. The experience of the Green Revolution has suggested that technological innovation can increase agricultural employment and productivity, provided that the technology and the credit system are scale-neutral (that is, they do not favor large farms at the expense of small ones), and provided that the institutions are not too strongly biased toward the interests of the larger producers. The situation in Sub-Saharan Africa is particularly suited to such a measure since the poor performance of the agriculture and food sectors can mainly be ascribed to the lack of technological progress.

Second, the growth of agriculture-nonagriculture linkages should be fostered by the increase of effective demand by agriculture for the products of the nonagricultural enterprises, especially those located in the rural areas. There is solid evidence that agricultural growth, through production and consumption linkages, provides a major impetus to the growth of incomes and employment in the nonfarm economy.

Third, the domestic demand for agricultural output must grow rapidly. This can only occur through accelerated growth in employment in the nonfarm sector, facilitated, in turn, by the indirect effects of agricultural growth.

In implementing such a three-pronged strategy, certain considerations have to be borne in mind. First, this is not a universal recipe for all countries at all times: the role of agriculture in employment creation varies considerably between regions.

Second, in the long run, a shift out of agriculture toward industry and services is inevitable, for agricultural growth by itself cannot solve the problem of employment in the economy as a whole. A coherent long-term strategy needs to take this into account.

Third, the history and pitfalls of the Green Revolution should be kept in mind, especially its bias against small farmers and the high cost of using chemical inputs. Even when research produces scale-neutral technologies, these can acquire a scale bias in actual practice. This is because the benefits of credit and extension services tend to be distributed in the same manner as landholding, often despite the intentions of the governments. In addition, since the adoption of new technologies requires as preconditions both the acquisition of knowledge and the capacity to invest, the larger farmers have better access to credit and extension and are often better able to benefit.

Fourth, supplementary policies are needed to encourage the labor-intensive, nonfarm economy. On the demand side, raising the incomes of the rural poor will tend to increase effective demand for locally produced goods and services, and so support the growth of rural nonfarm production. But supply-side policies are also crucial. These include the provision of credit and marketing facilities and the improvement of skills through appropriate training and investment in human capital. Credit is particularly important, since the formal financial system often fails to support the smallest and most disadvantaged enterprises, especially in rural areas.

Public Works and Food-for-Work Schemes. Another example of a targeted approach to poverty reduction is found in labor-based public works and food-for-work.[5] This approach is based on the fact that the most abundant asset of the poor is their labor; consequently, the poor's entitlement to income can be expanded if demand for their labor rises. One way to increase such demand is to build sorely needed infrastructure, particularly in the rural areas.

Some public works programs have been used to improve the food security of the poorest people. In these cases, wages were paid in food instead of cash and were often financed by food aid. Food payments have often been seen as an incentive to encourage poor and undernourished populations to participate in self-help projects. Food-for-work programs have been widely promoted by the ILO, especially in Asia and Africa, to provide such demand for labor. Since the late 1970s, these projects have aimed to reduce poverty by providing poorer segments of the population with employment and access to basic infrastructure and services. A number of developing countries that have adopted structural adjustment programs have made use of labor-intensive investment policies.

There is no doubt that this approach has been effective in creating employment opportunities in rural areas, particularly during slack agricultural seasons. Some urban public works programs have also had a significant effect on employment. The public works approach is most appropriate where it is cost-effective and sustainable over the long term, and where the mix of labor and equipment can be adapted to the costs of various project components and the availability of labor. But success requires a positive policy environment in public and private-sector agencies and firms to cope with such new tasks. These programs also have limitations. In particular, their scale is often small in relation to the overall magnitude of the problem

---

[5]For an overview of this approach, see the special issue of *International Labour Review* 131 (1), 1992.

of poverty and underemployment. Where this is not the case, the expense of public works makes it difficult to maintain programs over the long run.

The balance of past experience indicates that public works programs have considerable potential for poverty reduction, though this potential is not always realized. Evaluations indicate that everything depends on the design of the program, on decentralized planning, and on the early involvement of local people. The fact that many labor-intensive infrastructure works do not live up to expectations is not an argument against them as such, but rather an argument for better design and implementation. In this context, it is significant whether the assets created by the poor are also controlled by them.

Labor-intensive investment policies have already proved to be a successful employment creation instrument, particularly when compared with the efforts and resources needed to design and implement alternative policies with a similar impact on the poor.

Labor Market Access and Vulnerability

In many parts of the world, there is a rapid growth in the numbers of rural landless laborers, and labor market outcomes are not usually favorable to the rural poor in view of their disadvantaged position and weak bargaining power (Radwan 1989). A central question, then, is how to improve the outcomes of both urban and rural labor markets, especially in terms of returns to labor, and particularly for the poor. Four broad areas of labor market policy with some degree of overlap may be identified. First, an area that has received considerable attention in ILO work concerns labor market information. But the impact on poverty of policy in this area is limited—the poor require not only information but also access. Employment services generally cannot tackle the structural barriers preventing poor people from obtaining decent jobs. A second area in which the ILO traditionally has been very active concerns the regulation of contractual relations in employment. This may involve outlawing some types of coercive labor contracts (for example, bonded labor), modifying the conditions of work or the way in which the employment contract is defined, and securing the right to negotiate terms and conditions. Again, much of this intervention would not directly affect poverty (because it would take place mainly in the formal sector, where poverty is less concentrated). But some aspects of the employment relationship are potentially important targets for antipoverty action. This is particularly true of the regulation of wage setting, especially policy on wage inequality and minimum wage legislation. Third, policies to strengthen the labor market position of groups that are vulnerable to discrimination, exploitation, or exclusion have direct implications for poverty. A fourth area concerns policy interventions designed to increase the bargaining power of low-income groups in the labor market.

Labor Market Regulation to Reduce Poverty: Minimum Wages and Other Interventions. The relationship between minimum wages and poverty is less clear than might be imagined (Starr 1981). One reason is that the impact on poverty of the wages of individual workers depends on the pattern of economic activity of different household members and household structures. Nevertheless, minimum wages can be an important labor market policy instrument for reducing poverty (this aim is implicit in the ILO Convention on the subject [No. 131, 1970] and explicit in ILO Recommendation No. 135). Whether this potential is realized depends on several factors: the extent of coverage; the extent of compliance; the level of the minimum wages; the indirect effects on labor demand, for example, an increase in unemployment or underemployment; the indirect effects on consumption demand of those receiving the minimum wage; effects on labor productivity; and the effects of minimum wages on wage demands of those receiving higher wages. The net outcome of such regulation is thus far from obvious.

A general problem in assessing the effects of minimum wages or other forms of labor market regulation on poverty is the extent of compliance. A minimum wage that applies to, say, 20 percent of workers, will have little effect on poverty, and may simply reduce labor absorption in large-scale industry. For minimum wages to be effective in action against poverty, they have to be widely applied, and too often governments are content with the appearance of action that unenforced minimum wage legislation provides. Such attitudes are facilitated by the difficulty of assessing and documenting compliance.

Similar concerns can be expressed with respect to other forms of labor market regulation, such as employment security legislation. Casual, unprotected, irregular work is an important cause of poverty, and carefully designed legislation to outlaw exploitative practices and precarious employment conditions can contribute to antipoverty policies, provided those practices are prevalent throughout the labor market (see, for instance, Siddiqui 1990). But certain preconditions in labor market institutions and economics must be met before legislation is likely to be effective. In this area, the mutual reinforcement of economic policy and legislation would be important.

Reducing Labor Market Vulnerability. Through poverty programs, the ILO attempts to target groups that are perceived to be vulnerable in the labor market. Vulnerability is most often related to age, gender, ethnic identity, or household status. Children and the elderly are both disadvantaged in the labor market, but in different ways; in both cases, their initial vulnerability places them in a vicious cycle of intensifying deprivation. When the elderly are forced to work for lack of alternative income sources, they face discrimination and risk illness, both of which undermine their productivity and increase their need to work at the same time. Understanding these interactions is crucial if the pattern is to be broken.

In addition to low-income and low-productivity jobs that trap the poor, other factors play important roles in labor market vulnerability, as is well-illustrated by the position of women in the labor market. It is now generally admitted that a "gender-blind" approach to labor market policy or other policy creates, in practice, a negative bias against women. Women often start from a weak position: they lack direct control of assets and access to training; they experience discrimination in the labor market, but are not organized to combat it; they have competing domestic and labor-market demands on their time; and they are subject to cultural and norma-tive constraints on their economic roles. As a result of these built-in biases, a policy that does not specifically discriminate in favor of women ends up reinforcing gender inequality and, to the extent that gender is a risk factor for poverty, deepening female poverty.

The labor market situation faced by women in poor households arises from a combination of the general mechanisms creating labor market vulnerability and the particular disadvantages of women. Labor market segmentation largely follows gender lines. This is because access to the labor market may depend on informal mechanisms imbued with cultural constraints and attitudes that reinforce discrimination against women. For example, labor market access may require formal educational qualifica-tions, but investment in boys' education is seen as offering a higher eventual return than investment in girls' education. As a result of these barriers to access, women are often squeezed into the last, least desirable spaces in the labor market. Women's domestic roles in any case interfere with career progression in regular wage work. Home-based work is an almost exclusively female labor market category, subject to very low pay and hidden but intense exploitation.

The ILO has paid increasing attention to women workers, though only a small amount of this work has stressed the link between women's work and poverty. A number of international instruments have been adopted to pro-mote equal employment opportunities for women and to protect their rights as workers. The instruments include the Equal Remuneration Convention, 1951 (No. 100); the Discrimination (Employment and Occupation) Conven-tion, 1958 (No. 111); the Human Resources Development Convention,

1975 (No. 142); and the Workers with Family Responsibility Convention, 1981 (No. 156). The adoption of these instruments, however, does not necessarily guarantee their implementation, and the number of countries that have actually ratified certain conventions is disappointingly small.

One program that has focused on the links between women's work and poverty is the World Employment Programme on Rural Women (Berar 1988), which combines policy advice, analysis, technical cooperation, and the promotion of standards. The main activities in the labor market area have consisted of assisting the formulation and implementation of programs and projects concerned with self-employment and credit schemes for poor women and female-headed households, and social protection of vulnerable groups such as home-based piece-rate workers. Much of the ILO's work in the late 1970s and 1980s focused on the survival strategies of poor women, bringing to light the diverse and rapidly changing nature of poor women's income-earning activities in various socioeconomic contexts. In the late 1980s and early 1990s, ILO's emphasis shifted to analyzing the impact of economic restructuring on patterns of poverty and employment among women, both new opportunities created and new forms of discrimination and exploitation emerging from economic restructuring.

Many of the determinants of women's vulnerability in the labor market are also relevant to other vulnerable groups. Child labor is a case in point. Whatever form it takes, child labor is an extreme manifestation of poverty because it is the poorest families that need their children's labor to survive. But child labor also perpetuates poverty because it prevents children from acquiring the skills and education that would equip them for gainful employment. The ILO's general legal instrument on the subject is the Minimum Age Convention (No. 138), 1973. This instrument aims at the elimination of child labor, but it also attempts to protect working children and to provide welfare and educational facilities for them.

How effective is labor market policy in these different circumstances? There is evidence that affirmative action policies can have positive effects, but they need to be systematically and vigorously enforced. This involves using administrative controls and inspections, as well as mobilizing the groups affected, public opinion, and nongovernment organizations. Even so, success is likely to be qualified. Labor market regulation is also a limited instrument in poverty reduction; it is often ineffective in situations where poverty is most extreme. However, regulation may be an important supporting policy where a broader economic strategy to reduce poverty is given high priority. In brief, labor market policies against poverty make sense as part of a package, but not as an independent, self-contained approach.

Social Transfers

Measures to improve the position of the poor in society by altering the distribution of assets, restructuring systems of production, or increasing their access to jobs imply fundamental changes in economic relations. Such measures may take a long time to become effective, and even when they do, political, cultural, and other factors may impede a generalized improvement. A more direct approach, and one that promises more immediate results, is to undertake measures and policies aimed at redistributing existing income and wealth. Such measures include direct transfers of income, financed out of general revenues or earmarked social security contributions; the direct provision in kind of basic commodities or subsidization of their cost; or modifications of general economic policies in ways that directly affect material standards of living at low-income levels.

Such approaches are not without problems. First, they depend critically on the willingness of the nonpoor to undertake such transfers, implicit or explicit. This goodwill may not exist, particularly if the nonpoor countries regard the higher living standards achievable in the advanced economies as models to emulate, and if they possess the economic and political power to block or limit such transfers in their own country. Second, transfers rely on the administrative capacity of governments to regulate, monitor, and implement measures that impose a significant degree of solidarity within the economic structure. An absence of solidarity among the poor themselves may represent a difficulty: labor market regulations or agreements on burden-sharing may be ineffectual and avoided by both employers and employees if it is to their joint advantage. In a number of countries, corruption can be a major problem. Finally, in modifying the rules of the game and undertaking commitments to public transfers, governments may be acting counter to current directions of economic reform, particularly those associated with structural adjustment programs.

The following sections amplify some of these issues. First, social provisioning, both directly and through subsidy and price policies, is discussed. The next section looks in more detail at social security and social assistance.

Supporting Social Consumption and Provisioning

Meeting Basic Needs Through Social Expenditures and Transfers. Work by the ILO in the mid-1970s suggested that targeted transfers were the most efficient way of reaching the poor quickly, but that, at the same time, programs leading to structural change, which would put productive assets in the hands of the poor, should be fostered. It was argued then that poverty reflected the basic needs (food, shelter, health services, and so forth), and therefore an antipoverty strategy should aim at meeting such basic needs, in the first instance through a redirection of public expenditure (ILO 1977).

In most countries, social expenditure continues today, though on a less ambitious scale, to provide services and public goods to the poor. Social expenditure as a share of total public expenditure varies considerably among developing countries. According to the *Human Development Report* (UNDP 1991), it ranges from as low as 13 percent in Indonesia to 50 percent in Chile and Costa Rica. The allocation of these resources among the social sectors is equally diverse. The scarcity of statistical information, however, makes it difficult to obtain indicators for an assessment of the effects that such expenditures have on the poorer sections of society. Some programs directed toward the poor—such as the Social Investment Funds, which focus on nutritional assistance and on investment in the creation of social infrastructure—have been shown to have had positive (albeit smaller than expected) effects in Honduras, Bolivia, and Costa Rica (see Wurgaft, Chapter 9 of this volume).

Social Security and Social Assistance. Attempts to reduce poverty through transfers of income rest on two broad types of programs: social assistance programs and social security programs. The former target individuals according to their need, are often means-tested, and are usually funded out of tax or general revenues. Other schemes, financed out of general revenues, include benefits such as child allowances and health care services (citizenship benefits), which are frequently available on a universal basis; in developing countries, such benefits reach only a minimal level. Social security programs, which represent an insurance mechanism for all members of society, including the nonpoor, can supply some of the income needs of old age and lessen the consequences of possible disability, sickness, or unemployment. In almost all countries, social security programs are financed by contributions from employers and/or employees that are tied to earnings; benefits are also usually calculated on the basis of earnings. Nonetheless, social security schemes frequently contain significant transfers between social groups, as well as between generations.

From an economic point of view, the two approaches present a strong contrast. Means-tested systems aim to focus limited resources where they are most needed and, consequently, to minimize any leakage of benefits to the nonpoor. Expenditure under such systems is usually quite limited. Social security programs, on the other hand, are a response to the demand for economic security on the part of the population as a whole. Here, the limit to expenditure is the highest level of compulsory contributions that society will agree to pay; this varies over time and between countries.

It must be stressed that no system of social protection can operate satisfactorily unless certain economic preconditions are fulfilled. Social security presupposes that income from work normally provides sufficient income to live on and that most people will have regular work. It aims to replace such income when people are not able (or expected) to work and to supplement it when they face the extra costs of supporting children. In developing countries, these conditions are often not met. As a result, in developing countries, a relatively small proportion of the population is covered by any kind of social security scheme. In these countries, social insurance constitutes the bulk of existing provision. It is, however, limited by the fact that few in the population are engaged in forms of employment or self-employment of a sufficiently formal character to allow the collection of contributions. The only citizenship benefit of much importance in developing countries is the public health service, though for many people, this benefit is more theoretical than real and the quality of the service tends to be low.

Individual social benefits for poor people in developing countries are still rare. What help they get from the authorities tends to be in the form of projects directed at local communities, that is, programs to promote development rather than to protect vulnerable members of society. It has been argued that much more could be done to extend protective measures to the unorganized poor (those outside sectors covered by existing social protection schemes), along the lines of the social assistance schemes operating in the Indian State of Tamil Nadu (Guhan 1995). Under this particular proposal, a basic package comprising a small pension for the elderly and disabled, a lump-sum survivor's benefit, and a maternity benefit would be provided, all on a means-tested basis, initially with the aim of covering 50 percent of those below the poverty line, that is, those who are not merely poor but destitute. The package is estimated in the Indian context to cost between 0.3 and 0.5 percent of gross domestic product, which puts it within the range of feasible options even in societies with low incomes and constrained budgets.

The main thrust of the ILO's work in the developing countries has been to establish, strengthen, and, whenever possible, extend the coverage of social insurance schemes.[6] The aim has been to spread protection over a broader geographical area (many schemes initially covered employees in

---

[6]The relevant convention is the Social Security (Minimum Standards) Convention No. 102, 1952.

urban areas only); to cover workers in small enterprises, also often excluded in the early stages; and to extend some protection to the self-employed. The needs of the self-employed, insofar as they can be ascertained from observation and from social surveys, differ to some extent from those of employees, as does their ability and readiness to pay contributions.

To date, the schemes proposed by the ILO have been mainly of a contributory character. This reflects the concern of most governments in the developing world not to commit themselves to higher public expenditure. The ILO has, nevertheless, underlined the need for some form of national solidarity to help finance benefits for the self-employed with the least ability to pay contributions. In its technical cooperation projects in Africa, the ILO has proposed more modest forms of protection for the self-employed. In Cameroon, the initial priority was identified as health insurance and, resources permitting, a grant toward expenses of pupils at the beginning of the school year (ILO 1989). Recently, a start has been made in giving the ILO's work on social security a broader focus, but much remains to be done.

The Organization of the Poor

While interventions help, organization of the poor holds greater promise for reducing rural and urban poverty. When the poor organize themselves, a new institutional agent is created with growing resources of its own, able to defend the interest of its members and to act as a pressure group for social and economic change (Maldonado 1993).

In their struggle for survival, poor households rely first and foremost on their own labor to make ends meet. The poor are often so involved in their daily struggle for survival that they have neither time nor energy left for organized contact with the outside world. Moreover, there may be simply a lack of awareness that they can actively change their life situation. But their individual efforts can be amplified when they organize themselves. The main interest of the poor obviously is to increase their incomes, but they may also wish to strengthen their cultural identity, raise their status in society, establish social rights, or gain political power.

The organization of the poor starts at the grassroots (local) level. Often, they will need a catalyst or outside motivator who helps them analyze their position in society and pool their initiative and creativity.

In 1977, the ILO launched a program to promote "participatory organizations of the rural poor" (Rahman 1984). In this program, participation consists of the organized activity of the rural poor, who create their own initiatives and control the content, pace, and directions of those initiatives.

A participatory research methodology was used: the poor undertook their own research, with the aid of an external researcher who provided the initial stimulus for the investigation and acted as a rapporteur of the results. In principle, the task of the external agent or motivator is to withdraw as soon as a group has acquired sufficient momentum and confidence to continue with their initiative; this strategy avoids the development of a dependent relationship or the situation in which the motivator becomes the group leader (Tilakaratna 1987; Rahman 1983).

Since the beginning of the 1980s, the ILO has also been involved in promoting the organization of women in the rural and the urban informal sectors. Women's organizations may provide a legal basis for access to land; enhance bargaining power with the local government and the state; foster assertiveness and self-confidence in dealings with local power brokers; and enable women to identify their own needs and priorities and set up projects. It is often important for women's organizations to obtain legal recognition. This goal is more often met in Asia than in Africa, where the organizational setting is more informal. Another benefit is the exchange of information and experience among women's organizations both within and between countries. International exchange has led, for example, to the replication of grassroots organizations similar to the Self-Employed Women's Association (SEWA), and the Working Women's Forum in India.

Cooperatives are another form of organization of the poor, though they require access to capital and assets. The role of cooperatives in poverty reduction through the promotion of employment and income is recognized by the ILO. The 1992 Report of the Director-General (ILC 1992) argued that cooperatives offered a special advantage—in terms of enterprise and job creation and, hence, poverty reduction—to developing countries undertaking structural adjustment programs and to countries that had rejected centralized economic planning. Traditional cooperative structures can be fashioned into new self-help organizations, which create self-employment and income for vulnerable groups and the poor. This is especially true in the rural and urban informal sectors. Some examples are savings and credit cooperatives, which represent self-help methods of finance and investment. But cooperatives can also serve the interests of the rich exclusively. Therefore, a careful and critical approach is needed.

The philosophy behind most of these activities is the idea that, through organization, the poor can increase their negotiating power. But, as is pointed out by the Convention on Rural Workers' Organizations (No. 141, 1975), the scope of these activities and groups are very different from those involved in traditional labor negotiations between wage workers and employers. Here, the negotiating parties may be wage earners, the self-employed, or female homeworkers, on one side, and employers, land-owners, suppliers, traders, and various government institutions, on the other. The representation of groups among the poor may be based on ethnic or community identity, a common pattern of discrimination with respect to rights or income sources, or other factors. The subject of negotiation can also extend far beyond wages and other employment conditions, to the provision of government services, training and credit, social protection, or employment opportunities.

In principle, trade unions are one type of organization that can be powerful allies of the poor, although the existing associations and trade unions do not always directly represent the interests of all the groups concerned. Indeed, a widespread complaint is that national trade union bodies represent mainly those in relatively better paid and more stable jobs. While in some countries this complaint is legitimate, unions have helped organize unskilled wage workers—often members of poor house-holds. Unions are best at organizing large enterprises and plantations, where many people are working in a limited space and where working conditions are similar. The role of trade unions in organizing labor is much more complicated in the rural, small-scale, and informal sectors where wage workers are widely scattered among many different enterprises, and where many workers are self-employed. The diversity of workers in the rural and informal sectors calls for a variety of organizations. For instance, among the self-employed, organizations aimed at community solidarity and mutual help may be most effective.

With the advent of greater democracy in many developing countries, various groups have greater opportunities to organize themselves openly. National or international NGOs can play a powerful role as representatives of these emerging groups, and so can political parties, even though they may wish to exert influence rather than to be influenced. The new wave of democratization can help the poor negotiate with political parties. In a democratic state, active bargaining takes place between voters, parties, candidates for office, and elected representatives. In a democratic society, politicians must be responsive to the voters. Poor people can wield greater influence if they organize themselves.

Poverty, of course, persists in democratic states, and something more than local organizing is needed to tip the balance of power in favor of the poor. Mobilizing support at the national and international level is a vital part of a comprehensive antipoverty strategy. Antipoverty policies are not always in the direct, short-term interests of all groups in society. Any government in a democratic society will therefore have to enlist support from a variety of socioeconomic groups and be prepared to stand up to conflicting interests, in order to implement an effective antipoverty strategy.

Conclusions: Toward a New Strategy
of Poverty Reduction

Previous approaches have not met with great success, and therefore there is a need for a fresh approach to poverty reduction that takes into account current features of the international and regional economies. What is needed is a new growth regime in which social objectives are treated as an inherent part of economic policy—both as targets of such policy and as contributors to long-term growth. It is argued that employment-intensive growth is the most effective way to combat poverty.

For developing countries, there is no alternative but to accumulate sufficient investments to generate a high rate of employment-intensive growth. Employment creation is a unique instrument for achieving such an objective since it is a vital input in the creation of wealth, and, at the same time, the most efficient mechanism for income distribution. Creating the conditions for a growth regime that maximizes employment and restrains unemployment and deprivation will require a coherent strategy for poverty reduction. The broad elements of such a strategy are outlined below.

The proposed antipoverty strategy starts from the premise that the macroeconomic framework is explicitly consistent with the objective of poverty reduction. Three microlevel conditions are required:

1. *A regeneration of demand on a worldwide scale.* The experience of the "lost decade" of the 1980s shows that a major constraint on growth was the decline of world demand. Declining demand has affected both developing and developed countries. There is thus a need to provide incentives for productive (as opposed to speculative) investment on a worldwide scale. The new world economic order with its trilateral structure (the Americas, Europe, and the Pacific Basin) is now in a position to engage in such a process.
2. *Redefinition of the roles of the main actors in the development process: the state, the market, and civil society.* A situation is envisaged where government plays the role of "development state," responsible for creating the conditions for freely operating markets that are at the same time socially responsive.
3. *Balanced macroeconomic policies.* Experience of the 1980s has shown that "getting prices right" alone neither generates growth in output nor creates employment. What is required is a broad-based macroeconomic policy (informed by the experience of the NICs), which contains incentives for sectoral growth with the explicit objective of maximizing labor absorption.

The brunt of the attack on poverty should come through increasing investments that maximize employment creation. ILO's standards can play an important role in ensuring the high quality of employment.

Designing strategies to promote employment-intensive growth involves several tasks:

- restructuring of developing countries' economies in such a way as to have built-in mechanisms for sustained redistribution, and
- achieving the right mix between the formal and informal economies, designing policies that address the specific problems of each.

Historical experience in industrialized countries and NICs has shown that poverty is not a necessary condition for prosperity. The so-called "golden age" of growth in the postwar period shows that growth was compatible with continuous escape from poverty, mainly through employment creation.

A poverty reduction strategy needs to be incorporated into the growth process. Such a strategy would be made up of four parts:

- establishing a policy framework that maximizes the incomes of the working poor through policies to promote self-employment, to upgrade the informal sector, and to improve labor market contracts (minimum wage, minimum age, equal opportunity, and so forth);
- investing in the next generation by increasing investment allocations for education and health (the provision of these services is an essential part of public action that should not necessarily be subjected to the law of the market);
- introducing direct transfers as social protection measures for those segments of the population that cannot be reached through conventional policy instruments; and
- encouraging resource transfers from rich to poor countries through reformed trade and aid regimes.

Monitoring poverty should be a complementary component of this strategy. International pressure should be mounted until poverty reduction joins growth of GDP as a yardstick of progress.

44

REFERENCES

Berar, A. 1988. *Women and rural development: What have we learned?* Swedish Agency for Research Cooperation with Developing Countries Seminar. Geneva: International Labour Office.

Chen, S., G. Datt, and M. Ravallion. 1993. *Is poverty increasing in the developing world?* Working Paper. Washington, D.C.: World Bank.

Collier, P., and S. Radwan. 1986. *Labor poverty in rural Tanzania.* Oxford: Clarendon Press.

Guhan, S. 1995. Social security options for developing countries. In *New approaches to poverty analysis and policy,* ed. B. Figueiredo and Z. Shaheed, 89–110. Geneva: International Institute for Labour Studies (IILS).

ILC (International Labour Conference). 1992. *Democratization of the ILO.* Report of the director-general. Geneva: International Labour Office.

ILO (International Labour Office). 1977. *Poverty and landlessness in rural Asia.* Geneva.

_____. 1982. *Job and skills programme for Africa, basic needs in danger: A basic needs-oriented development strategy for Tanzania.* Addis Ababa: Job and Skills Programme for Africa.

_____. 1989. *Rapport au gouvernement de la République camerounaise sur l'entension de la protection sociale aux populations non salariées.* (OIT/TF/CAM/R.13). Geneva.

_____. 1993. Poverty: New approaches to analysis and policy. Draft submitted to the Poverty Symposium, November, Geneva.

International Labour Review. 1992. 131 (no. 1): 1–43.

Maldonado, C. 1993. Rompre l'isolement: Une expérience d'appui aux petits producteurs urbains du Bénin. *International Labour Review* 132 (2): 275–295.

Radwan, S. 1977. *Agrarian reform and rural poverty.* Geneva: International Labour Office.

_____. ed. 1989. Rural labour markets and poverty in developing countries. *International Labour Review* 125 (6): 681–837.

Rahman, A. 1983. *A pilot project for stimulating grassroots participation in the Philippines.* Geneva: International Labour Office.

_____. 1984. Participatory organizations of the rural poor. International Labour Office, Rural Employment Policies Branch, Geneva. Mimeo.

Siddiqui, A. M. A. H., ed. 1990. *Labour laws and the working poor.* Bangkok: International Labour Office/Asian and Pacific Regional Project for Strengthening Labour Administration.

Starr, G. 1981. *Minimum wage fixing.* Geneva: International Labour Office.

Tilakaratna, S. 1987. *The animator in participatory rural development: Concept and practice.* World Employment Programme. Geneva: International Labour Office.

UNDP (United Nations Development Program). 1991. *Human development report.* New York: Oxford University Press.

World Bank. 1993. *World development report, 1992.* New York.

3

BANGLADESH'S FOOD-FOR-WORK PROGRAM AND ALTERNATIVES TO IMPROVE FOOD SECURITY

Akhter U. Ahmed, Sajjad Zohir, Shubh K. Kumar, and Omar Haider Chowdhury

Pervasive poverty and undernutrition are fundamental problems in Bangladesh. About one-half of the country's 112 million people cannot afford an adequate diet. There is a close relationship among poverty, landlessness, and unemployment. The rural landless, constituting about 50 percent of rural households, depend mainly on agriculture for employment. Since demand for labor in agricultural production is seasonal, during the slack season, the landless remain virtually unemployed. Even for most farmers, it is difficult to eke out a respectable living from the limited land that the average Bangladeshi farmer owns. Landless and marginal farmers must often resort to self-employment. But self-employment is often not profitable enough to allow them to step out of poverty.

It is therefore logical to expect that the public development strategy in Bangladesh would include programs designed to generate employment, particularly in rural areas, to reduce poverty. In fact, over the years, Bangladesh has accumulated extraordinarily rich, diverse experience in poverty-reduction efforts, many of which involve employment generation schemes.

The food-for-work (FFW) program and the rural maintenance program (RMP) are two nationwide programs that play an important role in the reduction of rural poverty, primarily through creation of employment opportunities. The FFW program has been operating in Bangladesh since 1975. It aims to create food-wage employment during the slack season, mostly in construction and maintenance of rural roads, river embankments, and irrigation channels. A major objective of the program is to provide income to the rural poor during the slack period when the unemployment rate in rural areas increases. Wage payments are made in kind (that is, in wheat) rather than in cash. Such a practice is thought to stabilize foodgrain prices in the market and to improve food consumption and nutrition of the participating households.

This chapter reviews the achievements of the FFW program in fulfilling this objective. After an assessment of the operational performance, employment and wage implications, and developmental impact of the program, the chapter suggests alternative policies for the future direction of the program.

Poverty and Unemployment

Magnitude of Poverty and Food Insecurity

In Bangladesh, a rural household's access to adequate food largely depends on its access to land and other sources of income, while individual food security is determined by intrahousehold distribution. Since the availability of food at the household level is the primary determinant of the incidence of poverty in a country, household-targeted interventions such as food-for-work are expected to have a positive effect on food security and poverty reduction.

The Household Expenditure Survey, carried out periodically by the Bangladesh Bureau of Statistics, is the main source of information for studies on poverty and inequality in Bangladesh. However, the estimates of the incidence of poverty from the same database vary substantially in different studies. The variations in the estimates are mainly attributable to differences in underlying assumptions regarding the minimum calories required for meeting biological needs, which items should be included in the minimum diet, and which prices should be used to figure the cost of the minimum diet. Recently, Hossain and Sen (1992) used an alternative methodology to estimate the incidence of poverty for rural areas for the period 1973/74–1988/89.[1] The findings of this study, as reported in Table 3.1, indicate that absolute poverty declined substantially from the mid-1970s to the mid-1980s. The marginal increase in poverty levels during 1988/89 is probably due to the devastating floods in 1977 and 1988. One would expect that the situation has improved recently due to improved performance of the agriculture sector since 1990.

---

[1]A poverty line was computed by costing the normative minimum consumption bundle for the Bangladesh population, which gives a per capita daily intake of 2,122 calories, and adding to it a 30 percent allowance for nonfood basic needs. The study derived prices from the Household Expenditure Survey data by using quantity and value of different food items.

Table 3.1—Trends in rural poverty, 1973/74–1988/89

Period	According to Per Capita		According to Per Capita	
	Expenditure	Income	Expenditure	Income
	(percent of rural population classified as absolutely poor)			
1973/74	71.3	n.a.	60.3	n.a.
1976/77	n.a.	n.a.	78.9	73.1
1977/78	n.a.	n.a.	77.4	72.8
1978/79	n.a.	n.a.	65.8	60.7
1981/82	65.3	60.0	55.3	51.3
1983/84	50.0	42.8	46.3	39.8
1985/86	41.3	38.9	37.3	35.9
1988/89	43.8	38.7	43.4	40.0

Source: Hossain and Sen 1992.
Note: n.a. is not available.

Rationale for Public Intervention
to Generate Employment

Overwhelming hunger and malnutrition continue to persist in Bangladesh. For the vast majority of rural poor, the only asset owned is labor power. Therefore, wage rates and employment opportunities determine, to a large degree, the welfare of the poor. One major factor leading to widespread poverty in rural Bangladesh is large-scale unemployment and under-employment. Poverty reduction depends on increasing the economy's capacity for absorbing the existing labor force and on the prospect for increasing the productivity of wage and self-employed labor.

According to national planning documents, targets for generating employment were not met in any of the past three five-year plans. In fact, the number of jobs created was lower than the number of new entrants to the work force, meaning that the number of unemployed increased over time. Using the highly disaggregated input-output table of the Planning Commission to account for effective labor use, Hossain and Akash (1993) estimate the level of underemployment at about one-third of the labor force. The increase in unemployment and the high level of underemployment have had a dampening effect on the average wage rate.

It is generally argued that economic growth is the ultimate solution for the poverty problem, but it should be recognized that the nature of growth is more important than growth rates in determining the impact of growth on poverty reduction. Economic advancement that would ensure full employment and better wages is not foreseeable in the short or medium terms. Recent estimates (Hossain and Rashid 1991) based on the potential for employment generation through the normal market mechanism suggest that about 29 percent of the labor force was involved in activities of very low productivity in 1989/90. This low-productivity, residual employment is poverty-driven. Hossain and Rashid (1991) project that poverty-driven, low-productivity employment will increase by 25 percent in the 1990s. They further estimate that, even if the government succeeds in accelerating economic growth to 5 percent per year, as much as 15 percent of the labor force will remain in low-productivity employment in 2000. Thus, the likelihood that market mechanisms will successfully tackle the problem of unemployment and poverty in Bangladesh in the medium term is slight.

This situation rationalizes public investment in employment-generating programs that normally will not attract private resources. Public works programs generate employment and, typically, create public goods such as physical and social infrastructure through labor-intensive techniques (von Braun, Teklu, and Webb 1991). The FFW program is one such public intervention that attempts to promote rural development by converting surplus labor into capital. The program has the potential to improve immediately and directly the food security of the rural poor who participate, as well as the potential to improve food security in society over the long term by facilitating national-level economic advancement.

Food-for-Work Program in Bangladesh

The FFW program was launched by the Government of Bangladesh in 1975 in response to the 1974 famine. The initial purpose of the program was to provide relief for the poor facing severe food insecurity, using food resources donated to the country. Over the years, the program's focus has been shifted from relief to development. Currently, the main objectives of the program are

- to improve the performance of the agriculture sector through the construction and maintenance of infrastructure for production and marketing;
- to reduce physical damage and loss of human life due to floods and other natural disasters through appropriate protective structures; and
- to generate productive seasonal employment for the rural poor.

The FFW program is one of the 11 foodgrain distribution channels of the Public Food Distribution System (PFDS). One of the major objectives of operating the PFDS is to achieve food security by ensuring adequate availability of foodgrains. The PFDS channels fall into two broad

Table 3.2—Distribution of foodgrains by channels and their relative shares in the Public Food Distribution System, 1991/92

Channels	Total Offtake			Share of PFDS		
	Rice	Wheat	Total	Rice	Wheat	Total
	(1,000 metric tons)			(percent)		
Flour mills	0	340	340	0.0	14.5	14.5
Open market sales	273	2	275	11.6	0.1	11.7
Rural rationing[a]	215	2	217	9.2	0.1	9.3
Other priorities	60	152	212	2.6	6.5	9.0
Statutory rationing	0	169	169	0.0	7.2	7.2
Essential priorities	91	60	151	3.9	2.6	6.4
Large employers	30	27	57	1.3	1.2	2.4
Total monetized	669	752	1,421	28.5	32.1	60.6
Food-for-work	29	512	541	1.2	21.8	23.1
Vulnerable group development	26	204	230	1.1	8.7	9.8
Test relief	4	94	98	0.2	4.0	4.2
Gratuitous relief	32	24	56	1.4	1.0	2.4
Total nonmonetized	91	834	925	3.9	35.6	39.4
Total	760	1,586	2,346	32.4	67.6	100.0

Source: WFP 1993.
[a]The offtake from the Rural Rationing Program was suspended in December 1991. The program was officially abolished in May 1992.

groups—monetized and nonmonetized. Each channel implicitly represents some target groups. The FFW program belongs to the nonmonetized channel of the PFDS. Table 3.2 shows the distribution of foodgrains by channels and their shares in the overall PFDS in 1991/92. The FFW program is the largest among all PFDS channels, accounting for about 23 percent of total PFDS foodgrain utilization in 1991/92.

Figure 3.1 illustrates the increasing trend in annual amounts of foodgrain utilization under the FFW program since its inception in 1975 (that is, fiscal year 1975/76). As estimated by Hossain and Akash (1993), the allocation of resources to the FFW program in the 1970s varied between 4 and 5 percent of total national development expenditures. The peak allocation was in 1988/89, which amounted to 11 percent of total development expenditures. The sharp increase in allocation in that year was in response to the devastating floods in 1988. Resource allocation was reduced to about 6 percent of total development expenditures during 1989-91, which were normal production years. Normally, wheat (mostly imported) is used to pay workers. However, in the 1992/93 season, FFW distributed mostly rice in order to dispose of surplus government stocks.

Figure 3.1—Trend in foodgrain offtakes under the food-for-work program

Offtake
(1,000 metric tons)

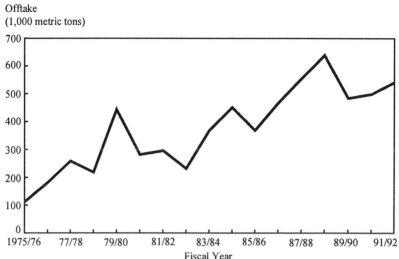

Source: WFP 1993.

Figure 3.2 shows the seasonal pattern of utilization of foodgrains in FFW during the initial three years of the program and the most recent three years. Besides the large increase in foodgrain utilization during recent years (especially between the months of January to May), the monthly utilization patterns in both periods are quite similar. Currently, about 85 percent of FFW foodgrains are used between January and May.

Table 3.3 presents an overview of the FFW program. A brief description of the implementation of the FFW program and the institutions involved, drawn mostly from Hossain and Akash (1993), follows.

The FFW projects are administered by the World Food Programme (WFP) and CARE. The WFP acts as both a conduit and an administrator for multilateral and bilateral food aid for the program. Major donors include Australia, Canada, the European Union, and the United Kingdom. CARE operates on behalf of the U.S. Agency for International Development (USAID) and administers projects using wheat supplied by the United States.

Projects administered by WFP are implemented mainly by three agencies: The Water Development Board, the Ministry of Relief and Rehabilitation, and the Local Government and Engineering Bureau. Water Development Board projects are often large projects that create coastal and

Figure 3.2—Seasonal pattern of foodgrain offtakes under the food-for-work program

Offtake
(1,000 metric tons)

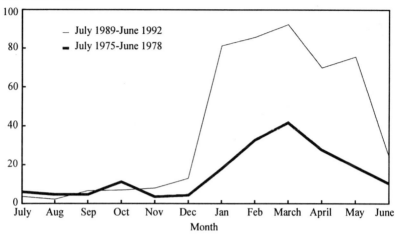

Source: WFP 1993.

flood-protection embankments along major rivers or reexcavate canals under large-scale irrigation projects, for example. The Ministry of Relief and Rehabilitation projects often involve the construction and repair of interior earth roads, and the digging and reexcavation of small irrigation channels. FFW schemes executed by the Local Government and Engineering Bureau include the construction and completion of roads connected to growth centers.

In addition to these major WFP projects, the Ministry of Fisheries and Livestock directs excavation and reexcavation of fish ponds, and the Ministry of Forests is responsible for forestry development and tree-planting schemes. Several nongovernmental organizations (NGOs) carry out even smaller schemes, including the rehabilitation of fish tanks, ground elevation for flood shelters, tree plantations, and pilot schemes.

CARE-administered projects are implemented by local government. Dirt roads dominate projects implemented by CARE.

The target group for FFW includes anyone who is poor, willing, and available to do mainly earthwork for food wages. Thus, participation in the program is self-selecting. Workers are mobilized by gang leaders *(sardars)* and supervisors.

The basic wage rate stipulated for Water Development Board projects is 40 kilograms of wheat per 1,000 cubic feet of earthwork, plus a variable

Table 3.3—Overview of the food-for-work program, Bangladesh

Program Features	Food-for-Work	
Source of funds		
Donors	USAID	WFP/donors
Local contribution	GOB	None
Commodities distributed	Wheat	Wheat
Program size (1991/92)		
Tons of grains (1,000 metric tons)		
Nonmonetized	120	400
Monetized	72	45
Value of grain (US$ million)	$33	$78
Number of beneficiaries (1,000)	600	3,400
Target group	Unskilled laborers	Unskilled laborers
Regional focus	National, 44 districts	National, 60 or more districts
Seasons	January–May	Predominantly December–April
Activities undertaken	Roads (80 percent) Canals (15 percent) Tanks, bridges, and culverts (5 percent)	Embankments and canals (40 percent) Roads (30 percent) Forestry (8 percent) Fisheries (7 percent) Other (15 percent)
Implementors		
Who handles the grains?		
Port to LSD	DG Food	DG Food
LSD to work site	PIC	PIC
Who identifies beneficiaries?	Self-selecting	Self-selecting
Who pays beneficiaries?	PIC sardar	PIC sardar
What commodity?	Wheat	Wheat
Who proposes schemes?	*Thana* (district)	WDB, LGEB, MF, MFL
Who reviews proposals?	CARE (100 percent)	Ministries/WFP (17 percent)
Who implements construction?	PIC: roads, contractors, bridges	WDB, LGEB, MFL
Who monitors construction?	*Thanas*	WDB, LGEB, MFL, and WFP/donors
Who monitors impact on beneficiaries?	CARE	WFP/GOB (selective)
Link institution		
Local level	*Thanas*	PIC
Central ministry	Local government	MRR, MF, MFL

Source: WGTFI 1993.
Abbreviations: CARE = Cooperative for American Relief Everywhere
                  DG Food = Directorate General of Food (Ministry of Food)
                  GOB   = Government of Bangladesh
                  LGEB = Local Government Engineering Bureau
                  LSD   = Local Supply Depot
                  MF   = Ministry of Forestry
                  MFL   = Ministry of Fisheries and Livestock
                  MRR = Ministry of Relief and Rehabilitation
                  PIC   = Project Implementation Committee
                  USAID = United States Agency for International Development
                  WDB = Water Development Board
                  WFP   = World Food Programme

allowance that takes into account such factors as the distance over which the earth has to be transported and raised. In Ministry of Relief and Rehabilitation projects, payments for allied factors are consolidated with the wage for the basic earthwork. The wage rate varies according to the type of project and the sex of the worker. For road and embankment projects, the wage rate is 47 kilograms of wheat for 1,000 cubic feet of earth for men, and 65 kilograms for women. For canal excavation projects, an additional wage of 4.65 kilograms per 1,000 cubic feet is paid. *Sardars* are paid 2.33 kilograms and supervisors are paid 0.47 kilograms per 1,000 cubic feet of earthwork done under their supervision, provided that each is supervising the specified number of workers or gangs. The average wage rate for the major FFW programs is estimated at about 4.6 kilograms of wheat per day.

Under the postmonsoon rehabilitation component of the FFW program, designed for women's participation, about 1.73 million workdays are generated for rural women from October to December. The postmonsoon rehabilitation primarily covers social forestry and fisheries development schemes. In some regions, women work together with male laborers in dry-season FFW activities as well. Moreover, FFW project implementation committees are encouraged to include women among their members, and these committees for postmonsoon rehabilitation, in principle, include at least one woman member.

Operational Performance of the Food-for-Work Program

Institutional Aspects

FFW is a large, umbrella-type program, under which several ministries, donor agencies, and NGOs operate various kinds of schemes, with wide variations in the size of these operations. One would, therefore, expect that the performance of individual schemes would also vary significantly. This section discusses the overall institutional performance of the FFW program in Bangladesh.

Over the past 18 years, seasonal employment has been created for large numbers of people under the FFW program. In recent years, the program has generated over 100 million workdays of employment in earthworks each year, directly benefiting about 4 million people. Indirect beneficiaries of the rural infrastructure works are the people living in areas in which the FFW schemes are undertaken. Their benefits include improved production in the agriculture sector, which benefits producers and consumers as well; enhanced marketing opportunities, as a result of road construction and rehabilitation; improved communications between communities; and reduced physical damage and numbers of human deaths as a result of structures that hold back floods. These achievements are significant. Over the long term, these accomplishments represent development gains and have the potential to facilitate a faster rate of economic growth, which should contribute to food security at both the household and national levels.

There are, however, several technical, organizational, programming, and institutional problems that limit the potential benefits of FFW programs. A report of the Task Force on Strengthening the Institutions for Food Assisted Development notes that FFW and other food-assisted programs have inadequate access to specialized planning, design, and supervision services, a fact that limits their technical strength. In addition, implementing organizations are inadequately staffed at both the central and local level. This technical weakness stems from the fact that food-assisted development programs are being isolated institutionally from the mainstream development effort. For example, the Bangladesh government made a fundamental decision to keep food aid flows separate from the national planning process. The capacity within the government to ensure compliance with program standards is weak. The ability to monitor program implementation and to ensure that any user of food resources can be held accountable for their proper use is also lacking (SIFAD 1989).

The management of the FFW program was critically evaluated on the basis of an in-depth survey of 32 sample projects undertaken during 1982 (Asaduzzaman and Huddleston 1983). Some observations from this study, most of which are still relevant today, follow.[2] Influential local people participated in the planning process in nearly one-half of the smaller projects implemented by the Ministry of Relief and Rehabilitation. In contrast, such local-level participation was reported in only about one-fourth of the large projects implemented under the Water Development Board, where technical considerations dictate minimum consultations with local people.

Delays in the project-approval process were a major problem. Projects that began late often faced difficulties in completing work before the onset of the monsoon season. Any work uncompleted is washed away by rains and floods during the season and has no longer-term benefit. There were two major factors that caused delays after the issuance of the government implementation order: formation of project implementation committees, and acquisition of land for lifting and depositing earth at the project site.

---

[2]This is adapted from a recent review report by Hossain and Akash (1993), which summarizes the findings of Asaduzzaman and Huddleston (1983).

Political motives for satisfying local clients were mentioned as the major factor behind the delays in forming project implementation committees. Many projects involved reconstruction or rehabilitation of an existing structure and compensation was not authorized for land from which earth was collected. Local officials claimed that such land was given voluntarily, while local farmers complained the project damaged standing crops and soil quality, and therefore compensation was needed. Negotiations with the affected people for settling the issues delayed land acquisition.

Asaduzzaman and Huddleston (1983) also noted that local government officials could not afford the time to monitor and supervise projects because they were too preoccupied with other administrative functions. Even the project implementation officers, whose main responsibility is the supervision of public works programs, were not able to visit all the projects under their jurisdiction once a month. Consequently, it was not possible to measure the quantity and quality of work done under the program, and there was considerable potential for malpractice and substandard work.

An institutional assessment of FFW road schemes administered by CARE was done by Management Systems International (MSI 1987). In general, the findings of this study conform to those of Asaduzzaman and Huddleston (1983). An additional observation of the Management Systems International study was that the presence of a strong union council in the *thana* and a motivated union council chairman was a key predictor of good FFW performance.

Targeting, Leakage, and Cost-Effectiveness

Well-targeted intervention improves the real income and food security of a target group without providing those benefits to members of the population who do not need them. Hence, successful targeting requires that leakage to nontarget groups be minimized. Leakage, when it occurs, increases costs and reduces the cost-effectiveness of targeted programs.

Targeting. The severity and magnitude of the poverty problem in Bangladesh dictate that public interventions target those whose needs are the greatest and provide a minimum income level. The FFW program in Bangladesh combines three types of targeting:

1. *The program is self-targeting.* Because of the nature of the work, only the poorest households tend to participate in the program. Various studies that have evaluated FFW projects suggest that the work requirement effectively discourages participation by the non-poor (Chowdhury 1983; Mitra and Associates 1991).

2. *The program distributes a self-targeted commodity.* FFW pays out wages in wheat. A recent study demonstrates that in Bangladesh, wheat is a better food for self-targeting than rice for improving food consumption and nutrition in poor households (Ahmed 1993a). Consumption studies in Bangladesh have shown wheat to have a negative income elasticity of demand in rural areas (Table 3.4). This indicates that wheat is an inferior good in rural areas and, hence, only the poorest would work for wheat.

3. *The program is partly seasonally targeted.* Over 85 percent of the FFW resources are used during January–May, which was the traditional slack season for agricultural activities during the early planning stages of the program. However, with the rapid expansion of cultivation of irrigated boro rice and wheat crops, employment opportunities in the agriculture sector in many areas have increased to substantial levels during this season in recent years, as will be discussed in detail.

Leakage. Leakage is defined here as the diversion of program resources intended for the target group to a nontarget population. However, only outright misappropriation of resources is considered here as leakage. Thus, for example, the use of wheat to compensate some of those who lose land in road construction work is not considered leakage, even if the compensated persons belong to a nontarget group.

Table 3.4—A comparison of income (expenditure) elasticities of wheat in rural Bangladesh

Author(s)	Estimating Model	Description	Expenditure Elasticity of Wheat
Pitt (1983)	Tobit demand system	Low–income	−0.10
		High–income	−0.24
Ahmed and Hossain (1990)	Working–Leser Engel function, modified by Hazell and Röell (1983)	Underdeveloped villages	−0.06
		Developed villages	−0.14
Goletti (1993)	Tobit demand system	Entire sample	−0.44
Ahmed and Shams (1993)	Almost Ideal Demand System (AIDS)	Entire sample	−0.22

Sources: Studies mentioned in the first column of the table.

In spite of the self-targeting characteristics of the FFW program, leakage of resources from the program is quite extensive and is a matter of concern. One major point of leakage in the FFW program is the overreporting of work done. FFW engages mostly in the reconstruction or rehabilitation of existing structures. Hence, underestimation of the condition of structures before work has begun and overestimation of the work performed can lead to a large amount of leakage. Another point of leakage is the practice of leaving the earth uncompacted, which makes it difficult to measure the actual volume of earthwork and the amount of work accomplished.

Leakage may also occur through underpayment to workers. According to Hossain and Akash (1993), the rate of underpayment in the FFW program ranged from 17 to 27 percent. Often, a portion of the allotted wheat wage does not even arrive at the project site: on average, the amount of wheat reported as not arriving was estimated at 18 to 35 percent (Hossain and Akash 1993).

In a recent study, the Working Group on Targeted Food Interventions, chaired by the International Food Policy Research Institute (IFPRI), estimated leakage of resources from various channels of the PFDS in Bangladesh (WGTFI 1993). Based on secondary sources of information on the two components of leakage—undercompletion of work and underpayment of workers—the study estimates a leakage of resources of 30–35 percent. Although this amount of leakage seems quite high, in comparison with other PFDS channels FFW is a moderate performer. At one extreme, the cash-based Rural Maintenance Program (RMP) operates at zero leakage (as claimed by CARE, the administering agency of RMP), while at the other extreme, the food rationing channels operate with enormous rates of leakage—70–95 percent. The Vulnerable Group Development (VGD) Program operates at a low leakage rate of 14 percent.

Cost-Effectiveness of Income Transfer. Two basic elements in the cost-effectiveness analysis of any program are its costs and benefits. The WGTFI 1993 study provides estimates of short-term cost-effectiveness of income transfers from various targeted intervention programs in Bangladesh. The cost calculations in that study include the cost of identifying beneficiaries, the cost of the income transfer itself, and the administrative cost of delivering cash or commodities to the beneficiaries. Training costs, if any, and other "development" expenditures are omitted from these "cost-of-relief" calculations. Thus, the cost of culverts and other construction materials, for example, are excluded from the FFW cost calculations. The benefits include only the direct income received from programs by the beneficiaries. For FFW, the benefits are wage incomes received by the program participants. Any leakage of resources to noneligible persons is deducted from the calculation of income benefit.[3]

The WGFTI (1993) study estimates suggest that the FFW program delivers one taka (Tk) of income to a participating household at a cost of Tk 1.8–Tk 2.4. Compared with FFW, the cash-based RMP is more cost-effective. RMP delivers one taka of income to a targeted household at a cost of only Tk 1.2. RMP delivers income relief at the lowest cost of any of the targeted intervention programs because it operates at zero leakage, and it avoids the cost of commodity handling by transferring cash income to beneficiaries through a bank transfer. Thus, as RMP has shown, "cash for work" can provide a lower-cost safety net than "food-for-work" schemes. In contrast, subsidized food-ration channels offer the least effective vehicles for delivering income to vulnerable households. Under the Rural Rationing Program, the government had to spend Tk 6.55 to transfer Tk 1.00 to an eligible household (Ahmed 1992). High system leakage (70 percent), combined with the costs of foodgrain handling, led to this high cost. The high fiscal cost of the ration subsidy ($60 million in 1990/91) and heavy leakage to the nonpoor brought about the abolition of the Rural Rationing Program in 1992.

Implications of Food-for-Work for Employment and Wages

The FFW program involves a number of employment-generating activities, primarily earthwork construction of rural roads and embankments. One main objective of the FFW program is to generate employment for landless and marginal farmers during the slack season when demand for labor in crop production is low. This section critically assesses this program rationale of the FFW and makes some observations about the implications of the program for the rural labor market.

---

[3]Because these benefits calculations ignore the second-round, income-generating effects of asset creation, the policymakers comparing programs will have to combine these short-term relief-effectiveness calculations with a subjective assessment of the development impact of the "for work" programs. Certainly, "for work" programs offer substantially more benefits to society than pure income transfers. Ahmed and Hossain (1990) documented the importance of the impact of rural infrastructure on income, wage rates, and the modernization of agriculture in rural Bangladesh. Of course, if cost-effectiveness calculations include the second-round benefits, then these calculations should also include all direct and indirect costs associated with "development."

Review of Studies

A number of studies[4] provide estimates of the employment generated under the rural works and FFW programs. There are, however, very few attempts to assess the net employment creation of these programs. Comparing "project" and "control" villages, Osmani and Chowdhury (1983) found that the number of days of employment did not increase significantly as a result of FFW activities. They argued that "FFW employment largely represents a shift from self-employment and to a smaller extent from other forms of wage-employment as well." While there may not be a significant net addition to the number of days of employment, some studies suggest a significant net addition to wage income (Osmani and Chowdhury 1983; Zohir 1990). Furthermore, the long-term effects of some of the development activities under FFW have favorably affected employment. For example, infrastructure development activities carried out under FFW have had a positive effect on output prices, a negative effect on input prices, and a positive effect on the adoption of improved technology. These positive and negative effects have generated new employment. Ahmed and Hossain (1990) found labor use per unit of cropped land to be 12 percent higher in infrastructurally developed villages, compared with underdeveloped villages. Another study by Zohir (1990) indicates that female participation in the workforce is significantly higher in rural roadside villages.

However, some recent studies (MSI 1987; Zohir 1990; Mitra and Associates 1991) indicate that the implementation period of FFW projects conflicts with crop production activities. The MSI study (1987) found that shortfalls in the utilization of wheat in several areas were caused by labor shortages in those areas. Mitra and Associates (1991) reported that over 80 percent of surveyed FFW laborers had alternative employment opportunities in agriculture. However, the majority of the respondents reported that agricultural wages were lower than FFW wages.

Implications for Slack-Season Unemployment

More than 70 percent of rural employment in Bangladesh is provided by the crop sector. Thus, labor demand is seasonal. It is believed that supply is also influenced by seasonal demand.

In the past, rainfed rice (aman and aus) dominated crop production. Peak periods for employment were (1) July–August, when aman is transplanted and pre-monsoon aus is harvested, and (2) November–December,

---

[4]See Hossain and Asaduzzaman (1983); World Bank (1990).

when aman is harvested. Thus, historically, September–October and January–March were identified as slack seasons in Bangladesh. Famine was more prevalent in the former season, since most of the crop production in any given year occurred during November–December. With the increasing prominence of dry-season irrigated boro rice cultivation, new peaks of labor demand have emerged during December–February (transplanting) and April–May (harvest).[5] In the changed situation described in the following paragraph, the role of FFW in providing slack-season employment has become limited.

Since it takes until October for floodwater to recede, earthworks in most parts of Bangladesh can only be carried out during the November–May period. Most FFW wheat is distributed as payment for earthwork. When monthly utilization of FFW wheat, expressed in person-days of employment, is contrasted with crop-sector labor demand (Figure 3.3), it

Figure 3.3—Crop-sector labor demand and employment under the food-for-work program (monthly averages)

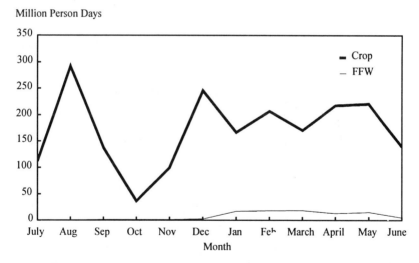

Source: Hossain and Akash 1993 and calculated from WFP 1993.
Notes: Labor demand in the crop sector is for 1990. Estimates for FFW are based on averages for 1989/90–1991/92, and the FFW wage is assumed to be 4.6 kilograms.

---

[5]In some northern districts, late boro is transplanted during February–March and is harvested during May. Wheat is harvested during March–April.

clearly shows that FFW fails to address the problem of slack-season unemployment. Rather, with the advancement of dry-season crops, FFW increasingly competes with agricultural activities. With the changing cropping patterns, aman harvest extends to December in many parts of the country. Given the extensive labor activities associated with irrigated boro, wheat, and some other dry-season crops, the January–April period may no longer be considered a slack season in many areas. Trends in the area covered by dry-season crops (as percentages of the net cropped area) suggest that the labor market has become tighter during this season in most of the districts of Bangladesh.

Implication for Wages

Daily wage rates in the rural labor market are more stable than the scope of employment.[6] Yet, seasonal wage fluctuations broadly follow the pattern of variation in crop-sector labor demand. Average monthly wages in three of the districts that are advanced[7] in agricultural technology are expressed as ratios of annual averages, and are depicted in Figure 3.4. The pattern in the mid-1970s reflects a period in which there were few crop activities during the dry season. The pattern of the mid-1980s reflects an increase in dry-season activities. The comparison shows that relative wages paid during the dry season (compared to other times of a year) have increased substantially, while the relative wages paid during September–October have fallen. This suggests that FFW, if it is intended to raise rural wages during the dry season, has lost much of its effectiveness relative to the mid-1970s.

Detailed data to estimate the effects of FFW on wages are not available. It is, however, expected that any additional demand for labor will have a positive influence on wages as long as the supply of labor is not simultaneously (positively) affected. Thus, FFW is likely to have a positive effect on wages during the period of its implementation.[8] However, the extent of such an effect will depend crucially on whether the program is competing

---

[6]One explanation for this is that supply may be responsive to demand. A more general explanation may be that supply decisions are influenced by expected annual income rather than the daily wage rate.

[7]These districts are advanced in terms of the adoption of irrigated, high-yielding varieties of rice, and other remunerative crops that are mostly produced during the dry season.

[8]It is quite possible that increased employment opportunity during one season may affect wage rates during some other season. If such effects are negative, a relative worsening of the wage situation during September–October (due to FFW employment during the dry season) may not be ruled out.

**Figure 3.4—Monthly wage variation in currently advanced
regions, 1975/76–1977/78 and 1985/86–1987/88**

Ratios of Annual Averages

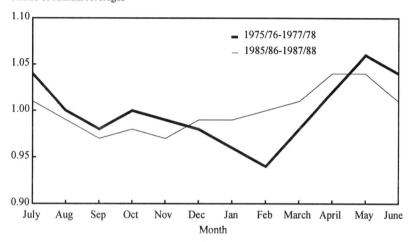

Source: Bangladesh Bureau of Statistics.
Note: Only Bogra, Chittagong, and Comilla districts are included.

(for labor) with activities where market wage rates prevail. If, instead, the program draws from a pool of unemployed or poorly remunerated self-employed labor, observed market wage rates may not be affected. Given the increasing market wage rates during the implementation period (Figure 3.4), FFW is now more likely to influence market wages. Zohir (1990) finds such conjecture to be true, and notes that increased wages have a negative effect on crop-sector labor demand, especially for weeding activities. However, no estimate of the magnitude of this substitution effect exists.

Implementing FFW during a period of peak crop-sector activities has several other implications. Since such a practice generally involves drawing labor from other employment, incremental gains in wage income due to participation in FFW activities are likely to have diminished. On the other hand, the same phenomenon may also induce increased participation of female labor in FFW activities. Such an increase is all the more likely if the stipulated female wage, which is 38 percent higher than that for males, is offered in reality. Unfortunately, no empirical research has been done in this area. If future research shows this conjecture to be true, positive social benefits from female employment may counteract some of the negative effects of the FFW program as it is currently implemented.

Developmental Effects of Food-for-Work and Food Security Implications

Benefit from Completed Projects

FFW plays a dual role: it provides employment to food-insecure house-holds and individuals, and it creates community assets for which private resources are difficult to mobilize. Historically, FFW resources have been invested in economic and social infrastructure. Such investments in "public goods" are essential for improving public welfare. Since these invest-ments generate externalities and are provided in large units generally ahead of private demand, they do not substitute for private initiatives. More recently, FFW resources have also been invested in natural resource conservation and management, which, like infrastructure development, has "public goods" characteristics.

In Bangladesh, a wide range of economic and social infrastructure development activities has been undertaken by public works and FFW programs. Detailed analyses carried out in Bangladesh have shown that physical infrastructures that improve access to markets and other institu-tions have favorable effects on (1) agricultural productivity, (2) employ-ment and wage income growth in the rural nonfarm sector, (3) food secu-rity for the lowest income groups, and (4) relative dietary adequacy of young girls and women (Ahmed and Hossain 1990; BIDS/IFPRI 1985; Kumar and Chowdhury 1985).

Several project-selection, project-implementation, and postproject conditions are important for the realization of the development impact of FFW. Experience in Bangladesh has shown that these include the mainte-nance of created assets and the management of the distribution of eco-nomic or social input or service. As with the "public goods" problem of private initiatives in the development of infrastructure, its maintenance and the management of its use require some form of public or community action. When this is not effective, there may be rapid deterioration of the asset, which in some cases leads to a worsening in economic indicators (for example, when a flood embankment is breached due to poor maintenance).

Effects on Agricultural Production and Income

Accelerated growth in agricultural production occurs with the increased use of improved technological inputs, accompanied by the commercialization of production. Use of these inputs has been facilitated by irrigation, flood protection, drainage, and other measures provided by FFW programs over the last two decades in Bangladesh. Moreover, the adoption of improved technologies is made more profitable by the reduction in transaction costs for inputs and outputs made possible by good physical infrastructure. Results from the BIDS/IFPRI (1985) study on the development impacts of public works showed that for a combination of irrigation/drainage/flood-protection types of "directly productive" investments, there was an increase in the gross value of crop production by 27 percent. Most of this increase came from greater land area committed to high-yielding varieties, increases in fertilizer use and labor per hectare, and an increase in cereal yields per hectare. The production increase was associated with a reduction of risk in agriculture, which led to greater use of improved agricultural inputs.

Results are substantially different when the economic infrastructure is made available with or without the availability of physical infrastructure of "overhead capital" such as access to roads, transport, markets, and communications.[9] Income from crop production increased 26 percent with the provision of economic infrastructure alone, and 41 percent when better physical infrastructure was also available (BIDS/IFPRI 1985; Hossain and Akash 1993). While the incremental effect of physical infrastructure is significant for crop output and agricultural income, its main effect is on nonagricultural income. Nonagricultural income increased by only 21 percent with improvements in irrigation-related (economic) infrastructure, but with the addition of physical infrastructure, nonagricultural income nearly tripled. Thus, both the returns to land and farm-nonfarm growth linkages are substantially increased when investments are made in both physical and economic infrastructure. The incremental income that results from this increased nonfarm employment is much more equitably distributed to low-income households than are the increments in farm income.

Physical infrastructure development is associated with changes in participation in output, land, and credit markets that contribute to the observed crop production and overall income response (Ahmed and Hossain 1990). First, there is an increase in output marketing and greater purchases of foods and other goods on the market. Since most of the incremental production is in rice, a basic food staple, this contributes to a reduction in the real price of rice and stimulates employment growth through the wage

---

[9]The term infrastructure includes a wide array of components, but a useful distinction has been made between those that contribute to "directly productive" activities, or economic infrastructure, and "overhead capital," or physical infrastructure. Examples of economic infrastructure include irrigation and drainage, while physical infrastructure includes transport, communications, and social services.

goods effect and through expenditures in consumer goods and services. Second, land markets are found to be more competitive, with land sales by small, nonviable farmers increasing as more profitable nonfarm opportunities become available. Third, there is improved access to institutional credit, and an increased credit demand for nonfarm investment.

Food Security and Nutritional Effects

The effect on development of FFW projects can be translated into improved food security and nutrition primarily through increases in real income and the participation of low-income households in these improvements. As shown earlier, these improvements are more likely with better physical infrastructure alone or in combination with investment in economic infrastructure. The latter, by itself, especially if aimed at increasing the returns to land, can be expected to contribute only limited income improvements for lower-income landless households in a land-constrained rural economy like Bangladesh. It is conceivable, however, that alternative types of public works that improve livestock, fisheries, or horticulture production for the landless and for small farmers would have very different results.

Improvements derived from greater agricultural productivity and employment can lead to better supply-and-demand conditions for food. An increase in the size of the rural nonagriculture sector provides more stable income sources and has a positive effect on wage rates. Improved market integration provides incentives for agricultural commercialization, better prices for food and nonfood items, dietary diversity due to more food purchases, and enhanced income opportunities for landless households. Finally, greater access and use of services, such as education and health services, can directly contribute to better nutrition.

There are also some possible detrimental effects from economic infrastructure, such as canal irrigation. Canals, for example, can contribute to the increased prevalence of waterborne diseases, especially when household water supply, sanitation, and housing conditions are poor. Also, if investments in economic infrastructure contribute to increased demand for labor, inmigration from areas with higher levels of poverty often occurs. This can often raise the measured levels of food insecurity and malnutrition even though the welfare of migrating households is likely to improve.

In the BIDS/IFPRI study, the baseline nutrition conditions were worse in FFW project areas than in areas without, suggesting that either these projects tend to reach worse-off areas, or they result in inmigration from poorer areas (Kumar and Chowdhury 1985). Water supply and sanitation conditions were poorer in areas where investments in irrigation infrastructure were made, indicating high population density and low income levels. Despite these inherent drawbacks, project sites had better short-term nutritional status, which suggests a more secure income stream and better ability to tolerate seasonality in income, food consumption, and health stresses. The nutritional improvements were significant for children past the weaning stage who could benefit from improvements in household food availability. However, there was no perceptible improvement for children who were not yet fully weaned. For this group, diarrheal disease, rather than household food availability, is a more important determining factor of nutritional status, and this disease was more widespread in project areas.

Consumption of calories and protein was raised for all age groups in project areas. However, if improvement in food security for those who are insecure is the objective, then the benefits are parallel to the income benefits obtained by the landless and other low-income households. Given their relatively high incidence of food insecurity, these households have a high marginal propensity to allocate income increments for food consumption. Reducing food insecurity, as defined by a household's ability to meet more than 80 percent of its food needs for the year, is therefore best achieved through investments in physical infrastructure, which contributes the most to income improvement for the landless and small farmers. Multivariate analysis shows that areas with good infrastructure had the largest improvement in calorie adequacy for the lowest income quartile. With physical infrastructure development, calories per capita improved by about 9 percent and adequacy by about 8 percent for the lowest income quartile. In contrast, agricultural productivity alone was greatest for the highest income quartile. Even though the result of infrastructure development was favorable to the adoption of agricultural technologies, the design of the study made it possible to test for the independent effects of both, while holding the level of the other constant (Kumar, forthcoming). The implication for the combined effects of both are clearly favorable for all income groups.

Multivariate analysis of the effects of physical infrastructure and technological change on intrahousehold calorie adequacy shows that physical infrastructure improves the diets of women, indicating the effect of infrastructure-led improvements in employment and educational opportunities for women. A similar improvement does not occur with technological change alone—with irrigation improvement, for example. Results suggest that while income gains are important, it is also necessary to increase the economic opportunities for women and access to the health services afforded by rural infrastructure development in order for household dietary improvements to benefit women and children.

Conclusion: Future Perspectives

Future Needs for Intervention

Bangladesh is on the verge of attaining self-sufficiency in foodgrain production. The recent trends in rice production indicate that the country may emerge as a surplus rice producer in the near future. However, the poor, who number in the millions, are unequipped to capture the gains from a rice surplus or self-sufficiency. Due to their inadequate purchasing power, they lack access to sufficient food and thus remain seriously underfed. Given the current level of poverty, it will take a long time to reach the goal of food security for all. A task force report, called "Strengthening the Institutions for Food Assisted Development," rightfully mentions that

> even if Bangladesh were to become self-sufficient in foodgrains in the very near future, this would not of itself solve the poverty problem. Nor would it necessarily call into question the future need for a labor-intensive public works program, a program of human resource development among the very poor, nor even the need to support such programs with special food-targeting measures. (SIFAD 1989)

Sustainability of Programs

FFW and other targeted food interventions in Bangladesh depend heavily on food aid provided by donors. With the increasing likelihood that there will be surplus rice production, one may consider the prospect of partly implementing FFW with internal food resources. That is, the government may distribute the benefit of increased rice production by supporting targeted programs with procured rice. However, given the serious budgetary limitations of the government, the general feeling is that the targeted interventions would have to draw on external assistance. If this premise is true, then the future of these programs would depend on the willingness of donors to sustain them. In this context, one would expect—since the food-assisted interventions are, in fact, donor creations—that the donors would feel somewhat obligated to continue to support them. The need for such interventions certainly will persist for the foreseeable future.

Apparently, the recent success of Bangladesh's Green Revolution, which has resulted in increased production of rice, has made it more difficult to continue to justify food aid. However, in spite of the likely self-sufficiency in rice production, the government argues that the wheat deficit still exists and, therefore, food aid continues to be justified. Furthermore, an IFPRI study by Ahmed (1993a) stresses that wheat, instead of rice, should be distributed for targeted food interventions to alleviate the protein-energy malnutrition at minimum cost.

Policy Implications

The FFW program has been an important instrument of employment generation in Bangladesh for most of the last two decades. The food aid supporting the program has helped Bangladesh raise the level of food security at the national level. The employment generation program itself succeeded at least partially in reducing food insecurity at the individual and household levels. More important, infrastructure development under FFW has facilitated noticeable growth in Bangladesh agriculture in the recent past. This has, in turn, reinforced gains in national food security. However, the changed production structure within agriculture and the limitations of FFW call for modifications of the program's design and a search for alternatives that more effectively address the continuing problem of food insecurity. The following suggestions are made in light of the discussion in this chapter and the recommendations made by the Working Group on Targeted Food Intervention (WGTFI 1993).[10]

The ability of FFW to generate slack-season employment is rather limited if resources are invested primarily in earthwork activities. In many regions of Bangladesh, the dry season is now a peak period in crop production and thus provides considerable employment opportunities. However, concentration of FFW resources in areas where irrigation-led technological change has not yet occurred in the dry season may serve the dual purpose of employment generation and diffusion of agricultural technology.

In all regions, the September–October period continues to be the worst season in terms of food insecurity. Lack of employment opportunities before the aman rice harvest in November makes this slack season especially acute for the rural landless, who depend on wage labor for their income. Also, foodgrain prices are typically high in this season. Consequently, real income and food consumption are at their lowest levels for the rural poor during these months (Ahmed 1993b). However, the bulk of FFW schemes involve earthmoving (road construction, canal digging, tank excavation, and embankment construction) and cannot operate during this wet, postmonsoon season of the year. However, there is some scope for FFW to switch from construction to maintenance activities during this

---

[10]The Working Group, chaired by IFPRI, consisted of technicians with a wide range of policy and operational experience. The WGTFI 1993 study reviews a complete spectrum of program options.

season. These activities could include maintenance of plantations, trees beside roads and canal embankments, roads constructed during the dry season by FFW schemes, and primary schools.

New activities in rural areas such as social forestry, latrine construction, and the construction of primary schools may also be worth exploring. Since construction and earthmoving activities are the most difficult to monitor, maintenance activities—such as rural primary school maintenance—present a lower risk of leakage.

The cash-based Rural Maintenance Program (RMP), a relatively small project of CARE and the Ministry of Relief and Rehabilitation, employs destitute women who are willing to work at low-paying manual labor. RMP-like "cash-for-work" interventions may provide the most promising alternative to FFW programs.

Cash-for-work can reduce program costs by 25 percent over food-based public works schemes by avoiding commodity-handling costs. A further switch from construction to more easily supervised maintenance activities lowers the scope for leakage, which might raise benefits by 30 to 35 percent. RMP disburses cash to the women's group bank accounts. In this way, the program also introduces a savings element. Through their accounts, the participants gain credit worthiness with local banks under normal circumstances. This group otherwise would never have the standing to gain access to formal financial institutions.

An appropriately targeted urban FFW to address the problem of urban food insecurity should be considered. Urban slums are currently untouched by labor-intensive works schemes. Environmental cleanup activities in urban areas involving slum dwellers could provide an opportunity to target the urban poor.

In all of the modified and alternative programs, greater opportunities for female participation should be created. Several studies document evidence that in both Asia and Africa, income controlled by women is associated with higher household food expenditures and caloric intake than is male-controlled income (Guyer 1980; Garcia 1990; Haddad and Hoddinott 1991; von Braun and Kennedy 1994). Thus, targeting transfer of income to women will most likely improve household food security more effectively than targeting it to men.

In order to realize greater benefits from FFW programs, it is also necessary to ensure accountability and reduce leakage. Since there are enormous difficulties in assessing the actual work performed in earthwork schemes, participation of local bodies (or, representatives of beneficiaries) at the stages of scheme selection and implementation should be strengthened. If the beneficiaries share costs, they are more likely to take an active part, be more accountable, and help reduce leakage.

If the FFW program in Bangladesh is to be made more development-oriented, some institutional rearrangements are in order. Given the relief orientation of the program in the past, the responsibility of coordinating the FFW program has fallen to the Ministry of Relief and Rehabilitation. This role may now be reduced to overseeing activities in some pre-determined regions where dry-season unemployment continues to be a problem. By and large, however, FFW should be brought into the regular development planning process, and its administration should be moved to a suitable development ministry.

REFERENCES

Ahmed, A. U. 1992. *Operational performance of the rural rationing program in Bangladesh*. Working Papers on Bangladesh 5. Washington, D. C.: International Food Policy Research Institute.

_____. 1993a. Food consumption and nutritional effects of targeted food interventions in Bangladesh. International Food Policy Research Institute/Bangladesh Food Policy Project, Dhaka. Mimeo.

_____. 1993b. Patterns of food consumption and nutrition in rural Bangladesh. International Food Policy Research Institute/Bangladesh Food Policy Project, Dhaka. Mimeo.

Ahmed, A. U., and Y. Shams. 1993. Demand parameters in rural Bangladesh. International Food Policy Research Institute/Bangladesh Food Policy Project, Dhaka. Mimeo.

Ahmed, R., and M. Hossain. 1990. *Development impact of rural infrastructure in Bangladesh*. Research Report 83. Washington, D.C.: International Food Policy Research Institute.

Asaduzzaman, M., and B. Huddleston. 1983. An evaluation of management of the food-for-work programme. *Bangladesh Development Studies* 11 (1 and 2): 41–96.

BIDS/IFPRI (Bangladesh Institute of Development Studies/International Food Policy Research Institute). 1985. Development impact of the Food-for-Work Program in Bangladesh. A Report prepared for the World Food Programme. Washington, D.C.: International Food Policy Research Institute. Mimeo.

Braun, J. von, and E. Kennedy. 1994. *Commercialization of agriculture, economic development, and nutrition*. Baltimore, Md., U.S.A.: Johns Hopkins University Press for the International Food Policy Research Institute.

Braun, J. von, T. Teklu, and P. Webb. 1991. *Labor-intensive public works for food security: Experience in Africa*. Working Papers on Food Subsidies 6. Washington, D.C.: International Food Policy Research Institute.

Chowdhury, O. H. 1983. Profile of workers in the Food-for-Work Programme in Bangladesh. *Bangladesh Development Studies* 11 (1 and 2): 111–134.

Garcia, M. 1990. Resource allocation and household welfare: A study of personal sources of income on food consumption, nutrition, and health in the Philippines. Ph.D. thesis, Institute of Social Studies, The Hague, the Netherlands.

Goletti, F. 1993. Food consumption parameters in Bangladesh. International Food Policy Research Institute, Washington, D.C. Mimeo.

Guyer, J. 1980. *Household budgets and women's incomes.* African Studies Center Working Paper No. 28. Boston, Mass., U.S.A.: Boston University.

Haddad, L., and J. Hoddinott. 1991. *Household expenditure, child anthropometric status, and the intrahousehold division of income: Evidence from the Côte d'Ivoire.* Discussion Paper No. 155. Research Program in Development Studies. Princeton, N.J., U.S.A.: Woodrow Wilson School of Public and International Affairs, Princeton University.

Hazell, P. B. R., and A. Röell. 1983. *Rural growth linkages: Household expenditure patterns in Malaysia and Nigeria.* Research Report 41. Washington, D.C.: International Food Policy Research Institute.

Hossain, M., and M. Akash. 1993. *Rural public works for relief and development: A review of Bangladesh experience.* Working Papers on Food Subsidies 7. Washington, D.C.: International Food Policy Research Institute.

Hossain, M., and M. Asaduzzaman. 1983. An evaluation of the Special Public Works Programme in Bangladesh. *Bangladesh Development Studies* 11 (1 and 2): 191–226.

Hossain, M., and S. Rashid. 1991. Labour force, employment, and access to income earning opportunities in Bangladesh. Bangladesh Institute of Development Studies, Dhaka. Mimeo.

Hossain, M., and B. Sen. 1992. Rural poverty in Bangladesh: Trends and determinants. *Asian Development Review* 10 (1): 1–34.

Kumar, S. Forthcoming. Rural infrastructure in Bangladesh: Effects on food consumption and nutrition of the population. *Economic Development and Cultural Change.*

Kumar, S., and O. H. Chowdhury. 1985. The effects on nutritional status. In Development impact of the Food-for-Work Program in Bangladesh. A report prepared for the World Food Programme. Bangladesh Institute of Development Studies/International Food Policy Research Institute, Washington, D.C. Mimeo.

74

Mitra and Associates. 1991. The labor survey 1991. Final report. Integrated Food-for-Work Project, Dhaka.

MSI (Management Systems International). 1987. Institutional assessment of food-for-work and feeder road programmes in Bangladesh. Washington, D.C. Mimeo.

Osmani, S. R., and O. H. Chowdhury. 1983. Short-run impacts of food-for-work programme in Bangladesh. *Bangladesh Development Studies* 11 (1 and 2): 135–190.

Pitt, M. M. 1983. Food preferences and nutrition in rural Bangladesh. *Review of Economics and Statistics* 65 (1): 105–114.

SIFAD (Task Force on Strengthening the Institutions for Food Assisted Development). 1989. Joint Government of Bangladesh/Donor Task Force on "Strengthening the institutions for food assisted development." Final report, vol. 1. Ministry of Planning, Dhaka.

WFP (World Food Programme). 1993. Bangladesh foodgrain forecast (July). Dhaka. Mimeo.

WGTFI (Working Group of Targeted Food Interventions). 1993. Options for targeting food interventions in Bangladesh. International Food Policy Research Institute, Dhaka. Mimeo.

World Bank. 1990. *Bangladesh: Poverty and public expenditures. An evaluation of the impact of selected government programs.* Report No. 7946-BD. Washington, D.C.

Zohir, S. 1990. Rural roads and poverty alleviation. Bangladesh Institute of Development Studies, Dhaka. Mimeo.

4

"YIGONG-DAIZHEN" IN CHINA: A NEW EXPERIENCE WITH LABOR-INTENSIVE PUBLIC WORKS IN POOR AREAS

Zhu Ling and Jiang Zhongyi

Poverty in China is concentrated mainly in certain regions and in rural areas. Unlike Bangladesh and India (Chapters 3 and 5), poverty in China has little to do with unequal land distribution, since rural land reform and the collectivization of land leveled differences in land ownership more than 40 years ago.

The market-oriented economic reforms that began in the late 1970s gave Chinese farmers decisionmaking powers in the management of farming activities; these reforms also enabled many to increase their incomes quickly through better use of resources, price increases, economic restructuring, and the development of nonfarm industries. However, about one-tenth of the rural population has scarcely benefited from these institutional changes; they remain food insecure (Chen Chunming 1992; Zhu Ling and Jiang Zhongyi 1994). This portion of the population inhabits areas that are poor in resources and infrastructure (Tong Zhong et al. 1994). Hence, there is a widening gap between the socioeconomic development of these areas and the national average.

To bridge this gap, the Chinese government has carried out large-scale antipoverty measures since 1985 to speed up development in poor areas and to ensure that the poor's basic requirements for food and clothing are met. The criteria set at that time for identifying poor households and poor counties were an annual per capita foodgrain ration of less than 200 kilograms and an annual per capita net income of less than 200 yuans. Poor counties designated by the central and provincial governments total 699.

The authors are indebted to Joachim von Braun for his valuable suggestions, comments, and editorial assistance. Special thanks are expressed to Lynette Aspillera, Yisehac Yohannes, Jay Willis, Zhang Ming, Li Yeuqin, Xie Changhao, Li Shi, and Kong Jingyuan for providing useful assistance. The authors are also grateful for the kind cooperation of the institutions and authorities interviewed at the central government level and in the Guizhou, Shandong, Ningxia, and Sichuan provinces of China. Deep gratitude is extended to the village committees and farmers' households visited in the four provinces.

"Yigong-daizhen," which means "to offer job opportunities instead of sheer relief," is one of the Chinese government's poverty-reduction programs. It consists mainly of government infrastructure construction investments in poor regions. It supplies the material basis for regional economic growth and provides short-term job opportunities and incomes for the local population. The projects carried out are similar to those known internationally as "labor-intensive public works" (von Braun, Teklu, and Webb 1991).

This chapter considers the effects of Yigong-daizhen projects on the employment, income, and nutritional status of households in poor areas. The organizational pattern of the Yigong-daizhen projects is described first. Then, data obtained from surveys of village communities and peasant households are presented and analyzed to identify (1) the targeting mechanisms of Yigong-daizhen projects and (2) the impact of the projects on the income and consumption of poor rural households. Finally, problems in the organization and operation of the program are assessed and measures for improvement are explored.

The Size and Organization of the Yigong-daizhen Program

Until the 1980s, the Chinese government's regional policies emphasized subsidies to and investments in less-developed regions, generally in the western areas of the country, through the national redistribution system of the centrally planned economy. Aid for the poor was distributed only as temporary relief. However, resources were not efficiently utilized and the goal of the central government was not attained. In fact, the regional gap in socioeconomic development between the east and west gradually widened and some poor areas of the west became poorer (Zhu Ling and Jiang Zhongyi 1994).

The main reasons for the failure of these policies were that

- subsidies failed to stimulate local initiative,
- investments in institutional and physical-infrastructure construction were inadequate, and
- investment projects were often not appropriate to the local environmental and socioeconomic conditions and did not tap the local resources.

During the 1960s and 1970s, roads, bridges, and water-diversion works were constructed and electricity was introduced in poor mountainous areas. However, these improvements served mainly military and state-owned industrial enterprises and benefited urban populations. They did not absorb local labor, nor did they promote socioeconomic development in poor areas. Often these projects were isolated from the social and economic context of the rural areas.

Policies for regional development were adjusted as part of broad economic reform in the early 1980s, and the philosophy of the antipoverty strategy changed significantly. A much stronger emphasis was placed on participation by local governments and the poor in organizing and implementing poverty-reduction programs, whose goal is local self-reliance. The design and organization of projects within the Yigong-daizhen program reflect these new principles.

The Yigong-daizhen program started at the end of 1984. Public investment under this program differed from formal capital construction projects of the state in the following ways:

1. The investment of the central government took the form of in-kind financing of the projects. These in-kind goods were surplus products created during a certain period under the planned economy. The investment plan depended on the availability of surplus goods. In many cases, several schemes operated during the same period (Table 4.1).

2. Rules stipulate that in-kind goods allocated by the central government are distributed as wages to those involved in construction

Table 4.1—Chinese government investment in Yigong-daizhen schemes, 1984–93

Scheme Number	Planned Period	In-Kind Goods Invested	Converted Value of the Goods	Project Focus
			(billion yuan)[a]	
1	1984–87	Cereals, cotton, and cloth	2.7	Roads and drinking water supply facilities
2	1989–91	Medium- and low-grade consumer goods	0.6	Roads and drinking water supply facilities
3	1990–92	Industrial goods	1.5	Roads and drinking water supply facilities, farm-land improvement
4	1991–95	Foodgrains	5.0	Terraced fields, small-scale water conservation
5	1991–95	Foodgrains and industrial goods	10.0	Big rivers
6	1993–97	Cereals, cloth, edible oil, medium- and low-grade consumer goods	10.0	Infrastructure, including clinics, health care stations for women and children

Source: Documents issued by the State Planning Commission referring to Yigong-daizhen schemes, 1984–93.
[a]In 1993, 5.8 yuan equaled US$1.00.

projects. Local governments are supposed to raise supplementary funds of an equal or greater amount to pay for project materials and other expenses. In practice, except for a few provinces with sufficient resources, most of the provinces and counties could not come up with the matching funds. To fill the gap, poverty-reduction funds from other channels (such as from line ministries responsible for economic sectors) were used and some of the transferred goods were monetized.

3. Local governments also mobilized the rural population to provide part of their labor free of charge or at reduced wages. These practices are not likely to work in the implementation of formal capital construction projects. But because the Yigong-daizhen programs were aimed at reducing poverty, local governments and the poor accepted these practices and participated in investment projects. Such flexibility played a positive role in pooling resources to improve infrastructure. However, employment of unpaid labor reduced the present income of the poor.

4. Yigong-daizhen projects mainly made use of simple, labor-intensive technology. Normally, construction was carried out in the slack seasons, providing varying amounts of additional income. Between 1985 and 1990, projects focused on building roads and drinking-water supply facilities (see Table 4.2). Thanks to this program, both transport facilities and social services in the poor areas improved, and human resources in project locales were enhanced. Specifically, farmers acquired technical skills on the job, and administrative cadres learned construction management; a specialized technical workforce was trained in infrastructure construction and water conservation.

Table 4.2—Major infrastructure achievements of the Yigong-daizhen projects, China, 1985–90

Achievement	Quantity
Public roads	131,000 kilometers
Bridges (number)	7,972
Dredged river navigation routes	2,400 kilometers
Public roads connected . . .	1,500 townships
	10,000 administrative villages
Drinking water supplied for . . .	20,970,000 people
	13,560,000 animals

Source: Data from the State Planning Commission, 1988 and 1992.

Implementation Rules of the
Yigong-daizhen Projects

Rules concerning the allocation and use of materials, the process of making investments, financial controls, and the duties of local governments and relevant departments are all stipulated by the State Planning Commission. Hence, there are similarities in project planning, organization, management, and monitoring among different programs in different places.

The implementation of projects involves a number of authorities and institutions with responsibility for planning, finance, banking, commerce, foodgrains, materials, sales and supply, agriculture, water and electricity, transportation, tax revenue, audits, and public security. Close coordination among relevant bureaus is necessary for an ensured supply of funds, materials, and laborers so that programs can proceed according to plan. For this reason, "leading groups for Yigong-daizhen" are established within the local governments concerned—at the provincial, prefectural, and county levels—to coordinate the program across different departments. Headquarters are established for the execution of each project and are composed of technicians in relevant professional bureaus (for example, bureaus of transportation, water conservancy, agriculture, and so forth), accounting personnel, and leading members of townships where the projects are located.

The process of the confirmation of a project starts with the township government developing the application. Then the county bureaus of transportation and water conservancy examine, separately, the subapplications involving matters within the scope of their respective jurisdictions and report their choices to the county's "leading group for Yigong-daizhen" for examination and approval. If approved, proposal papers are prepared by these departments and forwarded to the departments concerned at the prefectural and provincial levels. The final formula of the program must be approved by the provincial planning commission and then sent back to the county leading group, through descending levels of bureaucracy.

Local governments at various levels tend to concentrate resources on the most important projects, which can be easily implemented, and to carry out projects in stages. For road projects, efficiency is stressed and investment priority is given to the following categories of projects: (1) feeder roads linking villages and towns with main roads, (2) transportation roads in areas with rich resources but without accessible roads, (3) roads connecting existing public ways and transportation networks, and (4) renovation projects for existing roads that have heavy traffic but a low technical standard.

Drinking-water projects are selected based on the availability of water sources. The following categories of projects have priority: (1) projects with greater labor input (large employment generation), (2) projects matching existing infrastructure works (favorable complementary effects), (3) projects proposed by villages in which the leading body has comparatively great organizational efficiency and the households volunteer to collect supplementary funds or contribute their labor (low organizational and budgetary costs), and (4) water supply projects in townships or villages suffering seriously from water shortages (high public health and sanitation benefits).[1]

Contractors, Payment Regulations, and Compulsory Work

There are two types of labor required for construction work: skilled and unskilled. The former includes masons, carpenters, blacksmiths, and others who possess skills. In recent years, they have usually organized themselves into crews of contractors to take on tasks demanding higher technical standards, both locally and in more distant counties. Unskilled workers are local farmers who are recruited for manual labor, such as moving earth and stones.

Earthwork and stonework in road projects are usually contracted out by project headquarters to groups of villagers along the roads. The heads of the groups usually distribute the task to households, according to the number of laborers in each household. The labor of farmers is, to some extent, compulsory; this is embodied in unpaid work that is converted into the matching "funds" of the local governments. Those households with workers who are unwilling to work must pay a sum to the group to relieve themselves of work obligations.

However, due to the tradition of mutual enforcement of work obligations among community members, especially for projects that benefit the public, failure to work is rare. As for the drinking-water projects, which

---

[1]According to the stipulations of the Ministry of Water Conservancy of 1984, a water shortage exists when villagers must travel more than 1 kilometer (in a single journey) or climb a vertical distance of more than 100 meters to fetch water. There are standards that indicate what sufficient levels of water supply are; anything short of this qualifies as a "water shortage." During drought seasons, the standards call for a per capita daily water supply of more than 10 kilograms in northern regions and more than 40 kilograms in southern regions. For cattle, there should be a daily water supply of 20–25 kilograms per head. For pigs and sheep, a daily water supply of 5–20 kilograms per head is sufficient. In areas with an average rainfall of less than 600 millimeters—where dry wells and dry pits are usually used—it is necessary to store, each year, enough water for two years' consumption. In the southern regions, there should be a reserve capable of ensuring a supply of drinking water for 70 to 100 days, even if there is no rain.

belong to individual households or village communities after their completion, all the unskilled labor input contributed by the villagers is unremunerated—only the skilled workers are paid.

The labor payments are set by the project headquarters as task rates, with the work quotas set according to the amount and difficulty of the work contracted. The daily payment of a skilled worker is usually twice that of an unskilled worker.

The mode of payment varies with the kind of materials the central government has allocated. When foodgrains, cotton, and cotton cloth are used as the inputs, payments for project participants will be made in these materials. When stocks of industrial products are invested in construction work, workers receive "industry coupons" as wages; these have the same value as the official currency of RMB but function as a kind of banknote to be used only once. The industrial coupons are to be used within the county and in the shops run by government departments of commerce, agricultural machines, and production materials, or in county and township purchasing and marketing cooperatives (Zhu Ling and Jiang Zhongyi 1990).

Monitoring and Planning

The monitoring and control for approval of the projects is carried out by the professional departments in charge of engineering and technology works.[2] The whole process of project planning, controlling, organizing, and monitoring, along with the use of industrial coupons, has been the operational pattern for many years in the centrally planned economy; it is well known to the administrative cadres and the departments of the government at all levels. As a result, the organization of the program has been quite smooth. However, the process also has had the disadvantage of taking place in a planned economy. For instance, restrictions placed by authorities at higher levels on where investments are to be directed has made it difficult for the county and township governments to use resources flexibly according to local needs. As village communities have been excluded from the decisionmaking process, the programs approved at higher levels sometimes were not the projects most needed by local governments and the poor.

---

[2]The roads that meet grade 4 and above of the state technical standard are brought into the road maintenance plan of the county. The newly built drinking water installations are controlled by the users themselves, while the villager committees work out rules for the use of water and carryout supervision.

Regional and Household-Level Assessment

Sources of Data and Information

Interviews with officials of the central and provincial governments in 1990, and two case studies conducted in Guizhon and Sichuan provinces, form the basis for information at the macro level. Microlevel findings are based on data derived from sample surveys in Sichuan, Shandong, and Ningxia (see Figures 4.1 and 4.2) made in May and June of 1992.

The sample surveys were designed as follows:

1. One poor county was selected from each of three different categories of provinces—developed, somewhat developed, and less-developed—to compare differences among various poor regions. The three poor counties selected were Linqu County of Shandong, Wangcang County of Sichuan, and Xiji County of Ningxia. Several

Figure 4.1—Survey provinces of The People's Republic of China: Shandong, Ningxia, and Sichuan

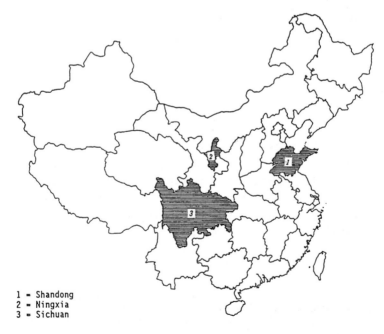

1 = Shandong
2 = Ningxia
3 = Sichuan

Note: Islands in the South China Sea are not shown on map.

Figure 4.2—Survey counties

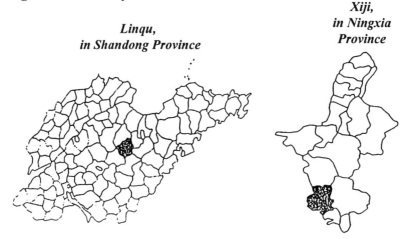

Linqu,
in Shandong Province

Xiji,
in Ningxia
Province

Wangcang,
in Sichuan Province

selected socioeconomic indicators of the studied provinces and counties and sample survey areas are compared in Table 4.3.

2. Twelve administrative villages were selected from each of the three studied poor counties and divided into three groups of four villages each. The first group consisted of villages participating in road projects; the second group comprised villages participating in drinking-water supply projects; and the third group comprised villages that were not participating in any Yigong-daizhen projects. Village questionnaires were designed to identify natural, economic,

Table 4.3—Selected socioeconomic indicators of the study areas in China, 1990

Location	Population	Area	Per Capita GNP[a]	Rural Poverty Incidence	Adult Illiteracy Rate	Farm Size	Per Capita Income of Farmers' Households
	(million)	(1,000 kilometers)	(yuan)	(percent)	(percent)	(mu)[b]	(yuan)
China	1,143.33	9,600	3,323.3	11.4	15.9	6.5	629.8
Shandong Province	84.93	156.7	3,825.5	6.8	16.9	5.6	644.7
Linqu County	0.88	1.8	2,389.1	8.0	19.3	3.6	565.0
Ningxia Province	4.66	51.8	2,502.4	18.9	22.1	15.8	534.2
Xiji County	0.39	3.2	332.0	43.5	37.0	16.8	212.0
Sichuan Province	108.13	570.0	2,090.2	11.2	16.2	4.2	505.2
Wangcang County	0.43	3.0	997.6	10.0	26.1	3.5	558.0
Survey data[c]							
Villages in Linqu	...	...	...	...	11.2	4.0	565.4
Villages in Xiji	...	...	...	...	57.7	20.7	350.8
Villages in Wangcang	...	...	...	...	23.2	4.9	914.4

Source: State Statistical Bureau, 1991a, 1991b, 1991c, 1991d; World Bank (1992); statistics of Linqu, Xiji, and Wangcang, 1991.
[a]Data used are the gross output value of agriculture, industry, construction, transportation, and commerce, which is termed "gross social products" in Chinese statistical sources.
[b]15 mu = 1 hectare.
[c]Survey data refer to 1991.

and social conditions of the village communities, and were used in interviews with chief members of the villager committees.

3. Household surveys: 10 households from each of the sample villages, selected through random sampling, were interviewed with structured questionnaires. Data collected related mainly to conditions in 1991.

The three sample counties were selected on the advice of the departments in charge of Yigong-daizhen projects in each of the three provinces of Shandong, Sichuan, and Ningxia. The selection of sample villages was the outcome of discussions with the departments concerned in the three counties in charge of the projects.[3] The data thus obtained were supplemented by information from government sources.[4]

Rural Households and Individuals
Participating in the Projects

When the main socioeconomic indices of participating and nonparticipating households were compared, few differences were observed in the size of household, per capita farmland area, or family labor resources. In two of the survey sites, the households with less land per capita participated more (Table 4.4). Here, "assets" means the sum of the original value of the household's productive and nonproductive fixed assets (such as machines, houses, animals, poultry, and durable consumer goods like bicycles or sewing machines), exclusive of land. Index of "income" here means the "net income of rural households," as defined in the *Statistical Yearbook of China* (State Statistical Bureau 1989).

About 40 percent of the participating households worked on obligatory workdays (without pay), so that the benefits they obtained from the proj-

---

[3]Due to problems with traffic, only two villages were selected for the reference group of Wangcang County of Sichuan Province. However, 20 households were selected instead of 10 in each of the two villages. So, the number of villages sampled in the three counties was 34 and the number of sample rural households was 360. Examination showed that 358 questionnaires were valid.

[4]These sources include the *Yearbook of Statistics* and other information published by the State Statistics Bureau, as well as materials provided by departments of the State Planning Commission, the Ministry of Finance, the Ministry of Communications, and the Ministry of Water Conservancy and Irrigation. The statistical yearbooks and Yigong-daizhen working reports of the sample provinces and counties, as well as local historical papers on the culture, geography, and economy of the three counties were another source of data.

Table 4.4—Comparisons between households participating and not participating in Yigong-daizhen projects, China

County/Province Household	Number of Households	Size of Household	Per Capita Farmland	Per Capita Assets[a]	Per Capita Income[b]	Earnings from Projects
		(persons)	(mu)	(yuan)	(yuan)	(yuan)
Linqu/Shandong						
Participating	58	4.2	0.7	1,183	613	15
Nonparticipating	62	4.2	1.2	958	520	0
Xiji/Ningxia						
Participating	39	5.2	3.1	634	366	66
Nonparticipating	81	5.2	4.5	580	344	0
Wangcang/Sichuan						
Participating	64	4.2	1.2	2,443	1,100	64
Nonparticipating	54	4.3	1.2	1,645	695	0
The poorest tercile of the total sample households						
Participating	46	4.4	1.8	318	330	18
Nonparticipating	73	4.6	2.8	293	287	0

Source: Survey conducted by the authors.
[a]Excluding land.
[b]Earnings from projects not included.

ects were only the improvement of local social services and not direct supplementary incomes. In principle, all farmers in the areas, including nonpoor ones, are obliged to contribute labor, so that participation in the Yigong-daizhen projects should not be discriminating.

Probit models are used to estimate the probability of participation in the projects for villages, households, and individuals, respectively. There are four conclusions that can be drawn from the village-level model (Table 4.5):

1. County and township governments do not necessarily choose the project sites based on whether or not a village established a "system of obligatory labor contribution," but do choose project sites based on village size. The larger the population of a village is, the more likely it is to be involved in projects.
2. Villages with favorable environmental conditions are more likely to get projects. The role of the irrigation index in the model, which indicates conditions for agricultural production in village communities, seems to testify to this point, but it is not statistically significant at the villager level.
3. Villages with more farmland per capita are less likely to get projects, which means that those with more (surplus) labor are supported more.
4. Distances from village to county seat and from village to township have been brought into the model as indices reflecting the relationship between villages and governments. (County seats and townships are places where the governments at the two levels are located.) The results suggest that within counties, the more remote areas get preferential treatment.

Table 4.5—Estimation of the probability of participation in Yigong-daizhen projects by village, Probit Model 1

Variable	Coefficient	t-Ratio
Population	0.31068E-02*	1.838
Distance from village to township	−0.13630	−1.396
Distance from village to county seat	0.25353E-01*	1.860
System of obligatory labor contribution	−0.94305	−0.622
Irrigation index of farmland	4.4919	1.404
Per capita farmland of a village	−1.3306*	−1.836
Constant	0.45017	0.177
N = 34		

*Significant at .10 level.

Table 4.6—Estimation of the probability of participation in Yigong-daizhen projects by household, Probit Model 2

Variable	Coefficient	t-Ratio
Per capita farmland of household	−0.17*	−3.30
Irrigation index of farmland	1.71*	4.80
Labor index of household (labor force/ household size)	0.44	1.30
Per capita assets	−0.45E-04	−1.05
Number of households in a village	0.21E-02*	3.10
Constant = −0.80		
N = 358		
Cases correctly predicted = 68.4 percent		

*Significant at .01 level.

In the household-level model (Table 4.6), two village variables, "number of households in a village" and "irrigation index," are included. Because both irrigated and rainfed areas of farmland tend to be distributed among households within a village according to household size, the index can be applied to all households in the same village. The significance of the two variables confirms the conclusion, derived from Model 1, that participating households are more likely to be located in larger villages. Yet, because the poor make up a larger share of the population in areas where the projects are carried out and because of the principle of equal opportunity for participation by all households and laborers enforced by village communities, the results of Model 2 indicate that households that are relatively rich in labor resources, poor in land, and low in per capita assets participate more in the projects. While this may be these households' free choice, it can also be interpreted as a result of the regulated access to participation.

Probit Model 3 was derived by estimating the probability of individual participation in the projects (Table 4.7). Data for the estimation are based on the records of individual participants and nonparticipants between 15 and 65 years of age—a total of 1,145 people. Several conclusions can be drawn from Model 3 to supplement those drawn from Models 1 and 2.

1. Laborers from households with less land tend to participate more in the projects. This may be because they have lower opportunity costs in agriculture.
2. Male laborers show a higher probability of involvement than females. The reasons for this may be twofold. First, the payments for

Table 4.7—Estimation of the probability of individual participation in Yigong-daizhen projects, Probit Model 3

Variable	Coefficient	t-Ratio
Age	0.19E-01**	4.94
Sex (1 = male, 0 = female)	0.47**	4.92
Years of education	0.32E-01*	1.89
Per capita farmland of household	−0.21**	−6.37
Constant = −1.41		
N = 1,145		
Cases correctly predicted = 78.6 percent		

*Significant at .05 level.
**Significant at .01 level.

moving earth and stones are according to task rates that may favor males (due to physical strength). Hence, the active participation of the male laborers can be seen as an efficiency decision by the household. Second, the conventional division of labor between males and females in farmers' families assigns household chores, livestock production, and fieldwork to women, limiting the extent of their participation in projects.

3. Laborers with a higher educational level and older laborers are more inclined to participate.

The analysis suggests that even within poor areas, the criterion for government approval for starting new projects is efficiency—the success of the projects and the effectiveness of the investments. This is consistent with the thinking of the central and provincial governments regarding allocation of resources for the projects: the order of priority among water-supply projects is "easy projects first," followed by difficult ones. Emphasis is also placed on the reliability of water sources. Among road-construction projects, priority has been given to roads that permit access to resources such as mines and forests and roads that strengthen the existing network. Furthermore, the success or failure of a project serves as an important indicator in assessing the achievements of government officials at the grassroots level. This also explains why township governments usually choose villages with better conditions to be the sites of new projects.

In contrast to this practice, village communities have practiced the principle of equality in the recruitment of the labor force for the projects, which means that rural households and individuals enjoy equal opportunities to participate in projects. However, households with a lower land and asset base actually turn out to be more involved in the projects than the relatively well-to-do people, according to the analysis.

Effects of Projects on Rural Household Income

The Yigong-daizhen projects have improved incomes of participating households (Table 4.4). In terms of relief, the poorer the area, the more important is the household income from the projects. The highest share has been about one-sixth of the disposable incomes of the households in Xiji County of Ningxia-Hui Autonomous Region.

It was mentioned earlier that, although the village communities covered by the projects are mostly those with comparatively favorable economic conditions, nonpoor households in the villages are not excluded from participating in the projects. Thus, it might be assumed that the distribution of project incomes among households may intensify the inequality of total disposable incomes. This possibility has been investigated through calculation of the Gini coefficients. Results of the calculations, listed in Table 4.8, indicate that farming constitutes the main source of income for the sample households. Since access to farmland is distributed on an equal basis to all households, income from farming does not vary widely among households. In comparison, degrees of disparity in nonfarm incomes are higher. The Gini coefficient of income from projects enlarges the overall Gini coefficient. It is only because of its small share that the impact on income distribution is limited.

It is worth noting that the Gini coefficient of earnings from public works in Wangcang County of Sichuan Province is as high as 0.974, indicating extreme inequality in the distribution of income, with a few people getting high payments from the projects. According to the data, the household with the highest income from the projects in the county (3,600 yuan per person) was a household that owned trucks that it used for transport. Therefore, the income of this household actually included the rewards for its capital.

Opportunity Costs and Net Effects for Income

The above discussion of rural household income from projects has not directly taken into consideration the farmers' opportunity costs for their involvement. To obtain information on this, the survey included some related direct questions to farmers.

Table 4.8—Income inequality among sample households in three counties, China, 1991

Source of Per Capita Income	Linqu County (Shandong)			Xiji County (Ningxia)			Wangcang County (Sichuan)		
	Share of Income	Gini Coefficient[a]	Contribution to Overall Gini	Share of Income	Gini Coefficient[a]	Contribution to Overall Gini	Share of Income	Gini Coefficient[a]	Contribution to Overall Gini
	(percent)			(percent)			(percent)		
Farming incomes	67.4	0.264	47.1	74.2	0.270	51.7	51.1	0.268	21.1
Family nonfarming incomes	6.9	0.961	16.4	3.2	0.947	6.6	19.4	0.930	39.8
Wages	15.1	0.767	25.3	9.2	0.836	14.8	16.4	0.776	20.6
Gathering earnings	0.8	0.960	1.0	0.2	0.981	0.6	1.8	0.929	1.6
Net public transfers	3.6	0.876	2.6	0.8	0.967	0.9	1.9	0.929	1.4
Private transfers	0.7	0.927	0.3	7.2	0.904	16.0	3.1	0.788	2.1
Rental from productive assets	2.1	0.974	4.3	0.1	0.992	0.3	1.4	0.986	2.7
Interests and others	2.7	0.825	1.4	0.8	0.986	1.8	1.5	0.925	1.8
Earnings from public works	1.3	0.803	1.6	5.6	0.837	7.3	4.2	0.974	8.9
Total disposable income	100.0[b]	0.304	100.0	100.0[b]	0.331	100.0	100.0[b]	0.437	100.0

Notes: For discussion of the method of calculation, see Fei, Ranis, and Kuo (1978) and Fields (1980); for details on the calculations, see Zhu Ling and Jiang Zhongyi (1994).

[a] Gini coefficient of each income component as well as that of the total disposable income.

[b] When a component income of a sample household appeared to have a negative value, it was replaced by zero. Thus, taking the total sample households as a whole, the overall disposable income would be less than the sum of all the component incomes, while the sum of the shares of the nine income components would be a little bigger than 100.0.

92

Table 4.9—Impact of participation in Yigong-daizhen projects on household work time and children's dislocation

	Question				
Reaction from Interviewees	Stopped Some Other Work (1)[a]	Women Work More (2)[b]	Children Work More (3)[c]	Child at Workplace (Women) (4)[d]	Child at Workplace (Men) (5)[e]
	(percent)				
Yes	21.9	45.8	6.5	6.5	2.0
No	78.1	54.2	93.5	93.5	98.0

Source: Survey conducted by the authors.
Notes: A total of 201 households answered these questions, representing 56 percent of the total sample. Among them, 40 households possibly participated in the projects, but due to their failure to answer questions concerning the number of days of their participation and their earnings from the projects, they were not included.
[a] Is there any laborer in your family who has stopped other production work to take part in the project?
[b] Have the female members in your family increased their working time in farming due to the participation of male laborers in the projects?
[c] Have the children in your family under 16 years of age increased their working time in domestic labor due to the participation of their parents in the projects?
[d] Do the female members of your family bring with them the children under 16 years old when attending project work?
[e] Do male laborers in your family bring with them the children under 16 years old when attending project work?

Several conclusions can be drawn from the responses to these questions in interviews with households (Table 4.9). First, for most of the laborers (78.1 percent), their participation in the projects resulted in a decrease in their leisure time. Because Yigong-daizhen projects were usually carried out during the slack season in farming, the opportunity cost of their participation in the projects was almost zero (the "leisure time" in this season was not the choice of farmers themselves but a manifestation of idleness of the labor force). This constitutes the rationale for low payment and the mobilization of the obligatory labor contribution commonly practiced in the construction works.

Second, the working hours of women in almost one-half of the households were increased—in other words, their leisure time was reduced in order to meet the time requirements of agricultural production while male laborers participated in the projects. The rural households made labor inputs by adjusting the deployment of the family labor force. In 54 percent of the rural households, participation in projects did not affect the amount of time worked by female laborers, perhaps because these households had more working members or because the timing of the construction work and the slack season in farming coincided.

Third, it was probably because of the abundant labor supply that the impact of farmer participation in the project on children's work (question 3) and children's dislocation from home (questions 4 and 5) was small.

The implementation of Yigong-daizhen projects has increased the immediate employment and the income of the participants, both of which represent short-term effects of projects on rural household income, or first-round impacts. Part of the increased income may be used by farmers for new investments in fixed assets or for the purchase of additional input materials, possibly leading to a further increase in incomes.

Infrastructure Effects

The execution of projects also improves infrastructure and social services in the villages, creating conditions for future increases in rural households' incomes. This is a long-term effect of the projects, which shall be assessed in the context of other income-determining factors. Village infrastructure was assessed on the basis of six factors: accessibility of the village by road (accessible by truck); the existence of supply stations for input materials (improved varieties of crops, chemical fertilizer, and other farm chemicals); and the availability of electricity, medical services, drinking-water supply centers, and village primary schools. To obtain an aggregate impression, each factor was assigned one point. Villages with all six kinds of infrastructure and services obviously received six points. The project villages among the sample generally got more than four points each, while the villages in the reference groups got around 2.5 points each, on average. There are, of course, correlations among these infrastructure conditions (Ahmed and Hossain 1990).

Studies in the past have indicated that income disparities among rural households are generally determined by differences in land ownership or access, capital, labor force, application of modern techniques and input materials in farming activities, as well as infrastructure conditions. A multiple regression analysis below has included indicators that represent the factors mentioned—including household per capita area of cultivated land, the ratio of area under improved varieties to total cultivated land, the irrigation index, household per capita fixed assets, the family labor resource index (labor force/household size), and the educational level of the household head, as independent variables; the dependent variable is household per capita disposable income. The results show the significance of per capita assets of rural households, infrastructure conditions of village communities, chemical fertilizers applied per mu,[5] and the counties with which sample households are affiliated (as dummy variables) to capture other regional influences. The regression model is as follows:

$$I = 121.23 + 0.11\ PCASSET + 50.59\ PCLAND + 0.79\ PMFERTI$$
$$(-0.885)\ (7.848) \qquad\qquad (2.191)^* \qquad\qquad (3.191)^{**}$$

$$+\ 49.14\ INFRA + 162.11\ COUNTY1 + 350.54\ COUNTY3$$
$$(2.253)^* \qquad\quad (1.573) \qquad\qquad (3.416)^{**}$$

$$+\ 47.59\ IMR;$$
$$(1.244)$$

$R^2 = 0.365;\quad F\ (7,350) = 28.777;\quad N = 358.$

Numbers in parentheses are t-ratios.
Two asterisks (**) indicate significance at the 99 percent confidence level and one asterisk (*) at the 95 percent confidence level.

Variables are

I	=	household per capita disposable income,
$PCASSET$	=	per capita assets (excluding land),
$PCLAND$	=	per capita cultivated land,
$PMFERTI$	=	chemical fertilizer applied per mu,
$INFRA$	=	points for infrastructure conditions of village communities in which the sample households live,
$COUNTY1$	=	Linqu County of Shandong Province,
$COUNTY3$	=	Wangcang County of Sichuan Province, and
IMR	=	inverse mills ratio for correcting sample selection bias (Dolton and Makepeace 1987).

The results concerning the dummy variables $COUNTY1$ and $COUNTY3$ in the model mean that the incomes of households in Linqu and Wangcang counties are generally higher than those in Xiji County. The results also imply that, apart from socioeconomic conditions, regional

---

[5]The amount of chemical fertilizer applied per mu might be partly influenced by infrastructure, but it also depends to a great extent on the financial resources of farmers, on prices, and on the type of fertilizer supplied. Since the use of chemical fertilizer affects farmers' income through its impact on crop production, it is kept in the income regression model here.

differences in features of the natural environment, such as topography and climate, decisively affect the household income. (Xiji is an extremely dry area, Linqu is located in a subdry region, while Wangcang has a mild climate, humid and warm, favorable for agriculture.) The regression results support the hypothesis that improved village infrastructure enhances household income.

The amount of farmland and the use of chemical fertilizers proved to be significant determinants of household income. Moreover, assets stand out as an important factor that determines income differences among households. This variable includes capital goods, housing, and durable consumer goods, but excludes land, because the land market is nonexistent under the present legislation and there are no prices for farmland cultivated by farmers in China.

Household assets are the deposits of incomes earned in the past, and represent the outcome of past economic activity. Therefore, assets indicate not only property amounts, but also farmers' knowledge, skills, and entrepreneurship. The latter items are difficult to measure, but they indicate the quality of human resources that can be mobilized for economic activities.

In the income regression equation, several independent variables (excluding two dummy variables) that are significant demonstrate, from different angles, that capital is the most important income determinant. These variables are "village infrastructure," which results from public investment; "assets"; and "fertilizer application," which represents not only material input in agriculture, but also the amount of circulating capital available to rural households. Often, funds allocated for fertilizer procurement make up the largest share of circulating capital for agricultural production in farm households. Considering that indicators representing asset value all have a positive correlation with income, it is likely that increases in capital possessed by rural households will promote income growth.

Credit and Investment

To determine how farmers could expand their own capital, relations among earnings from Yigong-daizhen projects, savings, debts, investment in the survey year, and the value of fixed assets are examined. The percentage of savings in rural household assets is lower than 6 percent, the smallest asset component. The shortage of cash funds is reflected in the expectations of interviewed Yigong-daizhen project participants with regard to the form of payments: 85.6 percent of them wanted cash payment rather than payments in kind.

Where does the capital for investment in fixed assets come from, besides savings? Income from projects by no means serves as the major source of investment for rural households: less than 4 percent of project participants invested their projects' earnings in fixed assets, while the majority spent the earnings on consumer goods. Loans are the main source of capital for investments.

During the period of the People's Commune (before 1979), the poorer rural households were, the heavier their debt burden became (Zhou Binbin 1991). Since the reforms, that is no longer the case. After the system of absolute egalitarianism was abolished, the ability to repay loans became an important criterion in rural households' eligibility for loans. A situation common in rural areas throughout the world emerged: the poor cannot easily acquire loans. Those who can are normally the nonpoor. In the sample, the correlation coefficient of loans and assets reaches as high as 0.5885. The formation of private assets of rural households has no strong connection to project earnings; rather, credit plays a determining role. The policy implication of this conclusion is that only when Yigong-daizhen projects are coupled with effective development of rural financial systems can these projects increase the future income of poverty-stricken households.

Food Consumption and Nutrition
in Sample Households

Food security in rural China has been improved through the equal distribution of land, the operations of the official food-supply agencies, and the relief operations of the civil affairs departments.

It is apparent that, among the various Yigong-daizhen projects, the construction of terraced fields strengthens the food security of the poor most directly. The road-building and drinking-water projects are not designed to solve food shortages directly, but to improve infrastructure and social services. However, these projects do affect rural household expenditures, including those for food consumption, through increases in farmers' incomes. In this section, the determinants of the consumption expenditures of sample households are explored. The food consumption and nutritional status of the sample population are analyzed and some insights relevant to policy in this area are considered.

The per capita consumption expenditure of the sample households of the three investigated counties was 426 yuan for Linqu; 402 yuan for Ningxia; and 825 yuan for Wangcang. The share of food-consumption expenses was 66.3 percent, 64.6 percent, and 67.1 percent, respectively, indicating that differences in the composition of expenditure among the three sample counties were not significant and that the conditions described by Engel's Law were not fully met. Engel's Law may not apply to populations that have not yet stepped over the threshold of poverty.

Only when basic requirements for food consumption have been met does the share of food-consumption expenses gradually decline as family incomes increase.

The food consumption of rural families is still strongly tied to self-production on the farm. The share of self-produced foods in the total food expenditures of sample households in the three counties was 69.5 percent, 87.6 percent, and 90.4 percent, respectively. It seems that rural household in-cash consumption expenditures are mainly for nonfood consumer goods and service payments (Table 4.10).

Since 1988, farmers participating in the Yigong-daizhen projects have been paid in "industrial product coupons," redeemable only for commodities purchased in appointed state-owned shops. Multiple-choice questionnaires on how participating households dispose of income earned from the projects showed that 3.8 percent of the households spent most of this income on farming machines, farming tools, and transportation equipment; less than 1 percent of households made investments in building residential houses; 21 percent bought other productive articles; 58.1 percent bought daily consumer goods, and the remaining 16.1 percent used the project income for other purposes. Thus, project income has obviously increased the consumption expenditures of rural households.

Although they have reinforced the purchasing power of participating rural households, earnings from projects have not necessarily played a decisive role in determining the nutritional status of rural families. This is because farm households do not rely on purchases for food consumption, for the most part. So, although Table 4.11 indicates that the nutritional status of households participating in the projects is better than that of those not participating, this difference may not be due to their different participation decisions. To explore the factors affecting the nutritional situation of rural families, the quality of diet of every sample household was assessed using the formula of Desired Diet Pattern Points designed by the Chinese Academy of Preventive Medical Science (Table 4.12).

All nutrition indices in Table 4.11 (except those in parentheses) have been calculated on the basis of the same data, that is, on three-day recalls of rural women on household food consumption. The survey was carried out in the middle of the farming season in Linqu and Wangcang counties, when the diet of farmers was of better quality than average. In Xiji County, the survey was carried out during the off-season, when the level of food consumption was comparatively low. These seasonal conditions led to an overestimation of the indices for Linqu and Wangcang counties and an underestimation of indices for Xiji County. Disparities in rural women's estimations of weights of consumed food in different areas may also have led to errors.

Table 4.10—Structure of annual per capita consumption expenses for sample households, China, 1991

Items of Expense	Linqu County			Xiji County			Wangcang County		
	Poor	Medium	Well-to-Do	Poor	Medium	Well-to-Do	Poor	Medium	Well-to-Do
Food									
(yuan)	224	286	339	195	259	320	374	596	678
(percent)	66.2	66.4	66.2	68.0	67.9	60.5	70.0	70.7	62.9
Share of food self-provided									
(yuan)	138	216	235	165	225	287	350	565	576
(percent)	61.6	75.5	69.3	84.6	86.9	89.7	93.6	94.8	85.0
Medical care									
(yuan)	20	29	24	42	51	71	58	27	42
(percent)	6.1	6.8	4.6	14.7	13.5	13.5	10.8	3.3	3.9
Cigarettes, wine, and presents									
(yuan)	28	34	39	15	19	65	48	83	157
(percent)	8.4	7.9	7.7	5.2	4.9	12.2	9.0	9.9	14.6
Other									
(yuan)	65	82	110	35	52	73	54	136	200
(percent)	19.3	18.9	21.5	12.1	13.7	13.8	10.2	16.1	18.6
Total									
(yuan)	337	431	512	287	381	529	534	842	1,077
(percent)	100.0	100.0	100.0	100.0	100.0	100.0	100.0	100.0	100.0

Note: Sample households are divided into tercile groups according to household per capita assets.

Table 4.11—Nutritional situation of participating and nonparticipating households (sample households), China

	Linqu/Shandong		Xiji/Ningxia		Wangcang/Sichuan	
	Participating Households N=58	Non-Participating Households N=62	Participating Households N=39	Non-Participating Households N=81	Participating Households N=64	Non-Participating Households N=54
Calorie intake per person[a]	2,423	2,358	1,708	1,469 (2,600)	3,490 (2,212)	3,223
Supplied by fat (percent)	22.2	21.7	14.9	14.6 (13.3)	22.1 (15.3)	20.1
Supplied by protein (percent)	14.3	13.3	11.7	11.3 (10.8)	10.3 (11.5)	9.6
Protein intake (grams)	86.7	78.3	49.9	41.4 (70.5)	90.1 (63.4)	77.1
Diet quality points[b]	87.8	84.8	67.0	66.8	82.5	77.2

Note: For the method of calculation, see The Institute of Nutrition of the Chinese Academy of Preventive Medical Science (date unknown).

[a] Data in parentheses have been calculated according to the sample household per capita amount of yearly food consumption, while the others are from three-day recalls on food consumption amounts in the survey season.

[b] The "diet quality points" can also be referred to as "points of desired diet pattern." Regarding methods of calculation, see Chen Chunming (1992).

All indices in Table 4.11 except calorie and protein intake closely conform to the results of surveys made by the Chinese Academy of Preventive Medical Sciences (Chen Chunming 1992). The Academy gave Ningxia 69.8 points and Sichuan 75.5 points for household diet quality (Shandong Province was not covered in the survey). Therefore, the existing data on the nutritional situation of sample households is used as the basis for the analysis in this chapter.

Compared with calorie, fat, and protein intake, diet quality points are a more comprehensive index of nutritional situation. This method of scoring points overcomes the problem of simplification that occurs when a nutritional situation is estimated on the basis of individual components. Because they have this advantage, diet quality points are used as variables in the regression analysis.

Through regression analyses, explanatory variables are identified. These are the household per capita predicted income *(PREDINC)*, the predicted income squared *(PREDINC2)*, and—representing, to some extent, dietary diversity—the number of poultry kept by the household *(POULTRY)*:

$$NUTRIT = 62.817 + 0.16\text{E-01 } PREDINC - 0.31\text{E--05 } PREDINC2$$
$$(20.731) \quad (3.890)** \qquad\qquad (-1.987)**$$

$$+ 0.30\ EDUCW + 0.44\ POULTRY - 0.36\ FNUMHH;$$
$$(1.112) \qquad\quad (4.545)** \qquad\quad (-0.740)$$

$R^2 = 0.174$; $F(5,352) = 14.884$; $N = 358$.

Numbers in parentheses are t-ratios.
Two asterisks (**) indicate significance at the 99 percent confidence level and one asterisk (*) indicates at the 95 percent confidence level.

Factors affecting the nutritional situation of the population are quite complicated. The regression analysis here only identifies some of the significant variables—higher per capita income and comparatively abundant farming products. In addition, predicted income squared appears to be negatively linked to a family's nutritional status, implying that the diet quality scores will not rise any further once income reaches a certain level. The number of years spent in school by women *(EDUCW)* and household size *(FNUMHH)* do not seem to be significant factors in determining nutritional levels in the sample. The positive relation of women's level of education with diet quality is consistent with the observations of the authors in the case studies. Due to the division of labor among family

Table 4.12—The formula for grading desired diet pattern points

Source of Calories (Food Varieties)	Optimal Composition of Calories	Grading Standards	Points (Total=100)	Maximum Points[a]
	(percent)			
Cereals, roots and stems of grains	60	0.5	30.0	40
Animal foods	14	2.5	35.0	40
Added oils and fats	9	1.0	9.0	10
Beans and bean products	5	2.5	12.5	15
Sugar	5	0.5	2.5	5
Nuts and oilseeds	2	0.5	1.0	5
Vegetables and fruits	5	2.0	10.0	15
Wines and beverages	0	0.0	0.0	0

Source: Chen Chunming 1992.

[a]Maximum points means that the points of a certain kind of food will no longer increase when the calories provided by it have surpassed its share in the optimal composition of calories.

members, the education level of rural women relates closely to the success of the livestock business, and is of key importance in the rationalization of the family food consumption and nutrient intakes.

This research provides some insights relevant to policy:

- Food consumption constitutes the biggest component of expenditure in sample households, and is determined mainly by family farming products. This relationship is as expected for the low-income economy of the sample households.
- General malnutrition persists in the poor counties (such as Xiji County) of the less-developed provinces, indicating that food security has not yet been achieved for the inhabitants in these areas. The nutritional intake of the population in poor counties of more developed provinces (Linqu and Wangcang counties) has reached the average national level (Chen Chunming 1992). The problem of food shortages has been solved in these areas.
- Farmers' earnings from Yigong-daizhen projects may not play a direct role in the improvement of the food consumption and nutritional situation of rural families, but the project itself has indirect effects on them. The regression analysis of the nutritional situation shows that rural household per capita income is an important determinant. Project earnings influence the nutritional situation through a chain of indirect effects:

- Rural household per capita income is largely determined by the village infrastructure. Improvement of infrastructure was a major objective of the Yigong-daizhen projects prior to 1991.
- Starting in 1991, project investments have concentrated on farmland and water conservancy capital construction to increase crop yields and, hence, to strengthen food security through improved food availability and income.

Village committees and local governments are better qualified than the national government to set project priorities based on whether villages are better served with infrastructure or land and water resource-focused projects or a mix of the two.

Conclusions

The introduction of freer markets in China during the economic reforms of the 1980s improved the efficiency of resource allocation and thereby promoted economic growth. However, in order to reduce poverty and to enhance the living standards of the whole nation, government interventions through income redistribution and public investments are still required. During the 30 years prior to the reforms, when incomes were low, China universally provided improved rural social services through government interventions—an achievement that has been seen as an example of support-led security (Drèze and Sen 1989). The antipoverty measures since the mid-1980s can be considered an extension of this tradition of public support.

However, in contrast to the past practice of only providing relief to the poor, the poverty-reduction policy produced by the reforms of 1979 placed particular emphasis on tapping existing potential. The results of the analysis suggest that the Yigong-daizhen projects' utilization of labor- intensive techniques mobilized the abundant labor resource in poor regions, helped improve regional infrastructure and social services, and increased job opportunities and incomes. Due to differences between poor regions and extremely poor ones, the effects of the projects also differed in certain aspects. Where food shortages were no longer a serious threat, the Yigong-daizhen projects for the construction of infrastructure gave impetus to economic growth.

In implementing the projects, about one-half of the labor inputs consisted of obligatory workdays contributed by the farmers. This practice is based on two preconditions: first, that farmers recognize their obligation to participate in public investment through labor contributions and, second, that farmers already have an income that basically meets their subsistence needs. In extremely poor regions, farmers' income from the projects functions as relief. In the absence of projects in these regions, civil affairs authorities of the state must continue to provide relief to the poor. In all project areas, any improvement in the social services signifies development. So, it can be argued that the policy of Yigong-daizhen combines relief, economic growth, and social development.

Yet, this research also shows that the policy guiding the implementation of Yigong-daizhen projects has limitations. For example, it has created only one of many essential conditions for poverty reduction. The poor need help in every aspect of culture, education, health, and production. Only by taking long-term, comprehensive investment measures can poverty be permanently reduced.

A distinguishing feature of the Yigong-daizhen projects in China is the nature of its targeting mechanism. Some researchers have recommended self-targeting through wages in public works fixed at a low level to ensure that those coming to work for the projects are the real poor (Ravallion 1990; von Braun, Teklu, and Webb 1991). In the implementation of the Yigong-daizhen projects, this kind of self-targeting mechanism has not been adopted explicitly. Some features of the targeting mechanism of the Yigong-daizhen projects differ from the targeting mechanisms of public works in other developing countries (for example, Bangladesh [Chapter 3] and India [Chapter 5]):

1. The Yigong-daizhen program in China was designed for the reduction of regional rural poverty, hence, the projects are targeted to specific regions. The primary purpose of the projects is to improve infrastructure and social services in poor regions and create conditions for regional economic growth. In other words, long-term goals of economic growth take precedence over increases in short-term job opportunities and the supplementary income of the poor. The principle of efficiency is followed throughout the establishment and construction of the projects, with the goal being a maximum rate of project investment success. This priority does not necessarily lead to the extremely poor villages and the poorest populations benefiting first or most.

2. Within the framework of poor regions, the project is aimed at village communities, that is, administrative villages, and not at rural households or individuals. During the implementation of the projects, the village communities are responsible for the mobilization of the labor force. Completed projects represent improved infrastructure (roads, for example), or supply services to village properties (water supply installations), or add value to farmers'

resources (for example, by terracing fields and improving soils). Thus, it is impossible to prevent the nonpoor of the villages from being beneficiaries of such projects.

This distinguishing feature of the targeting mechanism of Yigong-daizhen projects is determined by the organization and institutional arrangements of rural society in contemporary China. During the present period of transition from a centrally planned economy to a market economy, the village community is evolving into a self-governing body in rural society, while its administrative organ, the villager's committee, acts as a bridge between rural households and the government, in addition to managing public affairs in the village. Since a large number of rural households are drawn into project work, the Yigong-daizhen projects are difficult to operate smoothly without the mediacy of village communities. Furthermore, because the principle of equality is practiced in village communities and most of the rural households in the villages of poor regions are poor, the village communities are more helpful than any other kind of intermediary in enabling projects targeted to the poor. If individual brokers were relied upon for enrolling the labor force, those who would benefit most would possibly be the brokers themselves, the most mobile, and the nonpoor. Laborers with the highest mobility are presently not the poor, who generally limit their activities to their own village or township, because of their inability to pay the traveling expenses.

The Yigong-daizhen approach to targeting leads to a problem: how can extremely poor villages partake in the benefits of the projects? To address this problem, project rules stipulate that a certain proportion of the labor force must be from extremely poor villages; this promotes labor movement, and can gradually eliminate the barriers between village communities and improve the labor resource of extremely poor villages through their participation.

This problem can also be addressed if the areas covered by the projects expand to include extremely poor villages. The plan of farmland upgrading since 1991 has emphasized the stone mountain areas, deep mountain areas, and high and cold mountain areas. Yigong-daizhen projects might also aim to recruit labor mainly from among the poorest households within villages.

In the end, it should be stressed that, currently, poverty is mainly a regional characteristic in rural China. However, the new course of market orientation and related reforms may lead to the evolution of new poverty groups, characterized as follows: (1) urban poverty (depending on the outcomes of enterprise, employment, and wage system reforms); and (2) class-based poverty, originating from inequalities in property distribution (since private ownership of property now exists and capital returns increasingly influence personal income distribution). Therefore, the poverty problem will not be limited to the rural sector alone during the transition period. Thus, future antipoverty programs in China should include projects aimed at the urban sector. Yigong-daizhen programs may also be an appropriate measure to alleviate urban unemployment and assist the urban poor in increasing their income.

REFERENCES

Ahmed, R., and M. Hossain. 1990. *Developmental impact of rural infrastructure in Bangladesh*. Research Report 83. Washington, D.C.: International Food Policy Research Institute.

Braun, J. von, T. Teklu, and P. Webb. 1991. *Labor-intensive public works for food security experience in Africa*. Working Papers on Food Subsidies 6. Washington, D.C.: International Food Policy Research Institute.

Chen Chunming. 1992. The food consumption and nutrition conditions of farmers in the six provinces and a municipality. Research paper. Chinese Academy of Preventive Medical Science, Beijing.

Department of Regional Territorial Land under the State Planning Commission and the Sichuan Provincial Office for Yigong-daizhen. 1991. *A guidance for the work of Yigong-daizhen*. Beijing: Publishing House of Science and Technology Papers.

Dolton, P. J., and G. H. Makepeace. 1987. Interpreting sample selection effects. *Economics Letters* 24 (No. 4): 373–379.

Drèze, J., and A. Sen. 1989. *Hunger and public action*. Oxford: Clarendon Press.

Fei, J., C. G. Ranis, and S. Kuo. 1978. Growth and the family distribution of income by factor components. *The Quarterly Journal of Economics* (February): 17–53.

Fields, G. 1980. *Poverty, inequality, and development*. Cambridge: Cambridge University Press.

Institute of Nutrition of the Chinese Academy of Preventive Medical Science. Date unknown. *The table of food components.* Beijing: People's Health Publishing House.

Ravallion, M. 1990. *Reaching the poor through rural public employment.* World Bank Discussion Paper 94. Washington, D.C.: World Bank.

RCRD (State Council Research Center for Rural Development). 1984. The development studies on the western regions of China. Beijing: People's Republic of China.

Rural Investigation Team of the State Statistical Bureau. 1989. On the measurement of the Chinese poor areas. Beijing. Mimeo.

State Planning Commission. 1984. The notification on helping the poor areas to construct roads and water conservancy-irrigation system with grain, cotton, and cloth. Beijing. Mimeo.

_____. 1987. The notification on helping the poor areas to construct roads and water conservancy-irrigation systems with middle- and low-grade industrial roads. Beijing. Mimeo.

_____. 1988. The report about the performance of the public work projects by using grain, cotton, and cloth stock. Beijing. Mimeo.

State Statistical Bureau. 1982. *Statistical yearbook of China.* Beijing: People's Republic of China.

_____. 1989. *Statistical yearbook of China.* Beijing: People's Republic of China.

_____. 1991a. *Statistical yearbook of China.* Beijing: People's Republic of China.

_____. 1991b. *Statistical yearbook of Ningxia.* Beijing: People's Republic of China.

_____. 1991c. *Statistical yearbook of Shandong.* Beijing: People's Republic of China.

_____. 1991d. *Statistical yearbook of Sichuan.* Beijing: People's Republic of China.

Teklu, T. 1992. The experience of labor-intensive public works programs in the 1980s: The potential for improving food security in Botswana. International Food Policy Research Institute, Washington, D.C. Mimeo.

Tong Zhong, S. Rozelle, B. Stone, Jiang Dehua, Chen Jiyuan, and Xu Zhikang. 1994. China's experience with market reform for commercialization of agriculture in poor areas. In *Agricultural commercialization, economic development, and nutrition*, ed. J. von Braun and E. Kennedy, 119–140. Baltimore, Md., U.S.A., and London: Johns Hopkins University Press.

World Bank. 1992. *China strategies for reducing poverty in the 1990s.* Washington, D.C.

Zhou Binbin. 1991. Poverty problems in period of people's communes. *Economic Development Forum* 3. Beijing.

Zhu Ling, and Jiang Zhongyi. 1990. Impacts of Yigong-daizhen on poor areas of China. International Food Policy Research Institute, Washington, D.C. Mimeo.

_____. 1994. *Public works and poverty alleviation.* Shanghai: San Lian Bookstore and Shanghai People's Publishing House.

5

INDIA'S (MAHARASHTRA) EMPLOYMENT GUARANTEE SCHEME: LESSONS FROM LONG EXPERIENCE

S. Mahendra Dev*

By now it is well recognized that the instrument of rural works programs (RWPs) has become an important component of strategies to alleviate poverty and hunger in many developing countries. The case for RWPs lies in the self-targeting nature of the schemes (see Drèze and Sen 1990; Ravallion 1991; Besley and Coate 1992; Besley and Kanbur 1993). Also, discriminations prevalent in some agricultural labor markets can be avoided in public works programs (Foster and Rosenzweig 1992).

In India, employment provision has been used extensively as a tool for protecting entitlements for centuries. Since the fourth century B.C., when Kautilya, the ancient Indian political economist, wrote his *Arthasastra*, India's rulers and governments have emphasized public relief works, particularly during famine. Employment in public works later became the main element of strategies for famine prevention in India and it has proved effective (World Bank 1990). After India's independence in 1947, there were many central government-sponsored schemes, beginning with the Rural Manpower Program in 1960. The most important program at the state level is the Maharashtra Employment Guarantee Scheme (EGS), which was introduced in 1972. The Maharashtra EGS is one of the most researched and discussed programs in the country. The United Nations Development Program's (UNDP) *Human Development Report* (1993, 43) commends Maharashtra's EGS as one of the largest public programs in the developing world. Compared to the programs in other countries, the EGS has been in existence for a long time—20 years. The rest of the states in India and the other countries in Asia and Africa are eager to learn from the scheme's success, particularly its sustainability over time. The EGS is an especially interesting example of a public works program for poverty

*The author is grateful to Joachim von Braun, Jean Drèze, N. J. Kurien, Gustav Ranis, and T. N. Srinivasan and some of the participants at the workshop for comments on an earlier draft. The author alone, however, is responsible for any errors.

alleviation because it guarantees employment at a defined wage—an unprecedented feature in a public works program. It is considered a model because of this underlying philosophy of guarantee and because of its approach toward fulfilling this guarantee.

Due to constraints and backwardness, the employment provided by the agriculture sector in Maharashtra is not sufficient for laborers to earn an adequate living.[1] Hence, employment in agriculture needs to be complemented by government intervention. The EGS is one attempt to enlarge the scope of employment in order to alleviate poverty in the state.

During the drought period 1970–73, EGS mainly operated as a relief program (for details, see Drèze 1990, Osmani 1991, and Subramaniam 1975). "By any criterion, the drought of 1970–73 in Maharashtra must have marked an all-time record for the scale and reach of public works programs in a famine relief operation" (Drèze 1990, 89). Following the drought, the government continued the EGS and used it as an antipoverty program. The EGS began in 1972; it received statutory basis in 1977 when the Maharashtra Legislative Assembly unanimously voted it a law of the land. The law became operative from January 26, 1979, with the consent of the President of India, and Maharashtra became the first state in the country to guarantee work. This law declares that "every adult person in the rural areas in Maharashtra shall have a right to work, that is, a right to get guaranteed employment . . . in accordance with the provisions of this Act and the Scheme made thereunder" (Maharashtra, Planning Department 1981, 907).

The EGS provides a guarantee of employment to all adults above 18 years of age who are willing to do unskilled manual work on a piece-rate basis. The scheme is self-targeting in nature. It is totally financed by the state government.[2] The main objectives of the EGS are to sustain household welfare in the short run (through provision of employment) and to contribute to the development of the rural economy in the long run, through strengthening rural infrastructure. Works undertaken by the EGS have to be productive. There is an elaborate organizational setup for the

---

[1]Droughts occur repeatedly in the state. Rainfall in drought-prone districts is erratic and, consequently, agricultural production is unstable (PEO 1980). Twelve drought-prone districts (namely Ahmad Nagar, Solapur, Pune, Nashik, Sangli, Satara, Aurangabad, Beed, Osmanabad, Dhule, Jalgaon, and Buldhana) together accounted for about 60 percent of the state's net sown area, which highlights the fact that the bulk of the state's cultivated area is located in drought-prone area districts. If there is a breakthrough in dryland farming technology, agricultural productivity and employment prospects may improve in the state, but such a breakthrough does not seem imminent. Supplementary employment programs, therefore, may have to continue in the near future.

[2]See Dev (1992) for details on other salient features and on the resources of the EGS.

EGS. Initial planning is generally done by the Revenue Department while implementation is carried out by the Technical Department.[3]

The main objective of this chapter is to review the long experience of the Maharashtra EGS and draw lessons (do's and don'ts) for replicating the scheme in other states of India or other Asian and African countries. Using microstudies and secondary data,[4] the present study evaluates the Maharashtra EGS based on the following considerations:

1. What are the current developments in the scheme?
2. How well has the EGS succeeded in providing employment to the poor?
3. What are the direct effects of the scheme in terms of incomes and employment of the poor?
4. What are the secondary and general equilibrium effects?
5. How well has the scheme succeeded in providing food security and nutrition to the poor?
6. What are the opportunity costs of the program?
7. What are the delivery and recipient systems?
8. What lessons can be drawn from the experience of EGS to help replicate the program in other Indian states and in other countries?

The rest of the chapter is organized as follows. The next section gives a brief account of the political economy of the origins of EGS and its perpetuation. In the third section, some current developments in the EGS are presented. Direct and secondary effects of the EGS on the poor are analyzed in the fourth section, which also includes a discussion on the impact of the EGS on food security and nutrition. The fifth section provides a review of leakages, opportunity costs, delivery, and recipient

---

[3]See Dev (1992) for details on planning and organizational aspects of the EGS.

[4]The microstudies are Deshpande (1982); PEO (1980); ISST (1979); Dandekar and Sathe (1980); Dandekar (1983); Bhende et al. (1992); RDC and Kirloskar Consultants (1985); Deshpande (1988); Acharya and Panwalker (1988); Datar (1990); Sathe (1991); Deolalikar and Gaiha (1993); and Datt and Ravallion (1992).

Some studies and comments based on micro as well as aggregate data are Reynolds and Sunder (1977); Dantwala (1978); Abraham (1980); MHJ (1980a, 1980b); Tilve and Pitre (1980); Herring and Edwards (1983); Leiberman (1984); Bagchee (1984); Rath (1985); Dandekar (1986); Echeverri-Gent (1988); Acharya (1990); Drèze (1990); Drèze and Sen (1990); Ezekiel and Stuyt (1990); Gaiha (1991); Godbole (1990); Hirway et al. (1990); Kakwani and Subbarao (1990); Ravallion (1991); Ravallion, Datt, and Chaudhuri (1993); Subbarao (1992); Ahluwalia (1990); Bandopadhyay (1988); Bhatt (1991); Dev (1992); and von Braun, Teklu, and Webb (1991).

Some theoretical studies on rural public works are Sen (1975); Basu (1981, 1990); Narayana, Parikh, and Srinivasan (1991); Parikh and Srinivasan (1993); and Ravallion (1990).

systems under the EGS, while the sixth section concentrates on the lessons of the scheme. The last section offers conclusions.

Political Economy of EGS
Origin and Perpetuation

EGS as a public employment scheme originated in 1965, when it was designed as a state-level response to adverse economic and demographic trends in rural Maharashtra. A pilot project in Tasgaon Block of Sangli District was designed and operated as an Integrated Area Development Scheme, commonly known as a "Page Scheme," named after the late V. S. Page, the Gandhian activist who originally conceived it. Following enthusiastic public response, the pilot project was expanded to cover the entire Tasgaon Block in Sangli District. Subsequently, a modified EGS pilot project was initiated in November 1970 in all 11 districts of the state. During the elections in 1971, the State Congress Party committed itself to a 15-point program to tackle the problems of poverty and unemployment and, as part of this program, EGS at the state level was incorporated as a special program in April 1971 with an annual budget of Rs 50 million. To fulfill the election promise, the government extended the EGS to all rural areas in the state in May 1972. Soon after statewide adoption, the EGS was suspended during the peak drought period of late 1972 to early 1974. During this period, the EGS was superseded by central government programs. A novel element in this assistance package was the Crash Scheme for Rural Employment, introduced by the late Prime Minister Indira Gandhi in 1971 as part of her *garibi hatao* ("abolish poverty") program.

The government of Maharashtra, however, was not happy with the state's dependence on the central government for drought relief. In 1974/75, V. P. Naik, then the chief minister, backed by opposition parties, decided to set up a permanent scheme (using only state resources) to protect vulnerable groups in society and to create assets that would reduce effects of future droughts. Thus the government resumed EGS after two years.

There are different views on how much EGS has altered the political economy in the state. Herring and Edwards (1983) view EGS as a "manifestation of Kulak Power," and as inferior to genuine redistribution in terms of altering the political economy (p. 575). However, as mentioned in Hirway et al. (1990), Herring and Edwards did not consider the political implications of the EGS. By making employment an entitlement, EGS facilitates collective political action by the poor, and promotes the realization of their common interest. EGS can be viewed more as a promoter than a consequence of the poor's power. The EGS also makes rural politicians more responsive to the demands of the poor (Echeverri-Gent 1988). It provides the poor with opportunities for taking effective action and encourages the mobilization of their political resources. A number of organizations of the poor have come forward to help the EGS reach the poor. These include the Lal Nishan Party, which is active in Pune, Dhule, and Ahmednagar Districts. Bhoomi Sena is active in Thane District, while Development Group is active in Pune in educating the people about their right to work.

What are the reasons for the continued existence, or sustainability, of the scheme? The EGS has the support of all groups in the state: the urban population, rural rich, rural poor, and politicians. The politicians play an active role in the functioning of the scheme. They serve as members of various EGS statutory committees. A Committee of the Maharashtra Assembly inspects the EGS sites in different districts and reviews program operations. Committees made up of Members of Parliament (MPs), Members of the Legislative Assembly (MLAs), Members of Legislative Councils (MLCs), and *Taluka* (the administrative unit below a district) monitor and evaluate local EGS activities. Legislators see the EGS as a "prestigious" scheme that they have supported and from which they expect political benefits. Thus, MLAs support the program and are quick to claim credit for the operating of new projects.

The presence of politicians in the EGS has both positive and negative aspects. EGS operations are aided by the sense of urgency and purpose that is conveyed by the aggressive stance of politicians. At the same time, political leaders are disruptive elements when they create trouble at work sites and when they insist that projects be opened in areas already adequately served by ongoing works (see Leiberman 1984).

Political economy is also at work at the regional level. Relatively rich districts get EGS projects as a result of the lobbying of powerful politicians in those districts.

Quantitative Dimensions, Changes over Time, and Current Developments

Size and Cost of the Scheme

The following points emerge from Table 5.1, which gives some quantitative dimensions of the EGS for the period 1973–92:

1. From a modest beginning of only Rs 18.8 million in 1973, the scheme expanded to an expenditure of Rs 2,350 million in 1991 and from 4.5 million person-days of employment in the first year to

Table 5.1—Quantitative dimensions of the Employment Guarantee Scheme, 1972/73–1992/93

Year[a]	Total Expenditures	Percent of Wage Expenditures	Employment Generation	Nominal Cost Per Person Per Day	Nominal Wage Per Day	Real Cost Per Person Per Day[b]	Real Wage Per Day[c]
	(Rs million)	(percent)	(million person-days)	(Rs)	(Rs)	(Rs)	(Rs)
1973	18.8	n.a.	4.5	4.18	n.a.	3.64	n.a.
1974	18.9	n.a.	5.1	3.71	n.a.	2.73	n.a.
1975	137.2	n.a.	48.1	2.85	n.a.	1.73	n.a.
1976	346.1	90.95	109.5	3.16	n.a.	2.00	1.59
1977	511.0	75.04	136.5	3.74	2.81	2.23	1.75
1978	515.4	73.98	117.3	4.39	3.25	2.53	1.95
1979	741.7	79.58	163.5	4.49	3.61	2.50	2.19
1980	1,092.3	81.89	205.4	5.32	4.36	2.63	2.31
1981	1,221.2	75.90	171.5	7.12	5.40	3.04	2.56
1982	1,261.7	77.74	156.0	8.09	6.28	3.23	2.63
1983	1,309.3	76.20	128.0	10.23	7.80	3.90	3.29
1984	1,849.8	75.34	164.5	11.24	8.41	3.88	3.17
1985	2,320.4	63.68	178.0	13.04	8.30	4.15	3.06
1986	2,722.4	66.85	189.5	14.37	9.60	4.23	3.39
1987	2,434.3	63.47	187.6	12.98	8.23	3.56	2.72
1988	2,883.1	53.19	133.2	19.06	9.11	4.92	2.76
1989	2,542.3	50.00	81.3	31.27	15.02	7.52	4.09
1990	2,392.8	53.30	78.0	30.68	15.53	6.93	3.97
1991[d]	2,350.0	57.37	89.8	26.16	15.02	5.28	3.77
1992[d]	3,085.4	65.79	119.4	25.84	16.91	4.51	3.28
1993[d]	4,260.0	60.30	148.0	30.59	18.45	4.92	3.01

Sources: Columns 1 to 6, Planning Department, Government of Maharashtra; columns 7 and 8 calculated by the author.
Note: n.a. = not available.
[a]Years, such as 1973, refer to 1972/73, and so forth.
[b]Implicit price deflators for State Domestic Product of Maharashtra are used to obtain real cost per day.
[c]Consumer price index for agricultural laborers is used for obtaining real wages.
[d]Provisional.

about 190 million person-days in 1986, but declined to 80–90 million person-days after 1989.

2. The total amount spent on the EGS up to 1991 was Rs 27 billion, while the employment created during the same period was about 2.3 billion person-days.

3. The cost per person-day (in current prices) increased from about Rs 4 in the first year to about Rs 30 in recent years. The real cost per person-day increased mainly in the 1980s and the increase has been especially marked since 1988/89.

4. The average wage per person-day in current prices increased from about Rs 3 in 1977 to over Rs 16 in 1992. However, if these wages are deflated by the consumer price indices for agricultural laborers, the real wages (at 1971 prices) rose from Rs 1.7 in 1977 to Rs 3.3 in 1983, then fluctuated until 1988. Since 1988, real wages have been about Rs 4 because of the rise in minimum wages.

5. After gaining statutory status in 1977, the EGS has consistently claimed from 10 to 14 percent of the total development budget of Maharashtra State (not given in Table 5.1). One-half of the funds for the EGS are provided by the prosperous urban sector of the state in the form of taxes.

Changes over Time

The following changes in the EGS occurred over time:

1. *Composition of the EGS workers.* Data of the Planning Department show that, over time, the percentage of women participating in the EGS has gradually increased from 41.4 percent in 1979 to 53.3 percent in 1987.[5] The percentage of laborers from backward castes, however, declined from 41.9 percent in 1979 to 33.5 percent in 1986.

2. *Changes in the emphasis on assets.* Initially, the EGS's emphasis was on drought-proofing to create a permanent avenue for employment. In 1974/75, around 78 percent of expenditure was apportioned to irrigation, 12 percent to soil conservation and land development, and about 3 percent to afforestation. Thus nearly 93 percent of total expenditure was directly related to drought-proofing. Over

---

[5]It is useful to note here the trends in female participation in rural Maharashtra. The work participation rates for females in rural areas are 53.6, 54.6, 54.5, and 54.3 percent respectively in 1972/73, 1977/78, 1983/84, and 1987/88. They do not show any decline over time.

the years, however, the composition of expenditure has undergone considerable change. The expenditure on roads has risen from about 6 percent of the total in 1974/75 to about 40 percent in 1985/86. Since 1987/88, however, the percentage of expenditure on roads was less than 25 percent because of a government order.[6]

3. *Wage rates and employment.* The EGS experienced a major policy change in terms of wage rates in May 1988. EGS wages were doubled due to the revision of minimum wages for agriculture. The changes in EGS wage rates (in current prices) were as follows:

In 1976/77: Average EGS wages < Average market wages.[7]
 (Rs 2.81)   <   (Rs 3.20)

In 1989/90: Average EGS wages > Average market wages.
 (Rs 15.53)   >   (Rs 11.80)

The aggregate real cost of the scheme did not show any increase after the doubling of the piece-wage rates. Ravallion, Datt, and Chaudhuri (1993) found that average monthly expenditures on EGS fell after the increase in wage rates. Despite the doubling of all nominal piece rates in 1988, the real average EGS wage rate increased only 50 percent. Apart from inflation, the more important factor seems to be a shift in the EGS work toward activities that are paid at lower piece rates. Also, employment fell by one-third after the increase in the wage rate in 1988. This suggests that there might have been some rationing in employment since 1988 (see Table 5.1) due to the increase in wages.

Government officials, however, deny that there was any rationing following the 1988 wage increase. According to them, there are four reasons for the decline of EGS employment in recent years:

- As mentioned by Sathe (1991), demand for labor increased in the mainstream due to EGS's assets;
- Since the late 1980s, the government has been more vigilant toward EGS works, checking muster rolls, measuring work accomplished more exactly, and so forth;

---

[6]The government and the general population feel that roads are unproductive compared with land development works, since the roads sometimes get washed away during the rainy season.

[7]Total agricultural wage is obtained by combining the agricultural wages of males and females. The weights used are the proportions of females and males among all agricultural laborers.

- EGS workers now have to travel a greater distance than before to participate because work close to the village was completed in the initial stages; and
- Heavy monsoons in the last few years have increased demand for work in agriculture.

4. *Decline in the share of EGS expenditure on wages.* From 1977 to 1984, the share of EGS expenditure on wages ranged from 74 to 82 percent. There has been a significant decline in this share since 1985. The EGS secretary explained that unskilled wages are revised once in five years, whereas capital costs have to be revised every year. The latter have been increasing much faster than the wage rates. As a result, the share of wages in total expenditure has declined over time.

Most Recent Developments

In recent years, Maharashtra has shifted the emphasis of the EGS to new directions:

Village Development Through Labor (Shram Shaktidware Gram Vikas). This subscheme of the EGS was created by a special government resolution (Maharashtra Planning Department, June 22, 1989). The subscheme aims to enhance basic aspects of village development. These include optimum utilization of the water received during the year, well-conceived planning of the entire village, land utilization for optimum food production, and development of small labor-intensive industries like Amber Charkha, sericulture, and so forth. It is proposed that all developmental works in a village are executed in an integrated manner. There will be appropriate backward and forward linkages during implementation of the works. The program also envisages coordination with other developmental activities such as the Jawahar well scheme, Integrated Rural Development Program, and so forth. The objectives of the program are to provide employment to the rural people in their own villages, to reduce pressure on land, and to help develop the village (for further details, see Maharashtra Planning Department 1992). The government has also introduced a comprehensive watershed development program for irrigation works.

Horticulture Program Linked with the EGS. In June 1990 the government also launched a horticulture program linked with EGS. A plantation can be established with a minimum of 0.2 hectares of land per beneficiary. The program will be executed at 100 percent government cost on the lands of

Scheduled Castes and Scheduled Tribes and small farms per the definition of the National Bank for Agriculture and Rural Development (NABARD).[8]

Jawahar Wells under the EGS. The Jawahar well scheme is patterned on India's Jeevandhara well scheme. It was started by the EGS in September 1988. Under this program, wells are constructed on the land of small and marginal farmers who fall below the poverty line. However, since December 1991, the scope of this scheme has been widened. Under the modified scheme, the construction of wells is to be undertaken on the lands of small farmers as defined by NABARD.

These programs show that EGS made a clear shift in the late 1980s toward integrating EGS projects with other rural development activities.

Impact of the EGS on Poverty and Food Security

Does EGS Cover the Target Group?

The effectiveness of the EGS in covering the target group has been debated. Using landless laborers as the criterion for the target group, a study by the Programme Evaluation Organization (PEO 1980) shows that only 40 percent belonged to the target group under the EGS. Ravallion (1991, 159) questions this criterion and rightly says that "it is the poor whom we are trying to reach, not the landless per se." According to Ravallion, a better test would be to compare the income distribution among participants with that for the rural population as a whole. Using the results of micro-studies, Ravallion shows that EGS successfully targeted the poor.

Using International Crops Research Institute for the Semi-Arid-Tropics (ICRISAT) village-level data, a number of studies have examined the targeting performance of the EGS. Most have concentrated on Shirapur and Kanzara villages of Maharashtra. Walker and Ryan (1990) show that wealth in the form of total assets is strongly and inversely related to participation in the EGS. Their results also reveal that the extent of that relationship is greater for women than men in both villages. The inverse relationship is also much stronger in Kanzara, where the opportunity cost was higher because of an abundant availability of agricultural employment opportunities.

---

[8]The definition of small and marginal farmers, according to the criteria developed by NABARD, is based on how productive their land is and whether or not they live in drought-prone areas.

Deolalikar and Gaiha (1993) also examine targeting performance in these two villages. This study indicates that the scheme effectively targets young female agricultural workers who are household heads, who come from low-income and low-asset households, and who have low levels of schooling. A study by Datt and Ravallion (1992) on these two villages shows that, in general, low-wealth people participate in the program. However, according to this study, there are signs that social stigma and work disabilities offset targeting performance somewhat. In other words, low-wealth high-caste people and people with physical disabilities participate less.

The EGS provides employment at a prescribed wage for whomever wants to work. It is the individual (whether landless poor, low-caste, or female) who decides whether to participate in EGS after comparing the EGS wage and her reservation wage. As long as the EGS wage is very low compared to the market wage and the scheme has the guarantee feature without rationing, this debate is irrelevant, since targeting will be effective under these conditions.

However, since the late 1980s, there seems to be some rationing due to rises in wages. If the rationing is occurring in the selection of workers, government officials may show taste discriminations similar to private landlords. But Ravallion, Datt, and Chaudhuri (1993) show that the government has provided jobs relating to low wages and long distances for rationing the workers. However, these criteria might not have diluted the self-targeting of the EGS. In other words, these two criteria might not have induced the nonpoor to join the scheme.

Direct Benefits to the Poor

Mitigation of Underemployment at the Aggregate Level. A World Bank study (1980) shows that rural unemployment and underemployment in Maharashtra amounted to roughly 620 million workdays in 1978. EGS provided about 120 million person-days in 1977/78. EGS thus took care of about 20 percent of the unemployment and underemployment in the state in that year. Dev (1992) made calculations regarding the achievement of EGS in eliminating underemployment for the rural wage-employed in the state.[9] Dev concluded that "the scheme was able to eliminate approxi-

---

[9]The calculations made by Dev (1992) for 1987/88 data are similar to those made by Osmani (1991) for the mid-1970s. First, underemployment is estimated for the wage-employed using the number of days of unemployment per year and the number of wage laborers. This number comes to around 981 million person-days whereas the EGS employment to the target group was only 66.7 million person-days. It would thus appear that the scheme was able to eliminate (roughly) no more than 7 percent of unemployment among this group in 1987/88.

mately no more than 7 percent of unemployment among this group in 1987/88" (Dev 1992, 46). A study by Osmani (1991) concludes that the EGS was able to eliminate about one-third of underemployment in the state. Thus, based on the estimates of various studies at the aggregate level, it can be concluded that the contribution of the EGS to the reduction in total unemployment and underemployment in the state varies from roughly less than one-tenth to one-third. However, the equivalent of 10–30 percent of full-time employment has an impact on a much larger part of that group because the EGS employment is considered only supplementary or part-time employment.

The average labor attendance under the EGS was 0.52 million in the year 1987/88. In the same year, data from the 43rd round of the National Sample Survey (NSS) reveal that there were 21.2 million workers (self-employed as well as wage-employed) above 15 years of age (NSS 1990). Thus the share of EGS workers among total rural workers was only 2.5 percent in the state. Theoretically, in the absence of the EGS, unemployment among rural workers would have been up by 2.5 percent.

This is reflected in the trends in unemployment rates for Maharashtra in Table 5.2. The incidence of unemployment declined much quicker in Maharashtra than in India as a whole. The decline was particularly significant between 1983 and 1987/88.

Incidence of Rural Poverty. One criticism of the EGS is that, despite the scheme's existence, poverty in Maharashtra has not declined more rapidly than average. A comparison of the incidence of poverty in Maharashtra and in all India shows that from 1972/73 to 1983, the decline of poverty was greater in Maharashtra (Table 5.3). Between 1983 and 1987/88, the decline

Table 5.2—Incidence of person-day unemployment in rural Maharashtra and rural India

Year	Maharashtra		All India	
	Male	Female	Male	Female
	(percent)			
1972/73	7.7	11.7	6.8	11.2
1977/78	5.9	9.3	7.1	9.2
1983	6.3	7.2	7.5	9.0
1987/88	2.9	3.5	4.6	6.7

Source: Sarvekshana 1983, 1988, 1990.

Note: The incidence of person-day unemployment is defined as the ratio of days of unemployment to labor force person-days.

Table 5.3—Changes in incidence of rural poverty, Maharashtra and all India

Year	Incidence of Poverty		Change in Percentage Points	
	Maharashtra	All India	Maharashtra	All India
	(percent)			
1972/73	60.6	44.8	. . .	. . .
1977/78	54.1	40.5	−6.5	−4.3
1983	34.7	33.2	−19.4	−7.3
1987/88	28.1	25.6	−6.6	−7.6

Source: Calculated from different rounds of the National Sample Surveys on Consumer Expenditure.

Note: To obtain state-specific poverty lines, Rs 16 (for Maharashtra) and Rs 15 (for all India) in 1960/61 prices have been adjusted by the corresponding all-India and Maharashtra-specific Consumer Price Indices for Agricultural Laborers.

of poverty in the state was slightly lower than that for all India. The author's estimates of the incidence of poverty among agricultural labor households (not presented here) show that it declined from 64.1 percent in 1977/78 to 44.6 percent in 1983 for Maharashtra, while for all India, the corresponding figures were 55.9 and 40.7 percent, respectively. The decline of poverty among agricultural labor households was much more rapid in Maharashtra than in all India. However, given the existing wage rates it may be difficult for a very poor EGS worker to cross the poverty line (Acharya 1990).

A look at the trends in the Sen and the Foster-Greer-Thorbecke indices (which account for the intensity of poverty) for Maharashtra shows an unsteady decline, with fluctuations (see Dev, Parikh, and Suryanarayana 1991).

Employment and Income under EGS: Microstudies. Turning to microstudies, the employment provision of person-days per person in a year varies from 25 in PEO (1980) to 160 in Dandekar (1983) (Table 5.4). The differences in the estimates of the microstudies are due to differences in sample frame, sampling period, districts or villages covered, and so forth.

A study by Bhende et al. (1992) on Shirapur and Kanzara villages shows that over the five-year period from 1979/80 to 1983/84, days worked on EGS represented about 20 percent of the total employment in Shirapur and 10 percent in Kanzara. The scheme's effect was smaller in Kanzara because its agriculture was relatively prosperous. The same study reveals that the EGS was responsible for absorbing about one-half of the potential days of unemployment in Shirapur and about one-third in

Table 5.4—Results of some microstudies on composition, employment, and wages of EGS workers

Studies	Survey Period	Percent Belonging to Landless Households	Percent of Small and Marginal Farmers	Percent of SC and ST[a] in Population	Annual Person-Days of Employment	Wage Rate	EGS Contribution to Total Income
PEO (1980)	1976–78	24	40	n.a.	25	2.93	n.a.
ISST (1979)	1979	51	30	n.a.	157	2.75	n.a.
Dandekar (1983)	1979–80	45	42	42	160	3.60	65
Deshpande, V. (1982)	1976–77	31	31	31	50	2.00	n.a.
Maharashtra, Planning Department (1992)	1981	52	41	41	n.a.	n.a.	n.a.
RDC and Kirloskar, Consultants (1985)	1983–84	38	40	40	170	n.a.	n.a.
Deshpande, S. K. (1988)	1983–84	n.a.	n.a.	n.a.	23	5.50	21
Acharya and Panwalker (1988)	1985–86	34	46	46	54	5.30	31
Datar (1987)	1985–86	35	47	47	105	7.80	36
Sathe (1991)	1987–88	21	58	50	n.a.	n.a.	n.a.

Note: n.a. is "not available."
[a]SC is Scheduled Castes and ST is Scheduled Tribes, including other backward castes.

Kanzara. Datar's study (1987) shows that the reported contribution of EGS employment to the total employment of the participants was about 50 percent in the survey villages. Thus, if the results of the microstudies are accepted, the impact on employment for participating laborers is impressive by any standard.

Impact on Income. As Ravallion (1991) mentions, the EGS has to be judged by how effective it is in enhancing the incomes of the poor. The results of microstudies regarding the contribution of EGS to total income are given in the last column of Table 5.4. It shows a wide variation, from 21 percent in Deshpande's study (1988) to 65 percent in Dandekar's study (1983). Acharya and Panwalker (1988) compared a sample of 100 households with workers in the EGS to another sample of 100 households whose members had never participated in the scheme. The average annual wage income of the EGS households was Rs 32 higher than the wage income of the non-EGS households. According to this study, the average contribution of EGS to the total income of the household was about one-third.

For the households who also have some form of home production or family enterprise, the concept of total income is difficult to interpret. Therefore, the share of EGS income to total income has to be interpreted with caution, at least for these households.

Regarding direct transfers to the poor from the government budget, Ravallion's (1991) study shows that the direct gain to the poor (net of forgone income) is about 30 to 40 percent of the government's disbursement of the scheme.

Other Indirect Benefits and Stabilization Benefits to the Poor

It is important to note here that it is not enough to look at the amount of employment and income directly generated by the EGS. One has to look at other indirect or so-called "general equilibrium effects" and the stabilization benefits of the EGS on the poor.

Secondary or Indirect Benefits.

1. *Impact on agricultural growth.* One of the important second-round effects relates to the impact of EGS projects on the incomes of the scheme's participants. A criticism of the EGS is that the benefits of the created assets go to the nonpoor. This observation is certainly true, but is overplayed. From the point of view of the sustainability

of the scheme, it is important that some kind of benefits go to the rich. Moreover, as in the new subschemes, a part of the scheme should be consciously directed at improvements of land cultivated by the small and marginal farmers. Even if this is not possible, the poor could derive some continuing benefits from land improvements. There are different opinions on the effects of EGS-created assets on agricultural development itself. A recent study by Sathe (1991), however, demonstrates that the assets created under the EGS in the surveyed areas have led to positive developments in agriculture and rural nonagricultural activities. The study reveals that labor absorption increased in the mainstream and the need for EGS employment declined in the surveyed areas.

2. *EGS and agricultural wages.* There were complaints that agriculture lost some output due to the diversion of labor to the EGS. However, as Drèze and Sen (1990, 117) say, "the positive influences of this displacement (for example, an upward pressure on local wages) must be evaluated along with the negative ones (for example, a loss of agricultural output)." The guarantee part of the EGS increases unskilled laborers' bargaining strength in private negotiations with employers (provided that labor-displacing investment is not near their margin of profitability) (Lipton 1988).

Wages under the EGS are paid at a uniform piece rate for both male and female workers. Initially, wages were kept below agricultural wages in order not to disrupt agricultural operations. The official changes in EGS wage rates over time were due to the interventions of workers' organizations and court rulings. Maharashtra is divided into four zones based on minimum wages for agricultural laborers. Before 1985, the minimum wage, from which the piece rate was derived, was equivalent to the lowest official minimum wage in any of the four zones. The government had to revise this policy following a ruling of the Bombay High Court, which stated that workers must be paid minimum wages applicable in the zone in which they were located. As mentioned previously, the minimum wages for agricultural labor in the state were revised upward again and doubled from May 1, 1988. In 1993, the minimum wage levels in the four zones were Rs 12, Rs 14, Rs 16, and Rs 20. Thus, there is no unique wage for the EGS since wage rates differ depending on the amount of work and the area in which it is done. However, the average wage rate at the aggregate level can be obtained by dividing the total expenditure on wages by the generated person-days.

Real EGS wages and real agricultural wages are given in Table 5.5. Acharya (1990) feels that both the EGS and the agricultural

124

Table 5.5—Real wages (at 1970/71 prices) paid under the EGS and prevalent in agriculture, rural Maharashtra, 1975/76–1985/86

Year	Real Wages Under EGS for Both Sexes	Real Agricultural Wages	
		Male	Female
	(Rs)		
1975/76	1.59	1.79	1.29
1976/77	1.75	2.16	1.42
1977/78	1.95	2.32	1.57
1978/79	2.19	2.47	1.69
1979/80	2.30	2.27	1.52
1980/81	2.56	2.34	1.59
1981/82	2.63	2.26	1.51
1982/83	3.27	2.66	1.78
1983/84	3.20	2.79	1.84
1984/85	3.06	2.87	1.88
1985/86	3.39	3.75	n.a.
1986/87	2.77	n.a.	n.a.

Source: Calculated by Acharya (1990) by juxtaposing statistics from the Ministry of Planning, Government of Maharashtra, and the Labour Bureau's Cost of Living Indices for Agricultural Labourers.

Note: n.a. is "not available."

wage data suffer from uniform biases,[10] and therefore they may not represent the real wages in absolute magnitude, though temporal changes are comparable. Initially, EGS wages were beneath agricultural wages. Since the early 1980s, the EGS wage has climbed above agricultural wage rates. Recent data on agricultural wages by crop for the period 1985/86–1989/90, presented in Godbole (1990), also show that agriculture wages were lower than EGS wage rates. Acharya (1990) says that, because of the upward bias in the EGS wage, the actual wage received by the EGS workers may not be significantly different from the agricultural wages. It may be noted, however, that EGS wages acted as a floor wage for agricultural wages until the late 1970s and then, in the 1980s, may have put an upward pressure on market wages. This upward pressure depends on whether EGS has been meeting the work guarantee. In other words, it depends on whether it is true that there is no rationing in the EGS.

[10]According to Acharya, there is upward bias in the EGS due to the clubbing of expenditures, such as supply of material and transport costs of animal-drawn carts, within wage expenses. See Acharya (1989) for upward bias in the data on agricultural wages.

An important lesson one can learn from the EGS regards the wage rate that should be set for rural public works programs. The dilemma to be resolved is whether the wage rate should be below or equal to the market wage rate or a legally fixed minimum wage (generally market wages are below minimum level). Initially, the EGS wages were below market agricultural wages. In 1988, with the doubling of the statutory minimum wage rate, the EGS piece rates were doubled. The EGS is now required to pay wages at the statutory minimum rates, which are higher than market rates. "This requirement implies substantial budgetary outlays and potentially high social costs in lost output from alternative employment" (World Bank 1990). Ravallion, Datt, and Chaudhuri (1993) reveal that higher wages led to rationing of the employment guarantee. They argue that lower wages should be maintained in order to widen coverage; broad coverage, they argue, helps the poor more than rationing as a result of higher wages. There is some merit in the low-wage argument if one wants to concentrate on reducing the intensity of poverty. Ravallion, Datt, and Chaudhuri (1993) also show that after the increase in 1988, the EGS wages did not have an effect on agricultural wages. Rationing of the EGS also dampened the expected second-round income effects arising through the agricultural labor market and the insurance provided by the employment guarantee.

3. *Elimination of taste and statistical discriminations.* Foster and Rosenzwieg (1992), based on ICRISAT data, show that taste discrimination (which occurs when employers have a preference for employing certain kinds of workers) and statistical discrimination (which occurs when, among laborers with the same productivity, women are paid less) can be eliminated from agriculture labor markets in public employment programs like EGS.

4. *Social (nonincome) benefits.* EGS works have had a considerable impact on the social life of workers. Concentrating large number of workers in one place in similar conditions increases their interaction and helps to break down social differences. This can help expand the social awareness of workers belonging to various castes. The EGS also discourages sexual barriers to work and public activity, such as excluding women from certain wage rates. The large numbers of women on work sites has instilled confidence among them. Women's economic power has accorded them higher status in their families (Datar 1987).

Stabilization Benefits. One of the most important aspects of the EGS is its seasonal stabilization effects on the income of the poor. Reducing fluctua-

126

Table 5.6—Labor attendance under the EGS, by year and month

Month	1985/86	1986/87	1987/88	1988/89	1989/90	1990/91
			(1,000)			
April	731	686	957	535	534	331
May	820	765	940	532	532	347
June	748	740	769	333	332	297
July	515	621	523	174	173	148
August	475	523	411	129	129	114
September	587	482	357	80	110	90
October	549	420	227	85	97	84
November	505	374	266	90	96	75
December	696	494	361	151	123	104
January	649	601	446	182	186	190
February	639	739	472	238	246	247
March	668	1,061	493	309	307	253

Source: Data provided by Government of Maharashtra, Provisional Planning Department.

tions in income can be as important to the poor as raising average incomes. Stabilization can prevent acute distress and preempt the need for costly forms of adjustments, such as selling productive assets. In other words, even if the increase in employment and income is not very large compared with the aggregate need, the existence of any form of income/employment insurance could be quite significant. Table 5.6 shows that EGS is complementary to agricultural employment in the sense that EGS employment is high in the lean season (April to July) and low in the peak season (October to January). Bhende et al. (1992) reveal that in Shirapur Village, the two employment profiles appear to be strongly and negatively associated for men (r = −0.68) and for women (r = −0.64). In Kanzara Village, however, the association between the two employments shows weak complementarity (r = −0.33 for men and r = −0.40 for women). Walker and Ryan (1990) show that the risk benefits are quite high under the EGS. Landless labor households in Shirapur and Kanzara villages, where the EGS has operated since 1977, had about 50 percent less variable income streams than those in Aurepalle, where village employment guarantee programs were not available.

The extent to which EGS serves this insurance function in practice, and how valuable it is, depends on factors such as the ease with which employment can be obtained and on the costs of alternative mechanisms of coping (for example, credit).[11]

---

[11]Personal communications with Jean Drèze, 1994.

Effects of the EGS on Food Security and Nutrition of the Poor

What role has EGS played in providing food security and nutrition (inter- and intrahousehold) to the poor? Some indirect evidence on these issues is documented here since direct evidence is not available.

Food security in this context means a "household's permanent access to food in sufficient quantity and quality for an active and healthy life" (von Braun et al. 1992).

EGS seems to have played an important role in combating seasonal malnutrition among poor households by providing employment in the off-season or in the drought years or both when there is nutritional deficiency (Subbarao 1992). It has already been noted that there was a decline in income variability due to EGS and this could be expected to have a significant impact on seasonal malnutrition. Walker and Ryan (1990) and Bhende et al. (1992) show that the laborers in EGS villages had income streams that were almost 50 percent less variable than those of laborers in non-EGS villages. This finding indicates that the size of risk benefits is substantial, which is important for reducing seasonal malnutrition in poor households. So far, no one has been able to demonstrate that such risk benefits can be conferred more cost-effectively than via other interventions (Subbarao 1992). Walker and Ryan (1990) also suggest that measures to increase and stabilize consumption expenditure across years will do more to raise nutrient intakes than efforts to enhance income per se.

Sometimes it is difficult to draw conclusions about the nutritional impact of EGS because some evidence exists at the micro level that better-nourished laborers participate in the EGS projects. Deolalikar and Gaiha (1993) examined the determinants of EGS participants (particularly women) using the ICRISAT village-level data. Their conclusions include the following:

> Height plays an important role in determining participation in the EGS for both males and females. Insofar as height is correlated with better nutrition and strength, the significance of stature suggests that individuals with better nutritional status and greater strength and stamina self-select themselves into the EGS. This could occur because the EGS pays piece wage rates, thereby implicitly placing a premium on strength, briskness, and dexterity. Abler individuals who can perform a given task more briskly end up earning higher wages per unit of time than other individuals under the scheme. The fact that height continues to be a significant determinant of participation in the paid labor force suggests that the ability to draw taller and better nourished individuals is a characteristic that is unique to EGS employment. (Deolalikar and Gaiha 1993, 22-23).

This study also shows that the agricultural laborers who participate in EGS are, in general, taller than the participating farmers from small or large farms.

It is not clear whether ICRISAT village-level data are representative of all of Maharashtra. There is reason to doubt it, since the study by Deolalikar and Gaiha shows that female participation under EGS in the two villages was much lower than that of males. All other field studies have shown that EGS attracts female participation.

Intrahousehold Food Security. There is no direct evidence regarding the effect of EGS on intrahousehold inequalities in food security; female participation can be used as a proxy for increase in nutrition among women and children (see Drèze and Sen 1990). It is worth noting that in rural Maharashtra, the EGS is known as a women's program. Estimates on the proportion of women in the EGS vary: PEO (1980) finds a 39 percent share; Dandekar (1983), 51 percent; ISST (1978), from 49 to 80 percent; and Datar (1987), from 45 to 64 percent. These large percentages could be due to the predominance of female labor in casual unskilled work in rural areas. A recent study by Datar (1990) examining the effect of EGS on women indicates that EGS supplies a core income to many women.

Gopalan (1983) suggests that marginal increases in the incomes of men will not automatically be reflected in better health and nutritional status of mothers and children. In the Punjab and Andhra Pradesh, he observes that, in the absence of efforts to channel increased income toward the improvement of health and nutrition, income is often frittered away by the men on alcoholic drinks, while infant mortality rates remain high in these regions. Gopalan advocates that in all rural development programs, a portion of the budget should be earmarked to ensure that the benefits of the increased income are directed toward the upgrading of the health and nutritional status of mothers and children.

Little is known, however, about the social cost of women's participation in the EGS, that is, the resultant effects on child care and health. Deolalikar and Gaiha (1993) show that having children has not affected women's participation in the EGS. The provision of crèches (day nurseries) at EGS sites could be promoting female participation in the scheme.

A Review of Leakages, Opportunity Costs, Delivery, and Recipient Systems

Leakages under the EGS

Leakages under EGS can be divided into two categories: employment leaks to nontarget groups and misappropriation of EGS funds by implementive agencies. As already noted, employment leakage is not high under the EGS: studies show that more than 90 percent of the beneficiaries are poor (Dandekar and Sathe 1980). The second type of leakage presents the real danger. In Type 1 leakage, at least, employment is created, but in Type 2 leakage, no employment takes place. Corrupt practices can cause heavy leakage even before the resources reach the work site. Since its inception, corruption in the EGS has been an issue of major concern. An investigation by the state's finance minister found 341 cases of corruption at the end of 1983. Corruption occurs mostly through wage manipulation and falsification of expenditures. Compared with other antipoverty programs in India, however, EGS is better administered. The press can play an important role here in reducing the misappropriation of funds under the EGS by bringing about transparency.

Opportunity Cost of the EGS

What is the opportunity cost of the resources that are spent on the scheme? Would the short- and long-term effects have been different if the government had invested the resources in other ways? These issues are not widely recognized in the literature. The net impact of a project on the economy as a whole through direct and indirect effects cannot be captured through benefit-cost analysis of individual projects.

A general equilibrium approach is required to capture these effects. Such estimates are not available for the EGS in Maharashtra. But there are some estimates at the national level calculated by Narayana, Parikh, and Srinivasan (1991) and Parikh and Srinivasan (1993).[12] These may be the only works on India or elsewhere that analyze trade-offs among other policies and RWPs.

To compare the effectiveness of some policy interventions in alleviating poverty and hunger, Parikh and Srinivasan (1993) use counterfactual policy simulations with a sequential applied general equilibrium model of the Indian economy for the period 1980-2000.

---

[12]Also see Srinivasan (1989) and Parikh and Suryanarayana (1992).

The authors consider three broad sets of policies:

1. an *untargeted* policy of subsidizing part of the food consumption of the entire population, including the poor;
2. a *targeted* policy of providing additional employment opportunities for the rural poor; and
3. an *indirect* policy of subsidizing fertilizer or, alternatively, increasing the area irrigated to augment food production.

The study shows that among these three sets of policies, a targeted rural works program that is well designed and executed has the greatest effect on the poor.

The effect of alternative RWPs on growth of the economy and on the welfare of the rural poor can be seen in Table 5.7. The policy of rural works programs, denoted by RW, is introduced in the model analysis from the year 1980. Comparing a free-food scenario with alternative RWPs, Table 5.7 confirms that a well designed, executed, and targeted RWP not only improves the welfare of the rural poor substantially, but the economy grows slightly faster (because of the additional investment in rural works)—provided the resources needed for the RWP are raised through additional taxation. The study suggests that indirect poverty alleviation policies of subsidizing fertilizers or augmenting irrigation have only modest effects on growth and poverty.

While the estimates by Parikh and Srinivasan do overcome the limitations of partial analyses, they have other shortcomings. As Parikh and Srinivasan mention in their study, labor is not formally treated as a factor of production in any of the 10 sectors. This omission is a major limitation because RWPs are essentially interventions in the labor market. Also, there are ad hoc assumptions regarding leakages in the RWPs. The study considers leakages only in the wage component going to laborers. It may be mentioned that opportunity cost is also a part of the nonwage component of the funds. In other words, Type 2 leakage is not incorporated in their model.

Delivery and Recipient Systems

The framing of rules and enactment of laws is no guarantee of the effective delivery of EGS benefits. Delivery of benefits can be assessed relative to guarantee of employment, improvement of the incomes of beneficiaries (through wages adjusted to work accomplished), and creation of productive assets for rural development.

Elaborate arrangements are made to deliver the EGS benefits to the recipients. The Revenue Department must be prepared to provide work on demand, but it is the departments of irrigation, agriculture, forestry, and

Table 5.7—Impact of rural works programs on growth and the rural poor

Scenarios	GDP 70 Per Capita	Percent Change from Reference Run to the Year 2000				Rural Poor	
		Difference in GDP 70 Growth Rate, 1980–2000	Average EQY Per Capita	Calories Per Capita	EQY Per Capita	Poorest Class ENY Per Capita	Two Poorest Classes EQY Per Capita
With additional taxation							
RW100-1-1	3.5	0.22	2.2	5.7	67	70	39
With fixed tax rates							
RW100-1-1X	-4.6	-0.25	-0.2	4.7	67	70	39
RW100-1-5X	-8.5	-0.47	-2.6	3.8	67	70	39
RW100-1-0X	-13.2	-0.73	-5.4	2.6	67	70	39
RW100-0.5-1X	-3.7	-0.20	0.0	3.0	33	40	19
RW100-0.5-0.5X	-7.3	-0.40	-2.0	2.1	33	40	19
RW100-0.5-0X	-11.8	-0.66	-4.7	1.0	33	40	19
FF40X	-4.2	-0.23	-0.8	1.3	11	11	10

Source: Parikh and Srinivasan 1993.

Notes: GDP 70 = gross domestic product at 1970/71 prices; EQY = equivalent expenditure; ENY = energy intake (kilocalories per day). For details of the reference scenario, sell Parikh and Srinivasan 1993, 399. The reference scenario is built on a set of plausible assumptions about economic development 1980–2000 against which the alternative policies of rural works are compared.

(continued)

Table 5.7—Continued

Description of Policy Scenarios:

Run Designation	Quantity of Wheat Per Person Distributed as Wages	Targeting Effectiveness	Investment Effectiveness
	(kilograms)	(1.0 = 100 percent, 0.5 = 50 percent)	
With additional taxation			
RW100-1-1	100	1.0	1.0
Without additional taxation			
RW100-1-.5X	100	1.0	0.5
RW100-1-0X	100	1.0	0.0
RW100-0.5-1X	100	0.5	1.0
RW100-0.5-0.5X	100	0.5	1.0
RW100-0.5-0X	100	0.5	0.0
FX40X	40 kilograms of wheat is given free to the entire population.		

others that draw up advance plans for works in villages and then, on instruction, execute individual projects using EGS labor. Official instruction, informal guidelines, extensive monitoring, unscheduled field visits, vigilance tours by officials at various levels, and the advisory and supervisory roles of nonofficial statutory committees are all part of delivering the EGS benefits.

What distinguishes EGS from other rural employment programs is the statutory work guarantee. However, sometimes the "guarantee" and the delivery systems are not effective due to design and implementation factors.[13]

The delivery system is much better in areas where voluntary organizations are active. Deshpande's (1988) study on Jawahar Taluka of Thane District shows that the existence of a labor organization improved the delivery of the EGS benefits. The scheme was implemented differently in various parts of the taluka, depending on whether a labor organization was present. Other benefits of a labor organization include the following:

1. The organization helped spread awareness of the scheme among the poor and illiterate laborers.
2. It mobilized laborers to demand that the administration provide employment.
3. To an extent, it checked malpractice and leakages from the scheme and, on some occasions, helped the administration provide employment.

Deshpande's study also brought out the limitations of organizations in raising consciousness beyond the elementary level of making demands for the provision of employment. A study by Acharya (1990) also underlines the importance of voluntary organizations in delivering EGS benefits to recipients.

EGS Compared with Other Antipoverty Programs

According to various evaluations, the EGS has performed much better than other antipoverty programs in India, such as the National Rural Employment Program, the Rural Landless Employment Guarantee Program, and the Integrated Rural Development Program.[14] Although all the antipoverty programs are designed to provide a safety net, the EGS has been more successful than the others in controlling the type of works executed and the quality of implementation. None of the other programs has sustained large-scale opera-

---

[13]See Dev 1992 for details.

[14]See, for example, Acharya 1990 and World Bank 1989.

tions for a lengthy period or dealt with corruption and other administrative problems as effectively as the EGS (World Bank 1989).[15] Still, there is a lot of room for improvement in the EGS's performance.

Conclusions

The Maharashtra Employment Guarantee Scheme (EGS) has been in existence for 20 years. Urban-based finance and broad support for the EGS have contributed to the sustainability of the scheme. One-half of the resources for the EGS budget is provided by taxes on the urban population. The EGS is one of the state's most popular programs. It has gained widespread support because it offers something for everybody: the urban middle class and rich, the rural rich, politicians, the rural poor, and intermediate groups.

- The urban middle class and the rich pay for the EGS because they want to reduce overcrowding; rural employment opportunities are expected to restrict rural-urban migration.
- The rural rich support the program because they benefit from the assets created by the scheme. This may be one of the most important reasons for the sustainability of the EGS in Maharashtra.
- Politicians expect to receive political support because of the popularity of the scheme.
- Rural laborers support the program because they receive direct and indirect benefits from the scheme. Also, the number of potential participants in and supporters of the rural public works scheme may be larger than the actual number of participants at any one date (Ravallion 1991). In other words, many who rarely participate still value the scheme's insurance benefits.
- Intermediate groups, such as bureaucrats, support the scheme because they can claim responsibility for its success. For example, district collectors want to get credit for the benefits EGS provides in their districts.

But maintenance and utilization of assets created under EGS are often far from satisfactory. There are two problems in ensuring adequate maintenance. First, there has been considerable administrative delay in handing over completed works to the *Zilla parishads* (district councils) for maintenance. Second, when the works are handed over, local bodies have often

---

[15]In their reviews of poverty programs in developing countries, Osmani (1991) and Ravallion (1991) also feel that the performance of the EGS is better than that of other programs.

not allocated resources for maintenance of the EGS assets. Consequently, maintenance of assets is neglected. Acharya (1990) summarizes evaluation reports. Collectively, these reports show that the utilization of assets has not been uniformly satisfactory in all districts. A study by Sathe (1991), however, finds that the assets created under the EGS in the surveyed areas have led to positive developments in agriculture and rural nonagricultural activities. Other RWPs can learn lessons from EGS by studying its successes and failures in the maintenance and utilization of assets.

The following represent some of the specific conclusions of this evaluation of the EGS:

1. Over time, the composition of workers, composition of assets, wage rates, and employment have changed.

    - There has been a gradual increase in the percentage of women and a decline in the percentage of backward castes participating in the EGS.
    - Roads have assumed a large share of assets, rising from about 6 percent of the total assets in 1974/75 to about 40 percent in 1985/86.
    - A major policy change in wage rates occurred in May 1988. In the early 1970s, EGS wages were less than market wages. Beginning in 1988, EGS wages were raised over market wages.

    Some studies show that the decline in employment in the late 1980s was due to rationing, which, in turn, was due to an increase in wages.

2. Since the late 1980s, the government has changed the thrust of the scheme by introducing subschemes such as Village Development through Labor, Horticulture Program, Jawahar Wells, and so forth, which are supposed to integrate the EGS projects with the other rural development activities.

3. How effective EGS has been in its coverage of the target group has been debated. Using landlessness as the criterion, some studies have shown that only 50 percent belonged to the target group. Other studies, using poverty criterion, reveal that the EGS targets the poor effectively. As long as the EGS wage is very low relative to the market wage and the scheme has the guarantee feature without rationing, this debate appears gratuitous. The debate acquires relevance only when there is rationing of workers.

4. Turning to the direct benefits, the contribution of the EGS to the reduction of total unemployment or underemployment at the macro level in Maharashtra varies from 10 to 30 percent, depending on

assumptions and years selected. According to microstudies, the employment provision of person-days in one year varies from 25 to 160 days. The same microstudies reveal that the share of total income that comes from EGS (microstudies) has ranged from one-third to two-thirds. Although EGS income may not have allowed participants to "cross the poverty line," it has helped reduce the intensity of poverty.

5. The case for the EGS relies more heavily on secondary (or indirect) and stabilization benefits, rather than on direct benefits. EGS projects seem to have second-round effects on the incomes of the poor (although opinions are divided on this). There is evidence that the EGS wage rate has influenced the agricultural wage rate in the state.

6. The importance of the EGS lies in its guarantee of work. By making employment an entitlement, the EGS facilitates collective political action by the poor, and promotes realization of their common interests. The scheme makes rural politicians more responsive to the demands of the poor. Taste and statistical discriminations that are prevalent in agricultural labor markets can be avoided in a public employment program like the EGS. The EGS works have also had a considerable effect on the social life of the workers.

7. One of the most important effects of the EGS is seasonal stabilization of the incomes of the poor. There is evidence that the insurance benefits that result from the scheme are quite significant to the poor. Reduction in income fluctuations can prevent acute distress to the poor and preclude the need for costly forms of adjustment, such as selling productive assets.

8. There is no direct evidence on the impact of the EGS on food security and nutrition. The indirect evidence, however, indicates that the EGS played an important role in combating seasonal malnutrition of poor households by providing employment in the off-season and in the drought years when nutritional deficiency was widespread. If women's participation is used as a proxy for raising the nutritional status of household members, EGS seems to have reduced intrahousehold inequalities in nutrition.

9. Some studies based on ICRISAT village-level data show that height (a proxy used for nutrition) plays an important role in determining participation in the EGS for both males and females. It is not clear whether ICRISAT village-level data represent the whole of Maharashtra. One study by Deolalikar and Gaiha (1993) showed that the female participation under EGS in the study villages was much lower than those for males. But this study many not be representative, since all other field studies have shown that the

percentage of females under EGS was equal to or greater than that of males.

10. Regarding leakages, Type 1 leakage (employment going to non-target groups) is not high under the EGS. The real danger lies in Type 2 leakage—of the misappropriation of funds by the implementing agencies and the politicians. Corruption is lower in the EGS than in other antipoverty programs, however. EGS is better administered than other programs.

11. What is the opportunity cost of the resources that are spent on the scheme? Estimates for Maharashtra state are not available. Narayana, Parikh, and Srinivasan (1991) and Parikh and Srinivasan (1993), however, provide estimates at the national level. These studies compare the impact of food production subsidies, food consumption subsidies, and employment subsidies on poverty and hunger. The results show that among these three sets of policies, a well-targeted and efficiently executed RWP has the greatest impact on the poor. Some of the limitations of these studies (particularly the absence of a labor market) were discussed above. Extensions of this model can correct some of these limitations.

12. The rest of the states in India and other Asian and African countries could learn much from the experience of the EGS regarding the size of the program, the fixing of wage rates, how to achieve sustainability of the program, finance, the role of voluntary organizations, impact on famine prevention, and so forth. Finance provided by the urban areas and universal support, particularly the support of the rural rich, seem to be the main reasons for the sustainability of the scheme in Maharashtra.

Finally, the EGS has reduced the intensity of poverty and increased the food security of many households in Maharashtra. It may, however, be noted that one cannot expect the EGS to eradicate poverty in rural areas, since the scheme tends to bypass certain sections of the population. Therefore, along with the EGS, other programs that promote self-employment, improve the productivity of agriculture through development, and promote adoption of suitable dryland technologies and programs (old-age pension schemes, child nutrition, and other health improvement schemes) should be simultaneously implemented.

REFERENCES

Abraham, A. 1980. Maharashtra's Employment Guarantee Scheme. *Economic and Political Weekly* 15 (6): 1339–1342.

Acharya, S. 1989. Agricultural wages in India: A disaggregated analysis. *Indian Journal of Agricultural Economics* 44 (2): 121–139.

_____. 1990. *Maharashtra Employment Guarantee Scheme: A study of labour market intervention.* Delhi: International Labour Office-Asian Regional Team for Employment Promotion.

Acharya, S., and V. G. Panwalker. 1988. *The Employment Guarantee Scheme in Maharashtra: Impact on male and female labour.* Regional Research Paper. Bangkok: Population Council.

Ahluwalia, M. S. 1990. Policies for poverty alleviation. *Asian Development Review* 8 (1): 111–132.

Bagchee, S. 1984. Employment Guarantee Scheme in Maharashtra. *Economic and Political Weekly* 25 (41): 1975–1982.

Bandopadhyay, D. 1988. Direct intervention programmes for poverty alleviation. *Economic and Political Weekly* 23 (26): A77–A88.

Basu, K. 1981. Food for work programmes: Beyond roads that get washed away. *Economic and Political Weekly* 16 (1):37–40.

_____. 1990. The elimination of endemic poverty in South Asia: Some policy options. In *The political economy of hunger,* vol. 3, ed. J. Drèze and A. Sen, 347–376. Oxford: Clarendon Press.

Besley, T., and S. Coate. 1992. Workfare vs. welfare: Incentive arguments for work requirements in poverty alleviation programmes. *American Economic Review* 82: 249–261.

Besley, T., and R. Kanbur. 1993. Principles of targeting. In *Including the poor,* ed. M. Lipton and J. van der Gaag, 67–90. Washington, D.C.: Johns Hopkins University Press for the World Bank.

Bhatt, T. 1991. Employment programmes: An assessment. *Economic Times* 31 (209): 10.

Bhende, M. J., T. S. Walker, S. S. Leiberman, and J. V. Venkatram. 1992. The EGS and the poor: Evidence from longitudinal village studies. *Economic and Political Weekly* 28 (13): A19–A28.

Braun, J. von, T. Teklu, and P. Webb. 1991. *Labour-intensive public works for food security: Experience in Africa.* IFPRI Working Papers on Food Subsidies 6. Washington, D.C.: International Food Policy Research Institute.

Braun, J. von, H. Bouis, S. Kumar, and R. Pandya-Lorch. 1992. *Improving food security of the poor: Concept, policy, and programs.* Washington, D.C.: International Food Policy Research Institute.

Dandekar, K. 1983. *Employment guarantee scheme: An employment opportunity for women.* Pune: Gokhale Institute of Politics and Economics.

Dandekar, K., and M. Sathe. 1980. Employment guarantee scheme and food for work programme. *Economic and Political Weekly* 25 (15): 707–713.

Dandekar, V. M. 1986. Agriculture, employment, and poverty. *Economic and Political Weekly* 38, 39 (25): A90–A100.

Dantwala, M. L. 1978. Some neglected issues in employment planning. *Economic and Political Weekly* 23 (6 and 7): 291–294.

Datar, C. 1987. *Revaluation of the Employment Guarantee Scheme, Maharashtra.* New Delhi: Institute of Social Studies Trust.

_____. 1990. *Maharashtra Employment Guarantee Scheme.* Bombay: Tata Institute of Social Sciences.

Datt, G., and M. Ravallion. 1992. *Behavioral responses to work fares: Evidence for rural India.* Washington, D.C.: World Bank.

Deolalikar, A., and R. Gaiha. 1993. *Targeting of rural public works: Are women less likely to participate?* Discussion Paper Series 93-05. Seattle, Wash., U.S.A.: Institute for Economic Research, University of Washington.

Deshpande, S. K. 1988. Local-level management of a rural antipoverty programme: A case study of the Employment Guarantee Scheme of Maharashtra. A dissertation submitted in partial fulfillment of the requirements of the Fellow Programme in Management, Indian Institute of Management, Bangalore.

Deshpande, V. D. 1982. *Employment guarantee scheme—Impact on poverty and bondage among tribals.* Pune: Tilak Maharashtra Vidyapeeth.

Dev, S. M. 1992. *Poverty alleviation programmes: A case study of Maharashtra with emphasis on employment guarantee scheme.* Discussion Paper 77. Bombay: Indira Gandhi Institute of Development Research.

Dev, S. M., K. S. Parikh, and M. H. Suryanarayana. 1991. *Rural poverty in India: Incidence, issues, and policies.* Discussion Paper 55. Bombay: Indira Gandhi Institute of Development Research.

Drèze, J. 1990. Famine prevention in India. In *The political economy of hunger*, vol. 2, ed. J. Drèze and A. Sen, 13–122. Oxford: Clarendon Press.

Drèze, J., and A. Sen. 1990. *Hunger and public action.* Oxford: Clarendon Press.

Echeverri-Gent, J. 1988. Guaranteed employment in an Indian state. The Maharashtra experience. *Asian Survey* 28 (12): 1294–1310.

Ezekiel, H., and J. C. Stuyt. 1990. Maharashtra Employment Guarantee Scheme: Geographical distribution of employment. *Economic and Political Weekly* 25 (26): A80–A86.

Foster, A. D., and M. R. Rosenzweig. 1992. Information flows and discrimination in labor markets in rural areas in developing countries. *Proceedings of the World Bank Annual Conference on Development Economics 1992,* 173–204. Washington, D.C.: World Bank.

Gaiha, R. 1991. Poverty alleviation programmes in rural India: An assessment. *Development and Change* 22 (1): 117–154.

Godbole, M. 1990. *Rural employment strategy: A quest in the wilderness.* Bombay: Himalaya Publishing House.

Gopalan, C. 1983. Promoting child health and nutrition in India. *Food Policy* 8 (1): 23–30.

Herring, R. J., and R. M. Edwards. 1983. Guaranteeing employment to the rural poor: Social functions and class interests in Employment Guarantee Scheme in western India. *World Development* 11: 575–592.

Hirway, I., P. H. Rayappa, T. Shah, I. Khanna, N. Deshinga Raj, and S. Acharya. 1990. *Report of the study group of anti poverty programmes.* New Delhi, India: National Commission on Rural Labour.

ISST (Institute of Social Studies Trust). 1979. *Impact on women workers: Maharashtra Employment Guarantee Scheme, A study.* New Delhi.

Kakwani, N., and K. Subbarao. 1990. *Rural poverty in India, 1973–86.* Policy Research and External Affairs Working Papers WPS 526. Washington, D.C.: World Bank.

Leiberman, S. 1984. Maharashtra's Employment Guarantee Scheme: A case study of an employment security program in an Indian state. A paper prepared for the Conference on Population Growth and Labour Absorption in the Developing World 1960–2000, July 1– 6, Bellagio, Italy.

Lipton, M. 1988. *The poor and the poorest: Some interim findings.* World Bank Discussion Papers 25. Washington, D.C.: World Bank.

Maharashtra Planning Department. 1979. *The Employment Guarantee Act No. XX of 1978.* Bombay: Maharashtra Planning Department.

_____. 1981. *Employment Guarantee Scheme: A compendium of orders.* Bombay: Maharashtra Planning Department.

_____. 1992. *Employment Guarantee Scheme.* Bombay: Maharashtra Planning Department.

M. H. J. 1980a. Who pays for and who gains from EGS? *Economic and Political Weekly* 17 (31): 1226–1228.

_____. 1980b. Maharashtra II: Employment Guarantee Scheme: An evaluation. *Economic and Political Weekly* 17 (49): 2034–2045.

Narayana, N. S. S., K. S. Parikh, and T. N. Srinivasan. 1991. *Agricultural growth and redistribution of income: Policy analysis with a general equilibrium model of India.* Bombay: North Holland-Allied Publishers.

NSS (National Sample Survey). 1990. Results of the fourth quinquennial survey of employment and unemployment. *Sarvekshana,* special issue.

Osmani, S. R. 1991. Social security in South Asia. In *Social security in developing countries,* ed. E. Ahmad, J. Drèze, J. Hills, and A. Sen, 305–355. Oxford: Clarendon Press.

Parikh, K. S., and T. N. Srinivasan. 1993. Poverty alleviation policies in India: Food consumption subsidy, food production subsidy, and employment generation. In *Including the poor,* ed. M. Lipton, and J. van der Gaag, 392– 410. Washington, D.C.: Johns Hopkins University Press for the World Bank.

Parikh, K. S., and M. H. Suryanarayana. 1992. Food and agricultural subsidies: Incidence and welfare under alternative schemes. *Journal of Quantitative Economics* 8 (1): 1–28.

142

PEO (Programme Evaluation Organization). 1980. *Joint evaluation report on Employment Guarantee Scheme in Maharashtra.* New Delhi: Programme Evaluation Organization, Planning Commission.

Rath, N. 1985. Garibi Hatao: Can IRDP do it? *Economic and Political Weekly* 20 (6): 131–140.

Ravallion, M. 1990. On the coverage of public employment schemes for poverty alleviation. *Journal of Development Economics* 34 (1/2): 57–80.

_____. 1991. Reaching the rural poor through public employment, arguments, evidence, and lessons from South Asia. *The World Bank Research Observer* 6 (2): 153–175.

Ravallion, M., G. Datt, and S. Chaudhuri. 1993. Does Maharashtra's Employment Guarantee Scheme guarantee employment? Effects of the 1988 wage increase. *Economic Development and Cultural Change* 42 (2): 251–276.

RDC and Kirloskar Consultants. 1985. Impact of EGS on women workers. Pune. Mimeo.

Reynolds, N., and P. Sunder. 1977. Maharashtra's EGS: A programme to emulate? *Economic and Political Weekly* 12 (29): 1148–1149.

Sarvekshana (Journal of the National Sample Survey Organization). 1983. Vol. 6 (no. 3).

_____. 1988. Vol. 11 (no. 4).

_____. 1990. Special issue.

Sathe, M. D. 1991. Rural employment and Employment Guarantee Scheme in Maharashtra. Vijayanagar, Pune, Maharashtra: Development Group.

Sen, A. K. 1975. *Employment, technology, and development.* Oxford: Clarendon Press.

Srinivasan, T. N. 1989. Food aid: A cause of development failure or an instrument for success? *The World Bank Economic Review* 3 (1): 39–65.

Subbarao, K. 1992. Interventions to fill nutrition gaps at the household level: A review of India's experience. In *Poverty in India: Research and policy,* ed. B. Harriss, S. Guhan, and R. H. Cassen. Bombay: Oxford University Press.

Subramaniam, V. 1975. *Parched earth: The Maharashtra drought 1970–73*. Bombay: Orient Longman.

Tilve, S., and V. Pitre. 1980. Employment guarantee scheme and food for work: A comment. *Economic and Political Weekly* 15 (47): 1988–1989.

United Nations Development Programme. 1993. *Human development report*. New York: Oxford University Press.

Walker, T. S., and J. G. Ryan. 1990. *Village and household economies in India's semi-arid tropics*. Baltimore, Md., U.S.A.: Johns Hopkins University Press.

World Bank. 1980. *World development report 1980*. New York: Oxford University Press.

_____. 1989. *India: Poverty, employment, and social services*. A World Bank Country Study. Washington, D.C.: World Bank.

_____. 1990. *World development report 1990*. New York: Oxford University Press.

6
LABOR-INTENSIVE PUBLIC WORKS: THE EXPERIENCE OF BOTSWANA AND TANZANIA

Tesfaye Teklu

This chapter presents a review and assessment of the experience of labor-intensive public works programs in Botswana and Tanzania. The Botswana case represents a more advanced experiment with labor-intensive public works programs in Sub-Saharan Africa. Regular labor-intensive public works programs like the one in Botswana are integral components of a national development planning framework. The regular programs expand in times of drought to generate temporary employment for households experiencing drought-induced income shortfalls. Tanzania's LIPWP represents major donor-driven experimentation in Africa to generate employment and create assets.

This review focuses on the link between labor-intensive public works and household food security. These works programs are driven by a demand for the creation of productive assets and the generation of employment on the part of national planners and donors at the national level. Income generated through creation, utilization, and maintenance of public goods is linked to improved household food security. The food security outcome is conditioned by the public policy environment, particularly employment and wage policies; the functioning of the labor market; program-level parameters (choice of goals, choice of factor mix and technology, employment and wage policy, targeting rules, and so forth); and behavioral response at the household level (decision to participate, employment and income effects, and consumption response).

The chapter begins with a discussion of trends in labor market parameters, poverty, and food security that lay behind the increasing demand for labor-intensive public works in the 1980s. It then reviews the major labor-intensive public works programs in Botswana and Tanzania, focusing on the design and implementation of key program parameters. The effectiveness of public works programs' targeting of the poor and the programs' effect on household food security is discussed next. Evidence from the 1991/92 household survey by the International Food Policy Research Institute

144

(IFPRI) in Botswana is presented to show the short-term impact of a labor-intensive program on employment, income, and consumption at the household level. The chapter concludes by highlighting outstanding issues that require further policy consideration to improve and expand, in a cost-effective manner, poverty-focused labor-intensive public works programs.

Labor, Poverty, and Food Security

Demography and the Labor Force

Botswana and Tanzania are experiencing rapid population growth. In the 1980s, annual population growth averaged 3.5 percent in Botswana (Botswana CSO 1991) and 2.8 percent in Tanzania (Tanzania, Bureau of Statistics 1991). Population growth is higher in urban areas. For example, Gaborone, the capital of Botswana, averaged 8.4 percent, and Dar es Salaam, the capital of Tanzania, averaged 4.8 percent per year. By 1991, urban areas and large villages in Botswana accounted for 43.3 percent of the population (Botswana CSO 1991).

A sizable percentage of the population in each of the countries is below working age. The 1990/91 labor force survey for Tanzania indicated that 60 percent of the population is outside the working age bracket of 15 to 65 (Tanzania, Bureau of Statistics, undated). The 1984/85 labor survey for Botswana (Botswana CSO 1986) showed that the combined proportion of the young and the old who were not of working age was much greater in rural areas (63.9 percent) than urban areas (45.8 percent).

Labor force participation rates are, not surprisingly, much higher among those in the prime working age group than those outside of it. In rural Tanzania, they average at least 88 percent in the age group 15 to 65. The female participation rate in Botswana tends to be lower (65.9 percent) than the male participation rate (78.7 percent). In general, participation rates tend to be lower in urban areas, particularly among women, but there is an upward trend in the rates in urban areas (Van Demoortele 1991).

Growth in the size of the labor force is bound to accelerate in these countries for the foreseeable future due to continuing high population growth, a large presence of youthful labor outside the labor force, and an upward trend in labor force participation rates (urban female in particular). For Tanzania, for example, growth in the labor force averaged 2.8 percent per year in the 1980s, and is projected to expand to 3.3 percent in the 1990s (ILO 1991). For these countries, labor demand must grow to match the growth in labor supply—if falling wages or an increase in self-employment are to be prevented.

Economic Growth and Employment

Botswana is the fastest growing economy in Sub-Saharan Africa. Over the last decade and a half, it averaged an 8.8 percent annual growth rate of real gross domestic product (GDP) per capita (Botswana MFDP 1991). This was largely attributable to rapid growth in the mining subsector (22.1 percent) and the tertiary sector (9.5 percent), which together accounted for 93 percent of the GDP. Agriculture, which employed 70 percent of the labor force, showed a marked decline in share of GDP.

While the decline in agricultural growth appears to have caused little difference in overall growth in Botswana, the same is not true for Tanzania. The country averaged a 3.0 percent annual growth in per capita GDP between 1962 and 1967. Growth in the agriculture sector during 1962–67, particularly in export crops, spurred the rapid growth in national income (Coulson 1982). Economic growth tapered off during the 1967–85 period, when public policy shifted toward the implementation of socialist objectives and the economy experienced a series of crises: severe drought in 1973–74, the first oil shock in 1974, massive forced villagization programs in 1974–76, the war with Uganda in 1978–79, and the second oil shock in 1979. Average annual per capita GDP growth was 1.9 percent during 1972–79, and –1.4 percent during 1979–84 (the largest drop in growth occurred in 1983, when the per capita GDP growth rate was –5.7 percent). Agricultural food production barely kept up with population growth during 1972–84. The economy has improved since 1985, showing a positive real per capita income growth.

Although Botswana experienced rapid economic growth in the 1970s and 1980s, much of it occurred in the mining sector, where labor absorption is weak. Low and uneven growth in the agriculture sector in Tanzania and the decline of the agriculture sector in Botswana have coincided with rapid growth in the labor force. Although large-scale open unemployment is not evident in rural Tanzania (2.4 percent for men and 2.6 percent for women), some evidence indicates that there is a sizable amount of underemployment in rural areas (Kamuzora 1990).

In Botswana, on the other hand, unemployment in rural areas, which averaged 20.6 percent for males and 20.0 percent for females, is significant. A considerable amount of time is also unaccounted for in rural Botswana (Mueller 1985). High male migration to urban areas is changing the demographic structure of rural areas, particularly in poor, small villages. The recent 1991 population census showed a decline in rural self-employment from 140,805 in 1981 to 76,085 people in 1991 (Botswana CSO 1991).

Both countries face major urban open unemployment, which averaged 21.6 percent in Tanzania in 1984 and 31.2 percent in Botswana in 1984–

85); urban employment is particularly high among the young and edu- cated in Tanzania. The increasing pressure on the labor market is also manifested in declining wage rates. In Tanzania, for example, growth in formal sector real wages averaged 1.5 percent in 1967–72 and 0.6 percent in 1972–79. It declined 18.2 percent in 1979–85, and 20.9 percent in 1986–87. Botswana, despite increases in urban employment, continues to face sharp increases in urban unemployment, due to large migrations of people from rural areas to cities.

Linkages to Poverty and Food Security

Poverty is closely linked to employment and wages, particularly where labor is the main source of income, including transfer income. Income from self-employment accounts for a large share of income in rural econo- mies of both countries. Farm income is by far the dominant source of income in rural Tanzania. Analysis of determinants of income for rural Botswana, for example, shows labor is the major contributor.

The share of labor in total income depends on factors that influence duration of employment and wages. Findings from Mueller (1985) on rural Botswana, for example, show that the wealth of a household (as measured by ownership of livestock), the educational level of the working adult, and demographic factors influence the amount of time devoted to work. Those households with more livestock and educated members and fewer dependent family members spend more time working. The extent of the labor supplied is demand-constrained, particularly by the seasonality of farm work.

In general, a constrained labor supply and low return to labor (low wages) are the key contributing factors to poverty in these economies. In rural Tanzania, poverty is more pronounced in food-deficit, low-income regions. Although household members are engaged in their own farm work during the peak farm season, the return to labor is barely enough to cover household consumption needs (the wage market is not yet able to correct imbalances in the family labor-land ratio). And, because there is limited off-season nonfarm employment and income, farmers have to convert part of their produce into cash income to meet their basic nonfood needs. Even farmers in food surplus regions face a considerable food security problem, especially farmers located in areas of low infrastructure where sale prices for their produce are low. The problem of poverty in Tanzania is thus linked to insufficient family labor to produce enough for home consump- tion (at the existing low level of farm technology), limited off-season nonfarm employment, and the high cost of transportation. Poverty is particularly acute among labor-deficit female-headed households.

In short, the evidence from Botswana and Tanzania indicates that there is a close link between labor and poverty. This link is particularly evident in regions with low and variable agricultural production and limited off-season, nonfarm employment, and among the poor households. Households with a low labor endowment and few complementary inputs (livestock, level of education, and improved farm technology) face special poverty and food insecurity risks, particularly in drought-prone areas of Botswana and Tanzania.

Experience with Public Works Schemes

In such environments, public works programs may have multiple goals. Programs can be used as a vehicle for the provision of employment (to stabilize intrayear or interyear fluctuations in employment). They can also be an instrument to transfer employment and income to poor segments of the population, guided by a preferred poverty measure (to reduce the incidence of poverty or its intensity). And finally, such programs can be used as a low-cost method of producing rural assets that promote long-term growth. Although a range of public works programs can address these goals simultaneously, the program design requirements and implementation rules for each goal are not the same. The three case studies below—two in Botswana and one in Tanzania—demonstrate some variations of programs with these goals and the extent of their success.

Botswana has one of Sub-Saharan Africa's more extensive relief programs. It includes food distribution, direct income transfer for those who are destitute, labor-intensive public works schemes, and farm support schemes. These schemes have evolved out of the country's concern with chronic and transient poverty. The latter problem is closely tied to Botswana's recurrent droughts. The country has witnessed at least six droughts in the last three decades.

The relief program is designed to address both chronic and transient poverty by (1) transferring income to selected beneficiaries on a regular basis (for example, through a scheme for the destitute and through regular food distribution to primary school students) to increase their level of consumption; (2) providing short-term income support to stabilize current consumption (for example, labor-intensive public works programs during drought years); and (3) preserving assets and means of production to protect future consumption. With the exception of the latter, which has conflicting resource allocative and income transfer functions, the other components of the relief program are primarily designed as income transfers (Table 6.1). The public works program is the main instrument of income transfer during drought.

Program 1: The Labor-Intensive Rural Public Works Program in Botswana

This program emerged from the food-for-work program of the 1960s as a cash-for-work program during the 1978–79 drought. The program expanded and was tested during the drought years of 1982 and 1987. It was reintroduced on a much larger scale during 1992–93 as the principal instrument for income transfer to rural households.

During 1982–87, a variety of projects were implemented. Local government, that is, village development committees, played a significant role in identification and implementation of projects during the 1982–87 period. But in 1992–93, this role shifted to implementing ministries, as part of the new government policy to expand regular nondrought projects during droughts. Projects implemented under the 1992–93 relief program in Botswana were drawn from the regular national and district plans, with one exception. The exception was where the Ministry of Local Governments had to prepare separate projects to ensure that region-specific employment targets were met.

In this program, employment is open to all able-bodied adults seeking to work for wages. But, as the employment records of 1982–87 show, jobs had to be rotated to meet the excess demand for work in many locations. In 1982–87, only about 61,000 jobs were created. Due to sharing arrangements, each worker was employed, on average, 76 days per year (this was reduced to 45 days at the height of the drought period, during 1982–83 and 1985–86). Available information suggests that the 1992–93 rural works schemes created approximately 90,000 to 100,000 job opportunities (Manamela 1993). Preliminary reports indicate a much longer duration of employment during 1992, particularly in districts that did not fully use their employment quotas.

Uniform wages are fixed by the government. In the 1980s, the wage rates were kept at a fraction of the regular labor-intensive rural works schemes. In 1992–93, the wage rate was set at about 70 percent of the lowest minimum statutory wage rate for unskilled labor in the formal wage sector. Such a rate was considered low enough to make the program self-targeting.

Because of the uniformity of these wage rates, they affected the supply of unskilled labor differently, depending on the prevailing wages in the various project areas. The wages were often more attractive than market wages in rural areas, particularly in small villages (Valentine 1990; Quinn

Table 6.1—A profile of income-transfer schemes in Botswana

| Policy | Regular Operation (Nondrought) Since 1978/79 | | Implementing Institution | | Drought Relief Operation | |
	Type of Intervention	Objective	Central Government	Local Government	1982–88	1992–93
Food, water, and health services delivery	Food distribution to school children, medically selected children under five, and vulnerable adults	Improve nutrition and health status	Food Resources Department (FRD), Ministry of Local Government, Lands, and Housing (MLGLH)	Education and Health Departments of District Councils	Expanded to include *all* children under five, pregnant and lactating women, and children of primary school age. Includes inhabitants of remote areas and permanent, as well as temporary, poor. Increased size of food ration.	Included only medically selected pregnant and lactating women; eliminated take-home ration to school children; and eliminated feeding of inhabitants of remote areas and the destitute. (Option: working adults given employment in works schemes).
Employment through public works	None, except the rural roads programs (LG34)	Create rural assets, supplement income, compensate income loss (drought year)	Ministry of Local Government, Lands, and Housing (MLGLH)	Works Departments of District Councils	Provision of employment to working adults through rural works schemes. Village committees were vested with responsibility for identification of projects.	Expanded in 1992–93 as the main income-transfer instrument. Project preparation and implementation transferred to technical ministries. Ministry of Local Governments and Lands responsible for achieving district employment targets.
Direct income transfer to the destitute	Food stamp coupons to selected permanent poor	Income support to selected poor	Community and Social Department, MLGLH	Social Welfare Departments of District Councils	Expanded to include temporary poor from drought. Cash plus free food allowance.	Abandoned temporary poor. Cash for destitutes but no free food allowance.

et al. 1988). But they were also lower than market wages in areas close to large villages and towns. In the latter case, the wage rates probably contributed to the self-selection of poor households—particularly female-headed households with large families and low cattle ownership (Asefa 1989), which otherwise would have been engaged in unremunerative self-employment. The large presence of women in works schemes in 1992–93—averaging 60 to 70 percent—is an indication that the program did target the poor. Reports of the Ministry of Local Government and Lands indicate that several districts, particularly those close to major urban centers, experienced an acute shortage of male labor due to outmigration. Implementing public works programs in such areas would likely lead to high rates of female participation and effective targeting of poor, often female-headed, households.

Evaluations of the 1982–87 program identified some notable deficiencies (Hay 1988; Valentine 1990; Buchanan-Smith 1990). The program overemphasized the income transfer component at the cost of labor productivity. As Valentine (1990) described it, it was better for the government to pay rural inhabitants to do something constructive than have them depend on welfare transfers, even if what was produced was uneconomic. The program did little to raise future consumption because the assets created were poorly maintained. Also, the temporary nature of income did not translate into appreciable investment at the household level (Hay 1988; Asefa 1989).

Current reports on the performance of the 1992–93 program also suggest a low level of achievement, largely due to inadequate technical and managerial support in most districts (Manamela 1993). Many districts seem to have operated the program at a scale beyond their existing capacities. There is no concrete evidence to suggest that the 1992 program attained levels of productivity that surpassed those achieved in the program of the 1980s.

Financing and Implementation. Financing for the relief programs comes from the central government treasury (except for some donor food and technical assistance). Botswana spent well over 440 million pula (P) (in current prices) for its 1982–90 drought relief and recovery program. During the period between 1984 to 1987, for example, the level of expenditure represented 14 to 18 percent of total government development expenditure (Botswana MFDP 1991, 59).

The 1992–93 program was initiated against a backdrop of a general slowdown in economic performance and a projected increase in external funding of the 1991–97 development plan. In addition, government-sponsored evaluation underlined the possibility that the 1982–87 relief program could grow expensive and, therefore, difficult to replicate in the future. To contain program costs in 1992–93, the government dropped some components from the previous drought program, attempted to consolidate the various income-transfer schemes, and integrated relief and development through focusing on public works programs.

Preliminary assessment of the 1992–93 program suggests that there has been a substantial escalation of costs (Manamela 1993). The cost containment effort was, in part, compromised by reintroduction of some elements of the farm input subsidies, and by the low level of performance of the program. By May 1993, many districts had completed only 35 percent of their projects.

By and large, institutions that operate projects during nondrought years expand their operations in drought periods. A high-powered Interministerial Drought Committee, which is based within the Ministry of Finance and Development Planning (MFDP), coordinates these operations. It is responsible for the development of strategy and policy, the coordination and monitoring of relief activities, and the control and allocation of resources. The committee reports to the Rural Development Council, which is chaired by the vice president of the country. The Interministerial Drought Committee is linked to district and village levels through district drought subcommittees and village-development and extension teams.

Program 2: Engineered Rural Roads Program in Botswana

Botswana also runs a trial program that produces labor-intensive, low-cost, engineered earth roads (McCutcheon 1988). The program developed from an experiment tested in 1980–82 and expanded to all districts by 1986.

Design of Program. The program (LG34) (see Table 6.1) embodies three key, guiding principles: high labor content, compliance with a prescribed technical standard to ensure that roads are passable throughout the year, and low-cost maintenance (and, hence, sustainability) of roads (McCutcheon 1988).

Employment is open to all who are able-bodied. Typically, selection is done at village meetings. The process begins with a public announcement of conditions of employment and pay (participants must be able-bodied with no mental and physical disability). There are further screenings if there are more applicants than available positions. Random selection (a lottery technique) is widely employed, but other methods are also jointly or independently applied (for example, quota setting by sex, a limit on the number of participants per household, targeting of poor households with working adults). Hiring of labor continues at work sites.

At construction work sites, workers are organized into gangs. Each gang has 25 workers under the supervision of a gang leader. Above the gang leader, there is a senior gang leader, who supervises two gang leaders, or 50 workers. A technical assistant supervises the work of four to six gang leaders, or 100 to 150 workers.

Like the construction activities, maintenance work is implemented through the District Council Road Units. The workers are selected on a merit basis from the list of workers who were engaged in the construction work. The work is organized in small teams, typically in a team of five, headed by a team leader. Work allocation largely follows the length-per-man approach, where each laborer is allocated somewhere between 1.5 and 2 kilometers of road. A team leader is responsible for supervision of 25 kilometers of road.

Wage rates are determined as a fixed proportion of a minimum wage rate set for urban industrial workers. There is no explicit minimum wage for unskilled workers in rural areas; this represents a de facto minimum wage setting for the project. Wage rates are uniform, regardless of type of work, location of work site, and personal characteristics of workers (age, sex, education, experience, and so forth). Maintenance workers are paid at the same rate as construction workers. The wage is set on a daily basis, except in a few cases where task rates are applied. Workers are paid cash wages once monthly.

Financing and Implementation. The capital component of the road project is fully funded by the government of Norway. This funding covers the costs of technical assistance (ranging from 12 to 15 percent of total allocation), administrative overhead and training (together amounting to about 12 percent), and the direct costs for road construction work. Labor cost, according to guidelines, should account for 70 percent of the direct operational cost.

The program is coordinated at the central level by a district roads engineer, who reports directly to the undersecretary (rural) in the Ministry of Local Government and Lands. Each district has a District Council Road Unit, which is staffed largely by technical cadres. The chief technical officer in the District Council Road Unit supervises all roadwork, including LG34. Technical assistants, who directly supervise gang leaders at work sites, are responsible for ensuring the compliance of the roadwork with specified engineering standards, employing laborers, and managing overall activities at work sites.

Road sites are identified in consultation with local communities. The technical staff performs a feasibility assessment and prioritizes the roadwork. The ranked road links are then passed to District Development Committees for further evaluation. The final decision rests with district councils, whose members are elected representatives of the district population. Roads that are selected are eventually incorporated into district development plans.

Output and Distribution of Benefit. By the end of 1990/91, the program had created a total of 998 kilometers of earth roads in all districts (Table 6.2). Yearly output increased from 55 kilometers in 1983/84 to about 141 kilometers in 1987/88 and 177 kilometers in 1990/91. On average, annual output per year amounted to 106 kilometers of earth roads. Nearly one-half of these roads were constructed in the central district.

As of 1990, the project had created temporary employment for about 3,000 casual workers in construction and maintenance works. Over the years, there has been positive growth in employment, particularly in maintenance labor. Female participation is also rising, particularly in areas close to towns and major villages. By 1990, female labor accounted for 40 percent of all labor.

In terms of workdays, the project generated about 343,000 labor days per year between 1986/87 and 1990/91. Construction of earthworks utilizes, on average, almost 2,000 labor days per kilometer. There is little seasonal variation in workdays over the years, except for a slight decline in participation in the peak farm months of November and December (Figure 6.1).

Labor employed in maintenance works grew from 226 laborers in 1986/87 to 1,087 laborers in 1989/90. The number of labor days generated increased from 50,000 to 238,700 between the two years. By 1989/90, female laborers accounted for some 35 percent of total labor.

Growth in real project wages shows a weak but positive trend. However, this growth has not often been commensurate with the movement in the average productivity of labor. A decomposition of the growth rate of the unit cost of labor per kilometer (which is the difference between the growth rates of nominal wages and the productivity of labor) shows a close association between growth in the unit cost of labor and nominal wage rates. That is, what is driving growth in real wages is not productivity growth; it is the correction of wages for inflation. For example, annual growth rates for nominal wages and labor productivity averaged 7.1 and 4.4 percent, respectively. In 1990/91, the respective growth rates were 30.6

Table 6.2—Employment, output, and cost of earthwork access roads in Botswana, 1980–91

Year	Construction Labor Days Per Year	Length of Road Per Period	Labor Days Per Kilometer	Variable Cost Per Kilometer	Estimated Share of Labor Cost	Real Wage Per Day (1985 =100)[a]
	(1,000)	(kilometer)		(pula)	(percent)	(pula)
1980–83	77.78	39.0	1,994	10,380	40.3	...
1983/84	66.60	55.0	1,211	7,220	35.0	2.65
1984/85	152.03	89.4	1,705	10,088	...	3.02
1986/87	364.55	143.1	2,548	10,350	88.6	3.32
1987/88	305.18	140.6	2,171	12,810	67.1	3.38
1988/89	364.65	175.7	2,075	12,831	68.6	3.44
1989/90	341.53	158.6	2,153	16,172	62.1	3.49
1990/91	336.64	176.6	1,906	15,685	62.8	3.69

Sources: Hagen, Guthrie, and Galetshoge 1988; Solberg, Nteta, and Tessem 1990.

Notes: These roads were constructed under a program known as LG34. The ellipses (. . .) indicate a nil or negligible amount.

[a]The daily pula (P) real wage rate for workers on relief programs was P 2.21 in 1983/84, P 2.19 in 1984/85, P 2.07 in 1986/87, P 2.13 in 1987/88, and P 2.23 in 1988/89.

Figure 6.1—Casual labor force

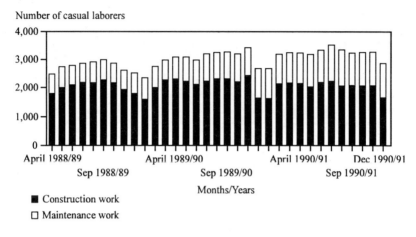

Number of casual laborers

■ Construction work
□ Maintenance work

Source: Brudefors 1991.

and 16 percent, respectively. Thus, there is an apparent overcompensation of workers beyond their contribution to project output.

Since labor cost constitutes at least two-thirds of the total variable cost, increases in wage rates translate into increases in the cost of construction per kilometer. This trend occurred particularly in the late 1980s and early 1990s (Table 6.2). For example, the cost per kilometer increased from P 10,350 in 1986/87 to P 12,831 in 1988/89 and nearly P 16,000 in 1990/91. In all years, the offsetting effect of productivity growth was much weaker, particularly in 1988/89 and 1989/90. In 1990/91, for example, the productivity index jumped by 16 percent, but it was overwhelmed by a 31 percent jump in the wage rate.

Compared with wages in small villages (for tasks including herding, domestic work, and sorghum stamping), project wages are much higher. They are even higher when the shorter workday on project sites (6 hours per day compared with an average of 10 hours per day in other occupations) is considered. On the other hand, project wages are lower than competing market wages in areas close to urban and large villages; in these areas, the project often faces a tight labor supply, particularly of male labor. A similar problem arises in sparsely populated areas, especially in the west, where the labor market is thin. The restrictiveness of uniform wage rates limits the program's ability to vary wage rates and improve labor recruitment in areas where the labor market is competitive.

Short-term benefits of the road program accrue to those engaged in construction and maintenance work. A recent IFPRI study of a sample of these project villages shows that the program has an unambiguous, positive, incremental effect on the income of participating households. Access to the program has improved the relative income position of participants, particularly those at the lower end of the income spectrum.

There is little information on the second-round income effects of rural access roads. However, project evaluation reports (Hagen, Guthrie, and Galetshoge 1988; Solberg, Nteta, and Tessem 1990) indicate that there are notable multiplier effects. Access roads facilitate easy links at low cost, particularly to large villages where services and employment are greatly concentrated. No less important for the rural households is the improved link between villages, cattle posts, and land areas. Because of the new road links, there is a greater demand for transport services, as evident in the greater use of bicycles, donkey carts, and light motorized vehicles. There is, again, little evidence on how much such services accrue to the poor in rural areas.

Household-level effects of this program are further analyzed below, based on a survey done specifically for this purpose.

Program 3: Special Labor-Intensive
Public Works Program in Tanzania

Labor-intensive public works in Tanzania date back to 1978, with the beginning of the Tanzanian special public works. This multisectoral scheme encompasses projects that focus on improving rural access roads (the Rukwa and Ruvuma projects); flood control and rehabilitation of irrigation projects (the Arusha and Dodoma projects); afforestation (the Ruvuma and Dodoma projects); water supply (the Rukwa project); and construction of rural housing (the Ruvuma project).

Design of Program. The labor-intensive projects share a common set of goals: (1) to rehabilitate and maintain rural assets (feeder roads, irrigation works, afforestation, and piped water supply); (2) to create employment opportunities for the rural unemployed and underemployed; (3) to provide supplementary income, particularly for low-income households; and (4) to build the technical and institutional capacity for future replication of labor-intensive public works programs. Poverty reduction is not explicitly featured in these projects, except in the stipulation of a gender balance in employment (a tacit assumption that poverty is closely correlated with gender).

The relative weights attached to these goals are not stated, but there is an apparent focus on employment creation for rural unskilled labor. (This is consistent with adoption of a uniform prescription of the 60–40 ratio of labor and nonlabor inputs across all projects.) But the goal of employment creation is not necessarily linked to the generation of income for workers. The projects, especially housing projects, are often considered "self-help" (as opposed to paid labor).

Employment is open to adults who are eligible for work. Initial selection is done at the village level. Involvement of the village government is often sought to ensure availability of labor for project work and "equitable" sharing of paid project work among the village population. Also, village governments play a major role in the mobilization of self-help labor.

Labor arrangements at work sites vary. The dominant mode, particularly in the road projects, is the technician-foreman-gang mode. For example, the Ruvuma road project has one foreman for every gang of 100 laborers. A variation of this approach is the length-per-man system. Typically, the length-per-man system is applied on road maintenance work and involves a foreman, a headman, and a gang of laborers.

The organization of community labor for self-help is aided by the structure of village government. Typically, every village has a three-tier administrative structure: cells at the bottom (each cell has 10 families); village council in the middle (the council constitutes political appointees and elected cell leaders); and village head at the top. A village council- or project-specific committee (for example, a forestry or irrigation committee) prepares the work plan and schedule, and then passes it to cell leaders, who are responsible for mobilization of their respective cell members. Typically, project work is rotated among village cells. Intervillage coordination is done at ward level, which represents a group of villages.

Official minimum wages are the established wage and are applied uniformly across projects, regardless of place and season. Within a single project, the wage is the same, regardless of the nature of the activity and workers' characteristics (for example, sex, age, education, experience, and so forth). Workers are mostly paid in cash, which is particularly attractive in rural areas, where cash incomes are limited. The only exception to this practice is the Pemba rice project (partly supported by the World Food Programme), where payment also consists of food.

To bypass official wage rates (these rates are sometimes considered too low to attract labor), some projects experiment with different compensation schemes. One mechanism is to switch to a task rate. The task rate permits workers to receive the same wage rate per day as other project workers, but for a shorter work time. Parity is achieved by adjusting the productivity norm downward. Also, each worker is free to take more than one task rate per day to maximize his or her income. Such a practice has been applied, for example, to the Mto-wa-Mbu Irrigation Project in Arusha (Martens 1989). A second method is to provide workers with food in addition to the official wage, which also minimizes absenteeism and drop-out rates. The Pemba rice irrigation project offers cash and an in-kind payment package.

Financing and Implementation. The program is jointly implemented by the United Nations Development Programme (UNDP), the United Republic of Tanzania (URT), and the International Labour Office (ILO), with financial contributions from the Netherlands, Germany, Denmark, and the European Union (EU). For 1979–91, the contributions of donors and UNDP amounted to US$12 million and US$6.2 million, respectively. The contribution of the Government of Tanzania was about US$2.4 million over the 1980–90 period, or about 11 percent of the total capital fund.

The funds are allocated to technical assistance (the whole UNDP contribution plus 13 percent of the donors' contribution to cover the service provided by ILO), project overheads (the contribution of the Tanzanian government), and operating cost of the projects (87 percent of the donors' contribution). A little over one-half of total funds go to finance the operational costs of projects.

Projects evolve through the country's decentralized administrative framework (village-ward-district-region) and then are coordinated within a special unit of the Prime Minister's office. At the national level, there is an interministerial coordinating committee responsible for overall policy guidance. While projects are not directly integrated within regional development plans, they are coordinated through regional development committees.

Output and Distribution of Benefits. The projects, as a whole, created 2.9 million paid workdays during the 1980–90 period (Table 6.3). Road projects absorbed 46 percent of the paid unskilled labor in 1980–86 (the Ruvuma road project alone employed 37.3 percent), followed by the irrigation projects, which accounted for nearly 40 percent. Forestry accounted for 10.5 percent in 1980–86, but its share expanded to 25 percent in 1987–90, especially with the Bareko project in Dodoma. The difference in scale of employment is related to the size of the project as measured by project cost (Table 6.4). There is little variation in labor intensity across projects.

The contribution of these projects to total employment is greater if self-help labor is also considered. For example, the housing project alone contributed 1.3 million unpaid workdays during 1981–88. Unskilled self-

Table 6.3—Share of employment generated, by type of project, UNDP/URT/ILO program, Tanzania

	Paid Unskilled Labor		Unpaid Unskilled Labor	
Project Type	1980–86 (Phase 1)	1987–90 (Phase 2)	1980–86 (Phase 1)	1987–90 (Phase 2)
	(percent)			
Road	46.0[a]	31.5	0.0[b]	0.0
Irrigation	39.9	39.5[c]	8.1	11.6
Forestry	10.5	25.4[d]	0.7	9.8
Water supply	4.5	3.6	1.0	4.5
Housing	. . .	. . .	90.2[e]	74.1
Workdays (thousands)	2,199.5	674.1	1,301.1	174.0

Source: Unpublished project reports.
Note: UNDP is the United Nations Development Progamme, URT is the United Republic of Tanzania, and ILO is the International Labour Office.
[a]Ruvuma roadwork alone accounted for 39.4 percent and 31.5 percent in Phase 1 and Phase 2 of the program, respectively.
[b]This includes a small activity (3,200 workdays) in Rukwa during Phase 1.
[c]This share is largely due to the addition of the Pemba irrigation project in Zanzibar.
[d]Indicates expansion of the Beriko afforestation project in Dodoma.
[e]The housing project in Ruvuma was entirely on a self-help schedule (unpaid labor).

help labor also accounted for at least 15 percent of total employment in irrigation and forestry projects in Dodoma.

Employment in these projects is temporary. This is, in part, due to the legal requirement that labor employed for over three months is eligible for benefits in the same way as permanent staff. Projects prefer to rotate labor to circumvent this legal requirement and to avoid extra costs. Poor infrastructure and the associated cost of transportation restrict additional labor supply (for job rotation) to adjacent villages. Furthermore, the practice of job rotation to reach all job seekers translates into low per capita days of employment.

The projects tend to stabilize fluctuations in agricultural employment that occur throughout the year. For example, a study of the Mto-wa-Mbu irrigation project in Arusha and the Mnenia irrigation project in Dodoma shows a counterseasonal employment pattern (Martens 1989).

Project wages are comparable with agricultural wages. For example, the project wage rates in Tanzanian shillings (TSh) in 1990 and 1991 (TSh 114 and TSh 159, respectively) were at least as high as the wages of farmworkers in maize and paddy fields. Although farmers are unlikely to move out of maize production at present (particularly when market risk is

Table 6.4—Employment and direct cost of special labor-intensive public works programs, Tanzania

Project Type	Location	Period	Paid Casual Labor Per Year	Share of Unpaid Labor	Share of Female Labor	Direct Cost Per Year	Share of Labor Cost
			(hours)	(percent)	(percent)	(TSh 1,000)	(percent)
Roads	Ruvuma	1980–86	123,893	0.0	n.a.	2,490	59
Irrigation	Arusha[a]	1980–85	76,347	16.7	12.0	2,358	49
	Dodoma	1980–90	17,696	16.2	25.0	935	49
Forestry	Ruvuma	1981–86	16,887	0.0	n.a.	938	46
	Dodoma	1986–90	21,317	15.4	37.0	2,523	49

Source: Tanzania, Labor Internal Public Works Program Unit in Prime Minister's office. Various years.
Note: n.a. is not available.
[a] Mto-wa-Mbu Project only.

high), current return differentials indicate that there is a potential conflict between farm and project work; this is especially true where the scale of project work is large and the demand for labor is seasonal. On the other hand, project wages are sometimes considered too low to attract labor, especially in areas where the population density is low and the mobility of labor is constrained because of poor infrastructure and high transportation costs. Projects may also fail to attract workers when they have to compete with profitable farm activities, such as coffee growing.

A direct comparison of output performance among projects is problematic because of differences in type of output, type of technology (mix of factors and efficiency of the production process), and organization of production (for example, communal versus private). However, the trend in physical output is uneven and slow growing. For example, the Mto-wa-Mbu irrigation project achieved 25 percent of its planned irrigation area. The Dodoma irrigation project, initiated in 1980, had reached only 29 percent of its target by mid-1991.

Various reports also indicate a substantial loss of created assets due to the lack of regular maintenance work. For example, only 34 percent of the total number of trees planted survived in the Dodoma community forestry project. The rate was lowest on communal woodlots. A substantial part of the investment in road rehabilitation and maintenance has also been lost. For example, a recent project document acknowledges that 2,903 kilometers of the 3,700 kilometers of roads in Ruvuma are in need of rehabilitation because of extensive deterioration (PMO/ILO 1989).

The main benefit of the project, then, is the short-term income increase gained by those engaged in construction work. A recent IFPRI village-level survey indicates that at least 64 percent of the villages in the project derive some income from rural works projects. Employment in labor-intensive projects ranks as at least the third most important source of income in these villages. Moreover, access to wage employment through the projects is the primary source of wage employment in project areas (in 64 percent of the villages).

Although the long-term effects are often diminished by poor maintenance of assets, there are a few exceptions where second-round income effects (income from created assets or labor market effects) are sizable. For example, access to irrigated land in Dodoma villages has made it possible for farmers to shift their crops toward labor-intensive, high-return crops. There is evidence that agricultural wages have increased because of the shift in crop mix, increased cropping intensity, and greater profitability of crops.

In addition, the project helps smooth consumption over seasons and reduces risk by minimizing the effects of droughts and floods. However, an inequitable distribution of land and water has contributed to an inequitable distribution of project-derived income. Although the poor may benefit from the increased demand for labor, the evidence shows that the project has aggravated income inequality in the village (Martens 1989; Van der Does and Kuik 1989).

Targeting the Poor and Food-Insecure

In the three programs reviewed, there is some evidence of reaching the poor through different modes of targeting that use the criteria of geography, gender, and self-selection through low wage rates.

Findings from surveys of female participants in Tanzania (Tamoda, Myovela, and Muijsers 1987; Scheinman, Hongoke, and Ndaalio 1989) show that female participation is high in areas with higher concentrations of landless or small farmers and no access to alternative wage employment. Where there are few employment options, a greater number of older women participate in rural works schemes. Women with children have a greater propensity to participate in poor areas. In areas where women have alternative employment with better returns, young females with no children tend to participate in rural works schemes (Scheinman, Hongoke, and Ndaalio 1989).

During 1991/92, IFPRI conducted a household survey in Botswana.[1] The purpose was to pose a set of specific questions to test the impact of the engineered road program on household food security in rural areas. These were some of the key research questions: What factors influence a decision to participate in public works? What are the gross and net effects of the

---

[1]The IFPRI survey covered about 350 households in eight project-participating villages in five districts. The villages were drawn from the category of small villages. They had experienced low population growth, partly due to net outmigration. Migration rates per household averaged 27 percent across the study villages. Within villages, there were sizable disparities in the number of working adults and livestock owned per household. At least 24 percent of the households had no adult male members and 30 percent had no livestock. Households in the survey villages were engaged in a variety of income-generating activities. The poorer villages depend on beverage trading and other low-paying wage work. Project income is a significant component of household income, particularly where alternative wage employment is scarce. Also, the villagers are highly dependent on private transfers, a phenomenon largely linked to net outmigration of working adults. Density of socioeconomic infrastructure varies, but it is sufficiently developed in all villages. For example, only 27 percent of the village population had no schooling and 56 percent had at least primary education.

project on household employment? What are the gross and net effects on household income? What is the project's effect on income distribution in rural areas? Has the project improved the food security of project participants?

Participation of the Poor

While job allocation is supposed to be accomplished in village meetings, the work site appears to be a focal point for entry and exit from project work. Jobs at project sites in the survey areas were generally available on demand. In fact, in some instances, projects faced labor supply shortfalls. Explanations obtained from nonparticipating households indicated the following reasons for nonparticipation: low wages for comparable skills (the segmentation of the market restrains those with a high labor supply price from entering roadwork); the menial nature of work (which screens out wealthy households with an established business and livestock); the physical intensity of the work (this excludes the weak and the old); the short duration of project employment (it attracts mainly those who are not regularly in the labor market—young adults, in particular); and the distance to the roadwork site (limits participation to households near the project sites).

The decision to participate in project work is determined by a set of household and individual characteristics. Results obtained from estimation of a probability decision model identify household size and composition, livestock ownership, and access to transfer income as key household characteristics (Table 6.5). The likelihood of participation increases as the number of household members of working age increases. The presence of children in a household diminishes the likelihood of participation, unless there is extra adult female labor to compensate for the mother's absence. The odds of participation fall with increasing livestock ownership. Access to transfer income also reduces the likelihood of participation.

At the individual level, the important explanatory variables are age, physical size and strength, and level of education. While the likelihood of participation increases with age, it does so at a decreasing rate. The likelihood of participation also increases with physical strength and height. Higher education levels reduce the likelihood of participation. Across villages, the likelihood of participation is higher for poorer villages.

Employment Share of the Poor

Project participation causes a reallocation of labor time within participating households (Table 6.6). A simple comparison of allocations of work time between participant and nonparticipant individuals shows that non-

Table 6.5—Maximum likelihood estimates of logit probability model for labor entry into rural roadworks

Variable Definition	Parameter Estimate	Marginal Effect	Elasticity of Participation at Sample Mean
		(percent)	
Age of working individual (years)	0.17 (4.02)*	0.02 (2.71)*	0.42
Age squared	-0.2×10^{-2} (4.16)*	-0.2×10^{-2} (2.77)*	. . .
Education level of working individual (1 if primary, 2 if secondary or above, 0 otherwise)	-0.37 (2.08)**	-0.05 (1.93)**	-0.19
Height of working individual (centimeters)	0.05 (2.96)*	0.4×10^{-2} (2.28)**	3.86
Share of children in household	-0.19 (1.53)***	-0.02 (1.44)	-0.14
Share of female adults in household	0.22 (1.90)**	0.02 (1.73)***	0.28
Dummy for livestock ownership (1 if middle tercile, 0 if lowest tercile)	-0.78 (2.60)*	-0.07 (2.26)**	-0.17
Dummy for livestock ownership (1 if upper tercile, 0 if lowest tercile)	-1.25 (3.81)*	-0.12 (2.85)*	-0.25
Dummy for village (1 if farther from town)	0.62 (2.38)**	0.06 (2.05)**	0.16
Share of transfer income in total household income	-1.07 (1.93)**	-0.10 (1.77)**	0.14
Constant	-10.67 (4.25)*	. . .	. . .
-2 log likelihood ratio	97.30*		
N	551		

Note: The dependent variable is individual-level project participation (yes = 1, no = 0). Numbers in parentheses are absolute t-statistics. Ellipses (. . .) indicate a nil or negligible amount.
  *Significant at 1 percent probability.
  **Significant at 5 percent probability.
  ***Significant at 10 percent probability.

Table 6.6—Time use for participating and nonparticipating individuals within project households, a 24-hour recall, Botswana

Activity	Participating Individual	Nonparticipating Individual
	(hours)	
Self-employment	1.23	3.53
Wage employment, project	4.76	0.16[a]
Wage employment, other	0.15	1.11
Domestic work/schooling	2.43	3.07
Nonwork	6.14	6.88
Average available time per day[b]	14.71	14.75

Source: IFPRI Rural Household Survey, Botswana, 1991/92.
Notes: The time allocated to project work comes from

$$T_p = (T_F^0 - T_F') + (T_W^0 - T_W') + (T_H^0 - T_H') + (T_L^0 - T_L') + (T^0 - T^1),$$

where T_F^0, T_W^0, T_H^0, T_L^0, and T^0 represent time allocated to self-employment, wage work, domestic work, nonwork, and total time endowment before the project, and T_p, T_F', T_W', T_H', T_L', and T^1 represent time allocated to project work, self-employment, wage work, domestic work, and nonwork after the project.

If the time allocation of the nonparticipating individuals within households is taken as a reference point for a pre-project situation, then Table 6.5 suggests that the time allocated to the project comes through reduction in nonwork (−0.74 hours), domestic work/schooling (−0.64 hours), self-employment (−2.3 hours), and other wage work (−0.96 hours).

[a]Dropped out of the project at the time of the survey.
[b]Day is defined as nonsleeping hours.

participating working members tend to allocate more time to income-earning self-employment and domestic work than do project participants, who concentrate more on project work. The direction of activity substitution is largely congruent with what the participants said were their major occupations before they joined the project (Table 6.7).

Although project wages and hours of work are fixed for all workers, there are sizable variations in the share of individuals' total work that is devoted to project work. The share of project time relative to total available time increases if the percentage increase in project work exceeds the percentage increase in the individual's total available time. There are several sources of these variations. First, some relaxation of individual total time endowment contributes to an increase in share. Second, workers who come from large households with many adult-equivalents can allocate a larger share to the project because they may share nonproject work with

Table 6.7—Previous primary occupation of road project participants, 1991/92, Botswana

Occupation	Share of Participants	Return to Labor or Wage Per Labor Day
	(percent)	(pula)
Own, crop	16.0	3.10[a]
Own, livestock	8.3	5.2[a]
Own, nonfarm	5.3	. . .
Wage, maid	6.5	3.5
Wage, herding	1.8	3.5
Wage, stamping	2.4	2.5
Wage, casual	5.3	. . .
Wage, other	1.8	. . .
Own, domestic work	23.7	. . .
Schooling	1.1	. . .
No work[b]	27.8	. . .

Source: IFPRI Rural Household Survey, Botswana, 1991/92.
Note: The ellipses (. . .) indicate a nil or negligible amount.
[a]The average 1985–88 return per person-day for sorghum and cattle production, respectively.
[b]Respondents tend to classify domestic work as nonwork since it does not generate direct income. Some of the time in the nonwork category may actually be in domestic work. The rest may be new entrants into the labor force.

other household members. Sharing appears more likely in poor households and villages. Workers from households with little livestock, particularly in remote poor villages, allocate a large share of their time to project work (large household size interacts with low employment opportunity for the poor in remote areas). Third, access to transfer income tends to decrease the share of project time (which may be due to an increase in nonwork time). Finally, it is easier to substitute labor within households if the participant is a young person or if his or her educational level is high.

Distribution of Project Income and the Poor

There are sizable differences in income levels across the survey households. For example, average per capita annual incomes range from P 670 for low-asset households to P 1,232 for high-asset households. For households that participated in the project, the average per capita income is P 740. The difference in mean incomes between low-asset households and households that participated seems small. This is in part due to the pres-

Table 6.8—Determinants of household-level monthly earned income, Botswana, 1991/92

Explanatory Variable	Parameter Estimate
Education of head of household (1 if primary and above; 0 if no education)	45.60 (2.64)*
Livestock per capita (LSU)[a]	46.84 (9.05)*
Share of transfer income	−162.64 (3.48)*
Village dummy (0 if MAHETWE, MOIYABANA, or MAKOBENG)	66.34 (3.00)*
Number of adult equivalents in household	15.05 (4.03)*
Predicted participation dummy (1 if project participant)	67.80 (2.47)*
Constant	41.18 (1.45)
F	29.79
$\bar{R}^2$	0.41

Notes: The dependent variable is household monthly earned income (household income less transfers). Absolute t-statistics are in parentheses.
[a]LSU is livestock unit (cattle equivalent).
*Significant at 1 percent probability.

ence of participating households in the low-asset group. However, if project-participant households are separated from the low-asset group, the gain in mean incomes may be greater.

The estimated determinants of the earned income equation (total household income less transfer income) equation in Table 6.8 show that ownership of livestock, level of education, household size (in adult equivalents), and participation in project work all contribute to an increase in earned income. Villages located close to major towns also enjoy a higher income level. The share of transfer income acts as a substitute to earned income.

It is plausible that participants were poorer to start with and that participation in roadwork improved their income level. In fact, the time allocation practices of the participants are very much like those of asset-poor households, which allocate more of their economic time (direct income-generating activities) to wage work and less to self-employment (Table 6.9). But, unlike the poor, who often engage in low-paying,

Table 6.9—Comparison of time and income distribution across low- and high-wealth groups, Botswana

Time/Income Category	Project Household	Group[a]	
		Low	High
	(percent)		
Total available time allocated to			
Self-employment (farm)	16	16	24
	(11)	(7)	(19)
Wage employment (project)	19	22	10
	(15)	(14)	(6)
Total household income derived from			
Self-employment (farm/livestock)	21	11	44
	(13)	(2)	(32)
Wage income (project)	47	39	23
	(41)	(27)	(14)
Transfers	21	35	25
Others	11	15	8

Source: IFPRI Rural Household Survey, Botswana, 1991/92.
Note: The per capita (adult-equivalent) annual income averaged P740, P670, and P1,232 for project-, low-, and high-income households, respectively.
[a]Bottom and top wealth terciles are determined by the distribution of livestock ownership in 1991/92. Both the low and high asset groups include households with project participants.

marginal-wage activities, access to a project allows the participants to move to better-paying project work. As Table 6.7 shows, alternative occupations pay less than the project daily wage (P 5.79 per day). Although an increase in transfer income partly offsets the gain in income, the increase in aggregate labor supply coupled with a shift to better-paying work have contributed to the improvement in household income.

Access to the project also appears to have improved the relative income position of the participants, particularly at the lower end of the income distribution. The percentages of participating households in the low- and middle-income terciles were 24 percent and 44 percent, respectively. The comparable percentages for nonparticipating households were 36 percent and 28 percent, respectively. The project thus appears to have contributed to moving some of the households to the middle-income group. This is confirmed also in decomposition of the Gini coefficient, which shows a source Gini coefficient of 0.68 for project income—a value that indicates the project helped to narrow income distribution. In contrast, transfer income appears to contribute to income inequality in rural areas.

Participation in the project also gives the added advantage of access to the rural credit market. There is a great deal of complementarity between public works and the village credit market. In 1991/92, 61 percent of the participants managed to obtain short-term credit from village shops, largely for food consumption, compared with 39.3 percent of the nonparticipating households. Access to a project thus serves as a substitute for loan collateral.

Policy Conclusions

Botswana and Tanzania have experimented with labor-intensive public works since the late 1970s. There are compelling reasons to continue with and even expand labor-intensive public works, given the low and variable incomes in rural areas, severe deficiencies in rural infrastructure, and rising unemployment and falling living standards in urban areas. However, it is necessary to take a fresh look at the objectives, design, and implementation of these programs, and the criteria for the evaluation of their performance. The following are some recommendations for the improvement of program performance:

1. Clearly specify concept and program objectives. The question of what a specific program stands for needs to be addressed early on. Program design and policies should then develop from such prescribed objectives and functions.
2. Move away gradually from fixed wages toward a market-based mechanism for wage setting. The specific wage structure (rate, type [time or task rate], mode of payment) will depend on the specific objective of the program and the functioning of labor and food markets.
3. Expand employment creation beyond merely allocating jobs equitably toward stabilization (employment to counter seasonal fluctuations); insurance (open when there is a demand for work); and targeting of the poor.
4. Determine program choice and size in the context of a sound macroeconomic and development framework. If the goal of a public works program is short-term transfer of income to the poor, it is crucial that design and implementation policies focus on minimizing the terms of the trade-off between current and future poverty-reduction goals.
5. Develop a sustainable technical, financial, and administrative capacity. The current provision of donor-supported technical and

financial assistance needs a greater emphasis on creation of "in-house" ability to ensure that programs are sustainable without recurrent donor assistance. Also, accountable financial management should be built into the program.

6. Emphasize targeting the poor, but at a minimum cost of participation. In Tanzania and Botswana, targeting the poor could make use of different poverty indicators. The initial effort could focus on geographic targeting—expanding projects in low-income areas, where the poor are concentrated. Within these targeted areas, targeting could be seasonal. Within a targeted season, wage rates commensurate with the poor's reservation wages could be established. The mode of wage payment should depend on the local food market.

7. Integrate a maintenance strategy (organization, financing, monitoring, and maintenance) into the project during its formation. The problem of devising an appropriate incentive structure for community-owned (communal woodlots) or community-maintained assets (access roads) requires special attention.

8. Identify criteria for the success of programs, develop a systematic monitoring and evaluation system, and devise a structured, evaluation-response procedure.

REFERENCES

Asefa, S. 1989. *Managing food security action programs in Botswana.* Michigan State University International Development Working Paper 36. East Lansing, Mich., U.S.A.: Michigan State University.

Botswana CSO (Central Statistics Office). 1986. *Country profile.* Gaborone.

_____. 1991. *1991 population census . . . Preliminary results.* Gaborone.

Botswana MFDP (Ministry of Finance and Development Planning). 1991. *National development plan (NDP7), 1991–97.* Gaborone: Government Printer.

Botswana MLGL (Ministry of Local Government and Lands). Various years. *Annual report, Department of Food Resources.* Gaborone.

Brudefors, U. 1991. Labor-intensive road program. Gaborone. Mimeo.

Buchanan-Smith, M. 1990. *Drought and the rural economy in Botswana: An evaluation of the drought program, 1982–1990.* Food Studies Group Study Paper 2. Oxford: Food Studies Group.

Coulson, A. 1982. *Tanzania: A political economy.* Oxford: Clarendon Press.

Hagen, S., P. Guthrie, and D. Galetshoge. 1988. LG-34 district roads labor-intensive improvement and maintenance program—Botswana. Paper prepared for the Norwegian Ministry of Development Cooperation. Gaborone. Mimeo.

Hay, R. W. 1988. Famine incomes and employment: Has Botswana anything to teach Africa? *World Development* 16 (9): 1113–1125.

ILO (International Labour Office). 1991. Tanzania: Meeting the employment challenge. Geneva. Mimeo.

Kamuzora, C. L. 1990. Constraints to labor time availability in African smallholder agriculture: The case of Bukoba District, Tanzania. *Development and Change* 11: 123–125.

Manamela, N. J. 1993. The 1992–93 drought in Botswana—The relief program components, process, and outcomes. International Food Policy Research Institute, Washington, D.C. Mimeo.

Martens, B. 1989. *Economic development that lasts: Labor-intensive irrigation projects in Nepal and the United Republic of Tanzania.* Geneva: International Labour Office.

McCutcheon, R. 1988. The district roads program in Botswana. *Habitat International* 12 (1): 23–30.

Mueller, E. 1985. The value and allocation of time in rural Botswana. In *The household economy of rural Botswana—An African case*, ed. C. Dov, R. E. B. Lucas, and E. Mueller. World Bank Working Paper 715. Washington, D.C.: World Bank.

PMO/ILO (Prime Ministers Office/International Labour Office). 1989. Project Preparation Report for Ruvuma Rural Road Program. Dar es Salaam. Mimeo.

Quinn, V., M. Cotten, J. Mason, and B. N. Kgosioinis. 1988. Crisis-proofing the economy: The response of Botswana to economic recession and drought. In *Adjustment with a human face*, Vol. II., ed. G. A. Cornia, R. Jolly, and F. Steward, 3–27. New York: Oxford University Press.

Scheinman, D., C. Hongoke, and A. Ndaalio. 1989. Female participation in the rural roads maintenance project: The impact of employment on the lives of participating women. Report prepared for the Norwegian Agency for International Development (NORAD). Dar es Salaam. Mimeo.

Solberg, K., D. A. N. Nteta, and T. Tessem. 1990. Project review for the Norwegian Ministry of Development Cooperation. Dar es Salaam. Mimeo.

Tamoda, S., H. Myovela, and I. G. M. Muijsers. 1987. Women and special public works programs: A case study of the Mto-wa-Mbu and the Rukwa water supply projects. International Labour Office, Geneva. Mimeo.

Tanzania, Bureau of Statistics. Undated. 1990/91 labor force survey— Mainland Tanzania. Dar es Salaam. Mimeo.

_____. 1991. 1988 population census: Preliminary report. Dar es Salaam. Mimeo.

Valentine, R. T. 1990. Drought, transfer entitlements, and income distribution: The Botswana experience. Gaborone. Mimeo.

Van Demoortele, J. 1991. *Employment issues in Sub-Saharan Africa.* African Economic Research Consortium Special Paper 14. Nairobi, Kenya: African Economic Research Consortium.

Van der Does, M., and M. Kuik. 1989. Mnenia small-scale irrigation project—An impact study. Dar es Salaam. Mimeo.

7

EMPLOYMENT PROGRAMS FOR FOOD SECURITY IN RURAL AND URBAN AFRICA: EXPERIENCES IN NIGER AND ZIMBABWE

Patrick Webb

The food security and poverty-targeting potential of employment-based income transfers has long been recognized in many African countries, not least in Niger and Zimbabwe. Niger's experience with public works dates from the 1930s. Beginning with the great drought of the 1970s, the Nigerien government has increasingly emphasized small-scale programs to generate labor for soil and water conservation and to minimize the effects of future droughts. These programs have been supported by donors and nongovernmental organizations (NGOs) with close government collaboration, and they have a growing focus on urban food security problems. Zimbabwe's history of employment programs is even older, dating back to 1903 (Iliffe 1990). It, too, has shown an increasing reliance on public works in recent years, both in urban and rural settings. However, in contrast to Niger, Zimbabwe has implemented two major public programs of its own, based primarily on domestic food and budgetary resources.

This chapter examines some of the public works experiences of these two countries, particularly with regard to their short-term impact on food insecurity. Three major questions are addressed in relation to projects in both rural and urban areas. First, who participates in labor-based works projects, and why? Second, what is the impact of the project on household employment and income? Third, what obstacles do employment programs face in alleviating food insecurity and lifting long-term constraints on growth in semi-arid environments?

Few in-depth evaluations of the effects of participation on food-insecure households have been undertaken in either country. Noting the scarcity of in-depth evaluations, Drèze (1989) argues for "paying greater attention to . . . important 'success stories,' because serious studies of costs and benefits are not available." Such information is urgently needed, according to Rukuni and Eicher (1991), so that researchers can turn their "attention to converting grain to calories via food-for-work . . . to combat hunger and malnutrition." Without such information, the debate on the effectiveness of projects is waged in an informational vacuum. The two studies described in this chapter were designed to fill a few of the identified information gaps, and thereby contribute to the improved design of interventions to create employment and enhance food security.[1]

Programs and Settings: Why Contrast Niger's and Zimbabwe's Experience?

The semi-arid zone of Zimbabwe has been called the "Sahel of the South"—an area in which rainfed cultivation is often possible but never fully guaranteed (Iliffe 1990). The comparison is not without merit. As in the Sahel, Zimbabwe's dry regions are landlocked, their average rainfall is low,[2] and a large share of the population is chronically food-insecure. Yet, Zimbabwe differs from Sahelian countries like Niger in that it possesses large tracts of higher-altitude land (600 to 1,300 meters above sea level) that are fertile and generally very productive.

Why then are these two seemingly different countries brought together here as case studies? A number of factors make it appropriate to compare and contrast Niger and Zimbabwe. First, both have dynamic labor markets and their economies rely heavily on international migration and remittance flows from absent men to de facto women-headed households. Second, although agricultural economies, both countries have important mining sectors, a fact that distinguishes Niger from most of its neighbors. Third, urban growth in both countries stands at more than 7 percent per year, more than double the national rate of population growth. The fourth reason is that both countries spent much of the 1980s focused on the goal of national self-sufficiency in food production. Since the late 1980s, they have deemphasized national self-sufficiency, shifting toward a more specific policy of food security at the household level. Fifth, until recently, the agricultural policy of both countries was marked by centralized control over the marketing of key commodities through a complex system of price control and trade legislation. Both governments have been changing their approach to food policy since the late 1980s, leading to price deregulation and the progressive withdrawal of public control over the economy. Sixth,

---

[1]For details of the two studies, see Webb 1992 and Webb and Moyo 1992.

[2]Regularly under 400 millimeters per year, and, in 1991/92, under 200 millimeters.

both countries are prone to drought. Given that food production in both countries is heavily dependent on rainfed agriculture, periodic droughts represent a regular threat to domestic food supply. The 1973/74 drought resulted in a 50 percent decline in food supply and the loss of 33 percent of the national livestock herd in Niger (Somerville 1986). In 1984, rainfall was again 40 percent below the long-term average at a national level, resulting in a 50 percent shortfall in cereal harvest (Niger 1991; Borton and Nicholds 1992). More recently, drought has devastated Zimbabwe. In 1991/92, rainfall was barely 50 percent of the average, resulting in a national harvest that was just 20 percent of the normal (USAID 1992; FAO 1992). By 1993, 5 to 6 million people were registered for food assistance (USAID 1992; Webb and Moyo 1992).

Drought years aside, Niger has a remarkable record of balancing aggregate food supply with demand over the past 30 years. Between 1960 and 1990, domestic production delivered an average of 2,300–2,500 kilocalories per capita, above minimum requirements (SBW 1987; FAO 1990a; CARE 1990). Unfortunately, even in good harvest years, average food-availability figures tend to mask problems of severe malnutrition. The prevalence of chronic malnutrition in Niger ranges from 20 to 40 percent, with wasting ranging from 10 to 38 percent. These are among the worst figures in Africa (UNDP 1990; Bread for the World 1992). Similarly, Zimbabwe is known for its "agricultural miracle" of the 1980s (Drèze and Sen 1989). Between 1980 and 1985, output of maize almost doubled, with production in the smallholder sector rising threefold. However, stunting is recorded at 29 percent (37 percent in some areas), with wasting at 16 percent (Zimbabwe 1989; Mason 1990; World Bank 1992).

Finally, interest in employment programs in these countries shows little sign of abating. Donors, NGOs, and the governments continue to line up to invest in public works activities. But there are differences in approaches taken by the countries that are spelled out in more detail below.

Public Works Programs in Niger

Most of Niger's labor-based work programs grew out of emergency projects initiated in response to the 1973/74 drought and famine. These programs did not emphasize the sustainability of assets generated and few were ever properly evaluated. By the late 1970s, most projects had gained a development focus. In 1985, 180 small projects, primarily under NGO management, were being implemented, most using food as an incentive for mobilizing labor (World Bank 1988). In addition to this, a large number of projects were funded by international donors, such as the World Food Programme (WFP) and the World Bank, operating in collaboration with government ministries. At least 14 donors and NGOs were supporting labor-based works programs at more than 100 sites in Niger during 1992.

Table 7.1 presents a profile of some of the programs implemented in Niger since the early 1980s. This incomplete list indicates that more than US$150 million has been invested in projects with a high labor content between the early 1980s and 1990s. This investment has generated more than 22 million days of work, which has mostly been applied to halting erosion and improving soil and water management in the semi-arid zones. This represents a significant development input via a single instrument. WFP alone supported 8.3 million workdays between 1989 and 1992 at a cost of more than US$19 million, 71 percent of which was dedicated to erosion-control activities (WFP/Niamey, unpublished records).

A number of important points emerge from Table 7.1. First, there is a distinct rural bias. Nine out of 10 projects are located in more remote, usually semi-arid, parts of the country. This pattern is partly the result of historical inertia: organizations that responded to previous famines have remained in areas likely to be vulnerable again (FAO 1990a, 1990b; WFP 1991). But the preponderance of rural projects also reflects the fact that urban food security has only recently become a public concern. More recently, the balance has shifted in favor of urban activities.

The second point is that most rural projects focus on natural resource conservation, rather than on road building, livestock projects, or irrigation development. Environmental degradation is one of Niger's greatest constraints and Lipton (1989) has argued that "public works programs have probably the best capacity for mitigating environmental degradation." This is because the most common, and most effective, measures against degradation cannot be implemented by machinery alone. The techniques employed for soil and water management require from 50 to 300 person-days of labor per hectare of "recovered" land (Derrier 1991). It is, therefore, these types of activity that dominate Niger's portfolio of labor-based projects.

The third point is that the mode and level of payment for project participants vary across projects. It is clear that food-for-work (FFW) predominates in the rural areas, while cash-for-work (CFW) has so far been associated with the urban projects. Voluntary labor inputs are universally wished for by project managers, and sometimes written into donor-community contracts.

The fourth point to be highlighted is that a large share of rural participants are women (60–80 percent). Most rural projects try to avoid direct competition with agricultural operations and, therefore, concentrate activities during the dry season. Since this is the season of male emigration, projects offering a low (usually food) wage are attractive to the poorest of the remaining workforce, namely women.

Table 7.1—Profiles of selected labor-intensive public works programs in Niger in the 1980s and early 1990s

Primary Task	Years of Operation	Area Covered	Participation	Work-days Created	Salary Type[a]	Female Involvement[b] (1,000)	Project Costs — Donor (percent)	Project Costs — Government (percent)	Main Donors (US$ million)[c]
Soil works, trees	1976–84	Tahoua	1,500 households	?	F	50	0.02	...	SWISSAID, Tahoua
	1985–2005				V		0.3[e]	?	Catholic Mission, WFP
Terracing, gullying	1981–87	Tahoua	148 villages	?	F, V	80	3.3	...	KFW, GTZ, WFP, DED
	1988–92						4.7	0.5	
Terracing, soil works	1984–91	Keita	5,000 households	4,200	F, C	65	33.0	1.2	Italy, FAO, WFP, UNDP
	1992–96		22,000 households	5,700	F, V	50	28.3	0.7	
Trees, soil works	1984–88	Tahoua	1,000 households	30	F	70	?	...	UNSO, Holland, UNDP
	1989–92			50[d]			0.2	?	SNV, Holland, WFP
Terracing, gullying	1986–90	Tillaberi	150 villages	6	F, V	50	3.3	?	KFW, GTZ, WFP, DED
	1991–95	Tahoua					10.5	0.2	
Terracing, gullying	1987–90	Galmi	11 villages	80	F	85	0.6	?	CARE, WFP, USAID
	1990–93			70			0.5	?	
Roads, wells, trees	1987–89	Maradi	300 households	36	F, C	5	0.4	...	ILO, UNDP, UNCDF
Trees, soil works	1987–93	Dosso	40 villages	?	V, FI	20	2.0	?	UNSO, UNDP
Irrigation, soil works, pastoral	1988–92	Tahoua	7,000 households	?	F, V	50	27.6	0.7	IFAD, WFP, UNDP
Irrigation, trees	1989–95	Dosso	7,000 households	?	C	40	17.1	0.9	World Bank, KFW, EEC
Urban sanitation, soil works, roads	1990–94		?	10,000	C	10	25.0	2.7	World Bank, EEC, KFW, UNDP

Source: Data obtained from the offices listed under "Main Donors" and from the Office of NIGETIP.

Notes: The list of programs is not exhaustive. The full names of the acronyms for donors are as follows: SWISSAID, Swiss Agency for International Development; WFP, World Food Programme; KFW, German Bank for Reconstruction; GTZ, German Agency for Technical Cooperation; DED, German Development Service; FAO, Food and Agriculture Organization of the United Nations; UNDP, United Nations Development Programme; UNSO, United Nations Sudano-Sahelian Office; SNV, Dutch Volunteer Service; USAID, United States Agency for International Development; ILO, International Labour Office; UNCDF, United Nations Capital Development Funds; IFAD, International Fund for Agricultural Development; EEC, European Economic Community.

[a] F = Food wage; V = Voluntary participation (no wage); FI = Food Incentive; C = Cash wage.
[b] Estimates based on project reports.
[c] CFA franc converted at a rate of 285/US$ (the rate for April 1991).
[d] Estimates based on averages for 1989–91.

In urban areas, by contrast, male participants predominate by more than 99 percent. The urban schemes were initiated on a pilot basis in 1990. They represent an attempt to organize private implementation of publicly funded projects. The Agence Nigerienne de Travaux d'Interet Public pour l'Emploi (NIGETIP) was created as a private NGO (supported by donors such as the World Bank and the European Community as well as the Nigerien government) to disburse funds through a bidding process to private agencies for public works. It is a small agency with less than 30 staff, organized into four departments: a director general's office, a finance and accounts department, a department for economic analysis and public relations, and a management and technical supervision department.

NIGETIP's three main objectives are to generate short-term jobs; to stimulate the private sector by funding the implementation of projects through small local enterprises; and to generate public goods and services through labor-intensive technology (World Bank 1990; Niger 1990). Private construction, architecture, and engineering firms make closed bids for the contract—the lowest bid by an accredited firm making a commitment to allocate at least 20 percent of total costs to salaried labor wins the contract.

In 1991, six pilot projects were implemented in the capital, Niamey. During their test operation, they generated 3,500 workdays, mostly in road construction, drain clearing, refuse collection, and soil conservation works. In 1992, NIGETIP went into full operation and expanded its coverage to all urban centers in the country. Over 200 firms have been accredited for placing bids for over 100 contracts during the year. For example, 27,000 workdays were generated by a dozen projects during the month of April alone (NIGETIP 1992).

At their outset, the urban schemes were overwhelmed by demand for work from the city's long-term unemployed males. Since the projects registered participants on a "first come, first served" basis, unemployed male household heads were usually first in line. Many women (nonhousehold heads) have expressed a desire to participate, but their involvement is constrained by the volume of male demand.

Public Works in Zimbabwe

Zimbabwe's rich public works experience is long and unusually rich. Labor-intensive public works programs have always played a major role in Zimbabwe's food security interventions through short-term employment provision and longer-term infrastructure development. Unlike Niger, Zimbabwe conceived two of its own large-scale programs based on interministerial cooperation for the disbursement of (largely) indigenous resources. The coverage of these programs has been considerable: between 1984/85 and 1991/92, more than 400 million in Zimbabwe dollars (Z$) has been spent by the government on wages, generating some 47 million days of work.

Food-for-Work Program. Initiated in 1989, this program was designed to supplant large-scale distributions of free food that had taken place annually since the 1981/82 drought (Bratton 1987). Over 2 million people depended on relief food for survival during the 1982–1984 period. A decade later, during the 1992 crisis, the number of people dependent on free food distribution had risen to 6 million. The government decided to suspend free food because of three problems: first, household targeting was thought to be inadequate, thereby spreading scarce resources too thinly; second, there was sometimes poor targeting at a regional level; and third, criticism of the perceived dependency of recipients on free food (Takavarasha and Rukovo 1990; Lenneiye 1991; Rukuni, Mudimu, and Jayne 1990; Moyo 1992).

The idea of basing drought relief on employment rather than on free food was implemented in October 1989. The program was designed to operate from the bottom up, with projects identified by villagers themselves and provincial technicians assessing, approving, and supervising appropriate plans. Appropriateness is measured in terms of community benefit, technical feasibility, and labor intensity. The latter is important because the government's budget allocation for the program only covers the purchase of food, its transportation, and the salaries of program staff. In other words, projects cannot require substantial material inputs. The largest number of projects in 1991, therefore, involved brick molding and small building construction, activities generally completed without additional material inputs. Other activities included water control projects (dam and weir construction or rehabilitation) and construction and maintenance of feeder roads.

Wages, initially set at 10 kilograms of maize per capita per month (supplemented where possible by beans and dried meat or fish), have varied since 1989, according to supply and demand constraints. Prior to 1992, only households that did not own livestock were eligible to be registered. In late 1992, this screening criterion was removed because of the danger of households selling animals at severely depressed prices solely in order to be accepted as participants.

The program has been both praised and criticized. Although proponents highlighted the "self-reliance" of the new program in contrast to the "dependency" of the earlier handouts, most praise is directed toward the program's food security impact during drought years (*Zimbabwe News* 1989; *The Herald* 1990). Sachikonye (1992), for example, argues that "what stopped [food shortages in 1990] from escalating into a widespread famine in the rural districts was the availability of 'food-for-work.'"

Table 7.2 shows the coverage and some of the costs of the program. Part of the large expansion in 1992 was supported by a US$23 million grant from the World Bank. This grant, and other donor support, is not fully reflected in the costs reported in Table 7.2. Thus, while nominal costs per capita of the food-for-work scheme appear to fall into the same range as those for the free food system, real costs are certainly higher and were still rising in 1993.

It should be underscored that the food-for-work program has reached more people than the free food system, both in absolute and relative terms. However, there are three important shortcomings in the program. First, less than two-thirds of officially recognized need is met by the food-for-work program. Second, productivity-enhancement based on structural output of the program is minimal. Third, it has proved difficult to expand the scale of the program to meet emergency needs. The 1991/92 drought exposed the static nature of the program.

Key constraints in all three cases can be traced to a lack of funding. For example, only 60 percent of the Z$25 million required for activities in May 1991 was released by central accounts—due to a shortage of funds for all programs because of structural adjustment effects either "compounded by" or "combined with" the drought. This lack of funding affects all levels of program operation, from staffing to transportation of equipment (Lenneiye 1991; Sachikonye 1992; Berg 1992).

Planning and operational constraints were clearly exposed by the 1991/92 drought. As the number of people who registered to participate rose from an average of 800,000 per month in 1991 to almost 3 million per month in mid-1992, the program had to expand rapidly to five times its

Table 7.2—Characteristics of Zimbabwe's food-for-work program, selected months between 1989 and 1992

	1989[a]	1990[b]	1991	1992[c]
		(1,000)		
People employed[d]	612	1,130	1,128	2,242
Food wages paid (tons)	5,973	9,938	10,983	20,761
Total cost (Z$)[e]	1,661	3,412	3,733	n.a.
Cost per capita (Z$)	4	3	3	n.a.

Sources: Compiled from data supplied by the Ministry of Labour, Manpower Planning, and Social Welfare.
[a]For October through December (the first three months of the program).
[b]For January through March and August through December (April to July was suspended).
[c]For January through September (provisional).
[d]Average number of workers per month.
[e]Averaged per month of operation.

predrought scale of operation—in essence, to convert from a prototype employment program back to a huge emergency relief program, but without the necessary resources.

The Public Works Program (PWP). This is Zimbabwe's second major national program. The program differs from food-for-work in several important ways. First, in contrast to the welfare orientation of the food-for-work program, Zimbabwe's national cash-for-work program was originally designed to accomplish development objectives. Although the government launched the program in 1984, when drought relief—not job creation—was high on the political agenda, the PWP is based on popular participation in labor-intensive activities.

Second, it relies less on participant selection of activities and more on a cadre of technicians to develop projects with high priority in national and regional development plans. Third, construction materials and tools are provided, including heavy equipment for digging, moving earth, and laying roads. Fourth, wages are paid in cash, originally at Z$44 per month but rising to Z$88 per month in 1989. Despite the program's emphasis on development, rather than relief, criteria for participation are the same as those for receiving free food: (1) no regular income, (2) no food stocks, and (3) no more than 10 head of cattle per household. Once participants are registered for the PWP, their names are removed from the free food or food-for-work registers.

The most recent phase was initiated in 1991, with plans for continuation into 1996. The 1991/92 national budget allocated Z$10 million to start the first phase of a "production-oriented Z$50 million Public Works Programme" (Chidzero 1991). At least 200,000 people are expected to benefit from the program. Moreover, these benefits are realized at a lower cost to the state than if the same activities had been implemented by the private sector (Zimbabwe 1990). In the first year (1991/92), work was pursued on 290 projects, 85 of which were completed.

There has been a clear emphasis since inception of the PWP on infrastructure creation, particularly the provision of water (irrigation as well as piped water and wells) and the development of roads and bridges. These two categories have accounted for more than 60 percent of program expenditure between 1988 and 1991, and will continue to represent more than half of the PWP's investments up to 1996. By contrast, no investments have been made in environment works (soil and water conservation) since 1988, and only minimal work has been done on projects designed to boost agricultural productivity.

In all cases, however, labor has constituted a relatively small component of project budgets, representing only 11 percent of the total in

1987/88, 24 percent the following year, and 17 percent for the 1991–96 phase. Materials take the lion's share of funds. This unequal allocation underlines the PMP's emphasis on infrastructure—and not employment creation objectives. But, it also points to a major obstacle to rapid expansion of the program as a mechanism for drought relief.

Household Participation and Household and Intrahousehold Effects

A question mark continues to hang over the issue of how best to measure success and failure in public works. The strength of well-designed public works—simultaneous action on several fronts—is also its weakness in evaluation terms.

The effect of a program on food security (a transfer of calories to vulnerable households) can be measured in terms of how effectively it delivered calories to target populations. The employment effect (how many jobs created, and with what income benefit) can be measured not just in costs per job, but also as a distributional outcome—how many of the poor received employment and to what extent has the distribution of jobs mitigated local poverty? And, asset creation (physical structures generated and resources enhanced) can be evaluated in costs per kilometer or costs per hectare, and also in regional economic multiplier effects and national-level food security. Few projects clearly specify their highest priority, although approaches to project design and implementation vary considerably according to these priorities. The result is uncertainty over which indicators of success need to be collected or represent the brunt of the project's effort.

The findings presented in the following section, based on surveys of five projects in Niger and surveys of each national program in Zimbabwe, relate primarily to one indicator, short-term food security. The surveys were done by IFPRI in cooperation with the Institut National de Recherches Agronomiques du Niger (INRAN) and with the Zimbabwe Institute for Development Studies (ZIDS).

Who Participates and Why?

The projects surveyed in both countries were highly effective in targeting poverty. For example, Table 7.3 compares selected demographic and income characteristics of participants heavily involved in the scheme versus those

Table 7.3—Selected demographic, income, and wealth characteristics of households in Niger and Zimbabwe with low or high participation in public works projects, 1990/91

Indicator	Zimbabwe Participation Groups		Niger Participation Groups	
	Low	High	Low	High
Demographics				
Attended primary school (percent)	83.0	65.0	10.0	0.5
Mean household size[a]	5.0	3.0	6.0	3.0
Wealth indicators				
Index of income per capita	100.0	67.0	100.0	48.0
Livestock assets (TLU per capita)[b]	1.2	2.0	1.1	0.7
Area cultivated (hectare per capita)	0.4	0.6	0.3	0.1
Crop income (US$ per capita)	160.4	120.2	128.0	139.0
Participation				
Days of project work per household per year	4.0	30.0	27.0	210.0
Project wages as share of income (percent)	8.0	33.0	4.0	20.0

Sources: IFPRI/ZIDS 1991 survey, IFPRI/INRAN 1991/92 survey.
[a]Members actually present during the previous six months.
[b]TLU refers to tropical livestock units, where small animals are expressed in cattle equivalents according to feed utilization.

less involved.[3] The table shows a strong correspondence between degree of participation and selected indicators of poverty. In Zimbabwe, the households that participate the most in public works tend to be smaller than richer households (three members versus five), the household heads are less well educated, and they are more dependent on agriculture. Dependence on agriculture is demonstrated by higher livestock holdings and greater area cultivated per capita, but lower productivity (measured in terms of income) and less land cultivated. Public works participants have an income that is only 67 percent of that of nonparticipant households.

---

[3]The degree of project involvement per household was assessed after the survey according to the total number of days worked on the project during the preceding 12-month period. For the cash-for-work participants, recall data were obtained on participation during the last six months of project operation (since these particular projects were suspended in March 1991). "Participant groups" were then divided equally from a ranking of all sample households. The "low participation" group includes households that did not participate in project work at all.

Some of these findings are similar in Niger. For example, heads of households most active in employment projects tend to be less well educated, even at a primary school level. Thus, they are at a disadvantage in the job market. This disadvantage is compounded by the fact that households with high participation in project work are half as large as those less involved. Smaller household size restricts nonfarm activities, thereby resulting in a lower income per capita and fewer livestock. The income index of project participants is, therefore, less than one-half that of households with little or no involvement in public works.

Other characteristics confirm the association between high participation and poverty. Table 7.4 shows the results of a dichotomous logit decision model for Niger. The estimated (log) odd-ratio parameters and associated mean-level probabilities provide preliminary predictions of whether a person is likely to participate in project work or not. The model, which explains 95 percent of 4,000 cases, indicates the following:

- The likelihood of participation increases with age (starting at six years), but, as would be expected, only up to a certain age; beyond this, the probability of participation decreases.

Table 7.4—Maximum likelihood estimates for project participation, logit model for Niger

Explanatory Variable	Parameter Estimate[a]	t-Ratio
Age (of individual)	0.68	0.10
Age squared	−0.40	−0.43
Household size	0.39	4.95
Own education (primary)	−0.25	−5.65
Head's education (secondary)	−0.41	−7.13
Gender of head (if male)	−1.78	−1.96
Child dependency ratio[b]	0.92	4.68
Female ratio[c]	2.23	2.45
Farm income[d]	1.83	3.23
Remittance income[e,f]	−1.84	−3.25
Body Mass Index[f]	−0.52	14.40
Log likelihood	−644.42	

Source: IFPRI/INRAN 1991/92 survey.
[a]Calculated for 3,810 individuals over 6 years old, of both genders.
[b]Number of children in household divided by household size.
[c]Ratio of adult women to total adults.
[d]Share of own crop and livestock income in total household income.
[e]Share of remittance and transfer income to total household income.
[f]Further estimations have to be run to determine the degree of exogeneity of this variable.

- Larger poor households with many adults are more likely to participate than smaller poor households, because there are more hands to earn an income and more mouths to feed.
- Education lowers participation: the more years spent in primary education by the individual and the higher the level of secondary education of the head of that individual's household, the less likely the person is to participate in the project. This aversion stems from the wage levels or wage expectations associated with having an education.
- The odds of participation are high for households that have a narrow or restricted income base and who are, therefore, heavily dependent on agriculture for most of their income. Where income is more diversified (for example, when it comes largely from outside remittances), households are less likely to participate.
- Individuals with a low nutritional status (low Body Mass Index) typically have the greatest need for employment income and are, therefore, very likely to participate in project activities.
- Households with a high child-dependency ratio and a high share of female adults and those that are headed by a woman (typically the poorest households) are more likely to participate than other households. This is driven by the strong need for income to compensate for that not provided by male adults.

Women-headed households are defined here as those in which no adult males have lived during the previous year. Households left without a male tend to be disadvantaged and poor. As a result, public works that target the poor also often target women. In the present survey, a larger share of households were headed by women in the high-participation group (22 percent) than in the low-participation group (10 percent).

In the urban projects, by contrast, few women participated. This was because the offer of a cash wage in an environment of high unemployment brought men into competition with women for limited work places. (Spaces are limited because projects are small and cash wages are supplied on a "first come, first served" basis.) Unemployed men quickly filled the available positions, squeezing women out of these projects.

In the rural projects, some of the poorest households sent up to five people to the same project to draw salaries. This nonscreened approach to participation probably improved the food security impact of employment on the larger households involved. However, given that scarce resources impose a limit on the size of each project, multiple salaries to the same household raise two problems: (1) they restrict overall coverage of the intervention, and (2) they encourage households to take advantage of salaries by sending elderly and child participants, thereby lowering the average productivity of project participants.

While children did not participate at all in projects in Zimbabwe, their participation was high in Niger (Table 7.5). Although most workers in high-participation households in Niger were women in the age group of 16-55 years (38 percent), the second largest group comprised children between the ages of 5 and 15 (25 percent). Of these children, more than 6 percent were aged 5 to 9. The youngest child working a full day and receiving a salary was only 6 years old. In the low-participation group, the share of children was somewhat lower, at roughly 18 percent. The largest share of workers in the low-participation households were men in the category of 16-55 years (67 percent of total workers).

There is great potential for making the exploitation of children (and women) a serious issue. More than 65 percent of the sample individuals were aged less than 15 years at the time of the survey, with 50 percent aged less than 25. This means that the pool of child labor is large. And, children are often more active and effective than the elderly men and women present at project sites (those aged more than 56 years). The latter slowly gather gravel and soil for filling holes between stones in bunds, or dig shallow pits for seedling planting. With explicit physical targets to be

Table 7.5—Involvement in public works by age, gender, and participation groups, Zimbabwe and Niger

Project Participants	Zimbabwe Participation Groups[a]		Niger Participation Groups[a]	
	High	Low	High	Low
	(percent of households)			
Males				
5–8 years	. . .	. . .	4.1	7.7
9–15 years	. . .	. . .	11.9	2.6
16–35 years	42.0	33.0	16.2	38.5
36–55 years	. . .	1.0	8.9	29.5
56–80 years	58.0	41.0	1.6	1.3
Females				
5–8 years	. . .	. . .	2.4	1.3
9–15 years	. . .	. . .	15.1	5.1
16–35 years	. . .	. . .	22.7	7.7
36–55 years	100.0	. . .	15.4	5.1
56–80 years	. . .	. . .	1.6	1.3

Source: IFPRI/INRAN 1991/92 survey.
Note: The ellipses (. . .) indicate a nil or negligible number.
[a]Each of the participation groups is divided into 133 households.

achieved, the advantages of younger (often more manageable) workers are obvious.

However, children were not hired in order to make up work quotas, to meet productivity deadlines, or to save capital. It should be noted that child participants were only found at the rural survey sites. Since there were no women participants in the urban projects, children were not to be found there either. The converse was true of the rural sites—the more women present, the more children present. In other words, most children were following their mothers and, if able, were working alongside them. It appeared that most children were hired for work only if their mother was present, only if household need was perceived to be great, and only if the child was deemed fit. These children are working for a salary when they should generally be attending school. But, there are few rural schools and the alternative to paid public works is usually unpaid household or farm-based chores.

It is clear that adult women make up a sizable share of adult workers— 60 percent of the sample if urban sites are excluded. The women work long and hard even after walking 8 kilometers from the village to the work site.

Figure 7.1 shows the characteristics of female workers during the dry season, broken down by regression tree analysis into clusters according to various demographic features. This figure demonstrates that, contrary to what many planners assume, the bulk of women participants are not of child-bearing age. The groups with the highest average number of days of participation are, first, adolescents (aged 10 to 17) in female-headed households with few adult women; and, second, older women (over age 41) from households with few young children and therefore no need for the attention of a grandmother. Child-bearing women aged 17 to 41 are apparently doing other things.

According to the figure, more than 220 girls less than 17 years old were working in these projects. (And that does not count the boys.) This means that the pool of child labor is large. More than 65 percent of the sample individuals were less than 25 at the time of the survey, with 50 percent less than 25.

A recent World Food Programme report (WFP 1991) recommends setting a lower age limit of 12 in order to reduce the number of children found at public works sites. Preventing small children from working for a wage at the site is certainly desirable. But, preventing children from coming to a site with their mothers may not be the best alternative. One benefit of such facilities would be to ensure that mothers with children retained access to jobs. The income earned from public works is substantial for the workers from the poorest households; preventing their access to such income must be carefully considered in the light of other income-earning opportunities for such households.

Figure 7.1—Regression tree analysis of days worked in public works by rural girls and women in Niger during the dry season of 1990

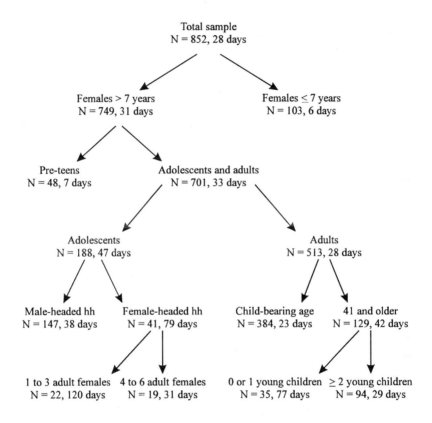

Total sample
N = 852, 28 days

Females > 7 years
N = 749, 31 days

Females ≤ 7 years
N = 103, 6 days

Pre-teens
N = 48, 7 days

Adolescents and adults
N = 701, 33 days

Adolescents
N = 188, 47 days

Adults
N = 513, 28 days

Male-headed hh
N = 147, 38 days

Female-headed hh
N = 41, 79 days

Child-bearing age
N = 384, 23 days

41 and older
N = 129, 42 days

1 to 3 adult females
N = 22, 120 days

4 to 6 adult females
N = 19, 31 days

0 or 1 young children
N = 35, 77 days

≥ 2 young children
N = 94, 29 days

Variables used in the analysis:
    Number of adult females in household
    Age of the individual
    Number of young children (less than 10 years of age) in household
    Female-headed households? (Yes/No)
    Number of adult males in household
    Number of old people (more than 65 years of age) in household
    Individual's years of formal education
    Anyone in household migrated for work? (Yes/No)

Source: IFPRI/INRAN 1991/92 survey.

The provision of child-care facilities at the work site would also benefit most households, by reducing the risk to newborn infants (carried on their mothers' back) of dehydration or a fall. Such facilities could serve as the focus for nonwage, resource transfers to the self-selected participants. These resources might include literacy training, general health care, supplementation and monitoring of child nutrition, adult education and training, and the provision of investment or consumption credit.

Income Effects

High levels of participation by poor households in public works can lift their salaries above those received by wealthier households. The public works income, which arrives in regular and small quantities, also serves to ease potential food shortages when household food reserves become depleted.

Project income represented 20 percent of total household income for the poor in Niger, while wealthier households earned only 4 percent of their income from project participation. Two-thirds of poor households' total income from the project was earned during the dry season. Thus, the poor, who have fewer nonfarm income sources, are far more dependent on public works for their short-term food security than are wealthier households. For the poor households in Zimbabwe, project income represented a significant 33 percent of total household income (total income here excludes unearned income, such as transfers and remittances). Richer households, by contrast, participate only minimally and so they derive a much smaller share of total income from public works employment.

It should be stressed that public works represent but one income-earning option among many. When income is broken down by farm and nonfarm sources (Table 7.6), nonfarm income plays a more important role among the poorer, high-participant households than among the richer, low-participant households in studies of both countries.

Crop and livestock husbandry represents the single most important source of income in both countries, amounting to roughly 45 percent of total income for all rural households in Niger and 70 percent in Zimbabwe. The latter figure is high because remittances and transfers are excluded from the calculation: if these were included, the relative shares would be quite similar. Other major income sources, aside from public works, include petty commerce such as food stalls in Niger and nonfarm labor wages in both countries. Despite this wide range of options for nonfarm activities, few poor households substitute public works for other activities.

Table 7.6—Income sources in Zimbabwe and Niger, by high and low participation in public works projects, 1990/91

Source of Income	Zimbabwe Participation Groups		Niger Participation Groups	
	High	Low	High	Low
	(percent of total income)			
Own-farm production				
Cropping	61.6	84.6	42.9	39.8
Livestock	1.0	0.1	2.6	4.1
Wage labor				
Public works	33.3	3.9	19.8	4.3
Nonfarm	3.9	5.1	0.8	3.4
Civil service	. . .	0.1	. . .	0.1
Trade				
Petty commerce	. . .	1.6	10.6	17.1
Restaurateuring	n.a.	n.a.	3.2	1.2
Artisanal				
Craft work	. . .	0.5	1.3	1.7
Small business	n.a.	n.a.	0.1	0.0
Remittances	n.a.	n.a.	11.5	15.2
Other	n.a.	n.a.	7.2	13.2
Total	100.0	100.0	100.0	100.0

Source: IFPRI/INRAN 1991/92 survey; IFPRI/ZIDS 1991 survey.
Note: The ellipses (. . .) indicate a nil or negligible amount.

Food Consumption and Nutrition Effects

The largest share of project income is spent on food. In Niger, the poor allocate almost 70 percent of total expenditure to food purchases, versus 43 percent for those with higher incomes. More than 90 percent of respondents reported that food consumption was the main reason for participation. In Zimbabwe, 95 percent of the food received by food-for-work participants was consumed at home. However, only 35 percent of the money received by participants in the cash-paying public works program was spent on food. In the wet season, almost 70 percent was reinvested in the farm through purchases of fertilizer and hired labor. In other words, relatively more of the wage is consumed at home if paid in food, but, at the same time, public works can serve to increase longer-term food security through agricultural development via the reinvestment of cash wages. Both outcomes represent important benefits.

Since increasing food consumption is a major reason given for partici-pating in public works, it seems logical that the most malnourished would have the highest rates of participation in public works. Determining whether this is the case is central to the issue of targeting—who should work and what subsistence wage should be provided? However, as Kennedy and Alderman (1987) recognize, "the nutritional effects of [public works] pro-grams . . . have not been studied" and, therefore, "virtually no evidence yet exists to document the effects of food-for-work projects on individuals within families."

Although it has been shown that caloric intake and nutritional status are not perfectly correlated (since morbidity, genetic, and behavioral factors play an intervening role), inadequate caloric consumption, linked with inadequate nutrient consumption, does play a major role in determining nutritional status (ACC-SCN 1989; Kennedy, Bouis, and von Braun 1992). While the present data are only cross-sectional in nature, they provide some very important insights into nutritional differences in different re-gions and households in the same year.

The results of anthropometric measurements taken from almost 1,000 children from 6 months to 5 years old in Niger at the time of the household consumption survey (Table 7.7) underscore the persistence of high levels of malnutrition among Nigerien households, even in a good harvest year. For example, there is a tendency for children in high-participation households to be more malnourished than children in low-participation households, and for children in rural households to show more signs of unsatisfactory nutritional status than those in households in towns. The differences be-tween groups are highly significant in terms of weight-for-height for both genders. Differences in weight-for-age (a measure of short-term wasting) are also highly significant for boys, but not for girls.

These results suggest that, without the 20 percent share of total in-come derived from public works, children in the poorest households might be more severely malnourished—as long as participation itself does not compromise child health and nutrition as a result of reduced care. This possibility must be examined through more complex analysis of the data in the future.

Children may not be the only ones suffering poor nutrition. Men in high-participation households show a significant tendency to have a lower Body Mass Index (BMI) (18.3) than those in low-participation households (19.7) (Table 7.8). (The average BMI of male and female adults was 19.0.) The same holds true, and is statistically significant, for women. Interest-ingly, when tested against the gender of household head, no significant difference was perceived between the BMI of women in male- and female-headed households.

Table 7.7—Z-scores for height-for-age, weight-for-age, and weight-for-height (all-round average) for preschoolers (6 to 60 months), Niger, 1990/91

	Average Z-Score[a]		
Child	Weight-for-Height	Height-for-Age	Weight-for-Age
Boys			
Participation groups			
High	−1.44**	−2.12	−2.35**
Low	−0.75**	−1.67	−1.66**
Location			
Rural	−1.35*	−2.13	−2.33*
Urban	−0.53*	−1.60	−1.44*
Girls			
Participation groups			
High	−1.48**	−1.19	−1.93
Low	−0.78**	−1.21	−1.41
Location			
Rural	−1.33**	−1.39	−1.94*
Urban	−0.61**	−1.20	−1.30**

Source: IFPRI/INRAN 1991/92 survey.

[a] $\text{Z-Score} = \dfrac{(\text{Actual measurement} - \text{50th percentile standard})}{\text{Standard deviation of the standard}}$.

The standard used is derived from NCHS (1977).

*Significant at the 5 percent level.
**Significant at the 1 percent level.

These findings confirm the successful self-targeting of public works. The poorest and most malnourished make the most use of the employment. But, they also raise the issue of how great is the project's net impact on food security. Nutritional status is the result of net energy balance; it is determined by energy expenditure as well as by consumption. This means that heavy activity in public works programs may fail to improve an individual's nutritional status if the increased labor effort required offsets the positive effect of the wage transferred (Higgins and Alderman 1992). Empirical evidence of this is, however, slim.

What is more, at least two other outcomes are also possible: (1) the individual's nutritional status may not improve because of the tax on energy, but children in that person's household may benefit from transfer of calories to them; or (2) the individual's own nutritional status may improve at the expense of other members of the household because of the unequal intrahousehold distribution of the income gained.

Table 7.8—Body Mass Indices for adults aged 15 to 65, by participation group, location, and gender of household head, Niger, 1990/91

| | Body Mass Index[a] | |
Adult	Males	Females
Participation groups[b]		
High	18.3**	18.7**
Low	19.7**	19.5**
Location		
Rural	18.6**	18.8**
Urban	20.1**	19.7**

Source: IFPRI/INRAN 1991/92 survey.
[a]Calculated as Weight (Height)^2. The "normal" range of the Body Mass Index (BMI) runs from 18.5 to 25.0. Individuals below 18.5 are bordering on undernutrition; those below 17.5 are likely to be considerably malnourished.
[b]The sample was truncated to exclude individuals with a BMI of less than 15 or above 28. Inclusion of these outliers would have unduly biased the sample results. Nevertheless, the number of valid cases used for these calculations was high: 454 men and 530 women.
*Significant at the 5 percent level.
**Significant at the 1 percent level.

It is worth noting at this point that a statistically significant difference (at the 5 percent level) was found in the BMIs of actual project workers and of other nonworking adults in participating households. The average BMI of a female worker in high-participant households was 18.4 compared with an average of 19.3 for women in the same households not participating in project activities. In low-participant households, the difference is greater still, with workers showing a BMI of 17.9 versus 20.2 for nonworkers.

These last findings suggest that it may be the more food-insecure individuals in food-insecure households, possibly junior members of the household, who participate most in public works in order to gain a private income that is not available elsewhere. An alternative reading would argue that workers do indeed gain a valuable income for food-insecure households, but that they themselves do not enjoy a net benefit in incremental calories consumed. Further analysis is required in order to shed light on this problem.

Conclusions

The results from these two case-study countries indicate that the short-term impact of wage employment on food security can be considerable. Households most involved in public works are poorer than households less involved; the heads of these households tend to be less educated than heads of relatively richer households (and are therefore less able to command higher wages elsewhere); and the poorer participant households have a less diversified income base, which means that income from public works represents a much larger share of total household earned income than it does among richer households.

These results suggest that if more food-insecure households were able to gain regular access to public employment, the short-term income (and food consumption) gains would be substantial. At the same time, if the technical viability of generated assets could be improved through neater dovetailing with regional development plans and a better supply of non-wage inputs, the longer-term food security effect of such programs could also be considerably enhanced.

Richer and poorer households obviously live side by side, but have very different income-earning options and expressed preferences. But in projects that are designed to target them, it is the very poor, urban and rural, who present themselves for work. In Niger, the effectiveness of poverty-targeting can be ascribed to a number of factors: (1) wage rates that are below prevailing market rates in real terms (despite minimum wage legislation); (2) limited administrative screening of prospective participants (that would exclude elderly women and children); (3) targeting public works to regions ranked by severe environmental degradation or food insecurity; and (4) a large coefficient of variation in incomes even in such regions.

In order to maximize food security through future programs, these conditions argue for greater targeting within food-insecure regions, as well as the setting of clearer guidelines for the targeting of individuals. One by-product of successful poverty-targeting is de facto age- and gender-targeting. This occurs because (1) women-headed households tend to be poorer than average, and their heads participate in the absence of male adults; (2) even in poor male-headed households, women participate when the husband's time bears higher opportunity costs or when he is temporarily absent from the house (migrating for work); and (3) participating women from poor households bring children with them, either to earn an additional wage or because there is no child care at home.

In Zimbabwe, the poverty effect is determined more by administrative screening and stronger geographical targeting. The national programs considered have succeeded in generating millions of person-days of work. Yet, both could achieve much more. The food-for-work scheme suffers from a distinct welfare bias in that the poverty-targeting effect of a low wage and self-selection mechanism has been diluted by a screening process that spreads scarce resources too thinly to help the large numbers of absolute poor. At the same time, technical and nonwage inputs to individual projects are insufficient and cannot generate productive or sustainable assets.

The Public Works Program, by contrast, has been constrained by its longer-term development orientation. The benefits of the Public Works Program are transferred to a narrow range of households, because the program employs far fewer people, placing greater emphasis on real ability to work for regular wages. The low employment ceiling set by this program (due to its reliance on heavy equipment) necessarily excludes large numbers of food-insecure households. Its own funding deficiencies have led to transportation bottlenecks—spare parts have always been scarce or faulty and the replacement of worn equipment has not been a priority. The potential for a rapid expansion of this program to meet food crises, consequently, is low.

Despite the difficulties outlined, both Niger's and Zimbabwe's employment programs have the potential to strengthen food security at a local level. A closer look should be taken at how to redesign both employment programs in order to maximize their effects on household and regional food security. Such a reorganization must begin with improved interministerial coordination between technical ministries in order to clearly define responsibilities for local participant targeting and supervision, materials transportation, operation-phase monitoring and maintenance, and strategic collaboration with other forms of public intervention.

One complaint often leveled at public works in recent years is that they have only a minor impact on unemployment, poverty, and resource degradation (Guichaoua 1991; Catterson, Wilson, and Gavian 1992). This is true, given the scale of the problems facing us today. However, these studies have shown that (1) at a local level, effects on employment, income, and food security are very high; (2) the scale of activities could be much larger, with greater and more clearly defined involvement of the public sector, donors, and private contractors; and (3) given the successful poverty-targeting of such programs, their effectiveness could be raised further by combining them with complementary activities in other fields. Even in sparsely populated areas such as Niger and southern Zimbabwe, labor-intensive activities are viable.

REFERENCES

ACC-SCN (United Nations Administrative Committee on Coordination-Sub-Committee on Nutrition). 1989. Malnutrition and infection: A review. Nutrition Policy Discussion Paper No. 5. ACC-SCN/ International Food Policy Research Institute, Geneva. Mimeo.

Berg, A. 1992. New and noteworthy in nutrition. World Bank Office Memorandum No. 18, Washington, D.C. Mimeo.

Borton, J., and N. Nicholds. 1992. *UN disaster management training programme: Drought and famine module.* London: Relief and Disasters Policy Programme, Overseas Development Institute.

Bratton, M. 1987. Drought, food, and the social organization of small farmers in Zimbabwe. In *Drought and hunger in Africa,* ed. M. Glantz, 213–244. Cambridge, United Kingdom: Cambridge University Press.

Bread for the World. 1992. *Hunger 1991: Uprooted people.* Washington, D.C.

CARE. 1990. CARE-International in Niger. Program Brief. CARE-International, Niamey, Niger. Mimeo.

Catterson, T., W. Wilson, and S. Gavian. 1992. Natural resource management and program food aid in Niger: An initial analysis of linkages. Report to the U.S Agency for International Development/Niger. Agricultural Policy Analysis Project. ABT Associates, Washington, D.C.

Chidzero, B. T. G. 1991. *Budget statement, 1991.* Presented to the Parliament of Zimbabwe 25 July 1991. Harare: Government Printer.

Derrier, J. F. 1991. *Conservation des sols et des eaux et ressources locales au Sahel: Enseignements et orientations.* Geneva: International Labour Office.

Drèze, J. 1989. *Famine prevention in Africa.* Development Economics Research Programme Paper 17. London: London School of Economics and Political Science.

Drèze, J., and A. Sen. 1989. *Hunger and public action.* Oxford, United Kingdom: Oxford University Press.

FAO (Food and Agriculture Organization of the United Nations). 1990a. Evaluation de la situation nationale de securite alimentaire et problemes a resoudre. Assistance a l'execution de la premiere phase et la preparation de la deuxieme phase de formulation d'un programme complet de securite alimentaire. Projet GCPS/NER/031/NOR. FAO, Rome. Mimeo.

_____. 1990b. *Le projet developpement rural integre de Keita.* Rome: FAO.

_____. 1992. *Food Outlook*, No. 4. Rome.

Guichaoua, A., ed. 1991. Investissement-travail et developpement: Des approches et pratiques renouvelees? *Revue Tiers-Monde* 32 (127) (Special issue): 485–631.

Higgins, P. A., and H. Alderman. 1992. *Labor and women's nutrition: A study of energy expenditure, fertility, and nutritional status in Ghana.* Policy Research Working Papers 1009. Washington, D.C.: World Bank.

Iliffe, J. 1990. *Famine in Zimbabwe 1980–1960.* Harare, Zimbabwe: Mambo Press.

Kennedy, E., and H. Alderman. 1987. *Comparative analyses of nutritional effectiveness of food subsidies and other food-related interventions.* Washington, D.C.: International Food Policy Research Institute.

Kennedy, E. T., H. Bouis, and J. von Braun. 1992. Health and nutrition effects of cash crop production in developing countries: A comparative analysis. *Social Science and Medicine* 35 (2): 689-697.

Lenneiye, N. M. 1991. Towards a food and nutrition policy for Zimbabwe. A draft Inter-Ministerial paper. Prepared for the National Steering Committee for Food and Nutrition and the University of Zimbabwe/Michigan State University Food Security Project for Southern Africa, Harare. Mimeo.

Lipton, M. 1989. New strategies and successful examples for sustainable development in the Third World. Testimony presented at a hearing on Sustainable Development and Economic Growth in the Third World held by the Joint Economic Committee of the U.S. Congress, Subcommittee on Technology and National Security, June 20, 1989, Washington, D.C.

Mason, E. 1990. The nutrition situation. Appendices for discussion at the National Consultative Workshop on Food, Nutrition, and Agricultural Policy, July 15–18, 1990, Nyanga. Mimeo.

Moyo, S. 1992. Public works program in Zimbabwe (1983–1991). Zimbabwe Institute of Development Studies. Mimeo.

NCHS (National Center for Health Statistics). 1977. *NCHS growth curves for children: Birth–18 years.* Vital and Health Statistics Series 11, No. 165. Washington, D.C.

Niger (Republique du Niger). 1990. Agenence Nigerienne de Travaux d'Interet Public pour l'Emploi, NIGETIP: Note de Presentation. Ministere du Plan. Niamey. Mimeo.

_____. 1991. *Annuaire statistique: Series longues.* Direction de la Statistique et de la Demographie. Ministere du Plan. Niamey.

NIGETIP (Agence Nigerienne des Travaux d'Interet Public). 1992. Rapport d'activité: Mois d'Avril 1992. Niamey. Mimeo.

Rukuni, M., and C. Eicher. 1991. Food security policy options in eastern and southern Africa. In *National and regional self-sufficiency goals: Implications for international agriculture,* ed. F. J. Ruppel and E. D. Kellogg, 89-106. Boulder, Colo., U.S.A.: Lynne Rienner Publishers.

Rukuni, M., G. Mudimu, and T. S. Jayne, eds. 1990. *Food security policies in the SADCC Region.* Proceedings of the Fifth Annual Conference on Food Security Research in Southern Africa, October 16–18, 1989. Harare, Zimbabwe: University of Zimbabwe/Michigan State University.

Sachikonye, L. M. 1992. Zimbabwe: Drought, food, and adjustment. *Review of African Political Economy* 53: 88-108.

SBW (Statistisches Bundesamt Wiesbaden). 1987. *Laenderbericht Niger: 1987.* Statistik des Auslandes. Wiesbaden, Germany: Statistisches Bundesamt (Federal Statistics Office).

Somerville, C. M. 1986. *Drought and aid in the Sahel: A decade of development cooperation.* Westview Special Studies on Africa. Boulder, Colo., U.S.A.: Westview Press.

Takavarasha, T., and A. Rukovo. 1990. Zimbabwe: Perspectives on food policy options. In *Food security policies in the SADCC Region,* ed. M. Rukuni, G. Mudimu, and T. S. Jayne, 63–72. Proceedings of the Fifth Annual Conference on Food Security Research in Southern Africa, October 16–18, 1989. Harare, Zimbabwe: University of Zimbabwe/Michigan State University.

The Herald. 1990. Pledge to help drought victims. October 12: 1.

UNDP (United Nations Development Programme). 1990. *Development cooperation: Zimbabwe 1989 report.* Harare.

USAID (United States Agency for International Development). 1992. Drought in southern Africa. U.S. Mission. Harare, Zimbabwe. Mimeo.

Webb, P. 1992. Food security through employment in the Sahel: Labor-intensive programs in Niger. Report to the Deutsche Gesellschaft für Technische Zusammenarbeit, Eschborn, Federal Republic of Germany. International Food Policy Research Institute, Washington, D.C.

Webb, P., and S. Moyo. 1992. Food security through employment in southern Africa: Labor-intensive programs in Zimbabwe. Report to the Deutsche Gesellschaft für Technische Zusammenarbeit, Eschborn, Federal Republic of Germany. International Food Policy Research Institute, Washington, D.C.

WFP (World Food Programme). 1991. Projet Niger 3579 (Elarg.1): Developpement rural integre dans les arrondissements de Keita, Bouza et tchintabaraden. 32nd Session of the CFA. Rome. Mimeo.

World Bank. 1988. Niger: Small rural operations project. Staff Appraisal Report 6910-NIR. Washington, D.C. Mimeo.

_____. 1990. Niger: Projet de travaux d'interet public contre le sous-emploi. Rapport d'evaluation. Infrastructure Division, Sahel Department. Washington, D.C. Mimeo.

_____. 1992. *World development report 1992: Development and the environment.* Washington, D.C.

Zimbabwe (Government of Zimbabwe). 1989. *Zimbabwe demographic and health survey 1988.* Central Statistical Office. Harare: Ministry of Finance, Economic Planning, and Development.

_____. 1990. Public sector investment: Public works programme 1991/92. District Development Fund. Ministry of Local Government, Rural and Urban Development. Mimeo.

Zimbabwe News. 1989. Masses show enthusiasm in food for work and self-reliance projects. December: 10–12.

8

FOOD AND CASH FOR WORK IN ETHIOPIA: EXPERIENCES DURING FAMINE AND MACROECONOMIC REFORM

Patrick Webb and Shubh K. Kumar

Between 1983 and 1993, Ethiopia witnessed three major droughts, one nationwide famine that left up to a million people dead, the escalation and culmination of Africa's longest civil war, experiments in the wholesale relocation of villagers, a reversal in government policy from centralization to decentralization, and, on top of all that, the recent implementation of structural adjustment. These upheavals have contributed to a depletion of household wealth on a massive scale and a growing food deficit. At no time during this 10-year period has the structural deficit between food supply and demand been less than 500,000 tons. As a result, as many as 5 million individuals (10 percent of the total population) were considered to be acutely food insecure in 1993 (World Bank 1993; USAID 1993).

Throughout this decade of crisis, the Ethiopian government and donors have relied heavily on labor-intensive public works. This paper examines the experiences of a number of large and small public works programs implemented in Ethiopia during the past decade and is divided into three sections. The first briefly outlines the changing design characteristics of programs as they have been adapted to perceptions of prevailing need. The second section examines targeting issues and the impact of participation on poor households. This analysis is based on the results of surveys at eight project sites around the country. The last section draws a number of conclusions from the Ethiopian case study.

The Changing Scale and Focus of Public Works

Ethiopia generally receives between 20 and 30 percent of all food aid arriving in Sub-Saharan Africa, the annual amount depending on the severity of prevailing drought or famine conditions. Figure 8.1 indicates that aid deliveries ranged between 200,000 and 300,000 tons until the

Figure 8.1—Food aid deliveries to Ethiopia, 1977/78–1990/91

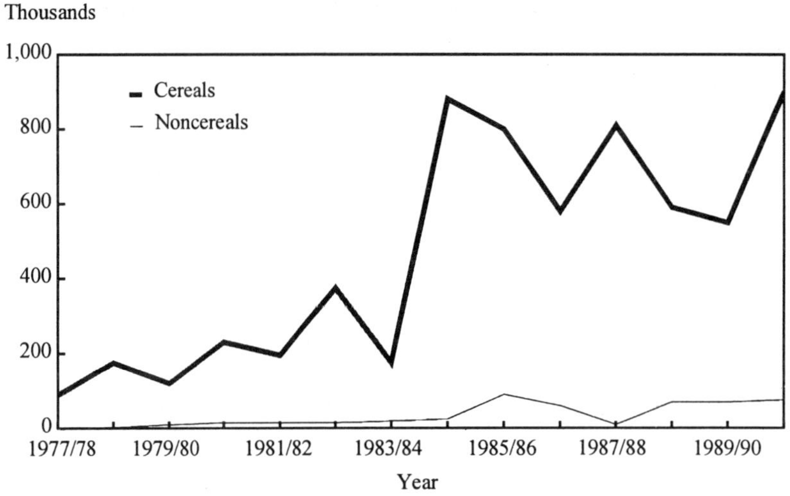

Thousands

Source: Aylieff 1993; FAO 1993.

large-scale famine of the mid-1980s, at which point they rose sharply to almost 1.0 million tons. In 1992, after three consecutive years of good harvest, food deliveries still amounted to 1.2 million tons—25 percent of all food aid to Africa in that year (FAO 1993; USAID 1993).

This heavy reliance on food imports has several explanations. The first is that, far from retreating, food insecurity is still on the rise. This rise stems from declining labor and land productivity (which are linked to a continued erosion of natural and human resources), falling per capita food production, growing unemployment, an erosion of purchasing power due to inflation and higher producer prices, and a weak institutional capacity to cope with any of these problems.

The second reason is that a rising number of nongovernmental (NGO) and donor organizations on the ground are making the detection and documentation of food insecurity more rapid and accurate than in the past (Aylieff 1993). There are now almost 100 NGOs operating in Ethiopia in addition to the usual bilateral and multilateral donors.

The third reason is that in Ethiopia, momentum for increasing the developmental uses of food aid through labor-intensive public works is mounting. More than 1 million tons of food were distributed during 1985/86 through feeding camps, supplementary feeding schemes, and dry ration distributions. Unfortunately, most of this aid arrived only after a rise in excess mortality and massive social disruption, including community dislocation. Very little of the food was used as payment for project work.

It was in the aftermath of the 1984/85 famine that the number of public works projects rose sharply. Most of Ethiopia's food aid is channeled through the World Food Programme (WFP), which uses 20 to 30 percent of the total to support the largest food-for-work (FFW) program in Africa. This activity started in 1979 and was planned to last four years. Far from terminating, the program began its second expansion in 1993, and it continues to generate millions of workdays per year.

At the same time, more NGOs are involved in public works. Up to 80 percent of the food aid not used by WFP is channeled to NGOs (UNEPPG 1989; Aylieff 1993). In 1984, only a handful of NGOs were active in food-for-work, but more than 50 operated relief projects. Most of these (82 percent) were medical operations and feeding programs (Webb, von Braun, and Yohannes 1992). Long-term rehabilitation programs necessarily had a low priority during the crisis period.

By 1986/87, when the peak of the crisis had passed in most regions, NGOs and government departments were faced with the question of how to redirect their efforts. The answer for most was to move from relief to rehabilitation. NGOs continued to receive large amounts of food aid. This raised the usual questions about the difficulties of switching from free food to food-for-work, due to disincentives of the former (Curtis, Hubbard, and Shepherd 1988; Elizabeth 1988). Although there was little empirical evidence to support the existence of a disincentive effect on agricultural production in Ethiopia, conventional wisdom had it that food-for-work would be better than food handouts (Webb, von Braun, and Yohannes 1992). Thus, a public works boom started. Of 65 NGO projects surveyed in 1986, only 3 had been initiated before 1985 (Hareide 1986b). Similarly, of 32 NGO projects still going on in 1992, only 1 had been in operation prior to 1986 (Berhanu and Aylieff 1992). The majority of these projects were small, with annual costs of less than US$1 million. Most had development objectives.

Carried by the momentum, the government in the mid-1990s became more committed than ever to a national public works program. An Emergency Code (similar to India's old Famine Codes that formalized central and local government responsibilities in the event of a crisis) relies strongly on the principle of public works. So does the proposed Social Safety Net Program that aims to protect the poor against the worst consequences of structural adjustment.

This growing interest in employment programs for the poor has been driven by recognition of three of Ethiopia's most pressing problems: acute rural food insecurity, a deteriorating natural resource base, and growing urban food insecurity.

Acute rural food insecurity continues to hobble Ethiopia's development efforts. Chronic and acute food insecurity persist across large swaths of the country even when there is no drought, the principal cause being poverty. When drought joins this endemic poverty, the results can be catastrophic. As an illustration, the 1984/85 famine was not an isolated incident. The peak of the crisis came after three successive years of drought had already exposed vulnerable households to the depletion of food and capital reserves, forced the sale of productive assets in order to purchase food, and caused a decline in food consumption.

Employment programs are seen as a useful way of reducing poverty without giving food handouts; at the same time, such programs attempt to remove the underlying causes of food insecurity, such as deficient rural infrastructure, environmental erosion, and low agricultural productivity.

The large-scale WFP/Ethiopian government food-for-work program makes an explicit attempt to attack these causes of food insecurity. Large-scale degradation of the natural resource base has long been recognized as a contributor to food insecurity. The (human) death toll associated with famine is only one part of the problem. Long-term depletion of resources carries the implications of a famine far beyond immediate suffering. The process of nation-building is severely set back not just by the loss of people, livestock, and savings, but also by the continued erosion of soil and vegetation that makes it difficult to rehabilitate the agricultural economy (FAO 1986).

From 1980 to 1990, WFP contributed more than US$230 million to labor-intensive projects aimed at rehabilitating farm and grazing lands by reducing soil erosion and improving soil and water management (Holt 1983; UNEPPG 1987; WFP 1990, 1991). In practice, this meant soil bunding, stone contour terracing, and afforestation. The program's most recent phase, costing US$78 million, was aimed at improving 2.6 million hectares of degraded land by offering 27 million workdays per year (WFP 1989).

Organization of Public Works and Institutions

The government implements WFP-supported activities through its ministries of agriculture and environment and through the Relief and Rehabilitation Commission. While the catalog of physical assets generated through these projects is impressive in quantitative terms, qualitative evaluations have tended to be less favorable. Survival rates of trees planted are low, maintenance of contour bunds is inadequate, and productivity gains often appear minimal (Webb, von Braun, and Yohannes 1992). On the other hand, when the projects are assessed in terms of their contribution to food security, the picture is quite positive. As noted in the next section, millions of days of employment have made a sizeable contribution to stabilizing consumption among poor households.

It is this food-security benefit of public works (employment in public works represents a relatively well-targeted income transfer to poorer households) that prompted the government to build its Emergency Code for famine prevention and its social safety net program around the concept of public works. Joint WFP/government activities are, by the nature of their objectives, focused on rural areas—the locus of severest famine and environmental degradation. However, the government has recently acknowledged a serious urban food security problem (Ethiopia 1992).

Since 1991, government policies have changed and now favor market liberalization, the dismantling of parastatals, and the disengagement of public-sector authorities from micromanagement of the economy. The plan is to support the urban poor directly with a targeted voucher scheme, urban employment programs (1,600 projects in 184 towns), a wage adjustment indexed to food prices for civil servants and others on fixed incomes, and cash and food grants to support demobilized soldiers (Morris 1992; Ethiopia 1992). The more numerous rural poor are to be assisted with a national employment scheme (food-for-work) and a targeted voucher scheme for fertilizer or oxen purchase. The latter scheme is intended to jump-start the agriculture sector. These measures, coupled with a reallocation of resources from military spending to smallholder development, have been essential first steps.

But these measures may in themselves be insufficient to deal with acute food insecurity in the short-to-medium term. Vulnerable households are not great competitors in the marketplace. They do not have the resources (or credit) to grow more food and to sell the surplus in response to higher prices. The transport and marketing infrastructure needed for the smooth flow of food, capital, and labor around the country are still missing. The costs of rapidly increased food production therefore almost parallels the heralded benefits. And, rapid urbanization has generated roughly 3 million urban poor—a number that rises daily (Ethiopia 1992).

The 1,600 planned urban projects are expected to generate 10,000 permanent jobs and almost 100,000 temporary workdays at a cost of US$35 million (Ethiopia 1992). The majority of the projects focus on low-cost housing construction, the provision of clean water, and road construction and maintenance. The rural projects involve natural resource management and road construction and maintenance. The roadwork was chosen because of recent calculations showing that labor-based methods of road construction are significantly cheaper than equipment-based methods for Ethiopia's rolling terrain; labor-intensive methods cost US$1,100 per kilometer, while equipment-based methods cost US$14,000 per kilometer (Morris 1992).

The following sections provide information on eight food-for-work and two cash-for-work projects that was gathered through detailed household surveys conducted between 1989 and 1991 (for details of survey design and methodologies, see Webb, von Braun, and Yohannes 1992 and Kumar et al. 1993). These projects were implemented prior to the recent macroeconomic reforms. The surveys make it possible to weigh some of the more contentious issues relating to public works in light of the policy environment of the late 1980s.

Three important issues are considered here: poverty targeting, the impact of participation on income and income use, and the cash wage versus food wage debate. The focus overall is, of course, on the project's effects on poverty reduction and food security rather than on the sustainability of assets generated. Analysis of the design and implementation of safety-net projects in postreform years would be required in order to assess the cost and targeting efficiency of public works in the new economic environment.

Household Participation and Impact

Poverty Targeting

Poverty targeting is an important criterion in the design of public works even in Ethiopia. Research findings from the late 1980s indicate that the top one-third of households in a stratified sample drawn from seven locations had an average annual income of US$100 per capita—more than double that registered by the bottom one-third of households in the same sample (who earned only US$42 per capita) (Webb, von Braun, and Yohannes 1992).

What is more, the wealthier households achieved drought-year cereal yields three times higher than poor households—300 kilograms versus 111 kilograms per hectare. As a result, output from the wealthier households was also higher, reaching an average of 38 kilograms per capita in 1985, compared with only 9.5 kilograms per capita from poor households (Webb, von Braun, and Yohannes 1992). These results suggest that, even where almost everyone is extremely poor, the degree of poverty is important in determining vulnerability to famine. This insight emphasizes the need to better target the absolutely poor in relief interventions and to target famine-prone regions as well as surplus zones of the country for productive investment.

The projects' success in targeting the poor was mixed. The average number of days worked in the projects surveyed was a little under 100 days per year per household. This figure concurs with previous estimates of average annual participation that ranged between 85 and 90 days (Holt 1983; Kohlin 1987). However, average participation rates mask considerable variation among years and seasons, as well as among socioeconomic groups. For example, during the 1985 famine, the average number of days of project work performed by households in the worst-hit survey site rose to 150 days per year; among wealthier households, this figure hovered around 100 days, while among the destitute, it reached almost 200. This need underlines the important role of public works, even during an extreme crisis. It does not, of course, rule out the need to transfer calories directly to those unable to work during a famine.

Participation also fluctuates within single years. Participation in projects that offer year-round employment declines during the main rainy season, when labor is required for planting and weeding. Peak project employment occurs in the period that just precedes the harvest, when all crop preparations have been completed and food stores are at their lowest (Figure 8.2). This confirms that participation is determined by need.

But is it the most needy who participate the most? There are no universal standards for the selection of participants in Ethiopia and very

Figure 8.2—Seasonal participation in food-for-work projects in Ethiopia

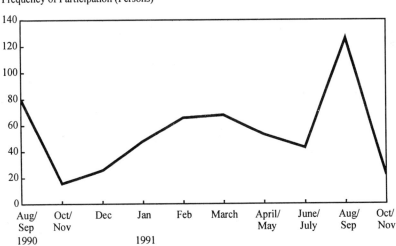

Source: Kumar et al. 1993.
Note: Taken from a sample of 650 households in three *awarajas* (districts) of South Shewa, in a survey conducted jointly by IFPRI and the Ethiopian Nutrition Institute in 1990–91.

few projects make an explicit attempt to target the poor (Berhanu and Aylieff 1992). A survey of projects in Wollo found that only 30 percent of respondents felt that the poor had preferential access to FFW (Kohlin 1987). A national survey similarly found only 17 percent of respondents reported a recruitment bias toward the poor (Admassie and Gebre 1985).

Some schemes set physical fitness criteria, thereby potentially excluding some of the food-insecure households that could have benefited the most from income transferred, such as households headed by women, the elderly, and the emaciated. Other projects take participants on a "first come, first served" basis (Kumar et al. 1993). There are a number of smaller projects that do allow community leadership to carry out the selection with the proviso that selection be equitable and take need into account, but these projects seem plagued by allegations of favoritism and bribery (Webb, von Braun, and Yohannes 1992; Kumar et al. 1993). Most programs rely on the assumption that the wage rate is sufficiently low to lead to self-selection of the poor.

Table 8.1 shows that this theory is not quite matched in practice. Although the poorest households in the survey sample (which is grouped into three equal income terciles) are not significantly disfavored in terms of participation (that is, the rich did not totally squeeze out the poor during the famine years), the poor did not benefit more than wealthier households during the late 1980s. This holds true for most sites even for the single worst famine year, and even when dependency ratios are taken into account. The

Table 8.1—Sample household participation in food-for-work projects at selected survey sites, by income tercile (average for 1985 to 1989), Ethiopia

Survey Site	Income Tercile		
	Lower	Middle	Upper
	(percent of participants)[a]		
Highlands			
Adele Keke	24 (54)	40 (60)	36 (55)
Gara Godo	31 (57)	39 (54)	36 (55)
Lowlands			
Beke Pond	33 (50)	27 (60)	40 (55)
Dinki	34 (50)	34 (48)	32 (32)

Source: Webb, von Braun, Yohannes 1992.
Note: Based on a survey conducted by IFPRI in 1989/90 in cooperation with Ethiopia's Ministry of Planning and Economic Development and with the International Livestock Centre for Africa (ILCA).
[a]The numbers in parentheses are dependency ratios (the percentage below 15 and above 60 years of age in the total population).

survey carried out at four different sites in 1990/91, a nonfamine year, found that poorer households had higher levels of participation (Kumar et al. 1993). However, a cross-section of rich and poor households participated in the available projects, with the degree of participation largely determined by the presence of able-bodied household members.

The explanation for this lies in the relative value of public works wages and other local wages, particularly those offered for agricultural labor. When the exchange value of a public works ration (be it food or cash) is higher than the prevailing market rate for manual labor, then a larger share of participants will come from wealthier households. Figure 8.3 underlines the importance of this point by comparing the changing value of (1) a fixed cash-for-work wage, and (2) the market value of a standard food ration. Each line on the figure indicates how much maize could be purchased on local markets (at free market prices), using the value of the different wages.

At the first market, food-for-work rations were of greater value than cash-for-work wages twice during the 1980s—during 1985 through late 1986, and again briefly during 1988. At other times, the cash wage was of more value in terms of maize equivalence. However, the story is different at the other two markets. At Hagere Mariam, the food ration was more

Figure 8.3—Comparison of food and cash wages in public works, and cash wages for manual labor, 1985–89, Ethiopia

Equivalent Market Value of Maize
in Kilograms/Month

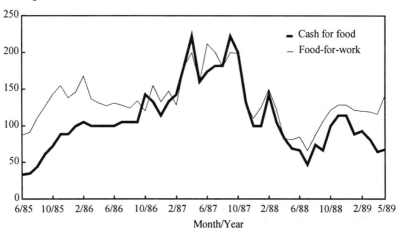

Source: Ethiopia, Central Statistics Authority.

valuable throughout the period except for a peak in mid-1987. At Alemaya, food wages remained more valuable than the fixed cash wage from 1985 through 1989.

These comparisons suggest that markets operate very differently from one region to the next, and food transfers via public works may have a valuable role to play in regions in which markets are constrained. The wage value itself may also be varied, depending on technical and social (targeting) objectives; that is, wage rates might be varied by season, or wages might be partly in cash and partly in kind (thereby conforming to the International Labour Office [ILO] requirements), or there might be employment guarantees against a fixed low wage. Given that income transfer is a key objective, determining the real (fluctuating) value of the wage is essential if wage rates are to be used to target the poor.

Public Works Income and
Food Consumption Effects

How is income used, depending on its source and content? The standard food wage across the country is 3 kilograms of grain and 120 grams of oil per day. However, Table 8.2 shows that there are many deviations from the standard because of constraints on availability and difficulties in estimating the numbers of potential participants (Hareide 1986a; USAID 1987). Payments did not vary greatly by gender of household head in the projects that operated between 1985 and 1989. Households headed by men or women both received the average wage for their particular locality.

Yet, wages did vary across income groups and also between projects. For example, the poorest households at two of the sites (Dinki and Gara Godo) received payments exceeding not only the standard payment for a day's work (an average of 3.6 kilograms per day at each site), but also the payments received by less poor households in the same communities (who received between 2.2 and 3.0 kilograms). By contrast, the poorest households at two other sites surveyed received payments of between 0.6 and 1.3 kilograms, below the recommended ration.

However variable, the payments generally represent a sizeable contribution to total household income for the poor; that is, the share of public works income to total net income was almost four times higher among the poorest households (in 1989/90) than among wealthier households. The 1990/91 survey concurs, finding that public works participation contributes to significantly higher net household income, particularly among poorer households.

Need for income (primarily used to increase calorie consumption) is the driving force behind most participation in these public works projects.

Table 8.2—Average grain payments received by food-for-work participants, by income tercile and gender of household head, Ethiopia

Survey Site	Income Tercile			Gender of Household Head	
	Lower	Middle	Upper	Male	Female
	(average kilograms/household/day)				
Highlands					
Adele Keke	1.3	2.2	1.4	1.9	1.6
Gara Godo	3.6	2.5	2.2	2.6	2.7
Lowlands					
Beke Pond	0.6	0.9	0.6	0.7[a]	
Dinki	3.6	2.8	3.2	3.4[b]	

Source: Webb, von Braun, Yohannes 1992.
Note: Based on a survey conducted by IFPRI in 1989/90 in cooperation with Ethiopia's Ministry of Planning and Economic Development and with the International Livestock Centre for Africa (ILCA).
[a]No female-headed households in Beke Pond participated in food-for-work.
[b]There were no female-headed households in the Dinki sample.

On average, participants in food-for-work projects from 1985 to 1989 consumed 95 percent of their food wage; participants in cash-for-work, by contrast, consumed an average of 82 percent of their wage in food (derived from IFPRI survey data in Ethiopia, 1989/90).

However, these are averages. While cash-for-work recipients in Ethiopia spent 82 percent of their wage on food at the sample mean, expenditure ranged from less than 73 percent in richer households to 94 percent among the poor. A similar pattern applies to food-for-work participants. In other words, the income and asset base of households, that is, their poverty level, determines how they allocate incremental income from public works.

For the poorest households, project participation can have a striking effect on calorie consumption, particularly in mitigating seasonal fluctuations in consumption. The 1990/91 survey found that calorie consumption among the poorest households can decline by as much as 50 percent between the postharvest and the subsequent preharvest period (Kumar et al. 1993). Figure 8.4 shows that while land-rich and land-poor households have a comparable level of calorie consumption immediately after harvest, better-off households maintain a relatively stable level of consumption throughout the year, dipping only slightly just prior to harvest. The households with less land exhibit a steady decline in their consumption level, with the trough also occurring at preharvest time (though at a much lower absolute level).

Figure 8.4—Calorie consumption among participants and nonparticipants of food-for-work projects in south-central Ethiopia, 1990/91

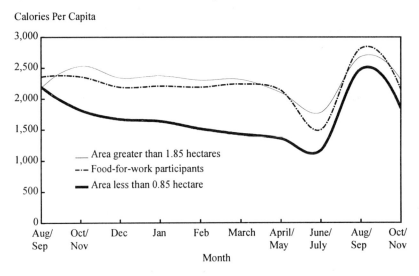

Source: Kumar et al. 1993.
Note: Taken from a sample of 650 households in three *awarajas* (districts) of South Shewa in a survey conducted jointly by IFPRI and the Ethiopian Nutrition Institute in 1990–91.

However, participation in public works projects appears to minimize the decline and thus raise the lowest consumption level, which is reached just before harvest. Thus, project participation, and consumption of the income, can have a marked effect on smoothing calorie intake over the year, thereby reducing physiological stress. This benefit may be translated into improved nutritional status of children in poorer participant households, compared with poorer nonparticipant households, although further analysis of the data is required to test this.

Cash Wage Versus Food Wage

If more of the wage is consumed at home when paid in food rather than in cash, are food wages a better means of achieving food security? Or, as is often claimed, do food-for-work activities and payments have a negative effect on local agricultural production?

The danger that food-for-work might have a depressing effect on agricultural production has been widely discussed (Maxwell 1978; FAO 1982; ONCCP 1986; Fitzpatrick and Strong 1988; Bryson, Chuddy, and Pines

1990). While this issue should not be lightly dismissed, there is evidence (at the micro level, at least) that the danger may have been overstated. Household interviews conducted by Holt (1983) and Kohlin (1987) in Wollo; CARE-Ethiopia (1988) in Hararghe; Erni (1989) in Shoa; EEC (1989) in Eritrea and Tigray; Maxwell, Belshaw, and Lirenso (1990) in Gamo Gofa; and Admassie and Gebre (1985) across the country all conclude that food-for-work has no negative effect on food production by participants.

The present surveys tend to concur. In the survey of participation during 1985 to 1989, only a handful of respondents reported that they farmed less when they participated in food-for-work (Webb, von Braun, and Yohannes 1992). Between 50 and 75 percent of participants spent the evenings cultivating their farms after working on food-for-work during the day. Households not farming in the evenings usually had other household members that took over farm activities while the head was away on food-for-work.

On the other hand, there is some evidence that income smoothing (through project participation) in favor of lean season consumption may be at the cost of lost agricultural output during the subsequent harvest in the unimodal rainfall areas of southern Shewa (Kumar et al. 1993). Loss of output, however, is limited to households that respond to immediate food needs only during the hungry season. Households that participate over longer periods show a positive interaction between project participation, labor input in crop production, and agricultural output, possibly due to an improvement in workers' food security and nutritional status.

When participants themselves are asked what their preferred form of payment is, there is a mixed response, depending on project context (Table 8.3). Food recipients preferred food, definitely. However, at one cash-for-work site, 81 percent of the cash recipients were in favor of cash, while, at another cash-for-work site, 83 percent favored food. The reasons again relate to problems with food delivery and the value of the wage received.

At the first site, restrictions on private trade at the time of the survey forced villagers to travel up to 100 kilometers to reach markets where prices had not been inflated as a result of the local infusion of cash. Many households were unable to travel and so purchased food locally. More than 75 percent of households report that prices rose by as much as 100 percent around distribution times. This resulted in widespread borrowing from moneylenders against the value of the next payment, at interest rates averaging 100 percent. The need to turn to this borrowing facility (only available to cash-for-food participants because lenders were willing to accept UNICEF's credit rating) reduced the net welfare effect of the distribution program. Here, the low value of cash, coupled with the high opportunity cost of time taken to use it, resulted in an 83 percent vote in favor of a food wage.

Table 8.3—Participants' expressed preference for food or cash wage, Ethiopia

Country	Preference		
	Food	Cash	50/50
	(percent)		
Cash recipients 1[a]	83	17	. . .
Cash recipients 2[a]	19	81	. . .
Food recipients	90	6	4

Source: Based on a survey conducted by IFPRI in 1989/90 in cooperation with Ethiopia's Ministry of Planning and Economic Development and with the International Livestock Centre for Africa (ILCA).

Note: The ellipses (. . .) indicate a nil or negligible amount.

[a]The two groups of cash recipients indicate that two different project sites were polled.

By contrast, at a second, much more remote, site near the border with Kenya, the transportation of food was difficult and time-consuming, so almost 80 percent of the people preferred to get cash, which they could use to tap into nearby mountain markets that were not as strictly controlled by the police and militia.

Do these study results settle the question of whether cash wages are better than food wages? The answer is no. More detailed and extensive empirical research is required. However, it appears that the choice of wage should be guided by whether markets are functioning well (that is, whether they are constrained by policy restrictions or infrastructure deficiencies) and whether there is a crisis under way. In Ethiopia, food wages did play a crucial role when markets were constrained, either physically or by policy measures. Where markets do work, cash disbursal may be the better option, since it is more easily monitored and creates demand for local food. The drawback can be local inflation, a transferral of transport and labor costs from the project to the beneficiaries, and, probably, a smaller effect on consumption and nutrition than would be desired.

In other words, close attention must be paid to local conditions in order to tailor projects to each location. A mixed food and cash wage may be preferable to a single-commodity wage to allow greater flexibility in wage-value adjustments according to seasonal and annual fluctuations in purchasing power.

Longer-Term Food Security Benefits

The long-term development impact of public works comes from the generation of community assets that would not have been created through private initiative. However, while public works offer an attractive labor-intensive option for transferring income to the poor, they are also management- and material-intensive.

Management constraints are caused by a lack of skilled manpower at both field and ministry levels. Programs often substitute consultants and financial inputs for human resource inputs that are locally unavailable. Yet, such deficiencies could be rectified. More concerted donor and government investment is needed to develop human capital and to establish policies and institutions that (1) bring public works into the mainstream of national planning for public goods provision and for food security enhancement, and (2) facilitate, rather than hinder, positive multiplier effects from public works (on land and other resource tenure and on pricing and marketing policies).

Material constraints can also be rectified by removing supply bottlenecks for food wages, labor, tools and equipment, and construction materials. These are tremendous constraints at the field level, but they are merely logistical problems. By contrast, tackling motivation constraints is a much harder challenge. Community participation is crucial to success in both construction and operating phases of public works. Decentralized, popular participation in project identification, implementation, and evaluation is essential. Such participation would help ensure that the long-term benefit streams are not regressive. For example, whether the poor gain from improved and more productive natural resources (or not through improved soil and water management techniques and structures) can depend heavily on land and other resource tenure policies. Short-term measures may only be successful in the longer term in an appropriate policy environment.

Conclusions

This chapter has focused narrowly on the poverty-targeting and impact issues associated with public works in Ethiopia. The findings suggest that demand for participation among the food-insecure is high. The value of public works in transferring needed income, stabilizing food consumption, and generating income for reinvestment in agriculture is also high.

At the same time, the asset-creating potential of public works—aside from the social security potential—should not be underestimated. The potential employment associated with food aid delivered at the current levels is large. For example, assuming that only 600,000 tons of food (50 percent of total food aid in 1992) were used in food-for-work schemes that provided 3 kilograms of grain per workday, 2 million people would receive employment for 100 days (within one year) working on roads, irrigation perimeters, and agricultural enhancement activities (Morris 1992).

If the average cost of transferring income to participants through such schemes is approximately US$10 per person (US$50 per household), the cost of coverage using 50 percent of available food aid would stand at more than US$20 million (Webb, von Braun, and Yohannes 1992). To provide partial food security through 100 days' employment for the 10 million people most vulnerable to famine would therefore cost roughly US$100 million per year—just 10 percent of the total official development assistance received by the country in 1991 (UNDP 1993).

However, the food security potential of programs continues to be constrained in two key areas. First, the fixed wage rate (which is often superior to agricultural wages) dilutes the food security impact—the absolutely poor are not gaining more access to employment programs than the less poor.

The second constraint, common to most projects across Africa, is that too little attention is paid to nonwage inputs. Over the years, a great deal of attention has been paid to improving the delivery of wages to recipients with minimal leakage, while the need for cement, tools, vehicles, wire, wood, and other inputs has been neglected. Sustainable assets depend on more than labor, so the thorny issue of monetization needs to be faced in the near future.

In sum, labor-intensive works are a means of reducing poverty and enhancing food security, and they play a role not just in long-term development, but also in famine, post-famine rehabilitation, and the creation of safety nets during structural adjustment. But they are not an end in themselves.

Public authorities need to mobilize the construction, repair, and maintenance of public assets as well as protect the poor against acute food insecurity. Households need to invest in income growth and diversification as a means to protect themselves against acute food insecurity. It would be appropriate to assist both through labor-intensive technologies where possible.

But, while public works have clear income transfer and income stabilization benefits, other interventions should also be considered together with such transfers to multiply the positive effects of consumption stabilization. Some households cannot participate in employment programs. The food security of those who can participate depends on more than, say, a 20 percent increase in household income. The effectiveness of labor-intensive programs can be increased if they operate alongside other essential social security and development instruments; these might include credit schemes to assist reinvestment in farm and nonfarm activities, improved health training and vaccination, and improved access to inputs that farmers purchase out of public works income. In this way, the artificial divide between emergency relief and development can be effectively bridged.

REFERENCES

Admassie, Y., and S. Gebre. 1985. *Food-for-work in Ethiopia: A socioeconomic survey*. Research Report 24. Addis Ababa: Institute of Development Research, Addis Ababa University.

Aylieff, J. 1993. Statistical summary of food aid deliveries to Ethiopia 1977–1992. Food Aid Information Unit. World Food Programme, Addis Ababa. Mimeo.

Berhanu, A., and J. Aylieff. 1992. Inventory, map, and analytical review of food and cash-for-work projects in Ethiopia. Draft report. World Food Programme, Addis Ababa. Mimeo.

Bryson, J. C., J. P. Chuddy, and J. M. Pines. 1990. *Food-for-work: A review of the 1980s with recommendations for the 1990s*. Draft report for USAID. Cambridge, Mass., U.S.A.: WPI Inc.

CARE-Ethiopia. 1988. Preliminary review of results. 1988 CARE-Hararghe food programs impact survey. Internal report. Addis Ababa.

Curtis, D., M. Hubbard, and A. Shepherd. 1988. *Preventing famine: Policies and prospects for Africa*. London: Routledge.

EEC (European Economic Community). 1989. Evaluation of food-for-work programs in Eritrea and Tigray. Report to EEC by Environmental Resources Limited, Addis Ababa.

Elizabeth, K. 1988. *From disaster relief to development: The experience of the Ethiopian Red Cross*. Geneva: Institut Henry Dunant.

Erni, T. 1989. Preliminary final report on N. Shewa Relief and Soil and Water Conservation Project in Tegulet and Bulga Awraja, Shewa, Ethiopia. Lutheran World Federation, Addis Ababa. Mimeo.

Ethiopia (Transitional Government). 1991. Emergency code for Ethiopia: National disaster prevention and preparedness strategy. Final draft. Addis Ababa. Mimeo.

_____. 1992. Study on the social dimensions of adjustment in Ethiopia. Ministry of Planning and Economic Development, Addis Ababa. Mimeo.

FAO (Food and Agriculture Organization of the United Nations). 1982. *The impact of WFP food aid in Ethiopia: A study of the effects of the sales of WFP wheat under the experimental sales procedures and the*

WFP food-for-work. Project for erosion control and reforestation (ETH 2428). Rome.

_____. 1986. *Highlands reclamation study: Ethiopia*. Final Report, Vol. 1. Rome: FAO.

_____. 1993. *Food supply prospects*. Rome: FAO.

Fitzpatrick, J., and A. Strong. 1988. *Food aid and agricultural disincentives*. Addis Ababa: CARE (USA).

Hareide, D. 1986a. Food-for-work in Ethiopia: A short introduction. In Proceedings of the Workshop on Food-for-Work in Ethiopia. Office of the National Committee for Central Planning (ONCCP), 45–53. Addis Ababa. Mimeo.

_____. 1986b. Food-for-work in Ethiopia. Paper presented at the Workshop on Food-for-Work in Ethiopia, 25–26 July, Addis Ababa.

Holt, J. F. J. 1983. Ethiopia: Food for work or food for relief. *Food Policy* 8 (3): 187–201.

Kohlin, G. 1987. Disaster prevention in Wollo: The effects of food-for-work. Report sponsored by Swedish International Development Authority, Stockholm. Mimeo.

Kumar, S., H. Neka-Tibeb, T. Demissie, and S. Tapesse. 1993. Public works projects in Ethiopia: Potential for improving seasonal food security and agricultural productivity. Draft report. International Food Policy Research Institute, Washington, D.C. Mimeo.

Maxwell, S. 1978. *Food aid, food for work, and public works*. IDS Discussion Paper 127. Brighton, U.K.: Institute of Development Studies.

Maxwell, S., D. Belshaw, and A. Lirenso. 1990. The disincentive effect of food-for-work on labour supply and agricultural innovation in North Omo Region, Ethiopia. Institute of Development Studies, Brighton, U.K. Mimeo.

Morris, D. 1992. Towards poverty alleviation and a social action program: Employment generation through labor-intensive works. World Bank, Addis Ababa. Mimeo.

ONCCP (Office of the National Committee for Central Planning). 1986. Workshop on food-for-work in Ethiopia. Proceedings of the Workshop on Food-for-Work in Ethiopia, 25-26 July, Addis Ababa. Mimeo.

UNDP (United Nations Development Programme). 1993. *Human development report 1993.* New York: Oxford University Press.

UNEPPG (United Nations Emergency Preparedness and Planning Group). 1987. Food for Work: WFP signs a US$76.1 million project for rehabilitation of forest, grazing, and agricultural lands in Ethiopia. *UNEPPG Newsletter* (July).

_____. 1989. Summary of 1988 emergency relief operations in Ethiopia. UNEPPG Briefing Paper. Addis Ababa. Mimeo.

USAID (U.S. Agency for International Development). 1987. Final disaster report. The Ethiopian drought/famine. Fiscal years 1985 and 1986. Addis Ababa: USAID/American Embassy.

_____. 1993. *Vulnerability assessment.* Famine Early Warning System. Rosslyn, Va., U.S.A.: FEWS/Washington for the United States Agency for International Development.

Webb, P., J. von Braun, and Y. Yohannes. 1992. *Famine in Ethiopia: Policy implications of coping failure at national and household levels.* Research Report 92. Washington, D.C.: International Food Policy Research Institute.

WFP (World Food Programme). 1989. Mid-term evaluation by a WFP/FAO/ILO/UN mission of Project Ethiopia 2488/(Exp. II): Rehabilitation of forest, grazing, and agricultural lands, vol. 1. Draft report. Addis Ababa.

_____. 1990. Appraisal of Project Ethiopia 2488/(Exp. III): Food-assisted land improvement project. Main report (draft). Addis Ababa.

_____. 1991. Interim evaluation summary report on Project Ethiopia 2488 (Exp. II). 33rd Session of the Committee on Food Aid. Agenda item 3(d). Rome.

World Bank. 1993. Ethiopia: Toward poverty alleviation and a social action program. Green Cover Report. World Bank, Washington, D.C. Mimeo.

9

SOCIAL INVESTMENT FUNDS AND PROGRAMS IN LATIN AMERICA: THEIR EFFECTS ON EMPLOYMENT AND INCOME

José Wurgaft

The economic crisis that has affected the Latin American countries since the early 1980s, together with adjustment policies and efforts made to reorganize the structure of production, have imposed heavy social costs, which have been borne mostly by the lower-income sectors of the population (Programa Regional del Empleo para America Latine y el Caribe 1991).

Until the mid-1980s, the countries of this region had to adopt short-term adjustment policies, which slowed the rate of job creation, increased unemployment and underemployment, and caused steep declines in real wages and nonwage income. Simultaneously, there were cuts in social spending by the state in most Latin American countries. The effect of these trends on social indicators was an increase in the percentage of households falling below the poverty line and a worsening of the degree of poverty (Tables 9.1 and 9.2).

Beginning in the second half of the 1980s, Latin American countries began to apply policies for structural change, which involved a transitional period of declines in employment and income in some areas of economic activity; some of the areas affected were privatized public enterprises or sectors engaged in the production of nontradable goods and services. These policies of structural change also threatened to accentuate preexisting economic and social inequality within countries due to the existence of a high-productivity, well-paid modern sector linked to the international economy on the one hand, and, on the other, an economic environment marked by backwardness, underemployment, and income levels insufficient to satisfy the workers' essential needs (ILO 1992).

A number of governments in the region set up social investment funds to offset, at least in part, the negative impact of the adjustment and restructuring process. Some of these funds are of a temporary nature, scheduled to last three or four years with the implicit or explicit assumption that, once the macroeconomic adjustment and the transitional period of restructuring of

Table 9.1—Indicators of economic activity, population, and employment in Latin America

Indicator	1980–85	1985–90	1980–90	1990–91	1991–92
			(percent)		
Economic activity					
Gross domestic product (cumulative annual growth)	0.6	1.9	1.2	3.5	2.4
Inflation[a]	134.8	487.5	271.4	198.7	410.7
Inflation[a] (excluding Brazil) (cumulative annual variation)			49.0	22.0	
Net transfer of resources (annual average, billions of U.S. dollars)	–10.6	–24.0	–16.6	8.4	27.4
Population and employment (cumulative annual variation)					
Total population	2.2	2.1	2.1	2.0	2.0
Economically active population	3.5	3.1	3.3	2.9	2.9
Employment	3.3	3.3	3.3	2.4	2.8
Nonagricultural employment	3.5	4.4	4.0	3.0	2.9
Total number of unemployed	6.8	–1.9	2.3	6.9	8.8

Source: Based on official data of Programa Regional del Empleo para América Latina y el Caribe.
[a]Weighted average.

Table 9.2—Structure of employment and income in Latin America

Indicator	1980	1985	1990	1991	1992
			(percent)		
Employment structure					
Nonagricultural employment	100.0	100.0	100.0	100.0	100.0
Private-sector employment	58.7	53.1	53.5	53.5	53.3
Large enterprises	44.1	36.5	31.7	31.2	30.8
Small enterprises	14.6	16.6	21.8	22.3	22.5
Public-sector employment	15.7	16.6	15.6	15.2	14.9
Informal-sector employment	25.6	30.4	30.9	31.3	31.9
Own-account workers	19.2	22.6	24.0	24.4	25.0
Domestic service	6.4	7.8	6.9	6.9	6.9
Total employment	100.0	100.0	100.0	...	...
Primary sector[a]	28.3	27.2	22.4	...	...
Secondary sector	25.0	22.0	23.7	...	...
Tertiary sector	46.7	50.8	53.9	...	...
Unemployment					
Total unemployment (rate)	5.2	6.0	4.7	4.9	5.2
Urban unemployment (rate)[b]	6.7	10.1	7.9	7.7	7.4
Poverty, income, and wages[b]					
Total number of poor	41.0	43.0	46.0	...	...
Urban poor	30.0	36.0	39.0	...	...
Total number of poor households	35.0	37.0	39.0	...	...
Urban poor households	25.0	30.0	34.0	...	...
			(1980 = 100)		
Per capita gross domestic product	100.0	92.0	91.1	92.2	92.7
Minimum wage	100.0	86.4	67.0	64.7	64.8
Wages in industry	100.0	91.0	86.8	88.3	93.3
Wages in agriculture	100.0	87.2	72.1	71.6	69.4
Wages in construction sector	100.0	84.3	85.8	81.7	87.3

Source: Based on official data of Programa Regional del Empleo para América Latina y el Caribe.
[a]Includes agriculture and mining.
[b]The data on poverty refer to the years 1980, 1984, and 1990.

production are over, the development process will itself permit the reduction of the social debt. Their temporary nature determines the exceptional character of their organization and terms of reference. Most of their resources come from external donations or soft loans that will not be available on a long-term basis. Other funds, however, were set up as permanent institutions, since they are intended to be an effective means of channeling part of the social expenditure and investment, regardless of whether the economy is in a stage of adjustment or reactivation.[1]

In contrast to the specific employment programs for poverty reduction and food security in the Asian and African countries assessed in this volume, many Latin American countries have chosen a "social investment fund" approach, which also incorporates employment program actions. This chapter therefore provides a regional complement to the previous ones, but also reviews a different approach.

Social Investment Funds

Their Nature and Purpose

The first temporary fund, which served as a model for those set up later, was the Fondo de Social Emergencia (FSE), which was established in Bolivia in 1986 and concluded its operations in mid-1990.[2] The first example of a permanent fund was the Fondo de Asignaciones Familiares (FODESAF), which was set up in Costa Rica in 1974 and is still fully operative.

The establishment of these funds represented a new approach in the institutional field, although there had been concern about the negative social impact of adjustment policies and poverty reduction much earlier. The Community Development Programs of the 1970s and the Emergency Employment Programs of the 1970s and 1980s in Chile, Peru, and Brazil are examples of this concern (Programa Regional del Empleo para America Latine y el Caribe 1988a). Moreover, in view of the widening social deprivation and the shrinking resources available for social spending, there was a desire to improve the targeting of the employment programs to achieve greater efficiency in social programs.

---

[1]There is also a tendency for the temporary funds to be converted into permanent ones. This has happened in Bolivia, and is being considered in Honduras.

[2]This section is based on Martínez and Wurgaft 1992.

In comparison with these previous efforts, the funds represent a broader field of action inasmuch as they have become a substantive part of both economic and global policy.[3] They also represent a change in the form of operation, because of their more autonomous nature and because they seek to combine in a single body the financing and administration of both employment- and income-generation projects and social expenditure programs not directly connected with employment. They have been set up through laws or executive acts or decrees, and in many cases they have been organized with the support of international financial agencies—especially the World Bank and the International Development Bank (IDB)—and the technical cooperation of the United Nations Development Program (UNDP), the International Labour Office (ILO)-Programa Regional del Empleo para America Latine y el Caribe (PREALC), the United Nations Childrens Fund (UNICEF), the International Development Association (IDA), and other bilateral and multilateral bodies. The social investment funds[4] currently in operation are listed in Table 9.3.

Main Institutional Aspects

As already noted, an important new feature of these funds is their institutional organization and form of operation. Rapid and efficient attainment of results was desired, and it was assumed that this would be impossible under the regular system of public administration. The establishment of such funds was seen as a suitable alternative. The funds were intended to be a new kind of institution that would draw its strength from the combined efforts of the public and private sectors and the beneficiary groups themselves and that would decentralize project identification, design, and execution by inviting segments of the population that have been on the sidelines of state social policy to participate in these tasks.

It is hoped that this synergistic action, effected through the mechanisms and procedures described below, will permit extensive decentralization of fund activities and much greater participation by the beneficiary groups than regular state programs. It is also hoped that the juridical and functional nature of these institutions, as well as their operational procedures, will permit a greater degree of administrative flexibility than is seen in other public institutions.

---

[3]In some countries, these funds are now the main instrument of social policy, and are seen as the "social face" of the adjustment process.

[4]The ways in which these funds are denominated vary from one country to another.

Table 9.3—Social investment funds in Latin America

Country	Name of Fund	Date of Establishment
Permanent funds		
Bolivia	Fondo de Inversión Social (Social Investment Fund)[a] (FIS)	1989
Costa Rica	Fondo de Asignaciones Familiares (Family Allowance Fund) (FODESAF)	1974
Chile	Fondo de Solidaridad e Inversión Social (Solidarity and Social Investment Fund) (FOSIS)	1991
Mexico	Programa Nacional de Solidaridad (National Solidarity Program) (PRONASOL)	1988
Peru	Fondo Nacional de Compensación Desarrollo Social (National Compensation and Social Development Fund) (FOCONDES)	1991
Venezuela	Fondo de Inversión Social (Social Investment Fund)	1990
Temporary funds		
El Salvador	Fondo de Inversión Social (Social Investment Fund)	1990
Guatemala	Fondo de Inversión Social (Social Investment Fund)	1990
Honduras	Fondo Hondureño de Inversión Social (Honduran Social Investment Fund) (FHIS)	1990
Nicaragua	Fondo de Inversión Social de Emergencia (Emergency Social Investment Fund) (FISE)	1990
Panama	Fondo de Emergencia Social (Social Emergency Fund) (FES)	1990
Uruguay	Fondo de Inversión Social de Emergencia (Emergency Social Investment Fund)	1990

Note: Other names are given to these funds in some countries.
[a]This fund replaced the Fondo Social de Emergencia (FSE).

It is precisely these qualities of decentralization, flexibility, and responsiveness that justify governments' use of this scheme rather than channeling resources through the regular public institutions. They feel that the operational shortcomings of the public sector, caused by bureaucratic administrative regulations and by excessive centralization and concentration, limit their capacity to provide the rapid social intervention needed to secure social compensation objectives. At the same time, "reconverting" any of the regular institutions to attain the level of decentralization, flexibility, and responsiveness demanded by compensation programs would be slower and more arduous than setting up completely new institutions, such as the funds.

These new institutions operate essentially as financial intermediaries that receive or procure resources and channel them to social development through other private or public bodies, through a wide variety of options. At the same time, however, it is acknowledged that the funds cannot act exclusively as intermediaries, and that they must also engage in promotion, dissemination, and training activities, especially with regard to the design and presentation of projects and requests for financing. This feature represents an important difference from other types of social development activities, where the state organizations responsible for carrying them out are totally dependent for their financing on other public institutions, even in the case of nonreimbursable external resources.

Figure 9.1 presents a general scheme for procuring financial resources and channeling them to the poorest sectors. Each individual country has special features and specific characteristics. In Costa Rica, for example, the operational procedures are different: FODESAF distributes the resources to public institutions (and also sometimes to private organizations or even international cooperation agencies) according to a predetermined budget, so that these institutions can finance regular social compensation programs. In the case of Mexico's Programa Nacional de Solidaridad (PRONASOL), the beneficiary groups participate through Solidarity Committees whose members are elected by direct vote of the beneficiaries at public meetings, or are designated by municipal authorities or in accordance with predetermined structures. These committees, in turn, call meetings to decide on the characteristics of the projects and are responsible for monitoring—ensuring that the parties involved fulfill their commitment. In the case of Chile's Fondo de Solidaridad e Inversión Social (FOSIS), the beneficiaries gain access to the resources by participating in tendering contests, public invitations, or competitions—either through their own organizations or through a private executing agency; they may also gain access by presenting a project or stating a need to a public or private body with which FOSIS has a valid working agreement.

In short, the funds have adopted a form of institutional organization that stresses flexible procedures and decentralization. The funds' links to the public and private sectors are dealt with later in this chapter.

Projects and Activities

From the time that the first funds started operating right up to the present day, their priorities have constantly been evolving (Wurgaft 1992). To begin with, they were presented as an improvement on the large-scale employment programs that arose in the 1970s and earlier. In these earlier programs, the social effect was pursued through the increased income made available to beneficiaries in the form of wages paid for the construction

Figure 9.1—General scheme of social funds in Latin America

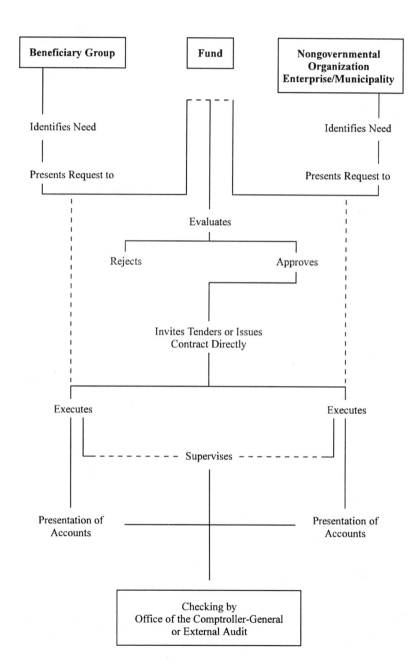

of labor-intensive infrastructural works or the provision of services, and through the social value of those works. The drawbacks of these programs were their very low productivity, the temporary nature of the employment provided, and generally low remuneration.[5]

In some of the funds, an attempt was made to shift the emphasis away from achieving social benefits through the employment generated toward pursuing those benefits through the magnitude and productivity of the works undertaken. In this new approach, a large part of the available resources are assigned to the construction of social infrastructure projects executed by private contractors who must fulfil certain minimum requirements of employment generation. Apparently, the purpose is greater efficiency of investments, but a limiting factor is their administrative focus on technical infrastructure achievements; employment and community participation and social organization are relegated to the background. Moreover, although there are successful examples of productive infrastructure projects—mostly in the areas of irrigation and local road building—that have generated stable indirect employment, most of the jobs created are of a temporary nature.[6]

In view of these drawbacks of infrastructure building, the most recent trend—especially for the permanent funds—has been toward the diversification of resource assignment, with special emphasis on projects designed to upgrade human resources through training, improved health, nutrition, and education, and the creation of stable productive jobs through the provision of financing and support for microenterprises, cooperatives, producers' organizations, and so forth. The aim is for social organization and participation to be the main instruments for social improvement; funds are assigned to infrastructure projects only when these complement the objectives.

The funds currently operating in Latin America follow some of these lines and use their resources to finance programs, projects, and activities, which correspond, in whole or in part, to the following classification:

1. Projects for the construction, repair, and maintenance of social and productive infrastructure, including projects for the construction, repair, or maintenance of schools, clinics, rural roads, small bridges, small-scale irrigation works, and so forth.

---

[5]Information on the experience of employment programs in Latin America, prior to the social investment funds, can be found in Programa Regional del Empleo para America Latine y el Caribe (PREALC) 1988a.

[6]Examples of infrastructure projects that generate permanent employment are the irrigation program for farmers and indigenous populations of FOSIS in Chile and the programs for access roads and irrigation and drainage of FSE of Bolivia.

2. Social assistance projects, including food aid projects, benefits for women heads of households, health, and education.
3. Projects designed to generate stable employment for poor sectors of the population. This type of project includes those in support of microenterprises (both urban and rural), rotating credit funds, formation of small cooperatives, and training programs.
4. Emergency employment generation projects, including projects in such areas as cleaning, landscaping, and urban tree planting.

In the case of the temporary funds, most of the resources have gone to finance economic and social infrastructure projects that generate temporary jobs during the construction stage. When these are properly evaluated projects, they can have permanent effects, due to the economic and social value of the work done. Some types of economic infrastructure projects, such as local roads or irrigation works, can also have a substantial impact in the creation of stable indirect employment. A further portion of the temporary funds has been channeled to various forms of social assistance in areas such as nutrition, health, or community organization that are not connected with employment. Finally, substantially smaller percentages have been channeled to support production activities in microenterprises, self-employment, cooperatives, and associative forms of production that provide stable employment or increase the income provided by these jobs. Although considerable importance has been assigned to these types of activities in the formulation of some temporary funds (FHIS 1989), the desire to get quick results has finally meant that priority has been given to infrastructure and social welfare.

In the permanent funds, the expenditure structure concentrates fewer resources on infrastructure projects. FODESAF of Costa Rica, for example, devotes one-half of its resources to social welfare unconnected with employment, 9 percent to support for production activities offering stable employment, and only 36 percent to social or economic infrastructure. Similarly, PRONASOL of Mexico devotes 57 percent of its resources to social welfare, 24 percent to production projects providing stable employment, and 18 percent to infrastructure. FOSIS of Chile, which is also a permanent fund, devotes almost two-thirds of its resources to the generation and improvement of stable employment through support for small production units and social welfare support programs (Table 9.4). Finally, Peru's Fondo Nacional de Compensación Desarrollo Social (FOCONDES) also gives high priority to the financing of production projects with a strong impact on the generation and improvement of stable employment (projects in the areas of nonindustrial fisheries, small-scale processing enterprises, marketing, and so forth).

Table 9.4—Resource assignment of social funds, Latin America

Type of Project	Bolivia FSE (1987–90)	Costa Rice FODESAF (1992)	Chile FOSIS (1991–92)	El Salvador FIS (1991)	Honduras FHIS (1990–91)	Mexico PRONASOL (1990)	Nicaragua FISE (1991)
				(percent)			
Infrastructure	88.0	36.0	23.2	80.8	79.0	18.4	87.0
Economic	43.0	...	20.0	25.6	16.0	...	55.2
Social	45.0	...	3.2	55.2	63.0	...	31.8
Social welfare	8.0	50.0	38.0	18.0	14.0	57.1	13.0
Stable employment	4.0	9.0	23.0	1.2	7.0	24.5	...
Other, unspecified	...	5.0	16.0	...	...	...	...

Sources: FSE: Buxel and Finot 1991; FODESAF: Draft Budget 1992; FHIS: World Bank 1992; PRONASOL: Peniche 1992; FIS: Siri 1992; FISE: Siri 1992; FOSIS: Prepared by PREALC on the basis of FOSIS 1992.

Note: The ellipses (. .) indicate a nil or negligible amount.

Availability and Procurement
of Resources

An essential function of temporary social investment funds is to obtain external resources in the form of donations or credits on concessional terms with regard to interest rates and repayment periods. Such resources have formed the major part of the capital of these temporary funds and have been a decisive factor in their forms of organization, objectives, and activities, ever since the initial experience of FSE in Bolivia. In contrast, permanent funds are financed primarily with domestic resources, although these have been supplemented with external credits in some countries. This difference in the source of financing means that temporary funds are mainly of a compensatory nature, whereas permanent funds also play a redistributive role.

FSE attained its resource procurement goals: altogether, it obtained more than US$200 million, mainly due to the support of the World Bank, both because it was the biggest external contributor and because of the importance of its backing in causing other multilateral and bilateral contributors to decide to provide resources. All in all, there were over 20 contributors, who provided practically one-half their assistance in the form of donations and the remainder in the form of credits with repayment periods of up to 50 years, lengthy grace periods, and very low interest rates.

In the case of the Fondo Hondureño de Inversión Social (FHIS) (Honduras), the amount of external resources that it hopes to procure during the fund's scheduled life is on the order of US$140 million, of which US$60 million was obtained at the end of 1992. As with FSE, the main contributors have been the World Bank, the IDB, the United States, the Netherlands, Canada, Germany, and other developed countries and multinational agencies, which have either made donations or provided soft loans.

The annual average amount of resources obtained by these two countries is equal to 1 percent of the GDP, so that it also has an impact at the macroeconomic level and on the balance of payments. In Bolivia, the contributions to FSE were equivalent, on average, to a 5 percent increase in exports of goods, while in Honduras, they were equal to a 3 percent increase, representing a positive contribution to economic activity in both countries.

External financing of social development on concessional terms is clearly a positive contribution to the beneficiary countries, both because of the amounts involved and the rapidity of the disbursements at critical times during the countries' adjustment processes. One drawback is that these contributions are made on a one-time-only basis or, in any event, they cannot be expected to become a permanent flow. This feature, which goes a long way toward explaining the temporary nature of the funds set up with external resources, raises the problem of how to continue the activities once the inflow of external contributions has ceased and the temporary funds have reached the end of their scheduled existence. One alternative is to consider temporary funds initial experiments that can be continued through permanent funds, financed primarily with domestic resources. These permanent funds would form part of a broad social improvement policy and help both offset the negative effects of the adjustment process and improve the distribution of the fruits of economic activities.

Of the permanent funds discussed here, the amounts involved were substantial in Costa Rica's FODESAF (1.7 percent of the product) and Mexico's PRONASOL (0.7 percent of the product and 7.7 percent of total social expenditure), totaling US$2.3 billion in 1992.

In contrast, the resources of Chile's FOSIS were slight, amounting to US$30–40 million per year (that is, less than 0.5 percent of total social expenditure and 0.1 percent of the product). This means that this institution's importance was of a qualitative nature: it was a means of trying out new forms of targeted social intervention and channeling resources of other institutions to social development purposes, rather than securing appreciable effects on income and employment.

The Effects of Social Funds on Employment and Income

The data available for evaluating the amount of employment created and the increases in the income of beneficiaries of the funds are clearly inadequate. No surveys or other procedures have been carried out for this purpose, and the existing information systems are designed merely to ensure that the programs and projects are carried out in accordance with the approved specifications. Because of this shortage of information, the existing evaluations are mostly limited to administrative, accounting, and operational aspects. Analysis of the real effects obtained and the benefits secured by the target groups is relegated to the background.

Employment Creation

This shortcoming is particularly marked with respect to employment generation. For the purposes of this study, only partial information could be obtained on the experience of Bolivia, Honduras, and Chile, which merely indicates broad orders of magnitude. This information primarily concerns temporary employment in the construction of infrastructure projects and global estimates of the new jobs resulting from the provision of loans to microenterprises.

Bolivia. Basic information about FSE comes from feasibility studies of the projects requesting resources from the fund, in which estimates were made, by types of projects, of the direct and indirect employment needed for their execution. These basic data were corrected on the basis of a study (Newman et al. 1989), which found that the workers on FSE projects worked an average of 50.3 hours per week, compared with only 46.8 hours for other workers. This implies that the number of jobs actually created was less than the figure assumed in the basic data. When the information was corrected in the main FSE evaluation study (Buxel and Finot 1991), in the period 1987–90, the total number of workdays was equivalent to 59,000 person-years of direct employment, an annual average of over 14,000 jobs.

The same evaluation mission estimated that in infrastructure construction projects, each direct job was accompanied by the creation of 0.75 indirect jobs (UDAPE 1989). Thus, over the period in question, 44,000 indirect jobs are estimated to have been generated (an average of some 11,000 per year), a total of nearly 103,000 direct and indirect jobs over the four years (that is, an annual average of 26,000). Although these figures are below the goal that the FSE originally set (20,000 direct jobs per year), they are nevertheless substantial; in 1990, for example, the number of jobs created was equivalent to 1.8 percent of the national employment and to almost one-third of the number of unemployed.

Some information is available on the prior employment status of those obtaining direct jobs: 55 percent already had a job when they joined the scheme, while 39 percent were looking for work. This suggests two conclusions: first, that the employment created by the fund served more to reduce underemployment than reduce open unemployment; and, second, that unlike other programs designed to generate employment through infrastructure works, which mostly attracted people who were previously inactive, almost all those employed through the FSE were active workers (Castaños et al. 1987; Newman et al. 1989). Most of them (90 percent of the total) were males of families located in the bottom deciles of the income distribution structure (Pollack 1992).

However, in the case of FHIS (Honduras), the available information indicates that from its inception up to June 1992, it generated 410,000 person-months of employment, equal to some 34,000 person-years and a little over 15,000 jobs per year. This average is a little misleading, however, since during the early months of the operation of FHIS, progress on the projects was very limited, so that the number of jobs actually generated in 1991 and the first half of 1992 must have been much higher than that average (Barahona 1993).

Even taking the annual average referred to above, the generation of temporary employment was relatively great and was equivalent to 1 percent of the employed population and 21 percent of the unemployed. Unfortunately, no information is available on the employment status of those obtaining jobs under FHIS before they were hired for its projects; therefore, it is impossible to determine the effective reduction in unemployment due to the fund's operations. Finally, according to FHIS estimates (Barahona 1993), 3,000 stable jobs were created up to mid-1992 through the loans made to microentrepreneurs under the Informal Sector Support Program.

Chile. The employment-generation effects of FOSIS were not very significant, first, because the fund's total resources are limited in terms of the country's total social expenditure and, second, because most of the investments were made in social improvement or training programs that do not have an immediate impact on employment. Among the productive programs, four are connected with job creation: those in the areas of irrigation, soil improvement, afforestation, and credit for microenterprises.

As of April 1993, 16 percent of the scheduled projects in the irrigation program had been completed, involving a physical area of roughly 23,000 hectares. According to the coefficients used by Instituto National de Desarrollo Agropecuario (INDAP) (Chile), the body responsible for executing the program, and in view of the fact that the projects involved the improvement of irrigation, and not the construction of new irrigation systems, it is estimated that the effect of the completed projects is equivalent to the incorporation of some 8,000 additional hectares. The ratio for the program as a whole is 5.3 hectares per stable job, so that it is estimated that some 1,500 stable jobs had been generated as of April 1993. If these figures are projected to the completion of the whole program, equivalent to the incorporation of some 41,000 additional irrigated hectares, this would represent the creation of 8,000 stable agricultural jobs.

The coefficient used in the evaluation of irrigation projects is 2.5 indirect nonagricultural jobs generated for each stable job created in agriculture (Maffei 1991). If this indicator is accepted, then the total effect would be the creation of 28,000 stable jobs (8,000 in agriculture and 20,000 nonagricultural jobs).

In the afforestation program, the figures indicate that some 400 stable jobs were generated in the maintenance of 17,000 hectares of tree plantations on nonirrigated land. Finally, the credit program for microenterprises is estimated to have generated between 4,500 and 5,500 stable jobs. This is a rather rough estimate, since a specific survey to be carried out by FOSIS is still being prepared.

This estimate is based on two factors: first, the credits granted under the program amounted to some 4.1 billion pesos (US$11 million), of which 3 billion pesos came from banks or financial institutions that received subsidies from FOSIS for this purpose, while the remainder came from FOSIS itself; and, second, in programs similar to FOSIS carried out in Chile and other Latin American countries, for which direct measurements have been made, for every US$1,500–2,500 of credit granted, one permanent job was generated (Fuenzalida and Fuenzalida 1992; Christen and Wright 1993; Jiménez 1993; Mezzera 1993). This is assumed to be the highest level of credit per job, since most of the loans were made to microenterprises of the largest capital and scale (around 10 employees) (Ruiz-Tagle and Molina 1992).

Cost of Job Generation

The temporary employment resulting from the infrastructure projects of FSE in Bolivia was equivalent to 103,000 person-years, for an expenditure of US$185 million during the four years that the project lasted (Buxel and Finot 1991). This represents a cost of some US$1,800 per job per year. The cost of the temporary employment generated by FHIS in Honduras was around US$1,000 per job per year.

In the irrigation program carried out by FOSIS in Chile, it was estimated that total investment of some US$25 million would generate some 8,000 stable jobs in agriculture by the end of the program, giving an average cost of US$3,000 per job. Irrigation alone, however, is not enough to create these jobs. Other investments are also required, such as the planting of crops, the purchase of agricultural machinery and equipment, the installation of irrigation systems on farms, electrical installations, and so forth. As the FOSIS program only involves the improvement of irrigation facilities, the investments for these purposes would amount to about 50 percent of the total (Maffei and Molina 1992).[7]

But, as already noted, the creation of jobs in agriculture is only one effect: a second, much greater, effect is the generation of nonagricultural employment. Taking into account the total investments and the total number of jobs generated, it may be concluded that each stable job from the

---

[7]Analysis of some agricultural development projects indicates that irrigation accounts for 30 to 70 percent of the total investment.

irrigation program costs around US$1,800 (total investments of US$50 million and a total of 28,000 stable jobs created).

Finally, various studies on microenterprise credit programs, to which reference was made earlier, indicate that one additional stable job is generated for every US$1,500–2,500 of credit made available to such enterprises.

Although these results only indicate orders of magnitude and are not strictly comparable, they show the advantages of programs that generate stable employment, compared with those that create temporary jobs. For example, to generate a stable job (that is, to provide employment for at least 10 years) by providing credit to microenterprises, it would be necessary to assign between US$1,500 and US$2,500 (a sum that can subsequently be recovered); in contrast, in infrastructure construction, it is necessary to spend between US$1,000 and US$1,800 to generate a single job that lasts one year. This does not mean, however, that one policy instrument should necessarily be preferred over the other, even when only their effects on employment are considered. Investment in infrastructure projects can deliver a rapid, large-scale response that cannot be achieved through credit to microenterprises. In the example from Bolivia, it is clear that the amount of employment generated through infrastructure projects funded by the FSE over four years could not have been achieved through the provision of credit to microenterprises. This latter instrument gives high yields, but its effects are only realized over the medium term; above all, it is difficult to apply to productive activities on a massive scale (Mezzera 1993). Besides, as has already been described, some infrastructure projects—such as irrigation, rural roads, drainage, and others—can have significant effects on the generation of permanent employment.

Effects on Income and Poverty

As in the case of employment, there is little information to evaluate the funds' effects on income, except for some data concerning FSE in Bolivia. It is therefore necessary to estimate the changes that would occur in the various countries and programs on the basis of different hypotheses.

Bolivia. In Bolivia, a study commissioned by the fund itself (Newman et al. 1989) concludes that there is an 82 percent probability that those employed on FSE projects would have found work in some other activity if FSE had not existed. In this instance, the estimated effect on income must be seen as the difference between the income received from working on FSE projects and the remuneration that would have been obtained if FSE did not exist.[8] The study concludes that the income "with FSE" was 67 percent higher than that "without FSE," because the jobs found outside

FSE would have been in low-productivity activities, mainly in the urban informal sector. The income provided by FSE was 67 percent higher than the average income of informal sector workers and peasants.

The question arises: did those employed by FSE belong to the poor sectors of the population? According to a study by Pollack (1992), 27.2 percent of the total income generated by FSE (Bolivia) went to persons in the first three income deciles; 51.3 percent to the fourth, fifth, and sixth deciles; and the remaining 21.5 percent was distributed to the seventh through tenth deciles. This means that, although nonpoor sectors of the population also benefited from FSE (at that time, the poverty rate in Bolivia was 64 percent, which may be assumed to correspond to the first six deciles), the greater part (78.5 percent) of the income generated by FSE did indeed go to the poor sectors of the population. At the same time, however, it should be noted that, within those sectors, those who benefited the most were in the higher strata (from the fourth to sixth deciles), while those in extreme poverty, who represented 33 percent of the Bolivian population (first to third deciles), received a smaller share.

In view of the fact that in Bolivia the first quintile of the population receives approximately 3 percent of total income, and that the investments made by FSE in 1990 were equivalent to 1 percent of GDP, it might be estimated that, if all those investments had been devoted to benefiting the population in the first quintile, the latter's income would have increased by one-third. Even so, the percentage of those investments destined for the payment of wages is not more than 50 percent of the total, so that the increase in wage income would have been only 0.5 percent of GDP, representing an increase in income of only 17 percent (see Table 9.5). If the investments had been distributed entirely over the first two quintiles (where the extremely poor are concentrated), which receive 9 percent of total income, the contribution of additional resources equal to 0.5 percent of GDP would have increased income on the order of 5.5 percent.

Costa Rica. Another country where it is possible to estimate the effect of the social investment fund on income is Costa Rica, where the fund in question (FODESAF) is of a permanent nature. In 1988, total social expenditure was equal to 19.2 percent of GDP, and FODESAF accounted for 8.9 percent of total social spending. Thus, in that year, the fund channeled resources equivalent to 1.7 percent of GDP (Table 9.5). However, taking

---

[8]It is assumed that the distribution of income by branches of activity is the same as in FSE.

Table 9.5—Estimated effects of social funds on incomes of the poor in selected Latin American countries

Fund	Year	Fund as Percentage of GDP	Degree of Actual Implementation	Administrative and Other Expenses as Percentage of Total	Income as a Percentage of GDP	Increase in Income	Percent Increase
FSE, Bolivia	1990	1.0	100	50		0.50	
First quintile					3.0		16.6
First and second quintiles					9.0		5.5
FODESAF, Costa Rica	1988	1.7	73	44		0.80	
First quintile					3.0		26.6
First and second quintiles					10.5		7.6
FHIS, Honduras	1991	0.7	100	50		0.35	
First quintile					2.5		14.0
First and second quintiles					7.5		4.6
PRONASOL, México	1992	0.7	100	45		0.40	
First quintile					2.7		14.3
First and second quintiles					8.7		4.6

Source: Prepared by the author on the basis of information provided by the funds, World Bank (1993), and ECLAC (1992).
Note: GDP is gross domestic product.

into account that the fund spent only an average of 72.8 percent of its budgeted resources and that 44 percent of the total amount spent corresponded to administrative expenses, materials, and equipment, the expenditure that actually reached the poor sectors was equivalent to only 3.7 percent of total social expenditure and 0.8 percent of GDP. Since the population grouped in the first quintile (where almost all the poor are concentrated) received 3.0 percent of total income in that year, devoting FODESAF's contribution (0.8 percent of GDP) entirely to that quintile would bring about an increase of 26.6 percent in the income received (Ramírez 1991). Assuming the hypothesis of a less favorable form of targeting of FODESAF's resources would give the estimated results presented in Table 9.5, which shows that in these circumstances the increases in income would be substantially smaller. Even so, these effects are significant since FODESAF is a permanent fund and similar results must therefore be achieved every year.

Honduras. In Honduras, the first quintile (where the poorest members of the population—assumed to be the primary target—are concentrated) has a share of total income of 2.5 percent. Until the end of 1991, the FHIS-financed projects cost nearly US$40 million, an annual average of US$20 million, equal to 0.7 percent of GDP. It is estimated that 11 percent of these totals represented administrative expenses, 39 percent was spent on materials and equipment, and the remaining 50 percent was the income of beneficiaries (Hurtado 1992); the total amount that directly reached the population came close to US$10 million, equal to 0.35 percent of GDP (see Table 9.5). If it is assumed that this amount went entirely to the poorest 20 percent of the population, then the income received by this group would have increased, thanks to the FHIS, by 14.0 percent, thus rising from 2.5 percent of total income to 2.85 percent. If, on the contrary, it is hypothesized that the resources of FHIS were not targeted so effectively, and that they were distributed among the first two population quintiles (in Honduras, the poor occupy the first four quintiles), then the income received by that poorest 40 percent (7.5 percent of GDP) would rise by only 4.6 percent.

Mexico. Similar estimates can also be made for PRONASOL (Mexico). In 1992, total social expenditure was equivalent to 9 percent of GDP, while PRONASOL's expenditure was 7.7 percent of total social spending, that is, 0.7 percent of GDP (Table 9.5). Of this amount, approximately 55 percent is channeled toward increasing the income of the target groups (the remainder is spent on inputs, administration expenses, and programs not connected with income). The total channeled to these groups was therefore equal to some 0.4 percent of GDP. If the whole of this amount had reached the first (poorest) quintile, which received approximately 2.7 percent of the product, then PRONASOL's effect would have been to increase income by 14.3 percent. If the same amount had been distributed among the first two quintiles, which received 8.7 percent of GDP, the effect would have been to increase their income by 4.6 percent.

It is not possible to make similar estimates for FOSIS (Chile), as its expenditure is very small compared with its country's total social spending and GDP, and its effect is therefore imperceptible in these terms.

In short, the transfer of income generated by most of the funds studied has a limited, but by no means insignificant, impact if the resources are properly targeted.

Other Considerations to Be Taken into Account in Evaluating the Funds' Effects

The Social Benefits of the Projects

Generally speaking, the evaluations of the projects financed by the funds are positive. The available studies focus on the number of projects carried out and the magnitude of the resulting physical works and services (Buxel and Finot 1991; World Bank 1992; FOSIS 1992; UAM 1992).

In the area of economic infrastructure, projects on rural roads and means of access, urban improvement, small-scale irrigation and drainage works, reforestation, and product collection centers predominate. In the field of social infrastructure, water supply and sewerage projects, housing, and the construction of buildings for educational and health purposes and for recreation and social organization are prevalent.

A leading concern in these experiences has been to avoid the concentration of resources and projects and to try to cover a wide range of social and regional needs. This is reflected in the number of projects carried out (more than 3,000 by FSE and more than 2,000 by FHIS, FOSIS, and PRONASOL), with relatively modest average investments per project (averages of US$60,000 for FSE, US$35,000 for FOSIS, US$20,000 for FHIS, and US$15,000 for PRONASOL). This concern is also reflected in the distribution of projects and resources among the different political and administrative divisions in line with the population distribution, more or less corrected by poverty levels, and in the distribution between rural and urban areas. In the latter respect, the evaluations emphasize the difficulties encountered in reaching the most isolated rural areas.

The technical and economic efficiency of the projects also seems to be satisfactory, although it is difficult to generalize, since there is a wide variety of types of projects. In Bolivia, evaluations by project and region highlight strengths and weaknesses and make recommendations for improvement, within a generally positive context. Consultation of the beneficiaries also elicits mainly positive opinions. The same is true of the evaluation of FOSIS, the main observations of which concern delays and administrative shortcomings due to staff shortages and lack of experience in the initial stages of some programs.[9]

An important criticism leveled at the funds that devote most of their resources to infrastructure projects is that they do not give beneficiaries sufficient opportunities to participate in decisions on which projects to adopt or on their form of execution. A related criticism is that they have taken a "paternalistic" approach and failed to contribute to community organization. This manner of operation is probably related to the need to get tangible results quickly, since the funds in question are temporary ones set up to deal with emergency situations.

With regard to social assistance or welfare programs, which form a prominent part of the permanent funds' activities, the available evaluations are also generally positive. The results depend essentially on the experience of the public or private institutions responsible for their execution. Evaluations of FSE and FOSIS have been made by project type, and in each case, different shortcomings, achievements, and recommendations are identified. There is no global overview, however, detailing the importance and incidence of the problems in question.

Finally, support projects for production, microenterprises, and informal activities are growing more important. In FSE, the rotating funds in these areas could be implemented only in the last years of the fund's operations, but they became a fundamental instrument of the social investment fund that succeeded FSE as a permanent body. Likewise, support programs for the informal sector are gaining importance for FHIS in Honduras and the permanent funds of the South American countries and Mexico.

---

[9] Evaluations of the infrastructure projects carried out by FSE of Bolivia in Potosi, Cochabamba, La Paz, Tarija, and Oruro (drinking water supply and sewerage, housing, access roads, irrigation, drainage, construction and repair of health and education buildings, control of erosion, and forestry) consider the quality of the execution by the contractors and the functioning and operation of the projects (Buxel and Finot 1991). For Chile's FOSIS, evaluations were made of the programs for forestry, training, nourishment and nutrition, development of indigenous communities, assistance to microenterprises, and so forth (FOSIS 1992).

Focusing on Expenditure and the
Role of Political Pressures

As noted earlier, the targeting of expenditure to the poorest sectors of the population, which are hardest hit by adjustment, is a primary objective of both temporary and permanent funds. Has this objective been attained?

This question is an appropriate one, because experience shows that decentralized forms of operation (which will be dealt with later) are not of themselves sufficient to ensure reaching extremely poor groups and the most severely marginalized sectors. In view of the desire to get quick results, programs and projects are selected largely in light of the demands of users who identify and design projects; this fact leads to the exclusion of some of the poorest groups because of their lack of capacity for proposing and running projects. NGOs are not always effective intermediaries because they also do not reach the most isolated areas. To tackle these limitations, the funds can promote the creation of such capacity, where it does not already exist, by promoting new NGOs, financing the activities of monitors, or taking measures for the direct organization of the target groups.[10]

Proper targeting of expenditure can also be hindered by political pressures: beneficiaries may not be selected from among the poorest and most vulnerable groups, but come from those affected by adjustment who have the greatest capacity to exert political pressure. The risk of political pressures may also play a role when decisions about the scope and location of programs are made; for example, there may be a bias in favor of nation-wide, urban programs because these are more "visible" than regional or rural programs. These are obvious risks that, up to a point, are common to all social development programs. They can be minimized by using broad-based institutions, by raising the political level at which decisions are taken, and by constantly promoting participation by the target groups.

The information available on the various funds shows marked differences in this respect. There are funds that seem to have achieved a high level of targeting of the poorest areas and groups, while there are others in which dissipation and leakage of resources to middle- and even high-income sectors occur.

---

[10]Chile's FOSIS created Centers of Entrepreneur Initiative to provide assistance to microenterprises in provinces and communities not considered by NGOs due to their geographical remoteness. Honduras' FHIS established a Program for Institutional Strengthening to support far-off municipalities. The primary objective of PRONASOL of Mexico has been organization of the community, which has led to the creation of more than 15,000 Solidarity Committees.

The Honduran fund (FHIS) is one that seems to be successful at targeting its social investments. It began by preparing a poverty map in 1990 to plot the location of the fund's investments. As of March 1992, FHIS had financed projects in all the municipalities of the country as well as in more than 1,000 villages and hamlets. Generally speaking, the municipalities and villages in the poorest areas are those that have received the most projects.[11]

In Bolivia, the evaluation mission notes in its report that "those who benefited most from the FSE projects were persons—generally of low income—living in cities with over 10,000 inhabitants" (Buxel and Finot 1991). With regard to geographical areas, the same report states that "the departments with the most beneficiaries were Cochabamba and Chuquisaca, as well as (but only in the last year) Santa Cruz and Potosí, the last-named being the poorest department in the country." Of the total of 947,000 permanent beneficiaries (direct and indirect) between 1987 and 1990, 53.6 percent were located in the capital (of the department) and the remainder in other areas. It may be noted that those in the capital were mostly benefited through drinking water supply and sewerage works. Of the 46.4 percent of beneficiaries located in "other areas" (representing approximately 25 percent of the national total), almost three-fifths were rural dwellers who benefited from afforestation and irrigation projects; one-fifth were urban dwellers located outside the capital; and the remaining one-fifth were urban children living outside the capital who received the meals program for children and school breakfasts. The spatial distribution of the permanent beneficiaries of FSE's investments is shown in Table 9.6.

The temporary beneficiaries, for their part, are estimated to amount to nearly 4 million, although this figure covers all beneficiaries of the projects, without distinguishing between those who benefited from only one project and those who benefited from more than one (and are therefore counted as many times as the number of benefits they received). The spatial distribution of these temporary beneficiaries appears to be similar to that of the permanent beneficiaries. Thus, the rural dwellers benefited from drainage, afforestation, and primary health care projects, and represented 25 percent of the total number of beneficiaries.

What economic and social strata do these beneficiaries belong to? According to Pollack's (1992) study, almost three-quarters of the income generated by FSE was distributed among people in the poorest 60 percent of the population. Bearing in mind that in 1991 the poverty rate in Bolivia

---

[11]Report by the executive director of FHIS to the World Bank advisory group, March 1992.

Table 9.6—Spatial distribution of beneficiaries of Fondo Social de Emergencia, Bolivia

Area	Number of Beneficiaries	Percent of Total Population
Urban	590,231	62.3
Capital	508,587	53.7
Others	81,644	8.6
Rural	264,694	27.9
Not specified	92,984	9.8
Total	947,909	100.0

Source: Buxel and Finot 1991.

was approximately 64 percent of the population, it may be concluded that most of FSE's resources were indeed focused on the "target" population. As already noted, however, it was the less poor sectors of this population that received the greatest benefits.

Maintenance and Development of Investments

A recurrent concern in connection with social investment funds (but one that is not usually taken into account in evaluations) is subsequent financing of the maintenance of social and productive infrastructure works whose construction was financed by the funds in rural areas.

Although the subsequent maintenance of infrastructure should be financed by the beneficiaries themselves, it is possible that, once the fund's action is completed, those sectors will not have the resources needed to finance such maintenance. The changes in productivity and income brought about through the application of adjustment policies are seldom significant enough to enable the poorer sectors to maintain infrastructure themselves. Without maintenance, the productive capacity and incomes of the families concerned would soon return to the levels that existed before the intervention of the fund.

In the short term, however, the effects of the adjustment policy on rural income are not evenly distributed over the rural production structure (Paz and Martínez 1992). On the one hand, there is the production segment made up of those who produce goods for export or goods for the domestic market that compete with imports (especially basic grains, whose "preadjustment" level of tariff protection is usually low); this segment profits from devaluations and tariff reductions on imported inputs, which enable it to increase its income. On the other hand, there are the producers of nontradable agricultural goods, subsistence farmers, and nonagricultural rural workers, who are adversely affected by those same measures and by the short-term contraction of domestic demand caused by the adjustment policy itself.

If the funds direct their investments toward the poorest population strata, these will comprise—in the case of rural areas—those engaged in the production of nontradable goods and subsistence farming. In these circumstances, it is hard to see how, in the short and medium terms, these sectors could finance additional expenditure for the maintenance and full utilization of the infrastructure built by the funds. In this case, it could be said that the funds' investments, while necessary, are in no way sufficient to bring about a sustained improvement in the quality of life of the sectors that benefit from them. If, however, the funds' investments in economic and social infrastructure also benefit sectors of the rural population engaged in the production of exportable goods and tradable goods for the domestic market, then this concern is much less justified because the incomes of these sectors would actually increase as a result of the application of the economic adjustment and restructuring policy.

If responsibility for the maintenance of the infrastructure constructed by the funds is not assumed by the state as part of its regular social expenditure, then it can be expected, in view of the income situation of the producers, that much of that infrastructure will be lost. What happened to the works constructed under the Temporary Employment Generation Program (PAIT) in Peru in the late 1980s is an example. PAIT was in operation from 1985 to 1987. Its purpose was to increase incomes of urban and rural poor families through wages paid during the construction of infrastructure. No funds were furnished for the work's maintenance, which ensured that shortly the new infrastructure was damaged beyond repair. Maintenance is a particularly important issue that does not receive enough attention when decisions on the nature of the fund are made or when the fund's activities are programmed and evaluated.

Public and Private Participation
in the Funds' Activities

The participation of regular public institutions and private organizations in social policy is another element that must be taken into consideration when evaluating funds.

In the debates prior to their establishment, it was noted that the funds could become institutions that complement, or even replace, the regular public sector, in line with strategies to reduce the state's role in carrying out social policy. Obviously, this risk does exist: the funds may take over the functions of ministries or institutions dependent on them, and they may lead to the postponement of action to improve regular state bodies, which would, in effect, be partly replaced by the funds. However, the funds were not set up with this objective; it is assumed that they have specific purposes and fields of action in which they will complement the rest of the public sector rather than compete with it.

As already noted, the funds operate with considerable urgency, on the assumption that the regular state organizations do not have the capacity to respond rapidly and efficiently to the problems of adjustment. This view is partly based on real or assumed shortcomings of the public sector, such as bureaucratic red tape, the narrow view taken by sectoral bodies, or the shortage of suitable staff. However, it is also based on the idea that the regular forms of organization are not capable of reaching the levels of decentralization needed to reach small communities or specific population groups. In contrast, this is seen as the inherent and specific aim of social investment funds. This is a matter that must be evaluated by governments, donors, and financing agencies in each particular case, comparing the levels of efficiency and rapidity of response that can be achieved by strengthening the regular bodies with the results expected from the creation of new institutions, that is, the funds.

If the option of setting up a social investment fund is selected, it is important that there is complementarity. The funds can provide resources to the regular state bodies for the execution of joint community support programs, help in their organization, and support small sectoral projects. They can develop ideas for programs and projects and work out methods and procedures for achieving direct access to the target population. Joint cooperation could involve the provision of financing by the funds and the actual execution of the projects by the regular state bodies, with the motivated participation of the beneficiaries. In short, they can provide a concept of decentralized and participative work at levels that the state does not normally reach. Once these programs have been tested, many of them can be handed over for subsequent execution by the regular bodies or municipalities themselves.

Private participation in activities promoted and financed by the funds is also related to the aim of improving the degree of targeting and decentralization. Infrastructure projects, which have received the major share of the resources of the most active funds, have been carried out primarily through private contractors. According to available information, this has permitted the attainment of adequate levels of efficiency in the execution of the projects, but it also has its limitations (Buxel and Finot 1991). It is not clear whether the employment generated and the wages paid really benefit the poorest groups. First, although the contractors have to comply with certain minimum requirements for labor intensity, they are not subject to any restrictions with regard to the nature of the income provided or the employment status of the workers hired. Moreover, part of the overall expenditure corresponds to the contractors' profits. Second, it is not clear how much participation the target groups have in the decisions on infrastructure works, how much communities and neighborhood organizations are actually consulted in the definition of the projects, or to what extent the projects really reflect their interests and initiatives. The field for participation is broader in the case of production activities, such as microenterprises or cooperatives, which are more in keeping with the criterion of promoting efforts by the target group itself. But so far it has been difficult for the funds to devote significant resources to these types of activities, even when they are highlighted as a fundamental objective. In the execution of social projects, the funds often act through NGOs. This has the advantage of permitting closer contact with detailed and specific problems and finding more concrete solutions to them, but it can also be a drawback. NGOs are often specialists in the problems they deal with and the geographical areas they cover. As a result, they are not suitable for the execution of some broader programs, in which case the funds must operate through the regular public entities.

Conclusions

The deterioration in Latin America's social conditions during the 1980s, together with the well-known effects of the adjustment policy on the incomes of wage earners and independent producers of nontradable goods, amply justify the need for social action. The details given in the preceding sections provide grounds for asserting that, in general, both the permanent and temporary funds have been or can be effective means of achieving the objectives for which they were established.

Regarding the efficiency of the funds, estimates of their effects on employment and income in the poorest sectors indicate that they are positive and by no means insignificant, provided expenditure is properly targeted. Thus, within the limits of the financial resources involved, temporary funds provide the desired compensatory effect and permanent ones provide redistributive effects. It should not be forgotten, however, that such targeting must take account of not only the degree of poverty of the target population, but also the particular nature of its productive activities and the (positive or negative) effects of the adjustment policy on that population. Only after such consideration will it be possible to plan the supplementary measures needed, once the operation period of the fund is over, to prevent a sudden reduction in the income obtained through the fund's activities.

Naturally, the fact that these funds are necessary and effective policy measures does not mean that they are sufficient in themselves. The operation of the funds reflects governments' interest in mitigating the social costs of the adjustment, but social funds are obviously too limited and insufficient an instrument to solve the problem of equity unaided. This is so, first, because of the limited nature of the resources at their disposal and of their operational capacity, compared with the size of the social debt amassed in the past decade. Funds are even more limited when the need to pay off long-term or structural social debt is also taken into account.[12]

Second, they are insufficient because of the complexity of the social problems connected with restructuring. These problems cannot be tackled with a single instrument, but call for a development strategy with concerted application of a whole range of instruments. The funds can complement and strengthen a global social development strategy, but they certainly cannot take its place. Sustained poverty reduction calls for action that goes beyond the potential of the funds. Specifically, it requires action to define the objectives of economic restructuring, macroeconomic policy, and specific measures concerning education and training the labor force; social security coverage; the institutions of the labor market; the design of employment and income programs for specific groups or regions; support for productive activities in marginalized sectors; and, above all, an increase in the size and efficiency of state social expenditure.

Finally, it seems necessary to improve the monitoring and evaluation systems of the social fund institutions. At present, information is available on the operative aspects of the funds, but there is little information on which to evaluate the economic effects of funds or their effects on poverty reduction. This gap must be substantially filled in order to quantitatively estimate the effects of the funds on income, on the social organization of the beneficiaries, and on their productive potential.

---

[12]The concept of social debt refers to the resources needed to overcome poverty and reach a socially acceptable level of equity. It distinguishes between long-term social debt, which corresponds to the cost of overcoming poverty existing at the beginning of the 1980s, and short-term social debt, generated as a result of the unequal distribution of the costs of adjustment during the last decade (Programa Regional del Empleo para America Latine y el Caribe 1988b).

REFERENCES

Barahona, M. 1993. *La experiencia del Fondo Hondureño de Inversión Social*. Santiago, Chile: Programa Regional del Empleo para America Latine y el Caribe.

Buxel, T. I., and I. Finot. 1991. *Informe de la misión de evaluación del FSE de Bolivia*. La Paz, Bolivia: Fondo Social de Emergencia.

Castaños, M. I., et al. 1987. *Evaluación de las acciones y proyecto del Fondo Social de Emergencia*. La Paz, Bolivia: Fondo Social de Emergencia.

Christen, R. P., and S. Wright. 1993. *Financiamiento de la microempresa: Papel y potencial del sector formal y financiero de Chile*. Working Papers Series/378. Santiago, Chile: Programa Regional del Empleo para America Latine y el Caribe.

ECLAC (Economic Commission for Latin America and the Caribbean [United Nations]). 1992. *Statistical yearbook*. Santiago, Chile.

FHIS (Fondo Hondureño de Inversión Social). 1989. *Propuesta de Fondo Hondureño de Inversión Social*. Tegucigalpa, Honduras: Proyecto SECPLAN/OIT/PNUD HON/87/009.

FODESAF (Fondo de Asignaciones Familiares). 1992. Draft budget.

FOSIS (Fondo de Solidaridad e Inversión Social). 1992. Evaluación de programas del FOSIS. Santiago, Chile. Mimeo.

Hurtado, Ch. 1992. *Informe de consultoría FHIS*. Tegucigalpa, Honduras: Fondo Hondureño de Inversión Social.

ILO (International Labour Office). 1992. *Memoria del Director General*. Décimo Tercera Conferencia de Estados Americanos. Caracas, Venezuela.

Maffei, E. 1991. *Riego y empleo: Proyecto Las Brisas, Santo Domingo y Cuncumen*. Santiago, Chile: October.

Maffei, E., and J. Molina. 1992. *Evaluación del programa de riego campesino*. Santiago, Chile: Convenio Fondo de Solidaridad e Inversión Social (Chile)-Instituto National de Desarrollo Agropecuario (Chile).

Martínez, D., and J. Wurgaft. 1992. *Fondo de inversión social. Situación y perspectivas*. Document presented at the Final Seminar of the Regional Project on Policies for Paying the Social Debt, Viña del Mar, Chile, November.

Mezzera, J. 1993. *Experiencias de apoyo al sector informal urbano.* Santiago, Chile: Programa Regional del Empleo para America Latine y el Caribe.

Newman, J., S. Jorgensen, and M. Pradhan. 1989. Como se beneficarios los trabajadores con el Fondo Social de Emergencia? Study presented to the Seminar organized by the Social Emergency Fund, La Paz, Bolivia 26–28 August. Mimeo.

Paz, J., and D. Martínez. 1992. *Política· de ajuste, empleo e ingresos rurales.* Programa Regional del Empleo para America Latine y el Caribe. Mimeo.

Peniche, A. 1992. El pronasol. Algunas notas y reflexiones generales. *El Cotidiano.* Revista de la realidad mexicana actual, July–August, Mexico City.

Pollack, M. 1992. *Los instrumentos compensatorios del ajuste: El FSE de Bolivia.* La Paz, Bolivia: Fondo Hondureño de Inversión Social.

Programa Regional del Empleo para America Latine y el Caribe. 1988a. *Empleos de emergencia.* Santiago, Chile.

_____. 1988b. *Deuda social: ¿Qué es, cuánto es, cómo se paga?* Santiago, Chile.

_____. 1991. *Empleo y equidad: El desafío de los 90.* Santiago, Chile.

_____. 1992. *Suriname: Policies to meet the social debt.* Working Papers Series/363. Santiago, Chile.

Ramírez, J. C. 1991. *Focalización del gasto del FODESAF.* San José, Costa Rica: Programa Regional del Empleo para America Latine y el Caribe.

Ruiz-Tagle, J., and J. Molina. 1992. Programa Nacional de Apoyo a la Microempresa. Evaluation report. Santiago, Chile: Fondo de Solidaridad e Inversión Social. Mimeo.

Siri, G. 1992. The social investment funds in Latin America: A critical appraisal. Study prepared for the Swedish International Development Authority (SIDA). Stockholm.

UAM (Universidad Autónoma Metropolitana). 1992. *El Cotidiano.* Revista de la realidad mexicana actual, July–August, México City.

Unidad de Análisis de Política Económica (Bolivia). 1989. *Evaluación macroeconómica del programa de inversiones ejecutado por el FSE.* La Paz, Bolivia: Fondo de Inversión Social.

World Bank. 1992. Staff appraisal report, second social investment fund project. Washington, D.C. Mimeo.

_____. 1993. *Poverty and income distribution in Latin America. The story of the 1980s.* Washington, D.C.

Wurgaft, J. 1992. Social investment funds and economic restructuring in Latin America. *International Labour Review* 131 (1): 35–44.

10
FUTURE DIRECTIONS FOR DEVELOPMENT AND RELIEF WITH FOOD AID

John Shaw

Poverty alleviation and food security are two prominent features on the international agenda. The provision of sustainable employment is seen as a major factor in the attainment of those goals.[1] Access by the poor to food and work, combined with the construction of essential infrastructure and accumulation of assets, has long been seen both in economic theory and practice to be an effective approach to poverty alleviation and the attainment of food security. This model is appealingly simple. Getting adequate food dominates the lives of poor, food-insecure people. Promoting the productive use of the most abundant resource that poor people have—their labor—in order to increase their income and assets can lead to self-reliance and to equitable and sustainable social and economic development. Constructing and maintaining basic infrastructure is an essential requirement for an economy's growth. Labor-intensive works programs that provide food and employment for the poor are therefore the cement that holds the model together (Gaude and Watzlawick 1992).

This chapter focuses on the use of food aid and the directions it might take both in development and in the provision of relief by contributing to poverty alleviation and food security. It concentrates on the direct uses of food aid in employment programs, while recognizing that there are other important benefits to be gained from this form of aid resource—particularly through the development of human resources—that have important indirect effects. The chapter begins with an analysis of current food aid uses and with the international policy context within which discussion and decisions are taking place. It notes the important global and regional

---

[1] "Everyone has the right to *work,* to free choice of employment, to just and favorable conditions of work and to protection against unemployment. . . . Everyone has the right to a standard of living adequate for the health and well-being of himself and of his family, including *food. . . .*" *Universal Declaration of Human Rights*, Articles 23 and 25, adopted by the General Assembly of the United Nations on 10 December 1948.

changes in vulnerability to food security and the international response; addresses the issue of targeting, which is central to the design and implementation of poverty-alleviating interventions; and describes and analyzes the use of food aid in employment creation in disaster mitigation and rehabilitation, gender concerns, structural adjustment, and environmental protection. The chapter ends by identifying some major principles and concerns to emerge from the experience of the World Food Programme (WFP) and other agencies.

Food Aid: Categories and Directions

Food aid is a controversial form of development assistance. Among the arguments against it, detractors point to the political and commercial motives that sustain food aid flows, its possible disincentive to local agriculture, and the risk of increasing dependence on imported foods. These dangers should not be ignored. But the value of food aid deserves equal prominence. Food aid plays a vital role in feeding the poor, saving lives in emergencies, and enabling countries to achieve economic growth and greater social equity (Shaw and Clay 1993).

The indications are that food aid will be required on an increasing scale during the 1990s (Shaw 1992). Increasing malnutrition, population growth, higher food imports, worsening balance of payments, debt servicing, and the burgeoning needs of victims of natural and man-made disasters are creating a demand in many developing countries for more food aid. Projections suggest the need for 20 million tons of food aid annually to meet market requirements throughout the 1990s and between 30 and 40 million tons to meet minimum nutritional requirements (NRC 1989; FAO 1991; USDA 1992). Total food aid deliveries in 1992 were 15.6 million tons, a level not reached since the 1960s and an increase of 15 percent over 1991 (WFP 1992a).

It is worth recalling that in 1991, cereal food aid deliveries (which make up the bulk of food aid) were 0.7 percent of world cereal production, 1.1 percent of cereal production in developing countries, 6.8 percent of world cereal trade, 8.4 percent of cereal stocks in developed countries, and 9.1 percent of developing countries' cereal imports—although these shares were significantly higher in the poorest countries, especially in Sub-Saharan Africa (WFP 1992b).

Food aid is an important and undervalued resource for development. In recent years, it has contributed more than $3 billion of assistance to Official Development Assistance (ODA) (Table 10.1). The net value of food aid to Sub-Saharan Africa in 1985–90 averaged $1 billion a year, about the same value as the net transfers to the region by the International

Table 10.1—Official development assistance (ODA) and food aid by members of the Development Assistance Committee (DAC) of the Organization for Economic Cooperation and Development (OECD), 1982–91

Net Disbursements	1982	1983	1984	1985	1986	1987	1988	1989	1990	1991[a]
						(US$ million)				
At current prices										
Total ODA (OECD members)	27,059	26,790	28,141	28,764	35,846	40,603	47,027	45,741	54,494	58,487
Total food aid[b]	2,363	2,405	2,853	3,079	3,031	3,035	3,829	3,240	3,166	3,558
Multilateral[c]	512	552	606	475[d]	655	589	861	741	810	817
Bilateral[d]	1,851	1,853	2,247	2,604[d]	2,376	2,446	2,968	2,499	2,356	2,741
Grants	1,130	1,122	1,499	1,706	1,621	1,849	2,320	1,989	1,824	2,026
Loans	721	731	748	898	755	597	648	510	532	715
						(percent)				
Food aid as a share of total ODA	8.7	9.0	10.1	10.7	8.5	7.5	8.1	7.1	5.8	6.1
Multilateral aid as a share of total food aid	21.7	23.0	21.2	15.4[d]	21.6	19.4	22.5	22.9	25.6	23.0
Grants as a share of total bilateral food aid	61.0	60.6	66.7	65.5	68.2	75.6	78.2	79.6	77.4	73.9
Multilateral plus bilateral grants as share of total food aid	69.5	69.6	73.8	70.8	75.1	80.3	83.1	84.3	83.2	79.9

Source: DAC/OECD data files.

[a]Provisional.

[b]Includes contributions by DAC members to multilateral agencies, but not actual amounts disbursed by these agencies.

[c]Includes contributions by the Commission of the European Communities (CEC) channeled through multilateral agencies (except for 1985), but excludes contributions channeled by EC member countries through the CEC to recipient countries.

[d]Includes bilateral grants by the CEC. For 1985, all CEC contributions are reported as bilateral.

Bank for Reconstruction and Development (IBRD) and the International Development Association (IDA) of the World Bank. An increase in financial aid to compensate for any reduction in food aid is unlikely. Owing to its history, constituency, and inherent nature, food aid has special advantages in sustaining a poverty focus, supporting food security programs, and attenuating the social costs of adjustment.

Yet most of food aid has not benefited poor and food-insecure people in sustainable ways. Historically, food aid has been classified into three categories: program, emergency, and project (Table 10.2). The boundaries between these categories have become increasingly blurred. Funds generated from the sale of program food aid have been used to meet the local costs of aid-financed development projects. Emergency food aid has provided balance-of-payments support and allowed the expansion of development projects. And project food aid has been used to support sector programs on a national or regional scale.

Table 10.2—Food aid deliveries by category and region, four-year average, 1989–92

	Region					
Type of Food Aid	Sub-Saharan Africa	Asia and Pacific	Latin America and Carib-bean	North Africa/ Middle East	Eastern Europe/ Former Soviet Union	World Total
	(1,000 metric tons)					
Total food aid	4,028	3,012	2,070	2,743	1,696	13,550
Program food aid	1,182	1,066	1,369	2,095	1,568	7,279
Percent of total	29	35	66	76	92	54
Emergency food aid	2,279	696	51	284	129	3,438
Percent of total	57	23	2	10	8	25
Project food aid	567	1,250	651	364	. . .	2,833
Percent of total	14	42	31	13	. . .	21
Agricultural and rural development	190	757	119	203	. . .	1,270
Percent of total	5	25	6	7	. . .	9
Nutrition intervention	110	180	189	41	. . .	520
Percent of total	3	6	9	1	. . .	4
Other	267	313	343	120	. . .	1,043
Percent of total	7	10	17	4	. . .	8

Source: WFP INTERFAIS data base.
Note: Figures may not add to 100 due to rounding. Figures in parentheses are percentages. Food aid is cereals in grain equivalents. The ellipses (. . .) indicate a nil or negligible amount.

Program food aid—the largest category of food aid—has been provided entirely on a bilateral, government-to-government basis. In the recent past, it has constituted over one-half of all food aid. This type of food aid has generally supported the balance-of-payments of recipient countries and generated local currency that has been used for public sector expenditures, which have often been attributed to development purposes. However, it seldom has made a large direct contribution to the alleviation of poverty and hunger. Program food aid has frequently been used to provide food at subsidized prices, mainly in urban areas, without much lasting benefit to the poor or to long-term development. Where the main objective of donors has been political or commercial, the aid has sometimes been erratic, and there has been little or no programming of generated funds. The result is often the dissipation of resources in general subsidies or undifferentiated budget support.

Emergency food aid—the second largest category of food aid—has provided life-sustaining food and short-term relief, but needs to be more closely tied to disaster mitigation and rehabilitation activities, which lead to sustained development. Refugees and displaced people needing longer-term assistance require an approach tailored to ensure not only survival but their health and nutrition, education and training, jobs and income, and basic social services. WFP, in cooperation with United Nations High Commissioner for Refugees (UNHCR), has developed a special category of assistance in these protracted refugee operations to meet these needs. The past five years have seen a massive increase in the provision of international relief food aid. Globally, some 4.4 million tons of relief food aid was delivered to afflicted countries in 1992 by the international community, an increase of nearly 50 percent over the previous five-year annual average. In Sub-Saharan Africa alone, it is estimated that more than 40 million people were at risk in 1992 because of drought and civil war.

Project food aid is the smallest category of food aid. Only a part of this type of food aid has been used to support food-for-work programs, mainly in agriculture and rural development projects. The remainder has been directed to supplementary feeding programs to improve the health and nutrition of mothers and preschool children, to primary and other schools, to training programs, and to food reserves.

There have been marked differences among the recipient regions in the ways in which food aid has been used (Figure 10.1). During the four years, 1989–92, most of the food aid to Latin America and the Caribbean, North Africa and the Middle East, and East Europe and the former Soviet Union has been of the program type. In contrast, more than one-half the food aid to Sub-Saharan Africa has been for emergencies, while the largest share of food aid to Asia and the Pacific has gone to support development projects.

Figure 10.1—Food aid deliveries by category and region, four-year average, 1989–92

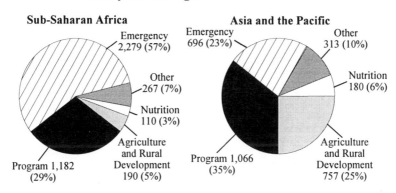

Sub-Saharan Africa

Emergency 2,279 (57%)

Other 267 (7%)

Nutrition 110 (3%)

Agriculture and Rural Development 190 (5%)

Program 1,182 (29%)

Asia and the Pacific

Emergency 696 (23%)

Other 313 (10%)

Nutrition 180 (6%)

Agriculture and Rural Development 757 (25%)

Program 1,066 (35%)

Latin America and the Caribbean

Emergency 51 (3%)

Other 343 (17%)

Nutrition 189 (9%)

Program 1,369 (66%)

Agriculture and Rural Development 119 (6%)

North Africa and the Middle East

Program 2,095 (76%)

Emergency 284 (10%)

Other 120 (4%)

Nutrition 41 (1%)

Agriculture and Rural Development 203 (7%)

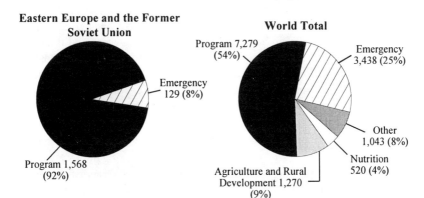

Eastern Europe and the Former Soviet Union

Emergency 129 (8%)

Program 1,568 (92%)

World Total

Program 7,279 (54%)

Emergency 3,438 (25%)

Other 1,043 (8%)

Nutrition 520 (4%)

Agriculture and Rural Development 1,270 (9%)

Source: WFP INTERFAIS database.
Notes: Agriculture and Rural Development, Nutrition, and Other = Project Food Aid. Cereals are in 1,000 tons in grain equivalents.

As a result, while one-quarter of the food aid to the Asia and the Pacific region has directly supported employment programs for agricultural and rural development, only small proportions of the food aid provided to the other regions—and about 9 percent of global food aid deliveries—have been used for this purpose.

Changing Global and Regional Dimensions

Important changes in vulnerability to poverty and food insecurity are taking place, which call for adaption in the national and international response (Crawshaw and Shaw 1993). Some of the more prominent changes relate to (1) regional variations, (2) the causes of vulnerability, (3) the most vulnerable populations, and (4) the ability to cope with both chronic and transitory food insecurity, and to the changing relationship between them.

Regional Variations

According to FAO/WHO data, major improvements in the world nutrition situation have occurred primarily in the Asia and the Pacific region, where the number of chronically undernourished has declined by nearly one-third over the past two decades (FAO/WHO 1992). In Africa, on the other hand, the number of chronically undernourished has steadily increased; it was nearly two-thirds higher in 1988–90 than 20 years previously. In the regions of Latin America and the Caribbean and the Near East, reductions in chronic undernutrition achieved in the 1970s have been followed by increases in the 1980s. In addition, there has been a recent and dramatic decline in the situation of people in many of the countries of eastern Europe and the former Soviet Union. Food aid to those countries more than doubled in 1992, representing almost 18 percent of world food aid flows, close to the level received by the Asia and the Pacific region.

Causes of Vulnerability

Drought was the primary cause of the African food crises of the early 1970s and the mid-1980s. Since the mid-1980s, armed conflict and civil unrest have come to dominate the food insecurity problems of a number of countries in Sub-Saharan Africa and elsewhere. In other countries, emergency situations have arisen as a result of major economic disruptions.

This process has also resulted in the increased vulnerability of population groups not normally considered at risk. It has particularly hurt the urban poor and societies shifting from a largely subsistence to a cash economy.

Vulnerable Groups

Poor rural populations continue to be the group most affected by food insecurity. Among the socioeconomic groups most at risk are the landless; women-headed households; small-scale, single-crop farmers; and small-scale pastoralists. Relief agencies generally concentrate on these groups. However, rapid urbanization has been followed by urban unemployment and poverty, with accompanying food insecurity (von Braun et al. 1993). The situation is particularly acute in periurban slums and shantytowns, areas that usually house recent immigrants. In conflict situations, urban populations are often swollen by refugees displaced by fighting in the countryside and seeking shelter and assistance. Urban areas are more dependent on functioning markets and stable economic conditions. They become particularly vulnerable when these conditions are disrupted, whether by changed government policies, warfare or civil unrest, or changing international economic circumstances (Jamal 1988).

Chronic and Transitory Vulnerability

Given the general expectation that aid budgets will decline, and the projected increased needs of countries in Eastern Europe and the former Soviet Union, there is concern that the pressing political and humanitarian need to meet relief requirements will jeopardize development programs that seek to overcome chronic vulnerability. What does seem to be true (although it has not been possible so far to quantify the shift) is that relief needs are assuming greater importance within aid agencies, attracting additional resources and staff attention. Since staff levels at most aid agencies have been frozen (or even reduced), this shift must inevitably result in decreased attention to development assistance to overcome chronic vulnerability. Even if resource flows to development activities remain unaffected, the benefits of those resources may be reduced because less staff time is available to ensure that resources are used in the most effective and creative manner. The resources of national governments may be similarly diverted by increasing pressure to meet immediate relief needs.

This shift in emphasis from chronic to transitory food insecurity is occurring despite much recent work pointing to the complex interrelationships between the different causes of chronic undernutrition, and hence the need for more sophisticated approaches (see, for example, Drèze and Sen 1989). Just as the causes of vulnerability to chronic food insecurity are better understood, fewer resources and less manpower and attention may be available to help fight the problem.

The international community has not shown itself to be able to cope with the recent shifts in vulnerability. New approaches are needed to identify the changing incidence of poverty and vulnerability to food insecurity as national and international situations evolve.

In allocating and utilizing food aid, donor and recipient countries are asked to give priority to (1) emergency requirements; (2) activities designed to increase agricultural (especially food) production, to raise incomes, to meet basic needs and stimulate self-reliance, and to create employment in developing countries (particularly in rural areas, including education and training geared to the achievement of these objectives); and (3) targeted nutrition intervention programs. Food-aided works programs, discussed in more detail below, may provide a bridge between these three priorities.

Targeting

Who are the poor? What causes their poverty? And what policies and intervention programs are needed to address their specific problems? It is important to disaggregate the poor both to understand the problem and to design and implement action programs that can best improve the condition of specific groups of poor people in ways that match their specific local and country characteristics. The poor are not a homogeneous group: there are significant differences in causes of and remedies for poverty among, for example, small farmers on resource-rich or resource-poor land; pastoralists; landless workers; the urban poor; and women who are single heads of households. A distinction should be made between the poor and the "poorest"[2] and between transitory and chronic poverty.

Targeting is a paramount concern in the design and implementation of poverty-specific interventions. It is key to ensuring access by, and outreach to, the poor.

A balance must be struck between criteria that focus action on the very poor and less exacting criteria that address poverty on a community or area

---

[2]Wilmshurst, Ackroyd, and Eyben (1992) define the poorest as those who have the least assets and are more prone to mortality, illness, and inadequate physical performance associated with chronic malnutrition. They may therefore be unable to respond to new economic opportunities.

basis without dissipating the effects or biasing the benefits in favor of any particular group. Risk and vulnerability mapping can be useful for focusing action on people and areas most in need, and for determining quickly the type and amount of assistance needed when disasters strike. In the absence of reliable data, appropriate rapid appraisal techniques can establish parameters for targeting, which can be refined once intervention programs begin.

Food-Aided Works Programs

A number of approaches to poverty alleviation and achieving food security have been developed and implemented, supported by food aid.

A special feature of labor-intensive works is their implementation by poor households and communities through food-for-work (FFW) programs. The rationale for these programs lies in the principle of additionality. Such programs result in *additional* consumption by participants whose incomes are too low for them to buy sufficient food for a healthy and fully productive life. Participation in works also results in a significant *addition* to their income. *Additional* employment is created and construction works are extended. This multifaceted additionality of FFW programs permits the extension of the limits of consumption, income, employment, and investment beyond what would have been possible without the programs (Shaw and Crawshaw 1993).

FFW programs are not without their problems. Where the rural poor are scattered over vast areas, the programs have been relatively small and costly. With a few exceptions, therefore, FFW in Africa has been much smaller and less structured than in Asia (World Bank/WFP 1991).

The concept and practice of FFW raises complex political, social, and cultural issues. Food may not be a satisfactory way to reimburse productive labor. On the other hand, as an addition to cash wages, or as an incentive to self-help ventures, it is widely acceptable; in some circumstances, it is preferred, particularly when food is in short supply, and when the benefits go directly to women to improve household food security, as they often have more control over food than cash (WFP/African Development Bank 1987).

A review of FFW conducted in 1990 by Bryson, Chudy, and Pines (1991) observed that WFP and nongovernmental organizations use FFW in development projects and emergency operations as a mode of food aid delivery that requires work from the recipient for the food received. This was regarded as an effective way to reach the truly needy in poor households and communities in food-deficit areas. The review found that FFW was successful in reaching poor areas and people, including women. FFW provided a useful device for identifying the needy in emergency situations. Development benefits significantly improved when food was combined with other resources (tools, materials, technical and administrative supervision), and when FFW activities were coordinated with the development program of the recipient government. The review recommended using FFW in conjunction with other activities (for example, mother and child supplementary feeding programs) to provide sustainability through the creation of employment, income, and assets, and to better target benefits to the poor.

However, controversy still surrounds FFW. Three long-standing and separate points of dispute have been identified in the international debate (Clay 1986). First is the argument about employment creation versus income generation and the size and distribution of the longer-term income and asset stream. The second dispute concerns the usefulness of food as a wage good; generalized statements about the superiority of food as cash are not helpful because they do not take account of particular site-specific situations. The third argument is whether or not the relative success of major schemes in Asia, where food is widely used as wage good, justifies assessment of FFW programs both as food security mechanisms and as expanders of employment to disadvantaged groups affected by widespread structural underemployment.

Four approaches and concerns within the provision of productive employment for the poor in labor-intensive work programs are discussed next: (1) development–emergency linkages; (2) environmentally sustainable development; (3) gender and development concerns; and (4) structural and sector adjustment measures. The discussion mainly draws on WFP experiences with these approaches.[3]

---

[3]WFP assists governments in developing countries in the implementation of their development projects. Requests for WFP assistance pass through an established project cycle. They are appraised by the appropriate United Nations specialized agencies for technical, economic, and social feasibility and soundness. They are also examined by the FAO Consultative Subcommittee on Surplus Disposal to determine that the food aid from WFP does not create disincentive to domestic agricultural production in the recipient country or disruption of commercial trade (FAO 1992). Appraisal missions organized by WFP are also sent to the requesting country to assess all aspects of the proposed WFP-assisted development project. WFP development assistance is approved by the Committee on Food Aid Policies and Programmes (CFA) on an individual project basis. Government ministries, departments, or agencies are responsible for the implementation of approved projects. Provisions governing WFP assistance to approved development projects for monitoring and evaluation are built into the legal document. Evaluation reports are submitted to the CFA for review.

Development–Emergency Linkages

The scale and intensity of poverty have been exacerbated in a number of developing countries (especially in Africa) by disasters caused by nature and by people. Conditions in many developing countries, especially in the poorest, call for a program of assistance that explicitly supports activities in the areas of disaster prevention, preparedness, mitigation, and rehabilitation. It is recognized increasingly that, while ad hoc relief is necessary in the short run, other measures are required that address the root causes of recurring emergencies. Many donors and aid agencies are therefore focusing on disaster mitigation and rehabilitation activities as major elements of their assistance programs. Because these activities are often labor-intensive and carried out in areas with food shortages, food aid is a particularly suitable form of assistance when labor needs to be mobilized and income provided.

Over one-half of food aid to Africa over the four years (1988–92) was for the victims of natural disasters and civil conflicts (Table 10.2). In consultation with other United Nations organizations and IFPRI, WFP has given special consideration to developing an approach to disaster mitigation and rehabilitation in Africa (WFP 1992c). WFP will examine on a regular basis how the development projects it assists might be used to mitigate the effects of disasters and, conversely, the extent to which the large flow of emergency food aid to Africa might serve both relief and development purposes. There is an increasingly tight connection between poverty and vulnerability to recurring emergencies, particularly those caused by drought. If the food security of the most vulnerable people was improved at the household and community level through development projects, the continued need for emergency assistance would be considerably reduced.

The major focus of this new approach is on supporting national disaster mitigation and rehabilitation strategies and programs through labor-intensive works that simultaneously (1) provide immediate employment and income, alleviate poverty, and strengthen self-help capacity; and (2) provide construction and improvement of infrastructure—particularly to increase agricultural production, stimulate rural development, and strengthen protective measures against drought and other disasters. Together with these labor-intensive works programs, targeted food, income, and health interventions could improve the well-being of the poor and enable them to withstand future food shortages. This approach draws from the results of IFPRI's research work on policy (von Braun, Teklu, and Webb 1991; von Braun 1991).

Development projects have been designed to expand rapidly when emergencies occur to provide additional food and employment when household food production or income collapses. Quick-action projects have been approved for disaster reconstruction and rehabilitation activities, to be followed by full-fledged development projects. Advance shipments of WFP commitments have also been made following early warning of an impending emergency; these help expand development project activities to accommodate disaster victims.

In Bangladesh, Burkina Faso, and Ghana, for example, WFP responded to the need for rapid food relief in 1991 by enlarging ongoing food-aided development projects, rather than by providing emergency food aid. A WFP-assisted project in the arid and semi-arid areas of Kenya that provides food to nongovernmental organizations involved in welfare-oriented activities includes contingency planning for food security during drought. In a seriously food-deficit area of Uganda, a 14 percent reserve was included in a WFP-assisted development project for relief works to be implemented during periods of drought. In a pilot multipurpose project for rural development in Djibouti, a FFW program is creating more employment opportunities in rural areas and reducing the need for recurrent emergency food aid.

In Burkina Faso, WFP is supporting government efforts to improve the living conditions of isolated communities and to check migration to urban centers. In a rural works program in drought-prone areas in Sudan, WFP is supporting labor-intensive activities that increase employment and incomes during the lean season, provide rural community facilities, and improve water supplies. In all these efforts, the coping strategies of poor households and communities faced with hunger have been supported. Employment has been provided during the agricultural off-season and in times of emergency to strengthen the local infrastructure's ability to sustain economic activities; as a result, people have been saved from migrating in search of food, thereby keeping the household unit intact and assisting the process of rehabilitation and, eventually, development.

WFP emergency interventions may be adapted, if the circumstances are appropriate, to facilitate development initiatives. For example, in the special emergency program for the Horn of Africa, WFP has collaborated with other donors in a preliminary identification of areas where, with recipient governments' agreement, emergency food aid might be joined with other technical and capital inputs in FFW activities.

In countries where civil strife is prolonged and food shortages are acute, but purchasing power exists, distribution of free emergency food aid is not always appropriate. In such situations, emergency food aid may be sold through the market. This approach would help meet food needs, restrain price inflation, encourage the revitalization of market institutions, and generate local currencies that can be used for humanitarian or reconstruction purposes.

In a WFP-assisted regional project for over 2 million Liberian and Sierra Leonean refugees and displaced people in Liberia, Côte d'Ivoire, Guinea, and Sierra Leone, many of the beneficiaries are engaged in a wide range of productive, self-employment, and income-generating activities in the development of basic community infrastructure, agriculture, water-supply systems, small-scale livestock, trade, and transport. UNHCR provides the nonfood inputs of seeds, tools, equipment, and other materials and technical assistance. The WFP ration scale of the basic commodities is being closely monitored and periodically reviewed with the aim of being gradually reduced as the refugees and displaced persons progressively work toward the goals of relative food security and economic self-sufficiency.

In protracted crises involving refugees and displaced people, beneficiaries have been engaged in crop production, infrastructure, and income-generating activities. In Malawi, for example, Mozambican refugees have been employed in long-term development activities, including building infrastructure and producing crops, which have increased employment opportunities. In addition, reforestation has helped offset the refugees' adverse effects on the environment. In Senegal, most of the Mauritanian refugees are farmers and pastoralists who have been encouraged to engage in agricultural, livestock, and other income-generating activities financed by UNHCR and nongovernmental organizations. Refugees in the Sudan, Tanzania, Uganda, Zaire, and Zimbabwe are similarly employed.

Another dimension of the emergency problem relates to returnees. With the end of hostilities in a number of countries, refugees, displaced persons, and former soldiers are returning to their homes. Food aid is required to tide them over the period of resettlement and to engage them in rehabilitation and reconstruction works. Working closely with the Cambodian Red Cross and other nongovernmental organizations, WFP provided food aid in 1992 that reached almost one-tenth of the entire population of Cambodia, including refugees returning from Thailand, internally displaced people, demobilized soldiers, and other vulnerable groups. Food is a major priority in this reconstruction program, but WFP also has arranged to provide seeds and funds to build houses and pay for trucks and transport in order to achieve self-reliance.

WFP has committed food assistance for over 800,000 Somalian and Sudanese returnees from Ethiopia and Ethiopian returnees from Somalia. In Mozambique, WFP has provided food aid since 1987 to support displaced persons in temporary settlements so that they can resume normal activities. Part of the WFP aid is used to help returnees from neighboring countries resettle in Mozambique.

In summary, where necessary, emergency food aid should be distributed as relief to ensure survival but, to perform optimally, it should be provided and used in ways that promote self-reliance, attack the root causes of emergencies, support national food security, and reinforce long-term development efforts (WFP 1992c). These aims require a considerable measure of organization to achieve. They are difficult to pursue under the pressures of sudden emergencies caused by either nature or by human activities. And they are a formidable challenge for governments in poor countries faced by economic crises. A key to success is advance preparation (Thimm and Hahn 1993).

Effective disaster prevention, preparedness and mitigation activities are immensely aided by a national legislative framework, adequate financial provisions, strong local administration and technical services, and well-designed projects that can be brought to implementation speedily when disasters strike. The importance of these elements has been underlined by experiences in many countries, particularly India (WFP 1991) and China (WFP forthcoming). The afflicted population can then be quickly employed in construction projects and assisted with food aid, which together provide sustenance and income. People would then be less likely to leave their homes in search of work or relief, their health would not be impaired, and household assets would be protected and augmented. Such a disaster response will require a training program for personnel at all levels.

Environmentally Sustainable Development

The United Nations Conference on the Environment and Development (UNCED) in June 1992 paid special attention to the problems of drought and desertification. "Agenda 21," the action program adopted by the Conference (United Nations 1992), notes that, apart from the human toll, the costs of drought-related disasters are also high in economic terms—lost production, misused inputs, and diversion of development resources. The action program suggests that early-warning systems to forecast drought will make possible the implementation of drought-preparedness schemes.

Developing countries also need to promote and support activities for environmentally sustainable development including forestry, watershed management, and associated soil conservation works; increasing agricultural productivity, including training of small farmers in sustainable agricultural techniques; and rangelands management. These activities may particularly benefit from food aid. Food aid can help offset the local costs of environmental protection works at the household, community, and national levels. These works are largely labor-intensive and can be carried out by unemployed and underemployed workers when there is little other productive employment. Employment in these works can help address the seasonal dimensions of hunger and poverty by providing food and work during the off-season. As such activities are often required in poor marginal areas, the provision of food and employment is automatically targeted at the poorest and most vulnerable groups. Funds from the sale of food aid commodities to project workers can help purchase locally produced tools, equipment, and materials needed in environment protection works, thereby creating additional demand and employment opportunities (WFP 1989b).

The rural poor helped by WFP often live in areas where the soil is depleted, erosion is advanced, rainfall is inadequate, and access by roads is limited. To assist such groups, WFP must support activities with inherent environmental risks. A study to examine the environmental implications of WFP-assisted projects concluded that avoiding such risks depends primarily on attention to the design, implementation, and maintenance of the projects. A checklist highlighting the types of projects supported by WFP that are particularly sensitive to environmental concerns has been devised for WFP's project preparation and guidelines (WFP 1989b).

Development activities designed to protect or improve the environment must also address issues of poverty and food security if they are to be sustained. That is why WFP development assistance focuses on enabling poor people—women and men—to be more productive and to obtain assets such as technical skills or essential material goods. Only then will they be in a better position to overcome their poverty.

Gender and Development

Women play a pivotal role in alleviating poverty and food insecurity because of their strategic position in the household and the productive work they do outside. Although there has been much recognition of this role, there remains a great deal of tokenism in supporting and strengthening their activities. Women continue to be "helped" through projects exclusively for them, thereby marginalizing their impact.

A comparative review of WFP-assisted development projects focused exclusively on women has shown that (1) such projects are neither automatically gender-responsive nor necessarily beneficial to women; (2) socioeconomic expertise and guidance are needed in the design, implementation, and evaluation of such projects; (3) social empowerment and economic viability often are difficult to achieve simultaneously through women's groups; (4) economic enterprises that benefit women should not be undercapitalized; and (5) the outreach capacity of mainstream economic institutions should be strengthened to deliver inputs and services to poor women (WFP 1989a).

A major failing of both national planners and aid programs has been to support women's roles in the household in the social sectors and their productive roles outside the home in the economic sectors. This approach dichotomizes in development planning and assistance what is not dichotomized in reality. Women's roles and activities are not dichotomized, but are part of a continuum of labor-time allocations in both productive and maternal tasks. Dichotomizing women's roles has the negative consequences of overtaxing women's physical capabilities, lowering productivity in the economic sphere, and diminishing their capacity to fulfil domestic responsibilities, such as child care and household security (Hammam and Youssef 1986).

Women represent about one-half of the total labor force—in some countries up to 90 percent—in WFP-supported FFW programs. This is not surprising. The structure of the regular labor market often excludes women. Only the very poor will work for food: women, especially when they are single heads of households, are too often in that category. FFW is flexible and women find the timing, particularly of off-season employment in FFW schemes, to be compatible with their domestic and other responsibilities. Payment in food is also attractive to them as women often have more command over food than cash in the household and a high propensity to attain household food security.

What might be somewhat surprising is the "nontraditional" nature of their work. Virtually the entire rural road network in Lesotho has been built mainly by women from the least privileged groups. A significant part of the labor force involved in the construction of the largest irrigation infrastructures in India consisted of women. Reforestation of large areas of Syria threatened by desertification has been accomplished through women's labor. In Egypt, women comprise 25 percent of landless and near-landless farmers who have acquired title to redistributed lands under a desert reclamation land settlement scheme. Food aid has helped defray the cost of infrastructure construction works and has tided women over until their own harvests can sustain them.

While women's participation rates in FFW development programs have been high, the goal should be to ensure that women not only gain employment but emerge with some new asset, be it improved land, or security of tenure, tools, or skills. The close interdependence between what women learn, produce, and earn and the size of the family, whether a family has sufficient food to eat, or whether daughters go to school, implies that there can be no stable, long-term response to the problems of poverty if the education, training, productivity, and incomes of women are not improved.

Antipoverty interventions should assist women in overcoming the obstacles to self-empowerment. There are several examples where such action has been taken. In the rural road construction project in Lesotho, daycare centers have been provided to look after young children while their mothers work. In El Salvador, Kenya, and Malawi, women are engaged in the production of weaning foods based on local crops. These products are manufactured at prices significantly lower than their imported equivalents, and at the same or higher nutritional value; meanwhile, additional employment and income are generated. In Bangladesh, poor women are being provided with a package of development services, savings, credit, functional education, and training in income-generating activities. The underlying premise is that, with this package, poor women will have the opportunity to join the mainstream of development (Islam 1991).

Structural and Sector Adjustment Measures

Experience with adjustment lending in the 1980s has been mixed, leading to the conclusion that it is both a potentially high-payoff and a high-risk instrument (World Bank 1988). The adjustment process often resulted in a shortfall in the real purchasing power of the poor and limited their ability to purchase food and other essential items. Adjustment programs have also been found to have a negative effect on food security (FAO 1989). In sum, there appears to have been an asymmetry between negative and positive effects. Negative effects of adjustment on the poor have often been certain and immediate, whereas positive effects have been uncertain and have long periods of gestation.

Two groups that tend to be hurt by adjustment measures and that may be appropriate beneficiaries of compensatory programs are (1) those who lose their jobs and (2) those who cannot afford price increases in basic food commodities (Singer and Shaw 1988). For each of these two groups, the most appropriate compensatory measures would be to provide income-earning, productive employment, whether in urban or rural areas. In the short run, however, it may be necessary in some cases to provide food supplements directly to those most adversely affected by the adjustment process. Two programs, from Ghana and Peru, may illustrate the scope for food-aided assistance under adjustment.

WFP's assistance in support of Ghana's efforts to restructure its economy entered a new phase in 1988, in keeping with the government's own moves to focus on the needs of the poor and those most affected by the adjustment process. An urban public works program, implemented in four major cities (Accra, Tema, Kumasi, and Sekondi-Takoradi), created, on a pilot basis, a stable labor force to carry out labor-intensive construction (and demonstrate its effectiveness), while providing temporary employment to cushion the effects of reductions in public-sector jobs. The project constructed 200 publicly owned houses and assisted in the upgrading of

400 serviced plots for low-income housing units. In addition, it helped rehabilitate urban infrastructure, including roads, drains, and waste disposal. WFP's support to secondary boarding schools enabled 80,000 boarders in 236 secondary schools to complete the full academic year. Without this assistance the schools would have been forced to shorten each academic term from 13 to 9 weeks. WFP assistance stabilized parents' contribution to feeding costs for two years, thereby cushioning the impact of the withdrawal of government subsidies. The counterpart funds created were used to rehabilitate and improve secondary school facilities through an investment fund.

The most serious drawback to direct employment programs is their high budgetary cost, particularly if the assets or services produced are public goods that do not generate revenue for the government. Since expenditure on public goods may run counter to adjustment's goal of reducing public sector budget expenditure, care is needed to strike the right balance in the economy and to meet the goals of adjustment. When carefully implemented during a recession, however, public goods creation can be a practical means of creating additional demand for labor and need not generate significant inflationary or balance-of-payments pressures.

Peru embarked on a structural adjustment program following the precipitous decline in its economic performance. One component of Peru's adjustment program has been a considerable reduction of government subsidies for basic foodstuffs, a step that particularly affected the poor. It was estimated that their purchasing power was reduced by approximately 40 percent in real terms. To offset the adverse impact on the poor's living standards and nutritional status, the government of Peru introduced a "social compensation program," a mix of income-generating, labor-intensive projects in urban areas and the provision of subsidized meals through canteens run by the Ministry of Health and women's associations. The immediate objectives of WFP assistance in Peru included encouragement of the formation of women's groups within the existing structure of the communities to facilitate access to health, education, and training services; increased school attendance and increased community participation in support of educational activities through the creation of parents' organizations; and an increase in the number of tuberculosis outpatients who start and complete their outpatient treatment as a result of nutritional support provided to them and their families during the course of treatment. The primary functions of WFP assistance were to serve as an incentive for the formation of women's groups, to provide a dietary supplement to the beneficiaries, and to provide a transfer of income to health and education promoters. About 10 percent of the WFP food commodities provided were sold to generate a fund, equivalent to about $2 million, to help meet the local costs of training courses; inputs for production and income-sharing activities of the women's groups; additional technical assistance and extension services; training courses for health and education promoters; health-related activities; and feasibility studies for productive and income-saving activities.

Conclusions

From the practical experience of WFP and others, five essential and interrelated principles that can alleviate poverty and food insecurity on a large-scale and sustainable basis can be identified:

1. Governments in developing countries should give their full commitment to alleviating poverty and food insecurity and making these goals central objectives in national development plans and programs.
2. The poor themselves should be intimately involved, through their own institutions, in the process of alleviating poverty and food insecurity.
3. Developing countries should be assisted in implementing poverty alleviation and food security programs with adequate international cooperation.
4. Coordinated action should be strengthened among government and nongovernment agencies and aid programs: no single organization has all the resources, expertise, and experience needed.
5. Appropriate monitoring and evaluation systems should be put in place to track and assess the impact of the measures implemented.

A significant increase above the current level of food aid would be required to support major programs of infrastructure improvement and environmental preservation as well as the human resource development needed for sustained development.

Countries in Asia and Latin America would be in a position to absorb large increases in food aid for development programs relatively rapidly, assuming that it is provided in appropriate and acceptable forms. Countries in Africa, on the other hand, would require more preinvestment activities and assistance to enhance national capacity before many of them would be able to absorb more food aid than they do at present.

An essential feature of the new food aid regime would be close coordination with financial and technical aid institutions and agencies. Coordination between the World Bank and WFP would be particularly important, both to ensure that the desired macroeconomic impact of enhanced food aid was attained and to ensure that financial and food aid were integrated in the implementation of development projects.

272

REFERENCES

Braun, J. von. 1991. *A policy agenda for famine prevention in Africa*. Food Policy Report. Washington, D.C.: International Food Policy Research Institute.

Braun, J. von, T. Teklu, and P. Webb. 1991. *Labor-intensive public works for food security: Experience in Africa*. Working Papers on Food Subsidies 6. Washington, D.C.: International Food Policy Research Institute.

Braun, J. von, J. McComb, B. Mensah, and R. Pandya-Lorch. 1993. *Urban food insecurity and malnutrition in developing countries: Trends, policies, and research implications*. Washington, D.C.: International Food Policy Research Institute.

Bryson, J. C., J. P. Chudy, and J. M. Pines. 1991. *Food for work: A review of the 1980s with recommendations for the 1990s*. Washington, D.C.: U.S. Agency for International Development.

Clay, E. J. 1986. Rural public works and food-for-work: A survey. *World Development* 14 (October/November): 1237–1252.

Crawshaw, B., and J. Shaw. 1993. Changing vulnerability to food insecurity and the international response: The experience of the World Food Programme. Paper prepared for the NATO Advanced Research Workshop on Climate Change and World Food Security, Oxford, July.

Drèze, J., and A. Sen. 1989. *Hunger and public action*. Oxford: Clarendon Press.

FAO (Food and Agriculture Organization of the United Nations). 1989. *Effects of stabilization and structural adjustment programmes on food security*. Economic and Social Development Paper 89. Rome: Commodities and Trade Division.

_____. 1991. *Prospects for food aid and its role in the 1990s*. CFS:91/3. Rome.

_____. 1992. *FAO principles of surplus disposal and consultative obligations of member states*. Third edition. Rome.

FAO/WHO (Food and Agriculture Organization of the United Nations/ World Health Organization). 1991. *Nutrition and development—a global assessment: International Conference on Nutrition*. Rome (Document PREPCOM/ICN/92/3).

Gaude, J., and H. Watzlawick. 1992. Employment creation and poverty alleviation through labor-intensive public works in least-developed countries. *International Labour Review* 131 (1): 3–18.

Hammam, M., and N. H. Youssef. 1986. The continuum in women's productive and reproductive roles: Implications for food aid and children's well-being. In *Food aid and the well-being of children in the developing world.* New York: United Nations Children's Fund and World Food Programme.

Islam, N. 1991. Bangladesh agriculture: Growth, stability and poverty alleviation. *Journal of International Development* 3 (5): 447– 465.

Jamal, V. 1988. Getting the crisis right: Missing perspectives on Africa. *International Labour Review* 127 (6): 655–678.

NRC (National Research Council), National Academy of Sciences. 1989. *Food aid projections for the decade of the 1990s.* Washington, D.C.

Shaw, J. 1992. Food aid in the 1990s. *Development Policy Review* 10 (2): 175–179.

Shaw, J., and E. Clay, eds. 1993. *World food aid. Experiences of recipients and donors.* Portsmouth, N.H.: Heinemann, A Division of Reed Publishing Inc., U.S.A., and London: Heinemann and James Currey.

Shaw, J., and B. Crawshaw. 1993. Overcoming rural poverty—Thirty years of World Food Programme experience. Paper prepared for the Symposium on Rural Poverty Alleviation, Agency Initiatives, and Popular Responses, University of Manchester, March.

Singer, H., and J. Shaw, eds. 1988. Food policy, food aid, and economic adjustment. *Food Policy*, Special Issue, 13 (February): 10–72.

Thimm, H. U., and H. Hahn, eds. 1993. *Regional food security and infrastructure.* 2 vols. Munster-Hamburg: LIT-Verlag.

United Nations. 1992. *Agenda 21. Rio declaration. Forest principles.* New York.

USDA (United States Department of Agriculture). 1992. *Global food assessment: Situation and outlook report.* Washington, D.C.: Economic Research Service.

WFP (World Food Programme). 1989a. *Comparative review of WFP-assisted projects in Latin America, focused on women.* CFA:28/SCP/3:3/3D/Add.A.1. Rome.

_____. 1989b. *Environment and sustainable development*. WFP/CFA: 27/P/INF/2. Rome.

_____. 1991. *Selected national experience with food aid. The Indian experience*. CFA:32/P/7 Rev. 1. Rome.

_____. 1992a. *Review of global food aid policies and programmes*. CFA:35/P/5 Add. 1. Rome.

_____. 1992b. *1993 Food aid review*. Rome.

_____. 1992c. *Disaster mitigation and rehabilitation in Africa*. CFA:34/P/7-B. Rome.

_____. Forthcoming. *China's national experience with food aid policies and programmes*. Rome.

WFP (World Food Programme)/African Development Bank. 1987. *Food aid for development in Sub-Saharan Africa*. Rome and Abidjan, Côte d'Ivoire.

Wilmshurst, J., P. Ackroyd, and R. Eyben. 1992. *Implications for U.K. aid of current thinking on poverty reduction*. Discussion Paper 307. Brighton, U.K.: Institute of Development Studies, University of Sussex.

World Bank. 1988. *Adjustment lending. An evaluation of ten years of experience*. Policy and Research Series 1. Washington, D.C.: World Bank.

World Bank/WFP (World Food Programme). 1991. *Food aid in Africa: An agenda for the 1990s*. A joint study. Washington, D.C., and Rome.

11
IMPLEMENTATION OF EMPLOYMENT PROGRAMS: KEY ISSUES AND OPTIONS

Jean Majeres

Labor and local resource-based works programs aim at several goals simultaneously. First, they aim to influence infrastructure investment policies to maximize employment and income generation, to create productive assets, and to reduce poverty. Second, they aim to create both public and private capacity for the effective planning and implementation of these employment-intensive policies and programs. Finally, while these programs do not explicitly attempt to improve food security, many of the infrastructure assets they create contribute directly and indirectly to this objective.

This chapter is based on International Labour Office (ILO) experience. It examines a number of issues that still require policy and operational attention if further progress is to be made in the use of employment-intensive investment programs for poverty reduction and the improvement of livelihood in the world's poorest countries. The ILO has been associated with employment-intensive works programs since the mid-1970s, mainly in Africa and Asia.[1]

The issues to be examined are, first, can investment policy and social policy be better linked or "reconciled" through appropriate employment policies and programs and what are the implications for technological choice, work organization, remuneration policy, and the targeting of poverty groups if these two policy areas are linked? Second, how can national (and international) investment policies be oriented (or reoriented) and local resources effectively utilized to make the most productive use of locally available resources and labor, in particular, to create productive assets? Third, if employment-intensive investment programs are to be given greater emphasis, what are the implications for the selection of investment schemes, decentralized planning and implementation, local

---

[1]This article draws on research published under the ILO's "Employment-Intensive Works Programme," in particular the special issue edited by J. Gaude and S. Miller (1992).

government and private-sector capacity, people's participation in decision-making, and their organizational and bargaining capacity? Above all, how can operational approaches be designed to pursue all of these goals?

International and domestic economic constraints have recently increased the awareness—both among policymakers in developing countries and among external funding agencies—of the potential advantages of employment-intensive growth strategies (see Radwan, Chapter 2 of this volume).

The scope for employment-intensive growth is particularly high in the rural sector, where many resources remain underutilized (ILO 1990; Egger 1993). Investments in land development, terracing works, rural access roads for the marketing of agricultural produce, irrigation, soil and water conservation works, afforestation, antierosion works, and storage facilities are examples of activities that catalyze agricultural production and related nonfarm activities in the rural areas (Egger, Gaude, and Garnier 1993).

In contrast to the special social safety-net type of program, the ILO has increasingly promoted labor-intensive approaches as a regular feature of infrastructure investment policies for structural poverty reduction. Indeed, more comprehensive policies are needed if the poverty issue is to be addressed—not with short-term measures, but with measures aimed at its very roots.

In the following sections, it will be argued that what is required for sustainable growth and poverty reduction are investments for the poor, not compensation (Miller 1992, 92), and that employment-intensive and local resource-intensive investments in infrastructure works that benefit the poor can be an important part of a longer-term development strategy aimed at reconciling economic growth with greater social equity.

After a brief presentation of the socioeconomic rationale for employment-intensive works programs and a clarification of basic conceptual options that underlie various types of employment programs, the chapter addresses the main issues confronting the implementation of labor-intensive works programs at the design, implementation, and post-implementation stages. Some options and practical approaches, derived from field experience, which might improve the design of policies and lead to more effective planning and execution of employment-intensive works programs are discussed.

The Concept of Labor- and Local Resource-Based Investments

The Evolution of ILO Approaches

During the 1970s and early 1980s, the main aims of the employment programs in developing countries that requested ILO assistance (particularly in Sub-Saharan Africa) were direct employment creation and income distribution. However, employment generation schemes were too often viewed by governments and donors only as short-term job creation, appropriate for emergency and relief situations.[2]

Subsequently, this approach was reviewed. The "labor-intensive" approach has been extended to a wider "local resource-based" approach[3] that incorporates local resources, including labor and, more generally, materials, tools and equipment, finance, know-how, and institutions. The aim is to maximize the use of all locally available resources, contributing to the development of the domestic market and, simultaneously, saving on foreign resources and exchange requirements. The local resource-based approach emphasizes the following objectives (Hertel 1991; Gaude and Miller 1990):

1. create immediate employment and income for the poor;
2. create the basis for permanent/longer-term employment and income opportunities for the poor (through the operation and maintenance of the assets created) and increased economic activity (especially in agricultural and related production);
3. ensure cost-effective construction and increase the sustainability of infrastructure works through optimum use of local resources—an objective that will also make maintenance affordable;
4. strengthen backward and forward linkages in the local economy by developing artisanal or small enterprise activities (such as the manufacture of tools, simple equipment, and so forth) and facilitating marketing of agricultural produce (creating storage, marketplaces, access roads);
5. promote the participation of decentralized government agencies and the local population in the selection, construction, and maintenance of infrastructure;
6. promote the involvement of private contractors using labor-based techniques in construction and maintenance works;
7. strengthen the local institutional and operational capacity of both the public and private sectors and local community-based organizations through technical, managerial, and organizational training;
8. contribute to the formulation of investment policy favoring the effective use and further development and protection of the local resource base; and

---

[2]Hence, the often used—and abused—term, "crash" employment schemes.

[3]In line with the concept of "employment-intensive growth," the "labor- and local resource-based" approaches and programs have also been called the "employment-intensive works programs." These expressions are used interchangeably in this chapter.

9. contribute to the creation of an overall policy environment favorable to large-scale replication of the approach.

During the 1980s, it was proven on technical and economic grounds that, in most construction and maintenance work, an end product of the same quality can be obtained using labor- and local resource-based methods instead of methods dependent on foreign-exchange and equipment. Substituting labor-intensive methods did not increase the total cost of the investment. It has been estimated that this fully applies to economies where labor wages are not higher than US$4–6 per day—but these wage rates are only indicative and depend on the relative prices of other factors of production. For example, comparative studies of labor-based versus equipment-intensive approaches to feeder road construction and rehabilitation carried out in Rwanda (Martens 1990), Ghana (Bentall 1990), and Botswana (ILO 1992) demonstrated the cost-effectiveness of labor-based methods, which (1) were in financial terms 10–30 percent less costly than equipment-based methods; (2) reduced foreign exchange expenditures by 50–60 percent; and (3) created 240–320 percent more employment—particularly benefiting unskilled labor and contributing substantially to poverty reduction among low-income target groups.

This cost-effectiveness was achieved using techniques and approaches developed by the ILO, the World Bank, and several major bilateral aid agencies in pilot programs. It is a major argument for a wider application of labor-based investment policies in the infrastructure construction sector; given this sector's importance in developing countries, local resource-based investment in this sector can and should become a central component of a sustainable employment-intensive growth strategy.

Indeed, this sector usually accounts for 3 to 8 percent of the gross domestic product (World Bank 1984), and 50 percent or more of domestic gross capital formation consists of construction output. In Sub-Saharan Africa, infrastructure works absorb up to 70 percent of public investment expenditure (World Bank 1983) and receive some 40 percent of total financial flows from international funding agencies.

These figures, based on World Bank estimates (Gaude and Watzlawick 1992), would provide even more valuable information if they were substantiated on a country-by-country basis. Unfortunately, such detailed analysis of individual investment programs and components and their effect on employment generation is rarely available. However, in Ghana, a recent European Community/ILO mission estimated that if only 20 percent of public-sector and 10 percent of private-sector infrastructure investment were implemented with labor-based methods, approximately US$100 million per year would be used for this construction technique and create an additional 50,000 jobs annually (that is, 70,000, instead of 20,000).

Obviously, a significant share of infrastructure investments can be executed with labor, using simple tools and light equipment. One could therefore expect that a major policy option for the 1990s and beyond should be that an increasing share of investments in infrastructure construction and maintenance works be carried out by labor- and local resource-based approaches and techniques.

The Need for Conceptual Distinction between Program Types and Goals

One of the constraints against the wider application of labor-based works programs is the lack of conceptual clarity that still prevails in many government and donor agencies at various levels:

1. the unclear distinction between social employment programs with predominantly short-term effects (for example, for relief) and cost-effective employment- and local resource-based investment programs with longer-term economic and social goals;
2. the unclear distinction between infrastructure works of general public benefit and works directly benefiting clearly identified community-based organizations (such as women's or youth associations, village development committees, peasant associations, and so forth, or identifiable individuals); and
3. the unclear distinction between sectoral programs, which are predominantly supply-driven, and area-based multisectoral programs, which are traditionally needs-oriented.

In the past, failure to distinguish between these categories has resulted in doubts as to the cost-effectiveness of labor-based approaches; the failure to integrate employment programs into national policies, particularly investment policy, food policy, and rural industrialization policy; the lack of efforts to create or strengthen local-level capabilities for sustained program action; ambiguities with regard to ownership and responsibilities for the management, use, and maintenance of created assets; and, often, the application of inappropriate remuneration policies. A discussion of related issues relevant for implementation follows.

Relief or Growth and Development? Employment-intensive public works programs have usually been seen as short-term measures (for drought relief, famine relief, and emergency operations) that have limited impact on long-term employment and income generation. It is essential to clarify this misunderstanding and draw a clear distinction between two categories: labor-intensive works as instruments of social policy and labor-intensive works as instruments of employment policy.

In social and compensatory employment programs, criteria of economic efficiency and viability, internal rates of return, and social and institutional sustainability do not necessarily apply. These programs correspond to the safety-net concept, redistributing income to special target groups, generally to compensate for lack or loss of income that these groups may experience for various reasons. Income may be replaced to offset a temporary crisis in a given sector, or—in the context of structural adjustment—to mitigate the negative effects of macroeconomic policy measures. Such programs are often characterized by poor project identification, low institutional sustainability and capacity building, and, occasionally, by very low levels of productivity and efficiency. Poorly run redistribution programs have undoubtedly contributed to a confusion between social policy and employment policy. While redistribution programs have a role to play, efforts can and should be made to overcome the chronic problems of low productivity and poor work organization.

The second category is labor-based works as an instrument of employment policy. These employment programs are linked to economic growth—employment policy and investment policy go hand in hand. These cost-effective investments create productive assets that are indispensable to employment-intensive, agriculture-led, or rural-led growth. Cost-effectiveness, technical feasibility and quality standards, and economic and social sustainability are main criteria for the application of labor-based methods.

Public Works or Works of Community or Household Interest? The confusion between public works and works of community or private interest has been detrimental to the design and implementation of a policy to develop the productive resource base, using the available labor force and other local resources. A clear distinction between the two types of works is essential for the design of more coherent policies—particularly appropriate remuneration policies.

Public works typically involve construction or maintenance of access roads, afforestation, soil conservation, and other environmental protection works on public land. Two characteristics of public works are that (1) the central, regional, or local government keeps ownership of these works, carrying out construction as well as maintenance requirements; and (2) the major motivation of the labor force required to work on such schemes is the wage received in compensation for the work done.

Works of community or private interest typically are small-scale irrigation works, small dam construction, afforestation on private lands or village and community woodlots, and so forth. Since the workers participating in such schemes are usually direct beneficiaries of the assets created, wage payment is generally not the motivating factor. This category of works has often—but not always correctly—been associated with the concept of "self-help."

Many community-based investments for the poor are not only of private interest, but also of wider interest to the society as a whole, and some form of public contribution or cost-sharing remains justified and required. Indeed, public investment in these works may serve as a catalyst for the creation of a dynamic process of local resource mobilization for productive asset creation (land development, irrigation schemes, dam construction) or for longer-term protection of the resource base (afforestation, soil and water conservation, protection of the environment). Moreover, for certain categories of works, such as village water supply and social infrastructure (schools, health centers), there is no sharp dividing line between public and community interests. Ownership of these types of schemes and revenue to cover operating and maintenance costs must be clearly identified, as this has important implications for the management, use, maintenance, and ultimate sustainability of the assets.

Clear policies and practical guidelines that serve to distinguish between works of public and private or community interest and to define the respective rights and obligations whenever these interests or responsibilities overlap are necessary to avoid problems in these programs at the operational and maintenance stage.

Sectoral or Area-Based Multisectoral Works? Sectoral programs are supply-driven in the sense that they are normally initiated and managed by the specific sectoral line ministries, and have a national or regional dimension generally reflected in the size of the investment and operating budgets made available through public expenditure or financial assistance from donors. There has been a tendency recently to shift from government execution of sectoral programs (road networks, irrigation, and so forth) to private-sector execution, through reliance on private contractors and community-based organizations.

Multisectoral area-based programs involve local communities and local government more directly. Demand-driven projects reflect a variety of needs felt at the village or community level. Local populations seek and expect to find financial or technical support at the nearest level of public administration—generally the commune, ward, or district in rural or urban areas.

Employment-intensive work methods can be introduced in both sectoral and area-based multisectoral programs. While the two types of programs should be seen as complementary, the objectives as well as the approach required to implement each category of works or to create the local capacity to do so differ substantially. In the first case, emphasis is on the introduction of labor- and local resource-based policies in technical ministries such as public works, irrigation, or agricultural departments, and on the establishment of small contractor and community and beneficiary training and capacity building for private-sector execution and decentralized contract management. In the second case, the emphasis is on promoting participation, people's organizations, decentralization, area-based funding facilities, and local government capacity.

Implementing Employment-Intensive Works Programs

The implementation of employment-intensive works programs raises both policy and operational issues that should be considered at all stages of program development—that is, at the design, implementation, and post-implementation stages.

Design Issues

Project evaluations carried out in several countries and documenting in greater detail the employment-intensive works programs in Burundi, Mali, Nepal, Rwanda, and Tanzania (Guichaoua and Thérond 1984; Guichaoua 1987a; Martens 1988; Gaude and Miller 1990) indicate that poor project performance is inextricably linked to deficiencies in program design. Such deficiencies have resulted in confusion among the parties concerned as to project objectives, approaches, responsibilities, and inputs. Poor design has also led to inappropriate scheme selection, inefficient implementation and maintenance, disagreements, disinterest, and subsequent unsustainability of the created assets.

Technical Appraisal. The detail of technical feasibility studies can vary depending on the size and complexity of a project. However, technical appraisals, particularly for small-scale investments, are often hastily prepared because of financial or time constraints; this leads to unrealistic targets, the underestimation of potential problems and constraints, the choice of inappropriate technology, and inadequate consideration of the local environment and ecosystem.

Alternative construction methods—and the extent to which labor can be substituted for equipment—are also often not sufficiently considered at the design stage. This can lead to the automatic adoption of conventional designs that are heavily biased against labor-based methods. The lack of technical expertise and awareness in the use of labor- and local resource-intensive methods in the public and private sectors is probably an important reason for this. However, the consequences of this ignorance are costly, and often adversely affect technical design and contract specifications.

Works constructed using labor-intensive methods should be adequate to the situation, and not—as is often the case—"overdesigned" and too expensive to construct and maintain. Because they are too costly for the local economy, overdesigned standards and construction methods that do not fully tap local resources imperil sustainability and reduce the likelihood that the project will be replicated. In a multisectoral, labor-intensive works program in Guinea, local cost-sharing that was systematically applied to all subprojects (according to a contract agreed upon by the target population) proved to be the best safeguard against overambitious designs; this program resulted in much lower construction costs than those of similar activities elsewhere in the country. Project evaluations of a labor-based, multisectoral works program in Madagascar have shown that the lack of participation of beneficiary communities and local government institutions in the identification of schemes and the absence of cost-sharing arrangements has led to a situation where project technicians and local consulting firms both selected the projects and overdesigned them. These two flaws resulted in unnecessary costs.

Environmental Considerations. Protection of the environment, poverty reduction, and overall economic and social sustainability are interwoven (Hertel 1991, 10). Because the rural poor often live on less fertile, erosion-prone soils, their future economic well-being depends on the protection of soil and water. Environmental concerns are essential to the long-term sustainability of productive and other assets, and can be approached from at least two different angles.

The first approach involves the target population directly. Infrastructure schemes to protect the environment have been identified as components in many programs: soil and water conservation and afforestation (for example, in Burundi, Mali, Rwanda, Sudan, and others), dune stabilization (in Mauritania), river training (that is, correction of the river bed) (in Nepal and Haiti), slope stabilization (in Rwanda and Nepal), and other antierosion works. Their common characteristic is that they are highly labor-intensive and require a major effort by the population concerned. Two key issues at the design stage are (1) to create awareness among members of the target groups of the need for environmental protection, and (2) to negotiate some form of agreement whereby target groups associate themselves with the construction and maintenance of protection works that are of vital importance to themselves and to society as a whole.

Indeed, a thorny question in many projects has been how effectively to combine local, short-term aims with wider, longer-term objectives. Protection of the environment and of the resource base are typically a long-term concern for society as a whole, but not necessarily for local communities that have to care for immediate needs. In fact, the poorer such communities are, the more their concerns and priorities for action will be short term.

In Burundi, peasants have agreed to protect forests planted on public land against bushfire in exchange for ownership rights to an already planted plot (about one-third of a hectare) situated between the state forest and their own fields. By 1992, three years after the introduction of an individual contract system, some 2,500 peasant households had joined the scheme, making the approach a success in terms of the linking of local and national interests and joint public-private management and protection of a national resource. Problems with this project may arise in the future because it has hardly been possible to create the managerial capacity for the exploitation and further development of the forest resource without any form of collective or group organization. However, economic interest groups or community-based organizations may form in the future because of common interests, such as charcoal-making, transport of timber and fuelwood, and marketing.

Environmental concerns can also be addressed in the engineering design of infrastructure works, since such designs may cause environmental damage. For instance, labor-based road construction techniques have a less detrimental impact on the environment than equipment-based techniques, mainly because different road alignments and drainage systems are likely to be adopted (the labor-based method follows the natural terrain much more closely than the equipment-based method, and avoids large cuts and fills and disruption of the natural drainage pattern). At the design stage, technicians may also decide between the use of local or external resources for construction. The choice will influence cost and maintenance requirements as well as the environment: the more external resources are used, the more maintenance is likely to be neglected and the more environmental damage will be caused. Involvement of local populations in such choices is therefore necessary.

Socioeconomic Viability. A preliminary assessment of the economic and social viability of selected schemes, along with technical appraisal, allows for discussion of the implications of possible alternative designs and approaches with the local communities and local government.

For small schemes, sophisticated estimates of costs and benefits are not needed. However, rough estimates are needed to weigh, in cooperation with the local population or institutions involved, the economic rationale for the investment; to make those concerned aware of the construction costs and expected operating and maintenance costs; and to reach agreement on responsibilities, inputs, and cost-sharing. For medium-scale or larger schemes, proper cost-benefit analysis is necessary but not sufficient. In fact, conventional project-appraisal techniques tend to overemphasize internal rates of return, while experience shows that—particularly for this type of slow-maturing project—feasibility and sustainability depend as much, if not more, on sustained interest on the part of users, appropriate extension and support services, and long-term upkeep. Because the employment-intensive approach tries to reconcile economic and social objectives, "the notion of efficiency" actually "goes beyond the conventional notion of cost-efficiency" (Gaude and Miller 1990, 212). Appraisals that integrate the institutional and organizational capacity of the local government and beneficiary groups, training needs, and social benefits predict whether or not a project will be viable more accurately than those that describe only economic benefits.

The assessment of social viability is usually the most neglected element at the design stage. This assessment by the people involved implies local-level discussions and agreements (that must be formalized in some way) on ownership, management structure, and who is responsible for the use and maintenance of the assets to be created. Cost-sharing arrangements or methods of remuneration must be agreed upon *before* the works start. The organizational capacity of the local communities or specific target groups must be known, and the required training to improve or stimulate this capacity must be included in the designs. In fact, experience shows that it is preferable that this social investment in support of community organizations be initiated before physical investment to ensure more genuine negotiations between local populations and public administration (Egger 1992a).

Target Groups. The question of targeting depends on whether the investment funds available are to be used for social as well as economic purposes. In a longer-term, employment-creation and poverty-reduction strategy, social policies must be integrated with economic objectives. Employment-intensive infrastructure works programs lend themselves to establishing this link between social policy and investment policy.

Questions of targeting, and modalities for effectively reaching specific groups among the population—for example, households below the poverty line, women (particularly female-headed households), tribal groups, or other disadvantaged minority groups—have to be discussed and agreed upon at the design stage with these groups' representatives, community leaders, or local government authorities. Selection criteria (for example, administrative or geographic selection and self-targeting through the setting of low wage levels) should be carefully defined. Preliminary surveys or data collection and studies are needed to select both the areas and target groups and to take into account the socioeconomic and cultural particularities of poverty groups.

Institutional Capacity of Local Government. The institutional capacity of local government to provide the technical, administrative, and financial support services required for efficient implementation will have to be assessed, and constraints should be identified. The more general question of decentralization, usually a very political one, depends on central government. However, basic requirements for the success of labor-intensive programs should be identified and documented to provide constructive policy advice to the central government and to build up support or pressure for appropriate decisionmaking. Training of local government planning and administrative personnel and of the technical staff of decentralized line ministries must also enter into program design.

Achieving Participation in Community Works. Work organization and definition of the modalities and terms of collaboration between public administration and community organizations or households participating in such joint ventures must also be addressed at the design stage. These modalities may include self-help, wage payment, and cost sharing. Failures, particularly with self-help on public works and state-initiated community works and with wage payment on community works, have shown that "official" self-help and wage payment should be discarded. These methods of work organization lead to ineffective participation and a lack of commitment to subsequent use and maintenance.

A more promising way of achieving participation, tested in a still limited number of ILO-supported pilot programs,[4] is the establishment of contractual agreements, which are simple, flexible, and binding, and promote local organization and negotiation. Such contracts specify the common objectives pursued and the responsibilities, rights, obligations, and contributions of each party involved. Work and cost sharing between the community and government or external assistance can be selected according to expected benefits, the size and the duration of the works, and the community's capacity to contribute in cash or in kind or both.

---

[4]For example, land development in Guinea, afforestation and environment protection in Burundi, management of forest reserves in Mali, irrigation in Nepal, and excavation of water reservoirs *(hafirs)* in Sudan.

In Sudan, village development committees entered into agreements with the provincial administration for the construction of *hafirs* (water reservoirs) on a cost-sharing basis—whereby these committees bore 25 percent of the total cost. Village development committees were involved in the whole chain of planning and implementing activities, from identification to construction and maintenance (Rice 1992, 6–8).

Above all, the project budget has to be prepared with those concerned. Test projects have shown that the question of remuneration is seen in a different light when all parties participate in this exercise:

1. Cost estimates of the works—unlike many community works undertaken now—become a normal component of the contract, and include the cost of labor, skilled labor being valued at the scale locally applicable or on a task basis, and unskilled labor, supplied in principle by the members of the community, at the level of the opportunity wage prevailing in the area during the works season.
2. The contribution of each party to meeting the costs can be negotiated on the basis of total cost sharing (as in the Guinea example), or as payment of one or several cost components, for example, labor or locally unavailable but indispensable inputs (as in the Sudan example).

Community members can then freely decide to contribute labor, or they can negotiate payment of the labor force and contribute other inputs.

In this context, the type of funding mechanism set up to support cost-sharing arrangements must also be considered. Preliminary assessments of the most appropriate terms of cost-sharing are required. The existence or creation of a district or area development fund to which proposals for cost sharing can be submitted, for example, by local communities, can facilitate initiatives from the grassroots level and improve microplanning. Ceilings for government contributions and subsidization can be set at different levels for directly productive investments and for social investments. Such ceilings may encourage local communities to select projects based on a thoughtful consideration of overall priorities (for example, agricultural production); and they may encourage several communities to collaborate on plans for certain types of investments, for example, access roads or health centers.

Subsidization levels can also be set higher if the community agrees to include long-term objectives, such as environmental protection works, in the plan of action. From a community's point of view, additional commitments to conservation efforts can be offered if increased resources can be secured to compensate for labor and forgone income.

Investing in People. Recent evaluations comparing several types of rural development projects with varying levels of local participation have observed that very different results have been obtained in the utilization and maintenance of the assets created, depending on the form and degree of community organization.

The lowest level of participation has been found in government-initiated or donor-dominated "microprojects," such as the microproject program of the European Development Fund (EDF) or the World Bank-sponsored Social Funds (at least those of the first-generation programs). Common shortcomings of these projects included (1) the lack of consultation with beneficiaries at the selection stage, and (2) emphasis on delivery, while involvement of the local population or their organizations and local capacity-building were neglected (Egger 1992a, 46–48, and Chapter 9 of this volume).

Programs that have promoted, from the outset, user groups or responsible development committees or have associated themselves with existing self-development associations (such as the Naams in Burkina Faso or the Young Farmers' Club of Walo in Senegal) have been far more successful, largely because the rights and responsibilities of both the beneficiaries and the financial or technical support program have been negotiated and clearly defined from the beginning. In some of the ILO-supported programs—forest development in Mali, irrigation schemes in Nepal—such agreements have been laid out in simple but binding contracts entered into with the users' groups. In a village water-supply program in Mexico, for example, representative village councils were vested with decisionmaking and bargaining powers according to revived Indian tradition. The organizational, technical, and managerial capacity of these institutions varies, and experience has shown that the development of this capacity may require support in stages, and the flexible integration of training programs into project designs.

Training needs assessments must therefore be carried out at an early stage. They should include (1) problem analyses and task analyses by technical activity; (2) population analyses, identifying skills and bottlenecks, training requirements by category of workers, and technical or other support personnel at various levels; (3) analyses of training needs by project phase (planning and grassroots project-selection phase and construction phase) and operation and maintenance phase; and (4) analyses of organizational and institutional needs, including community participation, village or local project committees, user groups, and local government institutions (Miller 1988).

For user groups, which generally have an immediate technical interest in, for example, water management in irrigation schemes, grassroots-level promotion is likely to be required to create awareness of the advantages of rural organizations. In the process of strengthening rural group formation, the interests and the social base of these groups are also broadened.

Self-development associations often still need flexible support to consolidate their structure and strengthen their organizational capacity at different levels. Training in organizational and management issues, in addition to technical aspects, further increases their influence and independence; they gradually become "development enterprises" capable of tackling an increasing variety of community problems (Egger 1992a, 54–58).

A favorable policy and institutional framework for negotiation of contractual agreements between local communities and the government or external funding agencies is needed to ensure local, participatory planning and the linking of local and wider interests. ILO-assisted programs have shown that success or failure of the program depends on consideration of the following critical factors at the design stage: technical appraisals, socioeconomic assessments, environmental concerns, and the people's organization and participation. Most important, each of these factors has to be linked to the development of operational modalities and procedures.

Implementation Issues

Most of the issues relevant to the design of employment-based works programs will, of course, arise again, to varying degrees, during the implementation phase. Central to successful implementation are work organization, remuneration policy, recruitment and targeting of poverty groups, community participation, capacity-building in the public and private sectors, and decentralization and microplanning.

Work Organization. The optimal method of work organization selected for program implementation at the design stage—direct execution by government, private sector execution, or community works—depends on the type and size of the works, the efficiency of technical departments, the presence or absence of enterprises or community-based organizations in the project area, and their organizational strength and managerial and technical capacity. Experience with public-sector (or "force account") execution[5] has shown that, in order for labor-based methods to be effectively introduced, proper training at the planning, engineering, and technical levels, as well as on-the-job training of foremen and workers, is required. Training packages for this purpose have been developed by ILO-assisted demonstration and training projects, and they are being used in many African and Asian countries.

---

[5]For example, rural roads programs in Kenya, Botswana, or Thailand.

Following program evaluations, several countries decided to shift from force account to private-sector execution. Sectoral feeder-road projects set up in the last five years in Ghana, Guinea, Madagascar, and other countries have successfully demonstrated that a package of support measures, based mainly on training and capacity-building, can be designed to help small firms under contract to public authorities to work cost-effectively. Of course, problems with small contractor execution have occurred in some countries (Sierra Leone and the microproject program in Madagascar, for example). These include mainly delays, noncompliance with quality standards, ineffective use of local resources, lack of technical supervision of the labor force, and overcosting.

The successful feeder road projects have consistently pointed to three prerequisites: first, at the enterprise level, the capacity of a small enterprise staff in the application of labor-based methods must be improved through technical and managerial training; second, at the government level, contract procedures and tender documents must be adapted (small contract lots, accelerated payment procedures) and contract management decentralized; and third, a progressive expansion of labor-based works should be planned with governments and donors to ensure that small- and medium-sized contractors, trained in labor-based techniques, have access to a sufficient number of contracts of this type, enabling them not only to survive, but also to acquire the necessary light equipment (Edmonds and de Veen 1992; van Imschoot 1992).

Remuneration Policy. Past and current recruitment and payment systems have been characterized by incoherent and often contradictory practices, and remuneration therefore often causes problems during project implementation. The difficulty of implementing an effective remuneration system is suggested by the wide range of payment methods used, such as payment in cash or kind; payment of the statutory minimum wage (generally the minimum industrial wage); payment of the agricultural minimum wage (if one has been defined) or, otherwise, of the going agricultural wage in the project area; partial wage payment or "incentive" payment; and "self-help." The self-help in this case is not in the sense of the traditional self-help among villagers (that is, an activity freely decided and undertaken at the ongoing initiative of a group of people), but in the sense of unpaid work inputs required by some local or national institution or authority.

Decisions on forms and levels of remuneration are often made without consideration of the type of works; who benefits from the assets created; who owns, operates, and maintains the infrastructure; how the work is organized—by a community or a local interest group, through some form of collective mobilization of the workforce, or through an individual employer-worker contractual relationship; and whether execution is public or private. In many countries, a clear and easily applicable remuneration policy remains to be formulated. Clarifications are often particularly needed regarding minimum wages in public works programs.

Wage Payment. In practice, public works programs employing wage labor have had to confront the following situations with regard to the application of minimum wages: first, in countries where real minimum wages were set too high, the richer part of the population, generally also more influential and better informed, often managed to have priority access to the jobs. The potential overall employment creation effects of the program are often not fully achieved, and labor is distracted from alternative productive—often agricultural—activities (this is the case, for example, in Senegal [Egger 1992b]). Also, labor-based methods risk being outperformed by equipment-based methods. Second, in countries where real minimum wages are too low, the programs are, predictably, faced with absenteeism and lowered productivity, which endangers the competitiveness of labor-based works. In Sierra Leone, Sudan, and Uganda, for example, where this situation occurred, governments that are supported by donors have resorted to payment or part-payment in food. According to an agreement between the ILO and WFP, payment in food is acceptable in projects employing wage labor if the food ration—whatever its price on the local market—is supplemented by "a cash payment of not less than 50 percent of the wage prevailing in the locality for the kind of work to be done" (Samson 1975). Food-for-work is often preferred by the workers in countries where food supplies are insufficient, or where food payments serve as inflation-proof wages (see Chapter 10 of this volume).

For public- as well as private-sector execution of public works, ILO guidelines stipulate that minimum wages should be paid and national wage legislation should be respected. Minimum wages should in principle be set at a level high enough to meet the basic needs of the worker and his family. It may be recalled that minimum wage legislation can, according to the International Labor Conventions on minimum wages (particularly Recommendation No. 135), "fix different rates of minimum wages in different regions or zones with a view to allowing for differences in costs of living"; for example, different wages may be set for urban and rural areas. It is important for optimal functioning of labor markets that such guidelines are applied. In theory, therefore, rural minimum wages could be set close to agricultural wages prevailing in the area. However, in practice, governments rarely fix region- or area-specific minimum wages (at least, this is the case in most of the Sub-Saharan African countries), which makes wage-setting a difficult exercise in the early stages of project implementation.

In pilot or test works in which the ILO has been involved, wages have generally been set at, or slightly above, the level of the agricultural wage (Miller 1992, Table 1, 87), while keeping labor demand at a level that would not distract workers from alternative agricultural activities. This has been achieved by concentrating on works as much as possible in the slack seasons when unemployment and underemployment are high, and avoiding peak periods of agricultural activity (Hertel 1991).

Self-Help. Decisions on the type of remuneration in community works, particularly with regard to self-help, are often made at a high level, without consulting those directly concerned. Even works of obvious public interest—such as road maintenance—may not be remunerated at all, having been "offered"—as self-help or community maintenance activities—by the government as the national contribution to a donor-funded road construction project (Majeres and Miller 1991; Miller 1992).

In projects where "officially" initiated self-help has been used, it has been virtually impossible to improve work organization, tools, skills, and productivity, with "beneficiaries" generally uninterested in providing unpaid labor inputs to projects not selected by themselves. In many cases, pressure has been exerted (by government or party officials) on the population to take part in the works that authorities have decided will benefit workers and the community (see, for example, Guichaoua [1987b] on Rwanda and Kjaerby [1989] on Tanzania and Chapter 4 on the Chinese experience). Over the past several years, participation of men and young people has continuously decreased in most countries that still mobilize the population for such unsolicited and unpaid works. It seems that women, because of their weaker social position, increasingly had to accept participation in self-help works.

Regarding policy recommendations on remuneration, it must be recognized that works of community interest are more difficult to handle. Such works can be of group interest only—for example, small irrigation schemes—or they may involve the responsibility of local government institutions and organizations representing the interests of the intended beneficiaries—for example, works that provide such basic needs as water, energy, transport, and access to services (Gaude and Watzlawick 1992, 10; India's and China's experience as outlined in Chapters 3 and 4 of this volume).

For community works, the following guiding principle seems to be self-evident: when the participant can establish a clear and direct link between the effort provided and the benefit obtained from the asset created, the remuneration of the work done can be limited to some contribution that may complement the benefits directly derived from the asset.

When this link is less clear and direct, remuneration should approach the level of a full wage. However, the application of this guiding principle obviously goes beyond mere payment of the workforce, and involves issues like responsibilities in project identification; cost sharing; mechanisms ensuring local communities' access to complementary resources and technical know-how; ownership; and responsibilities for management, use, and maintenance.

As a result of these difficulties and complexities, many governments are unable to formulate remuneration policies for public or community works and to enforce labor legislation—for example, normative standards for the setting of minimum wages. This failure has not only opened the door to incoherent remuneration practices, but has also led to abuses of various kinds—such as the extension, in many African countries, of the self-help concept to political mobilization of the workforce (Guichaoua 1991). It should be recalled that such a form of labor mobilization is considered forced labor in the ILO's Forced Labor Conventions (No. 29 and 105), which prohibit the use of forced or compulsory labor in any form, including "as a method of mobilizing and using the labor for purposes of economic development" (Picard 1991).

Recruitment and Targeting of Poverty Groups. Closely related to remuneration issues is the issue of labor force recruitment and targeting of poverty groups.

In specific emergency situations, which require particularly effective targeting of the most vulnerable groups, programs confronted with a high labor supply have set wages slightly below the going agricultural wage rates. This has reinforced the poverty-targeting nature of these programs in favor of the poorest households ("self-targeting" by the poor). Nevertheless, self-targeting through lower wage levels has its limits, for a number of reasons. First, going (agricultural) wage rates tend to be very low during emergencies. Second, in such situations, wages are often paid entirely or partly in kind, with daily food rations fixed at the subsistence level. Therefore, efforts are made to make use of other targeting approaches, such as careful selection of particularly poor areas for labor-based approaches, special targeting clauses in contracts with private contractors or executing institutions, or special selection criteria for particularly vulnerable or disadvantaged groups.

For works carried out by private contractors, the ILO has successfully tested, for example, in Madagascar and Nepal, the inclusion in contract documents of a clause requesting entrepreneurs to recruit unskilled labor in the immediate surroundings of the work sites, unless this is impossible. This policy is aimed at distributing income as widely as possible in areas where the labor supply is high and reaching target groups in poverty areas. However, this practice implies an increased need for training, the cost of which has to be borne by government or a cooperating agency. Also, in Madagascar, another clause required that at least 25 percent of the unskilled labor force in programs should be women. According to preliminary data, this target is being reached.[6]

In areas with large numbers of unemployed and underemployed people, rotation of the labor force has also been successful in works directly executed by government agencies. In Burundi, Rwanda, and Sierra Leone, the rotation period has generally been three months. However, rotation is only feasible if the workforce is employed by an institution or a project with a social purpose—not by contractors, unless the latter are directly or indirectly compensated (for loss in productivity, cost of repeated training, and so forth) by government or social institutions.

The application of a rotational recruitment system can cause problems, as already recruited workers may tend to resist it. The principle of such a rotation should be discussed with workers, local institutions, and traditional leaders—who in one way or another intervene in labor recruitment—and accepted beforehand.

The Need for Genuine Participation at the Grassroots Level. The concept of participation has often been espoused, but rarely operationalized, at least not on a significant scale.

The search for more participatory approaches is due largely to the problems encountered with work organization. Work organization based on an employer-worker relationship has proven inappropriate, and even counterproductive to works of community interest. Documented experience has shown that lack of genuine participation of local communities and potential beneficiaries has meant that the created assets have not been used to their full potential and have fallen quickly into disrepair.

Results obtained with community contract approaches, such as those already mentioned in Burundi and Sudan, confirm that successful implementation of community contracts depends, in the end, on the following three elements: (1) existence of well-organized community or interest groups; (2) scheme-specific agreement on inputs, cost sharing, and work sharing, and the rights and responsibilities of each party; and (3) decentralization. The three elements reinforce each other: the better these issues

---

[6]For the impact of employment-intensive works on women, see King-Dejardin 1994.

can be clarified and addressed, the easier it will be to agree on and implement a contract.

Contract execution has been an important factor in motivating local community organization. It has facilitated the mobilization of local resources, and has provided community organizations with improved bargaining skills, understanding of costing and budgeting, and access to external complementary resources, including technical know-how. Cost and work sharing have been negotiated and implemented according to contract agreements, even in areas with very scarce resources. Where the cost sharing was defined as a percentage share of total costs, unit costs have been kept very low. No case was observed where the communities committed themselves—through financial, labor, or material inputs—to sacrifices that did not correspond to their priority needs.

Contracts have been instrumental in combining local and national interests and in introducing joint public-private management of national resources (in forestry development projects in Burundi and Mali, for example). This approach has also succeeded in changing the relations between government departments and village populations, from authoritarian-subservient to more collaborative relationships. Contract execution has offered a new role to local government staff, who have by and large welcomed and supported it, sometimes enthusiastically.

In Mali, village communities, for decades accused of encroachment in state forests, have negotiated community contracts by which they assume responsibilities to protect, maintain, and develop a national forest reserve in exchange for certain felling and marketing rights (jointly defined with the Forestry Department) and an employment priority for their members in reforestation works. The contract approach has succeeded in substituting for the spiral of illegal land clearance and repression a participatory alternative that not only has altered relations between village populations and the Forest Department, but also has brought economic, environmental, and social benefits to the local communities and to the country.

In Guinea, village-level interest groups have entered into contracts with local government administrations in the districts of Dabola and Dinguiraye, and with external funding agencies to invest—on a cost-sharing basis—in agricultural, infrastructure, and forestry development activities. Because the cost sharing from the associations was defined as a percentage share of total costs, unit costs have been kept very low. The approach has facilitated the mobilization of local financial, material, and human resources. Technical support was an obligation of the district administration. However, to make sure that their obligations were actually fulfilled, a provision for technical support was included in the cost estimate and in the contribution of the external organization, but paid to the associations, which, in turn, paid the technician per service provided (Egger and Majeres 1992).

Tests have confirmed the superiority of the "contract approach" over implementation by wage labor directly recruited by the government or implementation by unpaid self-help. While not without problems, performance has been superior in terms of construction results during implementation and institutional and human development. For different activities, in diverse sociopolitical and cultural settings, and in a variety of economic conditions—including those marked by severe food deficits and poverty—contracts have been able to increase participation levels in target populations, while respecting the autonomy and priorities of community groups.

Decentralization and Microplanning. The success of area-based works is largely dependent on institutional efficiency at the local level. Decentralization is also a prerequisite for effective public-private association and participation—for example, for the establishment of contracts with communities or economic interest groups, or with private contractors.

For many infrastructure works of local interest, implementation responsibilities lie with local government. Responsibility for maintenance also usually remains at the local level. This applies to works carried out directly by the local administration under "force account" and to those contracted out to private firms, implying the use of official channels and government control of the funds allocated to the works.

Experience has shown that centralized procedures tend to be too cumbersome and too slow to support local works efficiently. Simultaneous improvement of administrative procedures and strengthening of decentralized decisionmaking power should be emphasized, since many programs face huge problems in this regard. While policies and procedures to ensure coherent planning and accountability have to be defined at the national level, allowance should also be made for decentralization of financial decisionmaking for certain categories of works and up to certain financial ceilings.

For effective decentralization measures to be taken by government, a precondition seems to be investment budgets made available for area-based funding with at least a medium-term perspective. Given the scarcity of resources in all the countries concerned, such policy decisions are not likely to be taken without the support and long-term commitment of external funding agencies. Experience with community contracts has shown that area-based investment funds, to which project proposals could be submitted, often lead to district-level planning and effective decentralization.

Finally, there is a basic dilemma that many programs face during implementation: the pressure from donor agencies to accelerate implementation and to enlarge programs quickly. Such requirements have prevented many programs from reaching their initial objectives, particularly those objectives related to people's participation, capacity building, and decentralization. An analysis by Gaude and Miller (ILO 1990) of evaluation reports covering nine country programs concluded that program objectives, approaches, and activities often proved to be unrealistic, or at least too demanding—shortcomings of the design phase—and proposed that the process of identification of investment schemes and their implementation take place over a longer period of time. Pressures for quick disbursements tend to go awry.

Postimplementation Issues

The key issue at the postimplementation, or postconstruction, stage is sustainability, which itself conditions the wider issue of replicability. Sustainability depends, above all, on local factors directly related to the program and its immediate environment. It can be evaluated in economic, social, institutional, and environmental terms. A project is sustainable if it can become self-supporting within a reasonable time period.

Social sustainability will to a significant extent be determined by the capacity of local communities to form autonomous organizations to defend the interests of their members in the most efficient manner (Gaude and Miller 1990).

Economic sustainability depends not only on choices made at the design stage, on the quality of preliminary technical and socioeconomic assessments, and on the cost-effectiveness of specific operations, but also on the general economic environment, which is largely outside the control of a project. This environment can change quickly, with risk growing as the use of imported inputs increases. Local resource-based approaches are therefore likely to become self-supporting more quickly. This point is obvious when considering material or mechanical maintenance requirements.

Environmental sustainability implies that labor-intensive works programs must, on balance, protect the environment. Measures for continued attention to this critical factor have to be integrated in operation and maintenance arrangements.

Institutional sustainability also may lie partly outside the control of the project, but can be supported by appropriate participatory arrangements and strengthening of technical and organizational skills. Longer-term viability of community-based organizations depends, in the end, on the members themselves; local government institutions are subject to changes in mandates, staff, and resources imposed on them by administrative or political structures. Hence, the participatory approach, which must aim to create a sense of ownership among the beneficiaries and to create partnership and responsibility-sharing with (local) government institutions, is important.

Replicability depends, in part, on the degree of success obtained in sustainability, but it rests first and foremost on the creation of national and local capacities in the public and private sectors, including the creation or strengthening of representative community-based organizations, farmers' associations, women's associations, and so forth. It requires the orientation of financial investments toward cost-effective, labor-intensive works programs, rather than toward capital-intensive, foreign exchange- dependent investments or social, compensatory programs. Above all, replicability requires government commitment to the approach and the adoption of appropriate policies and plans of action, from the selection of investment programs to the choice of technology in favor of employment-intensive methods, to decentralization and target group approaches for poverty alleviation (Gaude and Watzlawick 1992; Hertel 1991).

Conclusions

Employment-intensive works programs have been implemented in many developing countries because of their short-term job creation or income generation effects. These effects may indeed be appreciable from several points of view, particularly in emergency and relief situations. As this chapter has argued, such programs can also have a much more fundamental and long-term impact on the root causes of unemployment and under-employment and poverty. Poor rural people are by definition asset-poor. The programs should therefore be considered policy instruments intended to steer investments toward both the productive and social infrastructure necessary to provide the poor with access to long-term and sustainable employment and income.

The contribution employment-intensive programs can make to poverty reduction and food security (in contrast with social or compensatory programs) is then seen in the light of the development of the local resource base through cost-effective investments targeted at the poor, with a perspective of longer-term economic growth and greater social equity.

Given the potential of such programs to create employment and alleviate poverty, constraints and problems have been identified here so that local implementation can be made more efficient and so that this approach may be more widely applied.

These are the major policy conclusions:

- Past and current approaches to employment generation programs have often limited their scope to short-term measures with an immediate impact on unemployment and poverty. Policies and programs can and must be developed so as to give priority to cost-effective, labor- and local-resource-intensive investment programs targeted at longer-term employment-intensive growth and at poverty reduction.
- Employment-intensive works programs establish operational linkages between micro- and macroplanning and programming. In turn, area-specific experiences provide options for policy decisions that can strengthen local-level planning and implementation. Progress on the predominantly microlevel issues will largely depend on a favorable policy environment.
- Employment policies in the poorest countries often operate in a context of inadequate or nonexistent popular organizations, a weak private sector, and poorly functioning, if not completely paralyzed, public institutions. Labor-based and local resource-intensive works programs have proved to be powerful devices for promoting decentralization and activating local institutions. Institutional capacity-building and training are prerequisites to success. A major effort has to be made to develop rural people's organizations. Similar support must be provided to local government and decentralized technical staff, as well as to local contractors.
- There is a need to further develop district or area funds to support, basically through cost-sharing arrangements, small- and medium-scale local investments. Greater and more sustained support from the international donor community is required for this task, but policies have to be coordinated.
- More work needs to be done on operational instruments, systems, and procedures to translate policies into action. The example described is relevant: contractual agreements enable local communities and households as well as private contractors to enter into a freely negotiated association with public administration. This may lead to improved practices and modalities for public-private partnership, potentially replicable on a larger scale.

REFERENCES

Bentall, P. H. 1990. Ghana feeder roads project: Labour-based rehabilitation and maintenance. International Labour Office, World Employment Program, Geneva.

Edmonds, G. A., and J. J. de Veen. 1992. A labour-based approach to roads and rural transport in developing countries. *International Labour Review* 131 (1): 95–110.

Egger, P. 1992a. Rural organizations and infrastructure projects: Social investment comes before material investment. *International Labour Review* 131 (1): 45–61.

_____. 1992b. Travaux publics et emploi pour les jeunes travailleurs dans une économie sous ajustement: l'expérience de l'AGETIP au Sénégal. Geneva: International Labour Office.

_____. 1993. Travail et agriculture dans le tiers-monde: Pour une politique active de l'emploi rural. Geneva: International Labour Office.

Egger, P., and J. Majeres. 1992. Local resource management and development: Strategic dimensions of people's participation. In *Grassroots environmental action: People's participation in sustainable development*, ed. D. Ghai and J. M. Vivian, 304–324. London: Routledge.

Egger, P., J. Gaude, and P. Garnier. 1993. Ajustement structurel et compensation sociale: Etudes de cas au Honduras, à Madagascar et au Sénégal. Geneva: International Labour Office.

Gaude, J., and S. Miller. 1990. Rural development and local resource intensity: A case study approach. In *Human development and the international development strategy for the 1990s*, ed. K. Griffin and J. Knight, 189–214. London: Macmillan.

_____, eds. 1992. Production employment for the poor. *International Labour Review* 131 (1) (Special issue).

Gaude, J., and H. Watzlawick. 1992. Employment creation and poverty alleviation through labour-intensive public works in least developed countries. *International Labour Review* 131 (1): 3–18.

Guichaoua, A. 1987a. *Paysans et investissement-travail au Burundi et au Rwanda*. Geneva: International Labour Office.

_____. 1987b. *Travail non rémunéré et développement rural au Rwanda; pratiques et perspectives.* Série "Etudes et Débats." Geneva: International Labour Office.

_____. 1991. Les travaux communautaires en Afrique Centrale. *Revue Tiers-Monde* 32 (127): 551–573.

Guichaoua, A., and C. Thérond. 1984. *Entretien et mise en valeur des infrastructures réalisées dans la Province de Muramvya-Burundi.* Geneva: International Labour Office.

Hertel, S. 1991. Labour-intensive public works in Sub-Saharan Africa. ILO Note to the World Bank. International Labour Office, Geneva.

ILO (International Labour Office). 1990. *Advisory Committee on Rural Development, Review of ILO rural development activities since 1983.* ACRD/XI/1990/1. Geneva.

_____. 1992. Botswana road maintenance study. Report to the Government of Botswana. Geneva.

Imschoot, M. van. 1992. Water as a resource of employment. *International Labour Review* 131 (1): 125–137.

King-Dejardin, A. 1994. Public works programmes, a strategy for poverty alleviation: The gender dimension. Geneva: International Labour Office.

Kjaerby, F. 1989. *Unpaid self-help labour in rural roads construction and maintenance in Ruvuma Region.* Geneva and Copenhagen: International Labour Office and Centre for Development Research.

Majeres, J., and S. Miller. 1991. La rémunération dans les programmes d'investissement-travail: Entraide, rétribution ou salaire? *Revue Tiers-Monde* 32 (127): 575–595.

Martens, B. 1988. *Sustainability of economic development through irrigation projects: Case studies in Nepal and Tanzania.* Geneva: International Labour Office.

_____. 1990. *Etude comparée de l'efficacité économique des techniques à haute intensité de main-d'oeuvre et à haute intensité d'équipement pour la construction de routes secondaires au Rwanda.* Série Etudes et Débats. Geneva: International Labour Office.

Miller, S. 1988. Training needs assessment for special public works programmes. Working document. International Labour Office, Geneva.

_____. 1992. Remuneration systems for labour-intensive investments: Lessons for equity and growth. *International Labour Review* 131 (1): 77-93.

Picard, L. 1991. Investissement-travail ou travail forcé? *Revue Tiers-Monde* 32 (127): 617-625.

Rice, J. 1992. *Hafir: Employment generation in water supply works programmes for people of arid areas in Sudan.* Geneva: International Labour Office.

Samson, K. T. 1975. International labour standards and WFP projects: The distinction between wage-labour schemes and self-help projects. Note to the Third ILO/WFP Intersecretariat Meeting, Geneva.

World Bank. 1983. *Labor-based construction programs: A practical guide for planning and management.* Washington, D.C.

_____. 1984. The construction industry: Issues and strategies in developing countries. Washington, D.C.

_____. 1990. *World development report 1990.* Washington, D.C.

12
EMPLOYMENT FOR FOOD SECURITY: SYNTHESIS AND POLICY CONCLUSIONS

Joachim von Braun

The foregoing chapters have focused on employment policies and programs and actions for their improved effectiveness in pursuing the goal of eradicating poverty.

Chapter 1 highlighted a number of global trends that call for an increased focus on employment for poverty reduction in the 1990s and beyond. Prominent among these trends are the rapid growth of the labor force in low-income countries, the declining ratio of the cost of labor to capital, the growing need for infrastructure, and the increased dependency of the rural poor on labor, rather than subsistence farming (Box 12.1). They are to be considered in an employment-expanding growth strategy that is complemented by appropriate social security action for vulnerable groups (Radwan, Chapter 2).

In this chapter the findings obtained from the study of employment policies and programs in various countries are synthesized (Box 12.2) and conclusions regarding the design of policy are drawn from them. References made here to other chapters of this volume are also meant to refer to

---

Box 12.1
Factors Driving the Increased Focus on Employment at This Point in Time

- Huge growth in labor force
- Declining cost of labor versus capital
- Increasing asset-scarcity of the poor (for example, scarcity of land)
- Need for infrastructure and resource improvement
- Man-made crises and consequent reconstruction needs

Box 12.2
Overview of Experience with Employment Programs
in Selected Countries

Bangladesh
- Food-aided employment programs prove effective in reaching the poor.
- Infrastructure created by employment programs yields high pay-off in agricultural growth.

China
- Strong planning capacity represents a big plus for effective implementation.
- Monetization of food and other commodities works well.
- Poor areas are well-targeted, but not the poorest people in these areas.

India/Maharashtra
- Urban-rural political coalition plays an important role for program sustainability.
- Self-selection of poor works best with low wage.
- Flexible program size (employment guarantee) and large coverage a plus for addressing transitory food insecurity.

Botswana
- Integration in mainstream government administration good for asset quality.
- No need for food wages when food markets work.
- Extensive participation of women works well.

Niger
- Self-selection of the poor works well. Nutrition improved.
- Seasonal adjustment critical in semi-arid environments.
- Good experience with urban employment programs.
- Private sector can play role in implementation.

Tanzania
- Inflexible remuneration policy hinders programs.
- Deficient local institutions are a constraint on implementation.

Zimbabwe
- Food-for-work geographical targeting spread too thinly, but reach many.
- Response to drought crisis significant.
- Public works program had narrow outreach with regular wage employment.

Ethiopia
- In famine-risk situation, broad coverage needed; targeting of bottom-end poverty is insufficient.
- Scope for food wages in case of widespread failure of food market.

Latin America
- Scattered, ad hoc programs fail to create effective capacities.
- Doubts exist about employment programs as part of short-term social funds.

the extensive literature reviewed in the respective chapters, together with the original analyses presented.

The policy conclusions are divided into two categories: actions that may be taken by national and local organizations (governmental and non-governmental) and actions that may be taken by international organizations. The actions that could be undertaken by national and local organizations include steps to ensure that the political, economic, and social setting is favorable to effective implementation of employment policies and programs; to methods for incorporating elements that have proven crucial to program success into program design, such as participation; and to procedures for selecting appropriate criteria for effectively monitoring and evaluating program performance.

The proposed international actions are derived partly from experience with food-aided employment programs conducted by the World Food Programme (WFP) (see Shaw, Chapter 10) and partly from the implementation of pilot programs by the International Labour Office (ILO) (see Majeres, Chapter 11). They include improved mechanisms for sharing national experience and measures for overcoming the limitations of individual international agencies in a concerted effort to expand employment with a view to reducing poverty in low-income countries.

Employment Programs for Poverty Reduction: Typology of Program Efficacy

Employment programs are not a cure-all, but they are a versatile instrument that can be applied in a variety of contexts of poverty and food insecurity. In theory, it is as easy to design ideal employment programs for poverty reduction as to speculate about design flaws, particularly when adverse institutional or political economy conditions are also considered (Chapter 1). A careful assessment of the realities of existing employment programs in their diverse environments—the approach taken by the national studies in this volume—may provide a basis for drawing more constructive conclusions regarding program selection and design.

Two parameters, the food-security environment and the labor-market environment, determine to a large extent the optimal choice and design of labor-intensive employment programs. In particular, they determine the appropriateness of choosing long-term versus short-term program goals, the setting of wage rates, and the definition of program scale and coverage.

Table 12.1 summarizes the scope for employment programs in certain broadly defined institutional arrangements of labor-market and food-security environments. Widely varying pictures emerge under different conditions,

Table 12.1—Potential of employment programs under different food-security and labor-market conditions

Labor Market Conditions and Characteristics	Food Security Conditions		
	Crises and Famine Risk	Rural Chronic Food Insecurity	Urban Poverty/ Food Insecurity
Free labor market	++	+	+
Minimum wage policy and wage control	+	–	+
Job sharing, employment pooling, and community works traditions	+	+	–
Constraints in labor markets (for example, by gender, ethnic groups and caste)	+	+	–
Command systems and work obligations	+	+	+

++ = Strong potential.
 + = Some potential.
 – = No or little potential.

depending on whether labor markets can operate freely or are severely constrained (the rows in Table 12.1) and on whether food insecurity conditions are transitory crises, or chronic in rural and urban areas (the columns in Table 12.1). The empirical insights from national studies that provided the basis for categorizing the relative potential of the employment programs (strong potential, some potential, and little or no potential) in Table 12.1 under such varying conditions are elaborated below.

- Programs have a strong chance of ensuring food security in areas where labor markets can operate fairly freely. Under this condition, and assuming that an appropriate wage rate policy is applied (an issue discussed further on), the poor tend to be self-targeted by the employment programs (see Dev, Chapter 5; Webb, Chapter 7 of this volume). Free, interregional migration of poor people to work sites can mean that programs reach a large proportion of the poor. When poor people can move, programs need not move as close to the poor as under restricted labor market conditions. The location of the programs becomes less important under such conditions, and the programs can be directed more toward achieving a long-term return on investment rather than toward targeting local poverty. Free labor-market conditions consequently enhance the efficiency of employment programs both in targeting poverty and in developing assets. Restricted access to programs is common, especially when they are implemented at the community level (see, for example,

Teklu, Chapter 6; Ahmed et al., Chapter 3). Thus, there may exist a conflict between the freedom of access to jobs (which involves competition across communities) and local participation and control over programs (see Majeres, Chapter 11). Migration restrictions seem to have reduced the poverty-targeting effect of programs in, for instance, China (Zhu and Jiang, Chapter 4).

- Minimum wage polices or wage-control measures reduce the poor's self-targeting. Minimum wages are typically higher than the rural poor's returns to labor as a result of effective lobbying by (urban) formal wage labor. High wages would attract more than just the destitute, and with the typically constrained budgets of employment programs, the supply of jobs would not match demand and therefore would lead to the rationing of jobs. There is a high likelihood that the rationing of jobs works in favor of the richer, more influential members of society. Thus, higher wages may actually reduce a program's impact on absolute poverty, as in Maharashtra (Dev, Chapter 5) and Tanzania (Teklu, Chapter 6). But wage-rate policy is a protracted issue: in poverty-reducing programs, income from wages (earned in socially acceptable lengths of work days) should be higher than the poverty line for the working poor, but below a level that would attract the nonpoor. In this sense, a minimum wage policy is justified (Majeres, Chapter 11).

- Community works traditions and employment pooling can help employment programs reach the poor, as indicated for Niger (see Webb, Chapter 7). Communities with such work traditions are prevalent in many parts of Africa. They assist the mobilization of labor and facilitate the production of public goods such as local production on common fields for common stockholding or simple neighborhood-assistance schemes.

- In labor markets with gender, ethnic-group, or caste constraints, inefficiencies and inequality can grow more pronounced and impair the performance of employment programs. On the other hand, some of the studies in this volume suggest that employment programs can help overcome such constraints: the food-for-work programs in Bangladesh (Ahmed et al., Chapter 3), in which women played an unprecedented role, are one example. Another example of the positive effect of employment programs on gender equality is the Maharashtra Employment Guarantee Scheme (Dev, Chapter 5).

- Since free labor market conditions are an optimal context for maximizing employment program effectiveness, it would seem logical to conclude that command systems with work obligations would be particularly adverse for such programs. It depends, however, on how a given system works, that is, on the extent of local participation in decisionmaking on work obligations, on the ownership of the assets created, and on the effectiveness and trustworthiness of the system's administration. A restrictive institutional environment for labor markets can, under certain conditions (for example, when administrative capabilities are strong), also assure favorable outcomes of public works programs. China's employment program, which comes close to a command system with mandatory work, is one example of a program succeeding under restricted labor market conditions (Zhu and Jiang, Chapter 4). However, the presence of technically competent and administratively reliable organizations at the community level and an effective system of supervision of program administration are preconditions for favorable outcomes under command system-type labor markets.

Two other factors not shown in Table 12.1 may significantly affect the extent to which labor-intensive employment programs succeed. The first is the ability of the public works programs themselves to contribute to their own success over the long term as they evolve into stronger institutions with an established political support base. The second is the presence of strong organizational capacity at the local level, which can assist in program implementation. These two factors shall be elaborated on the basis of the findings from the various countries.

Over the medium term, only labor-intensive public works that create measurable assets will gain political support and so become sustainable in a political economy sense. While there tends to be quickly mobilized political support for programs designed to help during emergency situations, there is often little support, initially, for longer-term programs. This is because the asset creation of the latter shows its benefits only over the long run. Long-term commitment to more investment-oriented employment programs is required. Without such commitment, it is impossible to reap their full benefits either in asset creation or in institutional strengthening to enhance the programs' sustainability. In the past, unfortunately, the lack of political support for programs, combined with poor planning and hasty implementation on the part of the program administrations, has often led to poor performance and the further withdrawal of political support. This has particularly been the case when programs have been initiated by institutions that lacked the related experience and competence, regardless of whether they were national or foreign, that is, including NGOs, and in the context of hastily set up "social funds" (Wurgaft, Chapter 9).

The second factor in program success is the existence of organizational abilities at the local level, which contribute greatly to program effectiveness. In the studies of China (Zhu and Jiang, Chapter 4), for example, the local government's strong planning capacity clearly aided the program's success. In Botswana, as well, the mainstream government organizations into which the program was integrated aided program performance (Teklu, Chapter 6). Organizational abilities can be fostered successfully through training measures and stimulated sustainably in the context of program implementation and asset maintenance through carefully designed contractual arrangements (Majeres, Chapter 11). Such contractual arrangements are, of course, specific to each program's type, scale, and legal environment.

National Action for Poverty-Reducing Employment Policies

National governments can take certain steps to improve employment policies and programs and to make better progress toward the goal of poverty reduction. A first area of action consists of setting the social and political stage for effective implementation of employment programs. Another consists of incorporating key elements in program design and implementation. A third area includes developing appropriate processes for evaluating and monitoring program and policy effectiveness in order to facilitate "learning by doing."

Providing the Appropriate Social, Political, and Institutional Setting

Employment policies and programs cannot be designed in a vacuum, that is, programs have an impact on various aspects of development and social policy and vice versa. In addition, programs require favorable social and political settings in order to operate most effectively. A number of conclusions following from these observations are outlined in Box 12.3.

To elaborate on the issues in the box:

- There is a clear advantage to integrating employment programs into mainstream public planning. Programs that are planned separately, that are conducted by separate institutions, and that have independent budgets tend to be isolated and poorly designed because the responsible institutions lack access to planning capabilities and technical skill. This is especially true of programs designed to generate assets (this point will be explored later). Placing both the development-oriented and relief-oriented aspects of employment

---

Box 12.3
**Strategy and Institutional Design Issues of Employment
Programs at the National Level**

- Integration of employment programs in mainstream public planning
- A legal basis (law) for employment program implementation to
  prevent ad-hocism
- Participatory planning and implementation of programs
- Coordination of governmental and nongovernmental organizations
- Capability of programs to respond flexibly to crises
- Avoidance of "workfare" (that is, employment with little concern
  for the assets created) except by default in crises (when "workfare"
  is better than distress migration, camps, and so forth)
- Clear coordination of "development-oriented" and "relief-oriented"
  action, preferably under one umbrella-institution
- Political formation for sustainability of programs

---

programs under a single umbrella can add to their effectiveness in
reducing poverty, as in Botswana, for example (Teklu, Chapter 6).

- The implementation of employment programs requires a legal
  framework and may require the adjustment of existing regulations.
  Existing labor laws may, for example, prevent programs from setting wage rates to better target the poor (Majeres, Chapter 11).
- Attention to policies in other areas of development planning can
  extend the impact of assets generated by public works programs.
  For example, if employment programs created infrastructure, efforts
  to aid farmers in gaining access to agricultural technology will be
  easier and will pay off fast, as in Bangladesh (Ahmed et al., Chapter 3). Such complementary policies can stimulate growth and lead
  to a second round of asset generation through private investment.
- Decentralization of power and rural power, in particular, work in
  favor of efficient labor-intensive public works. Participatory planning and implementation has paid off in virtually all environments
  where it has been practiced (Majeres, Chapter 11). This is particularly true of small, local projects. The Chinese experience with
  drinking water projects at the community level supports this point
  (Zhu and Jiang, Chapter 4). Strong public administration at the local
  level tends to foster program designs that provide rural communities
  with access to appropriate services and assets.
- Appropriately defined roles for nongovernmental organizations
  (NGOs) are required. Where public institutions are weak or if crises
  arise, programs may operate independently of the government. Under normal circumstances, NGOs may carry out employment pro-

grams under the auspices of government organizations. Subsuming NGO activities within national public works programs can facilitate economies of scale (as in Ethiopia, for example) (see Webb and Kumar, Chapter 8).

- Empowerment of the poor and the demand for public works are intricately connected. The formation and mobilization of political coalitions are preconditions for the implementation of sustainable employment programs for the poor. Conversely, once implemented, public works themselves contribute to empowerment of the poor, which can increase the demand for the programs. Democratic processes at the local level have been the key factor in determining the poverty orientation of a number of programs, for example, the program in Maharashtra, India (Dev, Chapter 5) and the program in Botswana (Teklu, Chapter 6).
- Corruption in public works should be minimized the same as anywhere else. A strong judiciary system is an advantage in combating corruption, as are a free press and universal voting rights. There are no indications that corruption in employment programs is any greater than that in other investment programs. It is relatively likely that under conditions where the transactions are primarily wage payments and where the wage recipients know their rights, labor intensity will reduce corruption in investment (Dev, Chapter 5).
- Assets often tend to favor the rural rich. To some extent, however, it may be necessary to accept this in the short run in order to make programs politically sustainable. It is necessary to identify optimal levels of such implicit leakage effects in order to strike the best possible balance between short-term poverty targeting and long-term asset buildup. Financing public works from an urban industrial base can sustain programs over long periods, as shown by Maharashtra's and China's examples, but does not necessarily make them self-sustainable.

Key Elements in the Design and Implementation of Employment Programs

Certain elements of program design are of key significance in achieving program effectiveness in reducing poverty. Employment programs aimed at reducing poverty can succeed only to the extent that they, first, reach the poor, and, second, actually benefit the poor. One essential element of program design, therefore, is the means of targeting the poor (Box 12.4).

A second essential element involves the design of benefits, such as improved short-term food security or the generation of assets that ensure

312

Box 12.4
Targeting and Coverage

- Target poverty's causes
  - Infrastructure deficiencies (roads, water)
  - Resource constraints (land quality, irrigation, water)
- Target regions where causes are concentrated, but focus on high-return investments within those regions
- Self-target the poor by utilizing a (low) wage rate

---

future food security. Two other important features of employment programs that will also be discussed are adequate technical and managerial training of the personnel responsible for implementing the programs and the need for broader criteria for program evaluation.

Reaching the Poor. Targeting the root causes of poverty may be as important to reducing poverty over the long term as is the direct targeting of the poor themselves over the short term. Root causes of poverty that can be remedied by labor-intensive public works programs include weak infrastructure (roads, lack of piped water) and a degraded natural resource base (Radwan, Chapter 2).

The poor can be targeted directly if programs are located in regions where absolute poverty is concentrated. The effect is enhanced if labor movement is unrestricted. Within poor regions, it may be economically efficient to invest in programs that yield high returns and produce public goods. Examples of such investments might be the infrastructure and resource improvement activities mentioned above. The Chinese programs have adopted this approach successfully (Zhu and Jiang, Chapter 4).

The poor may be targeted directly, yet not administratively, through the setting of low wage rates (Box 12.5). The potential and limitations of this approach are addressed from different perspectives in the various national cases studied. Wage rates in publicly funded employment programs for poverty reduction should ensure food security but little more in order to ensure optimal use of program resources and broad coverage of the poor. This approach is exemplified in the programs in Maharashtra, India, in Bangladesh, and in Niger (Dev, Chapter 5; Ahmed et al., Chapter 3; Webb, Chapter 7). A food-security-insuring wage rate may actually be above market wage rates during crises when labor markets collapse (in a famine, for example). The level at which such a self-targeting wage level should be set depends on the local conditions regarding opportunity costs of time.

Box 12.5
Determining the Wage Rate for Unskilled Labor
in Programs

The food-security-insuring wage rate
- is just high enough to assure households' food security;
- may be above the market wage rate (of adults) in crises;
- tends to be below the "minimum wage" typically decreed by the government; and
- is an empirically determinable value, that is, the implementing organization must have suitable monitoring and analysis capability.

Any implementing organization must be able to monitor changing circumstances and adjust wage rates accordingly. Nevertheless, program participation should allow minimum basic needs to be met.

One issue with this wage-based targeting approach is that optimal wage rates often tend to be below typical minimum wage rates set by governments. Minimum wage rate policy needs to be reviewed in this context; such policy must not undermine the potential for the self-targeting of employment programs of the poor. A legal framework within which such wage adjustments can take place is critical for ensuring that those who are employed at a certain point in time do not have a stronger say about the wage rate than those who are not involved in the program at any given time, but are close to the threshold for being attracted to it under changing circumstances, for instance, when the opportunity cost of time diminishes in a drought. As much as possible, an employment guarantee should be aimed for at the level of the food-security-insuring wage rate. Of course, skilled labor is needed in labor-intensive public works programs, too, and must be remunerated at market wage rates appropriate to the levels of the skills involved.

Employment programs open to everyone have attracted a greater proportion of poor women than typically found in any other employment in the same countries or locations. Such programs have the capability of empowering women through off-farm, outside-of-the home employment (Ahmed et al., Chapter 3).

Child labor, however, remains a critical issue, not just direct employment in programs, but also when home tasks are shifted to children because adult household members are absorbed in employment programs (Webb, Chapter 7). Child-labor problems need to be addressed with explicit incentives for education that work in the short run. Such strong incentives need to be developed alongside employment programs.

Benefiting the Poor: Relief versus Generation of Assets? In general, the mobilization of labor without creating assets, that is, "workfare" or "make-work" projects that keep workers busy but produce nothing of value, as a form of welfare appears neither economically convincing nor politically feasible. Labor-intensive employment programs should serve the dual function of short-term relief and longer-term asset creation. In order to meet these two aims, employment programs must be flexible enough to respond to changes in the labor market, that is, to expand their activities in the event of sudden crises. In order to realize their full potential for providing short-term food security, employment programs need a flexible response capability, especially in crises. The advantages of quick response have been proven in Maharashtra, India, for example (Dev, Chapter 5).

Employment programs that provide workfare, that is, which disregard the asset-generation component, are generally undesirable. A correct economic judgment concerning them, however, depends upon the appropriate point of reference; for instance, in crises, this option may be preferable to distress migration and famine feeding camps. Experience in East Africa during famine supports the judicious use of a workfare design in crises (Chapters 6, 7, 8). However, workfare should not be considered a viable option for dealing with chronic food insecurity and poverty.

Figure 12.1 outlines the design of a flexible program system designed to provide short-term relief and to generate high-quality assets. A core program focuses on the creation of high-quality assets with labor-based technology. This is surrounded by a second set of programs that is aimed at stabilization and the mitigation of (seasonal) stress. In this second circle, the choice of asset creation changes. Here, asset-generation is deliberately designed to absorb large amounts of labor quickly to increase short-term transfers. Activities such as land development, forestry, and similar programs are likely candidates for asset components in this circle. The share of labor in these activities tends to be twice as high as that in road programs, for instance.

A third circle addresses large-scale relief needs that result from natural or human-made disasters. In this outer circle, the priority is to maximize employment. Often, the asset components of the programs cannot facilitate the program's being geared toward the production of lower-quality assets. The decision to pursue programs located in the outer circle is made after weighing the costs (including human misery) of alternative scenarios during a crisis. These scenarios include relief camps, large-scale migration, or the burgeoning of slums around urban centers that often follows an emergency. Such scenarios are seen with increasing frequency in famine-prone parts of Africa (Webb and Kumar, Chapter 8).

Figure 12.1—Poverty targeting and asset quality

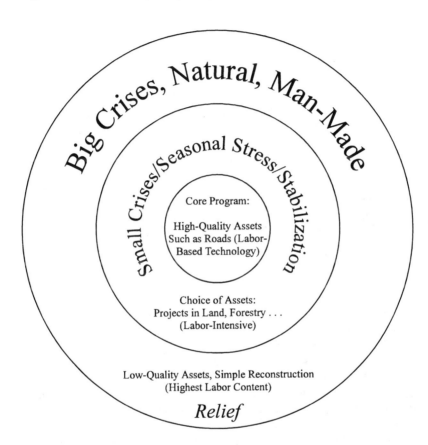

Asset quality is not the only feature that changes as program focus is shifted across circles. The optimal degree of local participation may change, too. Under normal circumstances, participatory planning is greatest in programs in the inner circle. In the relief circle (the outer circle), participatory planning may have to be reduced because of the need to react rapidly and to protect the interests of the most powerless because, in a crisis situation, community-level decisionmaking may not take the poorest in the community into account, and different social safety nets may be needed.

Training Needs and Evaluation Problems. The ability to generate high-quality assets presupposes technical training of the supervisory staff at

---

Box 12.6
Issues of Improved Technical Standards
and Evaluation

- Investment in management for technical quality of assets
- Training at project level
- Evaluation with respect to goal(s) and considering real alternatives—not theoretical "dream options"
- Time horizon of effective alternatives is relevant for evaluation

---

work sites and of the staff responsible for planning the asset-generation component of the program (Box 12.6). It also requires management training. Often, unfortunately, both the technical and the managerial capabilities of labor-intensive public works programs tend to be too weak to handle their respective tasks. In particular, programs that are created outside mainstream government-run public works programs seem to suffer from inadequate training. The long-standing training initiatives of the ILO for labor-based technologies, for example, have strengthened the capabilities of organizations implementing employment programs (Majeres, Chapter 11).

The approach to evaluation leaves much to be desired in many of the reviewed programs. Often, labor-intensive public works programs are criticized because the assets they create are not sustainable. Generally speaking, the dual purpose of employment programs (that is, asset creation and short-term poverty reduction) leads to unrealistically high expectations. The implementation of labor-intensive public works entails the acceptance of real trade-offs between such short and long-term goals.

Accordingly, evaluations of these programs must consider how well they have met their designated goals and succeeded compared to program alternatives. In addition, evaluations must take into account the time frame of the respective program's goals. For instance, an evaluation would have to be considered flawed if it criticized a program that had been implemented in a crisis with a short-term focus on food security for its failure to generate lasting assets of perfect quality with a high internal rate of return of, say, some infrastructure.

It would be equally inappropriate to assess a program's effectiveness over the short term when the program's objectives were designed to be met over the medium or long term. The indirect effects of employment programs can also be quite substantial over the short term—but these effects can easily be overlooked in evaluations. Improvements in rural infrastructure, for example, can spur growth in agriculture, as was the case in Bangladesh (Ahmed et al., Chapter 3). Employment programs that accompany and support institutional change can also have significant, indirect effects. The study from China demonstrates how the monetization of commodities in labor-intensive public works programs boosted the growth of the rural cash economy and led to greater integration of markets. The programs in both Bangladesh and China had a wide variety of developmental effects. This suggests that evaluations based solely on the short-term, direct effects of projects can be myopic and lead to the undervaluation of the real benefit of such programs.

Another potential indirect effect of public employment programs that should not be overlooked in program evaluation is the stimulation of private-sector activities. In Niger (Webb, Chapter 7) and in Bangladesh (Ahmed et al., Chapter 3), the private sector played a significant role in the implementation of employment programs. Such involvement can stimulate the development of growth and skills in the private sector, especially if companies enter areas of activity that have traditionally been the exclusive domain of the state (such as the development of infrastructure). Private-sector involvement can subsequently strengthen the overall competitiveness of the economy and open up new areas of private-sector activity. Such stimulation would be a significant positive effect of employment programs.

Evaluations must also take into account large seasonal fluctuations, which can offset or entirely reverse the accomplishments of employment programs (Shaw, Chapter 10). For example, dramatic changes in the opportunity costs of labor, as in Niger (Webb, Chapter 7), could adversely affect program performance. Seasonal adjustment of employment programs is, of course, critical in such environments, but may increase overhead costs. Evaluations should, in general, consider a broader set of criteria and, in particular, take into account the institutional changes fostered by employment programs.

International Action for Effective Employment Policies

Although the planning and implementation of employment policies and programs is essentially a national government activity, concerted action by a group of countries and action on the part of international agencies can enhance national programs and policies in a number of ways (Box 12.7). Countries that have experience with employment programs should share and pool their experiences. This would enable countries to learn from each other's successes and mistakes. A multitude of labor-intensive public

---

Box 12.7
International Actions for Effective Employment
Programs for the Poor

→ Promote networking among employment program policymakers
- Facilitate global learning from national experiences
- Overcome individual agency limitations by combining their
  strengths and experiences relevant to employment programs:

• World Food Programme	food for work, operation in food crises
• World Bank	infrastructure investment, financing, complementary programs, evaluation
• International Labour Office	conceptualization, training

→ Form a task force of agencies
- Develop a role for bilateral agencies, for example, to assist in
  long-term institutional strengthening of employment programs
- Encourage use of NGOs at national and international levels in
  policy mobilization and capacity building

---

works programs were tried in Africa in the 1980s, for example, without much consultation between or among national governments. A network of employment-program-managing institutions could facilitate the sharing of experience, and the ILO would be the obvious organization to support such a network's operation.

International agencies that support different aspects of employment programs should cooperate to maximize individual agencies' strengths (and minimize their weaknesses). The follow-up to the employment goals set at the Social Summit of 1995 in Copenhagen would benefit from such concerted efforts. The WFP, for example, which is active in supporting food-for-work programs, provides a key resource for wage earners, but often lacks the money and expertise to design the asset-generation component of labor-intensive employment programs (Shaw, Chapter 10). This component is crucial to the sustainability of programs focused on improving assets. The World Bank has the power to mobilize resources and has the expertise to design high-quality assets, such as well-engineered roads and dams and other infrastructure improvements, but it is not particularly strong in designing assets that can be built and maintained with labor-intensive technology. The ILO has been developing relevant training capabilities for two decades

(Majeres, Chapter 11), but lacks the capacity to mobilize financial resources to actually establish large employment programs. In addition, the ILO has occasionally been hamstrung by its constitutionally stipulated adherence to labor laws that allow little flexibility in program design, for example, in the area of minimum wage rate policy.

Bilateral agencies could help, over the long term, to strengthen the institutions that implement employment programs. Some agencies might compensate for the weaknesses of the international organizations in specific program environments. NGOs can play an important role in national and international policy mobilization in this field (including the mobilization of trade unions as well as donors) and actually do so already to some extent. Specialized NGOs could also enhance the training and capacity building of implementing these programs and strengthen the capacities of labor organizations, for example, trade unions.

In conclusion, the problems of absolute poverty and food insecurity are combined with and related to a massive and growing employment problem in low-income countries. Tackling the employment problem appears more and more to be the most effective means of addressing the food security problems of the poor. This focus on employment, however, must not lose sight of the key role of agriculture and rural growth stimulation for poverty reduction and food security. A combination of long-term efforts for improvement of human resources, especially education and agricultural growth, and short- and medium-run job creation for buildup and maintenance of productive resources is required. While this has been recognized by many countries, there continues to be a lack of a concerted multinational effort by the appropriate international agencies. Taking stock of the broad range of often impressive experience that has now been gained, as has been attempted in this volume, is but the first step toward more effective action.

List of Contributors

Akhter Ahmed of Bangladesh is a research fellow at the International Food Policy Research Institute (IFPRI) in Washington, D.C. Ahmed has undertaken a number of in-depth studies on the public food distribution systems of Bangladesh.

Joachim von Braun is a professor at the University of Kiel, Germany, where he holds the Chair for Food Economics and Food Policy. Until 1993, von Braun was director of the Food Consumption and Nutrition Division of IFPRI. His research focus is on food security policies, famine prevention, employment policies, rural finance, and food policy reform issues in transforming economies.

Omar Haider Chowdhury is a senior research fellow at the Bangladesh Institute of Development Studies, Dacca, Bangladesh, where nutrition and poverty alleviation are his major research concerns.

S. Mahendra Dev is an associate professor at the Indira Gandhi Institute of Development Research, Bombay, India. His research is focused on employment and social security issues in development.

Jiang Zhongyi, a citizen of China, is division director of the Research Centre for Rural Economics, Ministry of Agriculture, Beijing, China. His research includes agricultural policy reform matters in China, employment program analyses, and rural credit, especially in the poorer regions of China.

Shubh K. Kumar, formerly a research fellow at IFPRI, concentrates her research on assessing implications of different food distribution policies. A native of India, she has worked on research projects on a range of food policy issues in Ethiopia, Nepal, Zambia, and Bangladesh.

Jean Majeres, a citizen of Luxembourg, joined the International Labour Office (ILO) in 1974. At its headquarters in Geneva, he works on development issues, particularly those related to employment policy and poverty alleviation.

Samir Radwan, a citizen of Egypt, is director of the Development and Technical Cooperation Department at the International Labour Office. Radwan, who has acted as a consultant to numerous international organizations, was a member of the Brundtland Commission's panel on Food Security, Agriculture, Forestry, and Environment.

John Shaw has been associated with the World Food Programme, Rome, almost from its inception in 1963. In 1993 he was chief of its Policy Affairs Service, Policy and Public Affairs Division. Shaw has also been a consultant to numerous international institutions.

Tesfaye Teklu, an Ethiopian citizen, is a research fellow at IFPRI. Teklu's work includes research on famine prevention, employment policy, and rural finance.

Patrick Webb is a policy analyst in the policy affairs service of the World Food Programme in Rome. Before 1994, he was a research fellow and acting division director at IFPRI. Webb has guided research programs on food policy topics in The Gambia, Ethiopia, and Niger. His research includes themes such as famine prevention, employment, and irrigation policy.

Jose Wurgaft, a Chilean citizen, joined The International Labour Office's Programa Regional del Empleo para America Latina y el Caribe (PREALC) in 1978. He has worked mainly on employment and wage policy, and lately on special employment schemes and social investment funds. He has also been a member of the secretariat of the Andean Pact Integration Scheme.

Zhu Ling, a Chinese citizen, is a senior research fellow at the Chinese Academy for Social Sciences, Beijing. Her research focus is on poverty reduction, employment policies, rural finance, and agricultural development topics.

Sajjad Zohir, a research fellow at the Bangladesh Institute of Development Studies, primarily works on food and agricultural policy research.